STATE AND PUBLIC POLICY

STATE AND PUBLIC POLICY

Editor
Dr. Kamlesh Gupta

PENTAGON PRESS

STATE AND PUBLIC POLICY

Editor: Dr. Kamlesh Gupta

ISBN 978-93-86618-23-8

First Published in 2018

Published by
PENTAGON PRESS
206, Peacock Lane, Shahpur Jat
New Delhi-110049
Phones: 011-64706243, 26491568
Telefax: 011-26490600
email: rajan@pentagonpress.in
website: www.pentagonpress.in

Printed at Aegean Offset Printers, Noida

Contents

Message ix

Acknowledgements xi

About the Contributors xiii

Introduction xv

PART I
STATE AND PUBLIC POLICY IN NEW GLOBAL ERA

1. Public Policy Processes in Globalized India 3
Kuldeep Mathur

2. State and Public Policy: Contemporary Debate 17
Kamlesh Gupta and Manjri Damele

3. Public Policy and Globalization: An Emerging Framework of Global Public Policy 34
Abhishek Pratap Singh

4. Globalization of State Policy Agenda's 41
R.K. Sapru

5. A Borderless Internal Federal Space? Reorganization of States in India 56
Mahendra Prasad Singh

6. States' Paradiplomacy in India: Prospects and Pitfalls 76
Prakash Chandra Jha

PART II
GOVERNMENTAL POLICIES AND EXPERIENCES

7. Regional Disparities of Public Policy in India 97
Manoj Sinha

8. The Systemic Sources of India's Nuclear Policy 107
Abhay Kumar

9. Indian Nuclear Strategy: Pokhran II and Beyond 128
Minu Jha

10. Globalization and Tribal Development in India 157
Krishan Gopal

11. Population Policy of India: A Critique 169
Archana Srivastva

PART III
PUBLIC POLICY, DECENTRALIZATION AND DEVELOPMENT

12. Governance, Public Policy and Peace-Building in India: Exemplifying Status of Decentralization Policy in J&K State 183
Ashish Saxena

13. Minority Policies in India: The Post Sachar Scenario 195
Muneer Illath

14. The Oncoming Challenges of Public-Private Partnership into Rural Drinking Water Supply: A Case Study of District Sehore, Madhya Pradesh 206
Manzoor Ali

15. Globalization and its Effect on Local Self-Government: The Ideological Value of Democratic Decentralization in Question 222
Sibtosh Bandyopadhyay

16. Issue of Land and Forest in NREGA & FRA: Study of Sonebhadra District of U.P. 232
Vinay Kumar Tiwari

PART IV
GENDER AND POLICY INTERVENTION

17. Gender Equality and Women Empowerment in India: With Special Reference to Millennium Development Goal 245
Sumit Saurabh Srivastava

18. Social Movements and the Gender Component 260
Sumita Parmar

19. Disability and Mainstreaming Gender: It's Linkage with Inclusive Development 268
Sudhir Singh

20. Gendering Public Policy in India: A Review 280
Koushiki Dasgupta

21. A Socio-Historical Underpinning of Public Policy for Social Justice and Women Empowerment 288
Vijaylaxmi Saxena

22. Impact of Central Sponsored Schemes on Women Empowerment with Special Reference to Health and Education 308
Renu Srivastava

Index 319

Message

I am happy to say that the Rajiv Gandhi Chair in Contemporary Studies is doing well from its inception. The Chair was established with the aim to conduct research work, organize seminars, training programmes and published books, research papers/articles on different issues relating to the thrust areas of the Rajiv Gandhi Chair in Contemporary Studies of the University of Allahabad.

In this sequence Dr Kamlesh Gupta, Post Doctoral Research Associate of the Rajiv Gandhi Chair is going to publish an edited book on "*State and Public Policy*" which is a compilation of the Papers of subject expert/ academician of Indian universities and some of papers of this volume are included from National Seminar on State and Public Policy in New Global Era. Subject of the book is very relevant and significant in the present context. I hope that this volume will play a vital role in enriching academic debates including quality research in future. I also hope this will provide guidelines to those who want to further study on Public Policy and State. I hope that this publication will definitely encourage academicians, researcher, and also students. I appreciate this commendable effort and hope that all research papers/articles of the edited book will be in consonance with academic standards.

I express my best wishes for successful publication of the book.

Prof Mridula Tripathi
Dean Faculty of Arts
University of Allahabad

Acknowledgements

This volume is an outcome of collection of papers from subject expert/ academician of Indian universities and some of papers of this volume are included from National Seminar on State and Public Policy in New Global Era organized by the Rajiv Gandhi Chair in Contemporary Studies of University of Allahabad in November 2013.

We thank to our Vice-Chancellor and Allahabad University Administration for their support and cooperation. We must thank Prof. Mridulla Tripathi, Dean Faculty of Arts, Allahabad University who always extended his guidance and support. We also must thank to Prof. Krishna Gupta for his support and guidance. We must thank these scholars who contribute paper in this volume and from coming different parts of India for taking all troubles and lighting the way ahead for us. This book could not have been possible without his constant support and encouragement.

I thanks to Prof. M.P. Dube, Former Dean, Faculty of Arts, University of Allahabad and Prof. A. Satyanarayana, Head, Department of Sociology, who always extended his guidance as well as academic and administrative support in organizing this seminar. I also thanks to Prof. Mohd. Asalam, Prof Sumita Parmar, Dr V.K. Rai, Dr Rajpal Budhania, Dr B.K. Singh (Deputy Librarian), Mr Rajeev Gupta (AR) and Mr Pradeep Agrawal (AR). I thank to all JRFs, SRFs, Technical Assistant, and Office Assistant Mr. Dasrath Yadav of the Rajiv Gandhi Chair. Finally, Mr. Rajan Arya, the Chief Executive Officer of Pentagon Press, deserves thanks for bringing the book within a short span of time.

Dr. Kamlesh Gupta

About the Contributors

Prof. Kuldeep Mathur, Former Chairman, Centre for the Study of Law, & Governance, Jawaharlal Nehru University (JNU), New Delhi.

Dr. Kamlesh Gupta, Former PDRA, Rajiv Gandhi Chair in Contemporary Studies, University of Allahabad, Allahabad (U.P.).

Dr. Manjri Damele, Presently working as Assistant Professor, Department of Economics, Bundelkhand Post Graduate Degree College, Jhansi (UP).

Mr. Abhishek Pratap Singh, Research Scholar, School of International Studies, Jawaharlal Nehru University, New Delhi.

Prof. R.K. Sapru, Former Head, Department of Public Administration, Panjab University, Chandigarh.

Prof. Mahendra Prasad Singh (Retd.), Department of Political Science, University of Delhi, New Delhi.

Dr. Prakash Chandra Jha, Presently working as Assistant Professor of Political Science and International Studies, Amity Law School, Amity University Rajasthan, Jaipur (Rajasthan).

Dr. Manoj Sinha, Principal, Aryabhatt College, University of Delhi, New Delhi.

Mr. Abhay Kumar, Research Scholar, School of International Studies, Jawaharlal Nehru University (JNU), New Delhi.

Dr. Minu Jha, Presently working as Post Doctoral Research Fellow (ICSSR), Department of Political Science, University of Allahabad, Allahabad (UP).

Dr. Krishan Gopal (Retd.), Deputy Librarian, Jawaharlal Nehru University, New Delhi.

Dr. Archana Srivastva, presently working as Associate Professor, Department of Sociology, Kumaon University, Nainital (Uttarakhand).

Dr. Ashish Saxena, presently working as Associate Professor, Department of Sociology, University of Allahabad, Allahabad, (U.P.).

Mr. Muneer Illah, presently working as Assistant Professor, Department of Sociology, University of Allahabad, Allahabad, (U.P.).

Dr. Manzoor Ali, Research Officer, Center for Budget and Governance Accountability, New Delhi.

Dr. Sibtosh Bandyopadhyay, Head, Department of Political Science, Vivekananda Mahavidhalaya, Haripal, Hooghly (West Bengal).

Mr. Vinay Kumar Tiwari, Research Scholar Govind Ballabh Pant Social Science Institute, Jhusi, Allahabad (U.P.).

Dr. Sumit Saurabh Srivastava, Presently working as Assistant Professor, Centre for Globalization and Development Studies, University of Allahabad, Allahabad (U.P.).

Prof Sumita Parmar, Director, Center for Women Studies, University of Allahabad, Allahabad (U.P.).

Dr. Sudhir Singh, Presently working as Assistant Professor, Department of Political Science, Dayal Singh College, New Delhi.

Dr. Koushiki Dasgupta, presently working as Assistant Professor, Department of History, University of Gour Banga (West Bengal).

Dr. Vijaylaxmi Saxena, presently is Guest faculty in Humanities at IERT, Allahabad (U.P.).

Ms. Renu Shrivastava, Research Scholar Govind Ballabh Pant Social Science Institute, Jhusi, Allahabad (U.P.).

Introduction

The concept of State has occupied a high position in the political arena of the traditional period but the state is a historical institution, it emerged in response to a particular set of circumstances in sixteenth century Europe and it has continued to evolve in the light of the changing circumstances. The State developed into a nation-state in the nineteenth century. During the twentieth, and the post 1945 period adopted socio and economic responsibilities and emerged as a welfare state. In period of 1980s in different countries, a general rolling back of the state took place through the adoption of liberalization and privatization and introduction of the market reforms in public service. Above ideological trends/factors were responsible to the rise of pro market and anti state ideas of the new right. Such developments have led, some argue, to the emergence of a new form of state, portrayed variously as the competitive state, market pro-state or post modern state. The rise of globalization has stimulated a major debate about the state and public policy.

In the era of globalization, the State changes its nature according to global forces. The focus of state is more on regulatory and controlling functions. So the nature of state has to continuously undergoing change. The welfare state, as an institution, guarantees social welfare and social justice to the deprived groups but globalization has not only threatened it but also made it weak. In the contemporary context, social welfare agenda is taken over by non-state organizations that need to be carefully critiqued. The older theories of state, which are either inadequate or inapplicable, today cannot cover the new developments that have taken place in the era of globalization and therefore they have to be reviewed, specifically in the contemporary context.

Globalization has not only affected state but also influenced the public policy to a great extent. It has challenged the nature of public policy by summoning a series of non –negotiable, external and largely economic imperatives that must be appeased in a technically proficient manner if good economic performance is to be maintained, at the cost of democratic accountability. Globalization necessitates a certain privatization and technicization of public policy rendering it publicly less accountable. Public character of public policy is potentially seen as a casualty of globalization. The neo-liberal economy has further compounded the unevenness and inequality in society. In the light of these changes, we need to rethink about these aspects of public policy.

Accordingly, the volume discusses contemporary Perspectives State and Public Policy, challenges of state in the era of globalization, Debate on State and Public Policy, Public Private Partnership, Democracy, Decentralization and Development, Governmental Policies and Experiences. The Book divided in four parts: State and Public Policy in New Global Era; Governmental Policies and Experiences; Public Policy, Decentralization and Development and Policy Intervention.

Part-I: State and Public Policy in New Global Era

The section begins with a theoretical aspect & conceptual analysis of public policy and state, *Prof. Kuldeep Mathur* started his paper "Public Policy Processes in Globalized India" with an argument that globalization has become a term which explains everything that is happening in society. The Author comprehensively elaborated the public policy in the new global era. According to him Globalization is debated and controversial issue having several meaning for various commentators and scholars. He significantly highlighted dimension of globalization in terms of comprehension of time and space, new liberalism, movement of capital and technology across the world. He also emphasized the role of globalization in bringing about changes in the public policy such as diminishing role of State expansion of market, role of civil society and NGO etc. Prof Mathur discussed about issues of public policy processes-technocratic view of policy analysis, policy as a process of negotiation, changing policy discourse in India, market for policy advice: rise of research institutes, civil society organizations and advocacy groups. He argues that the world views are open to debate and contestation and a policy is an outcome of one that prevails at that time. Changes occur because relationships among actors change and a new constellation of forces may emerge. Policy making is a dynamic process occurring in a network society rather than one within hierarchies. Policy changes may also occur as knowledge brings about shifts in the beliefs and perceptions of the actors. In a complex society that we are living in, this may happen due to various influences. Trans-border movements whether of ideas or labour or capital demand a state that can allow this without friction. It is for this reason that state and its actions/public policies need to be the primary focus of attention. The challenge before government is to be concerned about its national interests while at the same time open to global discourse. As we saw earlier, the policy research organizations wedded to this philosophy will tend to intervene in policy processes within that framework. Prof Mathur concludes his paper that globalization has become more intense in recent years also through informal networks that bring together the most influential people together to exchange ideas and experiences. World Economic Forum is an example of such a network. In recent years it has been involved in contentious issues of globalization and sovereignty of state.

In their article, "State and public Policy : Contemporary Debate," *Dr. Kamlesh Gupta & Dr. Manjri Damele* discuss Contemporary perspective of state and public policy in new global era. After a short note on the concept of state and public policy, they ask what is the need to debate on the state and public policy. The authors advocate that the rise of globalization has stimulated a major debate about the state and public policy. Globalization has not only affected the state but also influenced the public policy to a great extent. Authors argue that we need to rethink these aspects of public policy. There are three actors, whose roles are significant for the formulation of public policy. These are; state, society and market. In contemporary context role of state is to regulate and insures the implementation of public policy, for this purpose some agencies of the state are working as a controlling agency i.e., IRDA, TRAI, CCI etc. The paper are divided into the six parts: Introduction; Globalization, State and Public Policy; Main Issues of Redebate on State, Debate on Public Policy, Challenges of Policy Concern and Implementation, and Contemporary Reforms.

"Public Policy and Globalization: An Emerging framework of Global Public policy" is an article written by *Mr. Abhishek Pratap Singh*. He discussed that public policy has changed in the era of globalization. There are certain limitations with newly emerging framework for operation of public policy. He argues that it is perhaps hardly surprising that commentators like *David Marquand* have pointed to the notion of "decline of public" in public policy making. Yet before rushing to endorse such a pessimistic conclusion, it is important to acknowledge that most of the issues discussed above rest on strong assumptions as to the nature, extent, and consequences of globalization on public policy. Whether acknowledged as such, these are unavoidably empirical claims and, moreover, empirical claims that do not always stand up to a close consideration of the available evidence. Indeed, although the contemporary period is invariably referred to as one of globalization, and although globalization is invariably seen as placing stringent constraints on the size of the public sector, in aggregate terms states consume a larger share of global Gross Domestic Output (GDP) than at any previous point in their history. In addition, the scope and nature of public policy has widened as the new framework of global public policy has come to acquire larger space in global political and economic discourse including non-state actors as well. In this context the understanding of public versus private becomes complicated when we move to transnational global policy-making. In the realm of policy-making, now a potentially large and rather heterogeneous number of non-state actors are involved also. The policy problems and their solutions now are transboundary in nature necessitating supraterritorial efforts on a global scale. The policy problem arises independently in a number of different places in the world but cannot be systematically addressed without acting on a global scale. Thus, it may not be end of public policy as concept , rather an opportunity for the emergence of global public policy framework with more convergence of interests and actions.

Prof. R.K. Sapru, in his article, "Globalisation of State Policy Agendas" analyzes various aspects of policy agenda of state in global context. He argues that it is largely felt that in developing democratic countries, policy agendas are driven by global forces. Problems arise in a context in which economic and social conditions play a major role in shaping opinions and political strategies. Now since August 2008 most economies of the world are in the grip of recession. The nature of the crisis being faced today is different from the ones in the last 75 years. Hence analysts are groping for answers and especially those in policy making who led the world into this crisis. The nationalization / government takeover of major institutions and the introduction of regulation in the hitherto unregulated parts of the financial structures is itself changing the economy in fundamental ways but even this maybe mere tinkering and more basic change may be required. When those entities that were thought of as "too big to fail" actually fail, it signifies the failure of the system of which they are a part. But the power of decision or policy and the capacity to implement it remains largely within the nation states. There is therefore a tension between the spillover, which may be said to be taking place at the global level and the reality of the maintenance of national sovereignty. Against the pressure of global agendas the fact remains that at times of crisis "governments are prone to withdraw from intergovernmental cooperation and supranational policy making rather than move positively into closer collaboration." Common issues and problems within a global context may be increasingly identified in international terms, but policy making and implementation still remain largely within nation states. The global socio-economic framework interacts with the political processes and policies pursued by governments of nation states. Prof Sapru suggested the success of nation states in policy performance will diverge notwithstanding the convergence of the global policy concerns.

In the article "A borderless internal federal space? Reorganization of states in India" *Prof. Mahendra Prasad Singh* examines the issue of reorganization of States in independent India. The major hypotheses of his paper are that (i) the historical internal boundaries are more a reflection of accidents of war and conquest than physical and cultural and regional geography and demography; (ii) the reorganization of States in independent India suffers from hangovers of history and ad hoc decisions of the Centre under regional protests and passions of the moment than any comprehensive deliberative design of redrawing of internal boundaries; and (iii) the Constituent Assembly of India missed the opportunity of making a comprehensive reorganization in conformity to cultural, administrative, and fiscal rationales that may have been feasible at the constituent defining moment in the life of the Indian nation-state. That opportunity having been missed by a beleaguered and fatigued nationalist political elites, the only conceivable conditions under which a comprehensive perspective plan for internal territorial reorganization can be imagined is under conditions of unsustainable fiscal overload or further political fragmentation crippling governability and politico-economic management of India. Given the foregoing, the foresight of the article 3 of the constitution leaving the final authority of reorganization with the Parliament of India with the obligation to only "consult" the States concerned is a pragmatic feature of the Indian federal experiment, even though it is generally supposed to be an unfederal feature by scholars like K.C. Wheare (1964). However, as B.R. Ambedkar, the chairman of the drafting committee of the Constituent Assembly subsequently explained: "Article 3 of the Constitution gives power to Parliament to create new states. This was done because there was no time to reorganize the states on linguistic basis for which there was a great demand". In the conclusion of paper Prof. Singh for sees some major problems on the agenda of reorganization of states in India in the decades ahead.

Dr. Prakash Chandra Jha, in his article "States' Paradiplomacy in India: Prospects and Pitfalls" analyze some aspects of States' Para-diplomacy in India. He argues that notwithstanding the intensification of sub-national governments' (SNG) involvement in foreign policy, literature in this area is still inadequate given the dominance of state-centric approach in International Relations. The author argues that the traditional state-centric approach cannot adequately explain sub-national role in foreign policy. In the globalised world it is possible for states of India to interact with investors in foreign countries in de facto sense if not in de jure sense. Compared to other countries including China Para-diplomacy in India is still at the incipient stage. However, paradiplomatic initiatives by states, of late, have begun gathering momentum. It is evident from the states' high profile investment-promotion activities abroad. Dr. Jha makes modest attempt to see whether States' paradiplomacy, aside from becoming instrument of economic development, can also address some of the long-standing problems with our neighbouring countries such as water sharing, terrorism, and illegal cross-border migration, environmental protection among others. Further the paper also tries to discuss whether subnational economic diplomacy presents challenges too. It is taking place in unplanned and scattered manner without central government coordinating with states. Yet another objective of the paper is to see despite intensification of paradiplomatic activities by states in recent times, why there is hardly any debate or discussion either in academia or government over the need for the greater or lesser role of states in India's foreign policy.

Part-II: Governmental Policies and Experiences

Part second deals with the applied aspect of public policy, in his article, "Regional Disparities of Public Policy in India," Dr *Manoj Sinha* discussed various aspects of public policy. After a short note on the concept, Dr *Sinha* asks some question what has been wrong with strategy pursued for the development and removal of regional disparities? Why has the idea of regional balance, though all along with us, failed to work? What strategy would be effective in removal of regional disparities and for acceleration of overall process of development? The authors advocate that this paper would try to find answers to some of questions. He argue that the foregoing analysis of the public policy and its impact on regional and structural disparities leads to certain conclusions which have high policy implications. These are (1) In the pre-colonial days the question of regional disparities was insignificant. Certainly there was regional variation which was mostly the product of natural factors. (2) The regional and structural inequalities became very wide and stiff due to British political, administrative and investment policies. The independent India inherited inequality and regional disparities as colonial legacy. In post-independence period, Indian planning and development evolved with reference to and in the context of national needs and requirements. After 1960's suppressed regional disparities surfaced. A number of people in area-oriented programmes were initiated and positive discrimination in devolution of development funds started. But still existing gaps between developed and under-developed areas are too wide. There are many region for generate the problem. The plausible solution, therefore, would not be that each depressed region should seek solution within itself. Each backward region is unique. As such, a uniform strategy for the development of different backward regions, contemplated at the Centre, would not provide suitable answers at the grassroots level. Hence the area specific strategy for the development is the first necessity. What Centre can do is to provide each region with sufficient opportunity to develop its own potential.

"The Systemic Sources of India's Nuclear Policy" is an article written by *Mr. Abhay Kumar*. He tries to analyze the transformation of India's nuclear policy since the end of the Cold War. The shift in the nuclear behaviour of India can be seen as a transformation from moral principles based on global nuclear disarmament and sovereign equality of all states, to a completely different approach of declaring itself a nuclear weapon state. The purpose of the article is to explain the shift of the India's nuclear policy from deliberate ambivalence to measured participation. The focus of this article is to discuss the influence of the systemic factors on the transformation of India's nuclear policy. For this purpose the introductory part of the article focuses on the ambiguous nature of the India's nuclear policy, since independence, though briefly. It analyses various reasons responsible for the nuclear tests and tries to explain why nuclear option was always retained by India. The second part of the article provides a brief outline of the theories in International Relations which deal with the question of proliferation of the nuclear weapons. Thereafter, the ensuing section provides a brief analysis of various systemic factors responsible for the outbreak of nuclear explosion in 1998. The conclusion part of the article sums up the observations.

Dr. Minu Jha, in her article "Indian Nuclear Strategy: Pokhran II and beyond" discussed contemporary views on the Indian Nuclear policy. Dr. Jha describe that the nuclear action of India in May 1998 surprised both the world and the Indian public. In the wake of the tests a number of questions haunted the minds of Indian and the foreign analysts. The questions concerned India's thinking about nuclear weapons, its future planning regarding nuclear force deployment, the situations under which India shall exercise its nuclear option, will India depart from the path of disarmament, will New Delhi sign the Comprehensive Test Ban Treaty (CTBT) and adhere to the FMCT guidelines. The chapter under discussion is an attempt at understanding the government's response to these questions as well as taking an account of the opinions of the non-official brigade.

Dr. Krishan Gopal, in his paper, "Globalization & Tribal Development in India" intended to analyze various aspects of Globalization & Tribal Development. After introducing the subject, he discussed role of World Bank in development of developing countries particular in India then he highlights some facts of word bank in reference of infrastructure development and different rural development schemes. The author discussed contemporary perspective of tribal development in India and governmental efforts and outcomes. He argues that the Bank's social safeguard policies define higher standards than those found in most countries, including India, in terms of compensation for land acquisition (at replacement value) resettlement (livelihood restoration), and for citizen participation. Author concludes his paper by these words that tribal development should be effected without any imposition on the tribal communities and the tribal people should be allowed to develop along lines of their own genius and tradition. Besides safeguarding their interests and protecting their culture efforts must be made to bring them into the mainstream of the country's socio-economic-political process. But when deciding and implementing tribal development programmes the most vital fact to remember is to judge result not by statistics nor by the amount of money spent but by the quality of human character that has evolved.

In the article "Population Policy of India: A Critique," *Dr. Archana Shrivastava* tries to analyze the population policy of India. After the introductory part, she argues in modern societies, population is regarded as human capital, and therefore as a resource of development. However, if its growth exceeds the available means of its survival, it becomes a problem serious enough to cause concern and anxiety to overall social and economic development of society. She tries to examine the population policy of Indian government, particularly after its independence. It is being increasingly realised that unless population growth-rate is effectively checked and controlled, gains of additional production will be neutralised. In fact, population growth rate everywhere is faster than the growth rate of economy with the result that the masses are not able to enjoy the fruits of economic growth. Rapid population growth very adversely influences social, economic and political systems. It was on this account that leadership in India, even before independence, decided to have a firm population policy for the country as a whole. It is not only in India but all over the world that concern about population growth is being expressed, though the nature of concern might differ from one country to the other. In some countries people show more concern about it than in others. There are, however, countries like Japan and France where fertility rate is too low and they are concerned about that. But on the whole, concern is felt about high, not low, fertility rate, including in India.

Part-III: Public Policy, Decentralization and Development

The part third of the book throws light on Public Policy, Decentralization and Development. It begins with the paper titled "Governance, Public Policy and Peace-Building In India: Exemplifying Status of Decentralization Policy In J&K State" by *Dr. Ashish Saxena*. He argues that Scholars had only begun to analyze the beginnings of the "third wave" of democratization in the early 1980s, and the term peace-building only gained currency in the 1990s. By the early twenty-first century, the study of democracy and democratization had firmly become a subfield of political and sociological inquiry. Consequently, peace-building enjoyed a rapid rise, especially in policy circles, without the same degree of institutionalization. Specialists only recently began to pay more rigorous attention to the relationship between peace-building and political governance and, more specifically, the extensive research on democratization. Author argues that there is an urgent need of debating the successes of third-tier in delivering public services in different States and to examine extent of sub-State decentralization in different States. It is to be emphasized that decentralization must proceed with sensitivity to the specific context, only in functional areas and in societies where decentralization is likely to foster participation and peace. The usual question that is asked in this context is the following - has the state disappeared? Keeping in view the general understanding of governance and nation-state in the conflicting situation, the paper humbly addresses such issues pertaining to conditions of governance in Jammu and Kashmir State (J&K). It is to be emphasized that the said state had a contentious history and allied disturbances, especially conflicting issues and terrorism at large, owing to its strategic location and conflicting ethnic diversities. The paper analyzes the progression of local government and implementation of three-tier federal framework in India, with special reference to Jammu and Kashmir (J&K) State.

The last part of the book focuses on Gender and Policy Intervention. In this part, the article "Minority policy in India: A post sacchar scenario," *Mr. Muneer Illath* intended to analyse aspects of Minority Policies in contemporary context. The author attempts to investigate the actions and responses from multiple stakeholders in the policies aimed at addressing the socio-economic grievances of Muslims in India with a special focus on the policies and programs initiated after the publication of the Prime Minister's High level Committee Report headed by Justice Rajinder Sachar in 2006. Investigating government's response to Sachar Committee recommendations, Harsh Mander (2011) observes that solution to any problem begins with an acknowledgment that it exists and this public realization echoed in Sachar Committee report would have to be actualized through inclusive development, mainstreaming of community while respecting diversity as the way out of the deprivation trap. However, many such studies conducted after the publications of SCR and subsequent plan of action laid out find that such hopes of addressal of historical disadvantages stands substantially belied even after 7 years of the implementation of the recommendations of SCR. There are some other recent documents, especially the Social Development Report (2012) highlighting the misplaced focus of minority oriented programs and siphoning off schemes and funds intended for minority welfare in the country to majority population or non-Muslim minorities.

Dr. Manzoor Ali, in his artical "The oncoming Challenges of Public-Private Partnership into Rural Drinking Water Supply: A Case Study of District Sehore, Madhya Pradesh". His paper intended to analyse applied aspect of public private partnership in Madhya Pradesh. He argues that 'Libertarian' philosophy which advocates for 'free market economy' without any regulation from State, the Indian government in 1990 decided to change the policy from 'Import Substitution Industrialization' (ISI) to open market. After the short note on concept of PPP in India, Dr. Ali discussed about PPP in drinking water sector, PPP in rural water and status of water in Sehore district. He points out challenges and suggestions of PPP, these are: To attract the private investment government has to give a wide range of concession, which would be costlier for government; Private investment will not be held accountable in PPP mode; Jobs created under PPP would be of contractual in nature. No labour rights protection; To efficiently manage the existing institution/s may cause retrenchment of workers.

In the article "Globalization and its Effect on Local Self Government - the Ideological Value of Democratic Decentralization in Question" *Dr. Sibtosh*

Bandyopadhyay has tried to access the problem and prospect of democratic decentralization process under the banner of globalization. His paper is divided in to four parts; Globalisation and its effect on local democracy; crises of representation; study report and conclusion. The study further seeks to examine the political attitude of people towards local self-governing institution and their representatives. These attitudes have been examined in terms of confidence or trust of voters on their elected candidates.

In his article "Issues of Land and Forest in NREGA & FRA: Study of Sonebhadra District of U.P" *Mr. Vinay Kumar Tiwari* studies Sonbhadra District. He argues that Land and Forest has been an important source of sustenance and livelihood for millions of people across the world. Forest provides all the basic needs such as food, fuel, wood, fodder, medicine and timber etc. At the same time forest related activities are major source of income as the forest produces and products are sold in both rural and urban markets to meet the consumers need. Land is the important issue during the colonial and anti colonial period of the movement. During the colonial period agricultural was stagnation, as the Zamindar were interested only in rack renting of the peasantry. They were unconcerned about investments and the colonial states also was not favourably disposed towards agricultural development as Zamindari system on which they relied ,was itself the greatest drag on agriculture. In the post independent period Zamindari system was abolished but was not accompanied by any redistribution of land although its distribution was highly skewed. The author highlights the relationship of land and forest livelihood and a question of implementation of Government sponsored right based development programme like MNERGA and Forest right act through case study in Ghorawal block, Sonebhadra district of U.P.

Part-IV: Gender and Policy Intervention

Dr. Sumit Sourabh Shrivastava, in his paper "Gender Equality and Women Empowerment in India: with Special reference to Millennium Development Goal" attempts to analyse various aspect of Women empowerment. The Author focuses on the Millennium Development Goal 3 (MDG 3) which aims at promoting gender equality and empowering women. The paper attempts its achievements & pitfalls in the context of India. The introductory part elaborates on the concept of women empowerment in existing literature. Later on the paper builds upon the outlining the Target of MDG 3 and its indicators to monitor the progress of achieving the same. The paper posits the performance of India along with these indicators and presents its situational analysis. Simultaneously the paper also elaborates upon the impending challenges & obstacles in the process of achieving the broader goal of gender equality and empowering women. The author concludes by arguing that although many significant steps have been taken by the Indian State to promote gender equity which have manifested in concrete positive outcomes yet there is much to be done.

Prof. Sumita Parmar, in her paper, "Social Movements & the Gender Component" intended to analyze various aspects of social movement. After introducing the subject, Prof. Parmar discussed background of social movement with involvement of women movement. She argues that Movements comprised solely of women first, became visible in the nineteenth century in the west when educated women united over issues of double standards practised by men vis a vis marriage and sexualities. Ironically, more than one and a half centuries later, the double standard, both in marriage as well as sexual practices, although reduced, still persists. However, the nature of the movements themselves have undergone many changes. Given the pervasiveness of the secondary position of women in almost all societies, irrespective of what laws and constitutions promise, women's movements strive for equity and justice across the globe. She put some example in favour of women movement in world and specially India. Prof. Parmar conclude her paper with these words In more recent times disturbing trends vis a vis women entering the public space, the articulation of women's voices and the highlighting women's issues have become evident. There is an effort to push for and impose religious and caste identities on women by reactionary forces and vested interests. Fortunately, this is being countered at two levels- the micro and the macro. At the micro levels, grassroots organizations concentrating on sustainable development in the remote and rural areas dilutes the impact of the unprogressive forces. On the other hand, at the macro level, globalization and the growth of international trade and commerce make it possible to organize across boundaries. Growing awareness among people and the desire to live qualitatively and not simply materially better lives, has become an important factor in the dynamics of the contemporary social movements.

Dr. Sudhir Singh, in his paper on the "Disability and Mainstreaming Gender: It's Linkage with Inclusive Development" tries to analysis gender disability and its challenges in contemporary context. Dr. Singh argues that disability is one of the most vital human concern and 1993 Vienna Convention of international human rights has first time adopted disability as one of the most crucial component and more than 150 countries of the contemporary world are signatories of this declaration. Again under the aegis of the UN, majority of world governments have signed the declarations which ensure the compliance of all rights to disables in 2007. We believe in the concept of welfare state therefore it is the duty of the society to provide basic societal support to women with disability. Our traditional values propelled us to extend all possible support to women but women with disabilities need more support from the society than the government because government neither could nor be successful till we will be not providing positive support to women with disabilities. Author suggested that societal awareness could be pivotal for the compliance of this egalitarian goal. Consciousness is increasing in this field but more need to done to provide tenets of human rights to women with disabilities.

"Gendering Public policy in India: A Review" is an article written by *Dr. Koushiki Dasgupta* about gendering policy in India. She argues that the problems of locating women in public policies are connected with three general concerns. The first question is related with the construction of an exclusive category of 'women`. Since women are a heterogeneous category including different castes, class, religions and cultures, it is difficult to make women a singular category of enquiry. Patriarchal oppression or socio economic discriminations against women may have been taken as components of unity but it is not enough to describe women as a category in the public policy making projects. Secondly, women productivity or her involvement as a worker in both formal and informal sector has no yet been acknowledged properly and her contributions in the public and private work spaces are undercounted or underestimated. Therefore, the policy makers are sometimes caught into the quandaries of vague information that their knowledge on women looks too much flawed to make any decision. The third question arises out of the figuration of women identity within a framework of ambivalence. She has been looked at wearing a double mask—one identifying her to the national community and the other to the particular culture she belonged to. Dr. Dasgupta concludes his paper in these words Gendering public policy needs the women speak for themselves in all issues of the society and it would be possible only when there is a cultural change, a perception that women are not objects of control but an equal partner of the development process.

Dr. Vijaylaxmi Saxena discussed the women empowerment in context of Social Justice in her article "A Socio-Historical Underpinning of Public Policy for Social Justice and Empowerment of Indian Women." Dr. Saxena started her article with conceptual background of women empowerment after them, she argues that Indian nation's identify does lay in the culture and more specifically in its womanhood, however, most of the Indian women have been suffering from the lack of self and space, disempowerment, disprivilege, disadvantage, sexist discrimination, gender inequity, invisibility, asymmetries and marginalization. Action for gender equality does largely depend on empowerment of women that is "equitable access to resources, power, and decision-making". Women empowerment requires a realignment of power, decision making at the household, institutional and all levels of society. Consequently various women empowerment specific policies and plans have been executed. She discussed women require a safe and secure space to be able to reflect on their needs, to articulate their conclusions and to have them taken seriously in peace-building. Economic and social rights must be guaranteed to women on a non-discriminatory basis, although this principle is regularly ignored in peace-building. The paper is divided into the six parts: Background; Emphasizing Ambedkar's view on social justice and empowerment of women; Public Policy for Women Empowerment and Development – Global Context; Microfinance and Women; Transnationalism, Dalit women and mobilization and concluding remarks.

Ms. Renu Srivastava tries to examine health and education schemes for women empowerment in her paper "Impact of Central Sponsored Schemes on Women Empowerment with Special Reference to Health and Education". She talked that women constitute about half of the total population of country but they suffer from many disadvantages, so the empowerment of women is one of the central issues in the process of development of countries all over the world. Health and Education is the key factor for effective and inclusive empowerment and it is as a mean to promote development in social and economic condition therefore the government has been implementing various schemes related to women health and education. The paper highlighted the various approach based central sponsored schemes on the health and education as well as try to see the impact of these schemes on women empowerment in different time period, the study is based on secondary sources.

The above mentioned contributions focus on contemporary debates on State and Public Policy. We hope that this volume will help in enriching academic debates as well as quality research in future. We also hope it be proved as a guide to those who want to study more about state and public policy. We are glad to present it in front of you. We do not claim for the perfectness and all-inclusiveness of the book but we surely want it to be a serious & thought-provoking attempt in the field of state and public policy.

PART I

STATE AND PUBLIC POLICY IN NEW GLOBAL ERA

1

Public Policy Processes in Globalized India

Kuldeep Mathur

It is a truism to say that globalization has been a source of change in society and state actions in recent times. For many, globalization has become a term that explains everything that is happening in society. There are many dimensions of globalization that have received different kinds of emphasis in public discourse.

Globalization and Its Dimensions

Scholte (2000) has attempted to distinguish between five kinds of definitions. One common notion of globalization has been in terms of internationalization. From this perspective, global is simply another adjective to describe cross-border relations between countries and designates growth of international exchange and interdependence. A second usage views globalization as liberalization and refers to a process of removing barriers on movement between countries in order to create an open and borderless world economy. Economists refer to this dimension and emphasize the free flow of capital as evidence. A third conception equates globalization with universalization and refers to the idea of synthesis of cultures Globalization has also been associated with concept of modernization and westernization. In this perspective, globalization is a dynamic whereby the social structures of modernity (capitalism, rationalism, industrialism and bureaucratism) are spread the world over. For many of us in Third World, we have been exposed to such globalization for centuries in the form of colonialism. Finally, globalization is identified with the idea of deterrorialization where there is shrinking of time-distance dimension.

Each of these conceptualizations generates intense debate and discussion. Without going into these debates here, I want to underline some significant dimensions of globalization that are helpful in discussing the changing nature of public policy processes in India.

The compression of time-space is one of the most significant dimensions of globalization. Modern technology has played a crucial role in connecting geographical areas and people of the world living in far flung corners. Telecommunications, internet provide for instant global thinking. Wars, insurgency, rebellions are brought to your TV screen immediately. Protests and movements have world wide connectivity whether they are related to environment or WTO. These cross-national contacts began to intensify as transport and communications improved. We feel the intensity of globalization today because of the dramatic progress in technology.

A significant implication of this kind of globalization is the rapid exchange of ideas and experiences across the world. A local protest movement quickly acquires a global dimension. Both the goals and strategies of a movement are in a way internationalized. Environmental movements are a prime example of this kind of globalization. The protest movement at Seattle WTO meeting another. Narmada movement closer home or the anti-atomic plant in South India still another. One can think of many more. They play a significant role in public policy processes and what is more significant is that these influences bear the imprint of world wide experiences.

What is distinctive is the second dimension of globalization and, that is critical for our discussion, is that the current wave of globalization is embedded in neo-liberal ideology. In that sense, it is different from the phase of colonialism. There is a revival of arguments of Adam Smith for market driven development based on conviction that market will bring prosperity and democracy. Thus, neo-liberals advocate free movement of goods, services and capital among countries and any restrictions on these should be lifted. Ironically, cross-border movements of workers are not promoted. They have promoted the idea of restricting the public sector and urged reductions in welfare programmes and to rely on market arrangements for health, education, old age pensions etc. Neo-liberalism is the reigning framework in contemporary globalization and has powerful promoters in multi-national corporations and multi-lateral financial agencies.

The most important aspect of this dimension of globalization is the globalization of production chains. Industries in the West began to find increasing competition for their manufactured goods. After the Second World War, the colonial division of labour where raw materials were provided by the colonies and processing into finished products done by the dominant countries broke down. Search began for cheap labour and cutting down on costs. Transport and communication technology helped in this search. The impact of globalization was felt in those countries where cheap labour was available, was skilled or semi-skilled and was amenable to some discipline of the market. Therefore, the greatest pressure of incorporation into the process of globalization is on countries that can provide such labour and a semblance of laws that can manage it. Labour flexibility is the most important aspect of this dimension. SEZs in India provide this even in greater measure; hence greater is its demand.

The third dimension of globalization that I want to emphasise here is transformation of the perspective of state. In the neo-liberal ideology, state is seen as a problem and not a solution. It is perceived to create obstacles to free flow of goods and services and globalization should lead to large-scale retreat of state regulation and interventions. Essentially, the point is of reducing scope of state activities and allowing greater and greater role to market to provide goods and services in society. The role of state is redefined in terms of how it can support improved functioning of the market. State is now seen as an enabling state and not merely a welfare state.

To summarise this part of the discussion, global capital appears to be the engine of globalization seeking wider markets for its manufactured goods, promoting reduced scope of state activities, and enforcing a market led economy which is unencumbered by public concerns or government regulation. There are critics of this mantra and they offer arguments for framing policies that can enable developing countries to stand up to the challenges. Stiglitz is well known through his book 'Globalization and Its Discontents' as one of the prominent spokesman of this group. But the fact remains, that today there is a difference between the globalizers and the globalized. The impact of globalization depends on where you stand.

I want to discuss the changes that are taking place in public policy processes in India in this perspective of globalization. As a logic of neoliberal globalization, state is no more considered as the prime mover of public policy. Governance paradigm has delineated three actors state, society and market as partners that craft public policy. It is a partnership that is now officially recognised in India through new institutions of policy-making and delivery of goods and services. If there is a Council of Trade and Industry of the Prime Minister to advise on economic policy consisting of leaders of private sector, then there is a National Advisory Council of the President of the Congress Party consisting of leading NGOs. Apart from these institutions at policy level, there are public-private partnerships implementing infrastructure projects or delivering health or educational services.

Technocratic View of Policy Analysis

In much of the prevalent literature, a technocratic view of policy analysis was predominant. This view is closely associated with scientific decision-making. In this perspective, policy process is based on a rational choice of the alternatives available to the decision maker. It is assumed that goals can be identified in advance and all information is available to identify trade-offs of each alternative from which the best choice can be made.

To meet with the limitation of having availability of all information Simon introduced the concept of what came to be known as bounded rationality and conjured up the notion of an 'administrative man' in contrast to the economic man who was a maximizer when the administrative man was a satisficer. The steps in the rational decision-making were not abandoned. Two significant consequences took place. One, this approach helped demarcate various stages in the process of policy making beginning from the stage of agenda setting to that of evaluation and feedback. Each stage was perceived as independent of the other The stages approach led to growth of technically oriented analysis. Introduction of computer introduced and encouraged use of quantitative techniques and modelling. Cost-benefit analysis reigned supreme.

This approach is more often than not, associated with planners and professional policy analysts who see the possibility of identifying best solutions to social and economic problems. When these solutions are not implemented, or cannot be implemented they blame politics and its irrational manifestations. Much of the field of policy analysis has been dominated by the literature emanating from the scientific-rational perspective. As a matter of fact a distinctive area of research as implementation analysis emerged particularly after the publication of the volume by Pressman and Wildawsky (1973). Implementation researchers divided the policy process into one that of policy formation and policy implementation and raised questions of how policies were formulated and then once made into law got implemented. More attention was focussed how the intentions and goals of policy makers were translated into action and achievement. The approach forced the researchers to accept the goals of policy as given which in principle had to be followed because the legitimacy of the decision at the top could not be questioned. (Bogason, 2000:100)

Policy as a Process of Negotiation

Apart from the fact that top down approach precluded understanding of policy as a process of negotiation (Bogason, 2000:103), it reduced political and social issues to technical considerations for achieving goals through administrative means. Vexing social and economic problems were interpreted as issues that needed to be managed better with improved programme design; their solutions were to be found in the objective collection of data and the application of technical decision making approaches. This rational-technocratic approach in large part defined the policy sciences since the 1960s (Fischer, 2003:5). This approach found resonance in the value of efficiency embedded in all economic and managerial thinking and therefore dominated the way governments defined their problems and found solutions for them.

Several scholarly contributions in the past decade or so mark a shift in focus in the framework of policy analysis from what was known as top down approach. These contributions are critical of this approach which was closely associated with the idea of scientific decision-making or what Stone (1988) calls a 'rationality project'. What was lost sight of in this dominant theme, argued by most scholars, was that policy was an arena of contestation—of bargaining and compromises—of politics. Reducing conflict ridden questions to the bureaucratic imperative of impersonality and value neutrality inhibited understanding of how policies were formulated and implemented. It viewed social and political issues as questions of efficiency, performance and productivity amenable to bureaucratic methods of decision-making. Fischer (2003:14) has further argued that these positivist methods of policy analysis have served intentionally or unintentionally to facilitate and bolster bureaucratic governance. He goes on to suggest that the post-empiricist call for the use of interpretative (hermeneutic) and discursive (deconstructionist) techniques are an effort to demonstrate that politics and policy are grounded in subjective factors. It seeks to show that what is identified as 'objective' truth by rational techniques is as often as not the product of deeper, less visible, political pre-suppositions. Their analysis starts with the recognition that different discourses, definitions, and questions lead to different policy outcomes. What are known as 'facts' are social constructions and framed through the discourses of the actors themselves. It is important, therefore, to explore and investigate the pre-suppositions, values and beliefs on which empirical assertions rest and uncover the many dimensions inherent to many deliberations and debates relevant to most policy issues.

These scholars argue that as facts are social constructions the way these facts are interpreted and defined paves the way for a policy. This is a very important argument because what is important in problem identification is not facts as such but the meanings attached to them by various actors. What is called for then is an analysis of competing definitions, and values and beliefs that interpret the facts. As Fischer (2003:14) points out this includes the theoretical assumptions that underlie a political discourse and the way they shape the apprehensions of policy alternatives, and thus alter the available range of policy options. He further argues that analysis should start with the recognition that different discourses, definitions and questions lead to different policy prescritions.

What we are seeing is that problem identification is by itself a complex issue where intense negotiation and bargaining can take place. Meanings are contested and the government finds itself in a position of asserting a meaning not necessarily acceptable by all. It has to persuade and argue. In todays complex governance style then government is unable to provide for an authoritative meaning. We need to therefore unravel this complex social and political process that gives meaning to problems and leads to a policy prescription. Once meaning is given policy will follow.

The alternative perspective in policy analysis then seeks to provide an improved reflection of the world of practice as far as policy process is concerned. Instead of attempting to insulate decision-making from everyday politics, it attempts to show that policy problems are defined in a subjective fashion and are dependent on the world view of the actors involved. The world views are open to debate and contestation and a policy is an outcome of one that prevails at that time. Changes occur because relationships among actors change and a new constellation of forces may emerge. Policy making is a dynamic process occurring in a network society rather than one within hierarchies. Policy changes may also occur as knowledge brings about shifts in the beliefs and perceptions of the actors. In a complex society that we are living in, this may happen due to various influences.

Globalization has brought into focus a new range of relationships among governmental institutions and international institutions. Policies are open to global influences and government institutions have accepted formulations of policy framed elsewhere. This is particularly true in the sectors of environment, climate change, human rights etc. It has led critics to argue that policy-making sovereignty of government has been abdicated. One of the important political developments in the era of globalization has been the emergence of a global civil society which has had a great influence on policy goals and policy making processes in these sectors.

Changing Policy Discourse in India

Policy discourse in India bears heavy technocratic influence from the time the country embarked upon its strategy of planned economic development. Within this framework, policy-making was an internal task of the government where the policy makers sought advice from technical experts and then determined policy. Bureaucrats enjoyed considerable influence by acting as 'gatekeepers' sifting information, analysing it and finally presenting alternative choices. Policy making in this sense was a top-down affair and reflected the classical minister-bureaucratic relationship.

This tradition of policy-making that began in the planning era appears to have found easy acceptance in the current liberalization era. Economic policy making continued to be characterised as a technocratic process demanding inputs from experts, for, achieving higher rates of growth was seen as a technical problem. However, experts and technocrats did not have single point of view. They had differences and promoted their own solutions as the valid ones. In addition, the bureaucrats were not seen as neutral purveyors of knowledge and were assumed to be partisans of a particular view. The result was that a kind of market for policy advice developed.

Market for Policy Advice: Rise of Research Institutes

Competing policy advice from technocrats and economists tended to widen the participation of experts in policy debates. Policy makers began to reach out for policy advice from outside the governmental technical-bureaucratic system. A market for alternative policies and forums to articulate competing public choices began to emerge. The development strategy espoused during the period of planning era had neither alleviated poverty nor strengthened the country industrially. Considerable economic disparities among people and regions within the country had grown over the years and the politics began to be dominated by demands for greater equality, justice and development. Public discourse began to be concerned with 'what went wrong' and alternatives began to be articulated. In a related but an important development, research institutes proliferated to fulfil this demand for alternative policies and answer these questions of 'what went wrong'. A competitive policy environment has emerged in which experts and research institutes attempt to persuade the policy makers to accept their version of technical solution to a problem. Thus, policies began to be contested on technical grounds thus widening the debate among an expanding technical group of people and on competing base of influence on the policy makers.

What has happened is that alternatives also provided opportunities to experts with different political orientations to influence policy. Technocrats competed with each other for 'expert' political space and thus confirming that research findings or their conclusions were not necessarily neutral. The garb of expertise helped in offering policy advice that had political overtones. The complication in understanding the kind of influence based on technical advice emanated also from diverse sources of funding of these research institutes.

During the plan era the Planning Commission had initiated the establishment of several research institutes that were later funded under the umbrella of the ICSSR. These institutions were funded mostly by the government and carried out research under its sponsorship. With liberalization, many more research institutes came up that were financed by private sources or international funding agencies. These research institutes usually do not depend on government for financial support and have multiple sources of funding. Many of these institutions entered the policy discourse to promote liberal policies and support market oriented delivery of public goods and services. Brookings Institution, a leading think tank of the US has taken the opportunity in the liberalization era to establish base in India to influence policy. (see Businessline 29 January 2013) In a statement, it says that Brookings is making the move because of India's growing importance on the world stage as the world's largest democracy a rising power with one of the fastest growing economies.

Research institutes in India began as providing support to the policies initiated as government priority. This came through identification of problems and evaluations of performance of polices. At this stage government funding was probably the only source of financial support. In later phase when the Planning Commission gave up its funding role by establishing Indian Council of Social Science Research, broadening of the perspective on research took place and the focus was not related only to government programmes and activities. The liberalization phase opened up the space for offering alternative policy advice even further. Sources of funding diversified, donor agencies began to take interest in shaping government policies and a kind of a policy market emerged.

Civil Society Organizations and Advocacy Groups

The liberalization phase of the Indian economy also brought changes in the way government functioned. Civil society organizations were recognised as important institutions providing support to the implementation of government programmes. Traditionally, NGOs have worked with local groups providing services, supplementing efforts of the government in delivering services or enabling communities to organize themselves to procure services or access entitlements. Their impact was limited and whatever engagement they had with state or other groups was to facilitate their primary task of successfully working for their constituency. However, their micro-experiences began to question the very policies that were being implemented and thus arose their concern for changing policies that could serve their constituencies like rural labour, child labour, poor educational provision etc. With contestation for alternative policies in public domain and debates being carried on by experts from research institutes, many of the NGOs tranformed themselves into advocacy groups and began their own struggle for policy change through public action.

Civil society organizations may enter policy advocacy directly by organizing campaigns and protest themselves or joining policy networks or issue-based coalitions· In the context of poverty, participation, democratization and equity concerns, Indian NGOs have engaged in organized advocacy in fields as diverse as informal, unorganized sector and child labour; affirmative action and protection for the disabled; a wide range of women's issues; environment, forests and related issues such as displacement and rehabilitation; health; judicial reform; participatory management and governance; consumer rights; appropriate technology; shelter and other issues affecting the urban poor; and issues relating to their own working space.

The struggles to change polices took many forms. Many of them were protests through demonstrations, public meetings or strikes. The more important initiative, of interest to us, was that many grassroots organizations, began forging allinaces with research institutes to further their aim. Such an alliance gave a technical basis to their arguments and legitimacy in debating with experts. Indian Social Institute with Walter Fernandes provided a base to large number of NGOs to provide principles for evolving national rehabilitation polices. Another example where alliances among NGOs have made their voice more powerful is in the area of issues and struggles concerned with rights of women. The National Commission of Women and Centre for Women's Development Studies (CWDS) has supported NGOs as umbrella organizations providing research base and forum for influencing public policy. It was the initiative of several women's organization coming together that led to government's decision to show expenditure on women in all departmental budgets. The relevance of budget analysis lies in the fact that it has provided civil society with a tool through which it can effectively bring the perspectives and the concerns of the poor and marginalised into the process of policy formulation. More importantly, through budget analysis civil society organizations have successfully demonstrated the importance of strategic engagement with the state for promoting a people-centric discourse. (Aiyar and Behar, 2005)

Thus, what has happened is that NGOs have developed alliances with other non-state entities to further an alternative and particpatory discourse on public policies. In concrete terms, NGOs have developed relationships with research institutions that tended towards a more progressive policy outlook. In turn, these institutes have played a key role as nodal institutions in the formation of policy networks and coalitions.

A significant development has been emergence of National Advisory Council, largely consisting of representatives of civil society group under the Chairpersonhip of the President of the ruling party. This in a way legitimized the role of civil society organizations in having a say in policy-making. In its recent report, (Indian Express November 9, 2013), it takes pride over the fact that it was pivotal in the enactment of landmark legislation like the RTI Act, NREGA and the Forests Rights Act among others. It also promoted National Food security Bill and the Communal Violence Bill.

Supreme Court and Policy Making

If the civil society organizations have forged links with research institutes to join the public discourse with evidence based research, the Supreme Court in its changed role definition has been a source of great support to them in policy struggles. Many significant policy changes particularly in the social and the environmental sector have been effected in the recent times due to the support that civil society organizations received from the Supreme Court. The redefinition and expansion of the role came about with the acceptance by the court of petitions filed by those who were not necessarily victims of law but alleged infringement of their fundamental rights. It became possible for organizations or individuals to plead before the Court on behalf of a group thus affected. Such petitions came to be known as public interest litigation and the Supreme Court deviated from its traditional role of being an appellate court by admitting them under original jurisdiction and issuing directives to the government. Under constitutional law, environmental protection had already been accepted as part of Right to Life and thus civil society organizations have sought the support of the Court in directing the government to pursue environmental friendly policies.

A few further illustrations would suffice. Delhi was facing severe problem of air pollution and the civil society organizations were raising their voices for the government to impose mechanisms that would provide the residents with clean air. In 1985, M.C. Mehta as chairman of an environmental NGO that he helps run, filed an appeal in Supreme Court in 1985 to issue a writ, order or direction to the Government of India and Delhi administration and Delhi Electric Supply Undertaking, Delhi Transport Corporation to take action to close down hazardous industries located in densely populated areas, and to take action against vehicle owners who emit noxious smoke and pollutants from the exhausts of their vehicles.

This raised an intense public debate as the Court proceeded to enforce the Acts that had already been passed by the Parliament. It set a time table for the commercial vehicles to convert to more eco-friendly fuel like CNG. An intense debate followed on the choice of clean fuel that was joined by other experts apart from those who were members of the Court appointed committee. Other stakeholders also joined in but ultimately the efforts of civil society organization with the support of the Court were successful. (see Mathur 2013 for more details)

A more recent example is that of the passage of Right to Information Act 2005. Here the Supreme Court is seen to be prompting the civil society organizations to take up the cause of right to know and transparency in public transactions. As far back as 1975 the Supreme Court stated that " In a government of responsibility like ours where the agents of the public must be responsible for their conduct there can be but a few secrets. The people of this country have a right to know every public act, everything that is done in public way by their public functionaries. They are entitled to know the particulars of every public transaction in all its bearings." Another judgement coming in 1982 held that right to information was a fundamental right under the Constitution. It went on to say that the concept of an open government is a direct emanation from the right to know which is implicit in the right of free speech and expression guaranteed under Article 19(1)(a). There were other cases also in the 1980s that upheld the right to know. Significantly, the Supreme Court also established that access to information was a right as guaranteed under the Constitution. It was not merely a largesse that a benevolent government provided to its citizens. Thus fight for this right was a struggle for democracy and not for mere good governance.

Within this context, issues of right to know began to be raised sporadically, particularly in cases of environmental degradation where the government was not willing to give full information. Much of the information about the Bhopal gas tragedy was kept under the wraps leading to extensive disaffection among the civil society activists. What provided greater momentum to the RTI movement was the beginning of a rural movement in around 1990 started by Mazdoor Kisan Shakti Sangathan (MKSS) in Rajasthan demanding access to information on behalf of wage workers and small farmers who were denied benefit of their rightful wages or their just benefits under government schemes. Singh (2011:55) suggests that MKSS transformed the movement and it metamorphosed into a mass movement. The *jan sunwais* (public hearings) are mentioned as the core strategy that moved the Rajasthan government and caught the imagination of the people.

As the demand for transparency spread, a national body that brought the rural and urban activists was formed for coordinating efforts for the formulation of national legislation. The National Campaign for People's Right to Information (NCPRI) was established in 1996 and consisted of eminent lawyers, retired civil servants, eminent journalists and other activists who not only drafted a Bill but negotiated with the government for its passage.

Again in the case of Right to Education, Supreme Court played a significant role in giving strength to civil society organizations fighting for the cause of child's education and eradication child labour. The report of the Ministerial committee that recommended free and compulsory education for children in 6-14 age group was in major part a response to a 1993 ruling of the Supreme Court in the case of Unnikrishna J.P. *versus* State of Andhra Pradesh. The Court had ruled that though right to education is not stated expressly as a fundamental right, it is implicit in and flows from right to life guaranteed under article 21'. In other Campaigns for Right to Employment or Right to Health the Supreme Court has played a significant role too. (See Chandoke, 2007)

Thus the civil society organizations have found support from the Supreme

Court which redefined its role and then gave a liberal interpretaion of the fundamental rights guaranteed under the Constitution. This helped in mobilizing support and raising intense policy debate in public domain. Agendas were set and effort was to change the worldview of the policy actors.

Concluding Remarks

The alternative perspective in policy analysis then seeks to provide an improved reflection of the world of practice as far as policy process is concerned. Instead of attempting to insulate decision-making from everyday politics, it attempts to show that policy problems are defined in a subjective fashion and are dependent on the world view of the actors involved. The world views are open to debate and contestation and a policy is an outcome of one that prevails at that time. Changes occur because relationships among actors change and a new constellation of forces may emerge. Policy making is a dynamic process occurring in a network society rather than one within hierarchies. Policy changes may also occur as knowledge brings about shifts in the beliefs and perceptions of the actors. In a complex society that we are living in, this may happen due to various influences.

In dealing with large number of complex issues that plague the society, government in India in a way has opened itself to ideas that may not necessarily emanate from its own internal institutions. Globalization has been the driver of this kind of change. Further, policy ideas are not restricted by any national boundaries. They frequently cross them and are carried by academicians, think tanks, international organizations and civil society institutions. Such frequent transfer of ideas has been helped considerably by the modern means of communication. Another dimension of this diffusion of ideas is their coercive or non-coercive nature. Some of the transnational ideas are accepted because they come part of aid conditionalities while others can be part of voluntary acceptance. (see Dobbins, Simmons and Garrett, 2007). However, as Beland (2009:710) suggests, the recognition that many policy ideas spread beyond national borders should not obscure the fact that, as far as country-level politics is concerned, national boundaries and institutions remain central to the politics of policy change around the world. Despite the development of major transnational policy networks, national institutions and policy legacies still weigh heavily on the production of expertise and social learning.

State is the central part of the story of globalization. Transborder movements whether of ideas or labour or capital demand a state that can allow this without friction. It is for this reason that state and its actions/public policies need to be primary focus of attention. The challenge before government is to be concerned about its national interests while at the same time open to global discourse. As we saw earlier, the policy research organizations wedded to this philosophy will tend to intervene in policy processes within that framework. Civil society organizations have now global links and are not confined to the boundaries of a state. The international financial organizations, donor agencies carry this philosophy further.

Let me end by saying that globalization has become more intense in recent years also through informal networks that bring together the most influential people together to exchange ideas and experiences. World Economic Forum is an example of such a network. It brings together heads of state, business and civil society leaders, academics and policy experts in its meeting in Davos. In recent years it has been involved in contentious issues of globalization and sovereignty of state. (see Rupert and Solomon, 2006:57-59)

Endnotes & References

Aiyar and Behar (2005), Budget work in India: Civil Society Experiment in democratic engagement, Economic and political weekly, vol.40, no.2.

Beland Daniel (2009), Idea, Institutions and Policy Change, Journal of European Public Policy, vol. 16, no 5.

Bogason P. (2000), Public Policy and Local Governance, Institutions in Post Modern Society, Edgar Elgar, Cheltenham.

Businessline, New Delhi, January 29, 2013.

Chandhoke Neera (2007), Engaging with Civil Society: The Democratic Perspective, Prepared for the 'Non-Government Public Action' Programme, Centre for Civil Society, London School of Economics and Political Science.

Dobbins F.R., Simmon and Garrett G. (2007), The Global Diffusion of Public Policy; Social Construction, Coercion, competition or Learning?, Annual review of Sociology, Vol.33.

Ficher F. (2003), Reframing Public Policy: Discursive Politics and Deliberated Practices, Oxford University Press, Oxford.

Indian Express, New Delhi, November 9, 2013.

Mathur Kuldeep (2013), Public Policy and Politics in India: How Institutions Matter, New Delhi: Oxford University Press. 2013

Mathur Kuldeep and Björkman J W (2009), Policy-making in India: Who Speaks? who Listens?, Har Anand Publication, New Delhi.

Pressman Jeffrey and Wildavsky Aaron (1973), Implementation: How Great Expectations in Washington are Dashed in Oakland, University of California press, . Berkeley.

Rupert M. and Soloman M Scoat (2006), Globalisation and International Politics Economy, Rawman Littlefield, New York.

Scholte J. A. (2000), Globalisation: A Critical Introduction, Hampshire, Palgrave.

Stone A Deborah (1988), Policy Paradox: The Art of Political Decision Making, W.W. Norton & Company.

2

State and Public Policy: Contemporary Debate

Kamlesh Gupta and Manjri Damele

The concept of State has occupied a high ground in the political arena of the traditional period but the state is a historical institution, it emerged in response to a particular set of circumstances in sixteenth century Europe and it has continued to evolve in the light of the changing circumstances. The State developed into a nation-state in the nineteenth century, and during the twentieth, and the post-1945 period adopted socio-economic responsibilities and emerging as a welfare state. In period of 1980s in different countries, a general rolling back of the state took place through the adoption of liberalization and privatization and introduction of the market reforms in public service. Above ideological trends /factors were responsible to rise of pro market and anti state ideas of the new right. Such developments have led, some argue, to the emergence of a new form of state, portrayed variously as the competitive state, market pro-state or post modern state. In the era of globalization, the State changes its nature according to global forces. The focus of state is more on regulatory and controlling functions. So the nature of state has to continuously undergoing change. The welfare state, as an institution, guarantees social welfare and social justice to the deprived groups but globalization has not only threatened it but also made it weak. In the contemporary context, social welfare agenda is taken over by non-state organizations that need to be carefully critiqued. The older theories of state, which are either inadequate or inapplicable, today cannot cover the new developments that have taken place in the era of globalization and therefore they have to be reviewed, specifically in the contemporary context. The rise of globalization has stimulated a major debate about the state and public policy. Globalization has not only affected state but also influenced the public policy to a great extent. It has challenged the nature of public policy by summoning a series of non-negotiable, external and largely economic imperatives that must be appeased in a technically proficient manner if good economic performance is to be maintained, at the cost of democratic accountability. Globalization necessitates a certain privatization and technicization of public policy rendering it publicly less accountable. Public character of public policy is potentially seen as a casualty of globalization (Moren M., Pein M. and Goodin R.E., 2006). The neo-liberal economy has further compounded the unevenness and inequality in society. In the light of these changes, we need to rethink about these aspects of public policy.

This paper addresses the question, why to need debate on the state and public policy in new global era. The author advocates that the rise of globalization has stimulated a major debate about the state and public policy. Globalization has not only affected state but also influenced the public policy to a great extent. The paper is divided into the following parts: Introduction; Globalization, State and Public Policy; Main Issues of Redebate on State, Debate on Public Policy, Challenges of Policy Concern and Implementation, and Contemporary Reforms.

Since the beginning of human civilization to till the present government and state have been evolving and developing, as a result of which significant changes have taken place in nature. In the early stages of civilization there was tribal state but later it became society centered. With the changes in time and circumstances and development in ideas related to the state the police state emerged which gradually transformed into a welfare state. However this was not the end of change and the establishment of an administrative state according to public needs and demands was given recognition by the end of the twentieth century. With the efforts of Margaret Thatcher in Britain, Ronald Reagan in USA and Melroni in Canada the welfare state was transformed into an administrative state. The disintegration of USSR and the emergence of a unipolar system further influenced this notion. Alongside in 1980-90 the effects of privatization, liberalization and globalization became obvious in almost all the countries of the world, especially the developed countries, and also on public policy, started becoming visible. As a result, after the adoption of liberalization, privatization and globalization, a need for a redebate and further discussions on the significance of state and public policy has emerged at the global level since there is a definite decline in the role of state as an active agent but even then in the context of contemporary circumstances most countries would like to implement new ideas on good governance in the state and the concept implemented by the administration with transparency and economy. In this situation new pro rightist thinkers are the chief supporters of consumerism and they too much oppose interference of work load of the state (Heywood Andrew, 2010). As the effect of globalization different forms of the state have become obvious to us. These are: Competitive State, Post modern State, and Pro market State.

In developed countries, development is mainly a popular and continuously occurring activity but the state and the administrative policies have an important role in regulating the development. In the contemporary perspective state, development and public policies have all been influenced by globalization. In comparison to developed countries however there was to improve the role and size of bureaucracy for improvement of governance system in the developing countries. But in the present context of globalization there is a need for a re debate on state and public policy. "The biggest challenge of public policy at present is accountability and transparency. These challenges emerge as the effect of globalization" (Riggs FW, 2012). In the context of development the importance of public policy has increased but "due to globalization there is a challenge to its welfare nature and there is also a change in the idea of public security" (Bislon Seven, 2004). On the one hand the state wants to establish itself as a welfare state while on the other hand globalization wants to see itself in the role of a minimal legal state. In this condition there are two choices for developing countries. Firstly, there should be a change in the role of government and public policies due to the emergence of market economy, and secondly, redebate in the context of changes in nature of public policies.

The culture and values in reference of democratic system of developed countries are putting pressure on developing countries in the contemporary period. In developing countries there is an effort for developing basic sustainable development, as a result of which there is a pressure on developing countries to convert its capitalist policies into public policies which might not be able to sustain its nature of being a welfare state. As a result the state is adopting welfare measures with its minimum legal nature. The state is minimizing, its focus from productive activities to social and infrastructural services and is gradually moving towards importance of decentralization and local administration. In this context scholars of public administration have given the argument that it is now time to have a new debate on the role of all three namely state, public policies and development. In the context of the global market system, a scholar named James Stever in his book "The end of Public Administration" has declared the end of state and administration and has suggested that all the activities of the government should be left to market system (Stebar James, 1988). The prediction of the end of the state was first done by the followers of Marxism. In this context Lenin in his book "Socialism is the higher level of Capitalism" has emphasized on the development and role of multinational corporations and suggests that the state should take care of the needs of these multinational corporations and make them more powerful through its policies. Other scholars have also talked about the emergence of a new management system of whom the most important is Scolt who takes the position that in the era of globalization also state and state governance will continue to remain (Scoolt J.K., 2007). According to scholar Jismen even after the implementation of the practical form of globalization, state and administration will continue to remain strongly. Professor Rajni Kothari says in this context that "on one side the state is declining in its social transformative form while on the other side there is emergence of global political institutions. These institutions will be the possibilities of the future" (Kothari Rajni, 1996). Another thinker named Baldev Raj Nayar says that "it will be wrong that the functions of the state are become narrower due to the increasing function in the wake of globalization. Instead there is a possibility of increasing function of the institution named state" (Nayar Baldev Raj, 2009). After the implementation of the ideology of globalization usually three significant choices come to the fore. Firstly, a group of scholars talk of the end of the state, i.e., decline of the state and administrative activities. Secondly, a group of scholars talk about the strengthening of the government and administration. The third trends are the most important one, which negates the limited role of the state and accepts a minimal legal state in the context of globalization. Three aspects need to be studied in the fields of public policy in effect of globalization. They are: Public policy, development, and accountability; Administrative reforms and modernization; and Public Policy and Democratic institutes.

While discussing the main reasons for the change in the nature of modern states Farel Heddy says that the main reason is globalization (Ferel Heddy, 1996). In general there are three reasons for the changes in the role of state, public policy, and development. These are:

1. **Development of information technology:** The implementation of the market system has helped in the development of information technology the most. As a result of this advancement there has been tremendous development in the sectors of internet, satellite, and communication. Because of this advancement globalization has moved in the direction of unification (integration of global level) and the obstacles between various countries regarding communication has been reduced. The phenomenon of globalization received a great boost and a change in the roles of government and administration also took place. Alongside further discussions took place on public policy and administration and the concept of governance through network started coming into debate.
2. **Second phase of globalization:** In the first phase of globalization there was only economic liberalization and increase in trade and improvement in relation between various nations were given emphasis. However in the second phase now positive policies and stronger influence of international institutions have started becoming visible. As a result the concepts of global friendship and good relations between nations have started gaining ground. Alongside because of various function of the administration it has become more powerful. Also, the international policies are being recognized and accepted by all the countries (including developing countries).
3. **Downfall of socialist economy and move towards capitalist economy:** The downfall of the socialist economies was another reason for the inclination (trends) of most nations to move towards capitalism and global policies. They are now adopting positive policies which are taking their economies towards globalization. Thus in addition to supporting the policies of multinational institutions most nations are also tending to form policies that will provide infrastructural facilities to poor people.

As a result of the above mentioned reasons in the last decade a tremendous change has been observed in the state, government and administration and a further relook and discussions on their interrelationships has emerged. In this connection a group of scholars have started talking about having discussions on the condition of the state through the concept of the 'roll back state'. Some other groups of scholars are proposing a competitive state through new concepts of the relationship between state and public administration while still other group of thinkers are advocating a minimal right transformative state.

Globalization, State and Public Policy

In the present context comparison of the contemporary form of globalization can be done to a man of many disguises (Multi makeup man) who takes different disguises while appearing before us. However it is difficult to correctly define globalization. Economists have stated globalization to be a step towards the formation of a global market. Political scientists have described globalization to be part of the process of unification of all the communities of the world. The scholar Ferzmand has identified six meanings of the word globalization (Farzmand A., 1999). They are:

1. Internationalization
2. Opening of boundaries
3. A Process
4. An Ideology
5. A Phenomenon
6. Both a process and phenomenon

According to Farzmand, "the meaning of globalization is to move away from the process of state control and protection and by opening boundaries to a great extent, to make the relationships between business, culture and trade harmonious" (Farzmand A, 2001). It was Ferzmand's belief that this boundary less world could be unified by a globalised process that would include global economy, global government, and a public administration.

As a process the phenomenon of globalization has been existing since ancient time. However, in the present age it was the result of the efforts to make capitalist ideas more powerful and to reach the global market during the recession that occurred in 1970. Globalization is both a phenomenon and a process. In this context it is a process for expanding opportunities and forging new boundaries for the increasing capital accumulation at the global level. Alongside it is also a phenomenon that is occurring due to the capital accumulation. Thus, from the above discussions on globalization it is clear that in the present context of globalization the nation is giving importance to issues related to state, government and administration. The views of the scholars on the topic of globalization can be broadly divided into three groups since globalization cannot be accepted in its entirety. Firstly, Views support globalization; secondly, Views opposing globalization; and thirdly, Balanced view.

The scholars who supporting globalization view the world as one village and imagine the concept of a global village due to the advancement of internet, email and other technology. This view is supported by the capitalist ideology and they see the world as a consumer. This view supports western notions like liberalization, individual freedom, western ethics and consumerism etc. These scholars also argue that globalization as a process which does not accept national boundaries or they imagine foundries-less world. Huntington, one of the exponents of this view, sees globalization as a race (*bhagadad)* and declares the end of any force that comes in its path. He advices all nations to adopt globalization since this process has the capacity to run the economy and market processes (Hantigton Semuel 1996). Fukoyama, another scholar, also supports above argument.

The scholars who oppose globalization, they argues that it as a danger for the sovereignty of nations, administration, democratic processes, and for various communities. They believe that global institutions are trying to establish control over financial power and by imposing pressure on the socioeconomic policies of nations they are forcing them to take decisions in their favour. They are defining it is a new form of imperialism who's leader is US and the multinational corporations which are trying to westernize all the countries through globalization. Thus globalization can lead to a condition of economic colonization. These scholars have warned to states saying that as a result of globalization economic disparity will increase, and labour and capital will be exploited in developing countries, which can lead to political turbulence. Scholars like Ferzmand challenge to global imperialism and saying that in this process local and national sovereignty and attempts at decentralization will gradually decrease (Farzmand A., 1999). This view has been supported by Koreton while scholars like Sweater and Kalevar etc. give the argument that rather than peace and security, increase in globalization signals can increase in global insecurity and the death of public administration. Thus the scholars who oppose globalization see it as a global government but see it as a dictator who is being supported by powerful nations and capitalist imperialists.

At present globalization is definitely increase capitalism. More than 65% of the world's capital is in the hands of only 15 multinational corporations. Their strategy is expansion of multinational companies and accumulating capital which seems to be true in the case of developing nations.

The scholars advocating a balanced view include Skant and Ferzmand. Ferzmand believes that "globalization is a reality for socio-economic development." He feels that this process cannot be stopped, but in order to combat the challenges which emerge it is important to make changes in policies and form strategies accordingly (Farzmand A., 1999). This viewpoint can be applied to John Strauss views on slavery and globalization. In the context of globalization it is not necessary to think how to stop it but it is important to think how to control it. Thus it is important to form effective strategies to combat the contemporary challenges emerging from it. Globalization is a continual process which has both negative and positive effects on state, administration, and society. William Tab has taken a positive view of globalization and said that globalization is a process that reduces the hurdles between nations and through this process social, political and economic interaction increases (Mohanana B., 2000). In this context C.P. Bhambhris statement is also important; he said that "at present it is important to think how states facing the challenges because of globalization can attain their goal of social justice" (Bhanbari C.P., 1996).

Contemporary Debate on State

Globalization has emerged as a continually flowing process whose far reaching effects can be seen on the state, public administration and society. There are different effects on the governance of developed and developing countries and there are both positive and negative effects which are felt by society and governing system. The scholars who support globalization feel that globalization will bring about the end of state and its governance, but in the last few years it was observed that it is not so. On the other hand because of the emerging contemporary issues the state is emerging more powerful. The opponents of globalization also gave the argument that the state will turn into a corporate government and serve the interests of capitalist forces. However, at present the state is being seen as an administrative state or regulating state. Alongside the scholars had said that globalization might prove to be a threat to sovereignty of the state, democracy, and individual freedom and will be forced to accept the policies/decision of various international institutions like World Bank, IMF and WTO, and multinational corporations and the globalization policies of the developed countries. By encouraging the welfare of these institutions problems like poverty and unemployment will increase. The opponents of globalization, while giving this argument had said that due to globalization the multinational corporations are siphoning the capital of developing countries because of which economic disparity in these countries is increasing. Additionally increasing in technology and decrease in human resources is increasing unemployment.

On the other side the supporters of globalization talk about the transformation of state and public administration and they argues for a change in the role of the government for forming strategies for good governance and development of the state, since "in developing countries there is a long tradition of intervention by the government in the economic sector" (Dhameja Alka, 2004). The direction of these strategies has to be decided by the government policies. In the contemporary period public administration is responsible for the control of the state's economy. In the context of state's accountability a scholar named Ajrail talks about breaking the link between private sector, institutional function, legal controlling function, end of boundaries of competitive control and competition and un-legal boundaries of state activities which has competitive to private sector.

According to the famous economist Joseph Stigler "In the age of globalization there is a special responsibility of the government. For wording effectively it is important for the market has to create functional basic infrastructure" (Stigilor Joshef E., 2010). These infrastructural facilities include a functional legal system and institutions that will implement them. If the market has to work smoothly then definitely there has to be a well-established and well-functioning legal system, an effective competitive system for which necessary of anti-trust changes, and there has to be an environment of development, which means all the contract should be right way and laws opposing frauds have to be made stronger, which properly represent the accepted code of conduct. In the age of globalization the state can contribute towards training labour, technical innovations, and increasing small and medium industries, and development of import substitution goods. For example in the directive principles of the Indian Constitution it is mentioned that, "the country will fulfill its socio-economic responsibilities of which the main one is to remove social injustice, to bring about equal opportunities, and to ensure the health, education and housing of the poor" (Indian Constitution, 2010). These can be provided only by the state. In emergency situations there is an increase in the function of the state, but apart from them ensuring social justice, protecting minorities, and establishing a legal system for a multi-religious and multi-cultural society can be done only by the state. Thus, it can be said that in reality the state has emerged as a controlling agency for which there is no alternative to accepting global policies and coordinating controlling functions.

In the era of globalization discussion on the role of the state and public policies can be of two kinds:

1. What activities should be done by the state
2. What activities should be left to private institutions

In this context two streams of thought exist. The first is that the state should not interfere in the domestic activities of the citizens. The second is that the role of the state should be most important but decreasing the importance of administration would be incorrect. In reality administration is the key of the state and its activities but in the last two decades there has been a great impact of globalization on the structure, processes and behavior of administration. If this is the major debatable issue then two kinds of argument appear before us. The first is that a powerful role of the state is important for the proper organization of objects and services and those rules and institutions are more important which can protect the interests of the people along with the market. Second, the identity of public administration should be within the framework of the state otherwise there might be a change in its nature. A change in the nature of the state and public policy can be observed due to globalization. These changes are of three kinds: Development of information and technology; Positive reaction of global institutions; and Greater stress on efficiency, economy, effectiveness and production (3E&P).

There has been a definite effect of advancement of information technology on the state and public policy. Technology increases the skill and effectiveness of the activities of public administration, which helps the administration to provide better facilities to the people. At present the concept of e-governance is being given great importance which makes administration more friendly. The second reason is the effect of globalization on public policy and administration in developing countries. In general when finance is needed for the development of developing countries then the major global institutions provide finance for infrastructure, human resource development, and other sectors on their own terms and condition but the effect of these conditions fall on the policies of developing countries. Through the effect of these policies all the sectors/areas of developing countries have converted into laboratories. Alongside due to the third reason skill, friendliness and production are areas where there have been tremendous changes due to the effects of globalization. The people centered institutions are under pressure to increase their skills and production and compete with private organizations. These organizations are under pressure to reduce the staff structure, bureaucracy and implement new methods like new public management and corporate governance, and to link with public services as a result of globalization, but in developing countries there is a great role of the state in socio-economic development in addition to providing services. However, due to globalization the state has to take the roles of partner, coordinator and facilitator. Globalization has created new partnerships, new relationships, effects on policies and new institutions between the government, people and organizations which have increased the effect on the people.

In order to make the government a more effective partner in development the World Bank Report has recently drawn attention on two strategies. The first strategy stresses on main sectors like legal system, health and basic needs and collective and cooperative function and says that the state has to focus on four main activities (World Bank Report, 2012). These are: Rule and regulation has to be established in a strong way; To maintain public policies in social way; Investment on infrastructural social services in the basic sectors has to be increased; and Protection of environment and efforts for the welfare of marginalized people.

For implementing the second strategy includes forming the structure of effective rules and necessary sanctions, controlling corruption, capacity building of government servants, improvement of his salaries, decentralization, increasing public participation. In other words the state is not in a position to do all activities on its own in the era of globalization. The market, governmental and other organizations (non-governmental, community organizations, pressure groups, and civil society) have to also fulfill their responsibilities. The state has to function as a coordinative agency where on the one hand the state has to form such organizational infrastructure and policies in which the private sector can be encouraged to play a partnership role, and on the other the state has to ensure that most benefit of the governmental policies go to the marginalized section and poor. In this way poverty and inequality is reduced and the benefit of development can reach all sections of the society. The state has to invest more heavily investment in some basic sectors in which education and health are the most important.

Public Policy in New Global Era

The rise of globalization has stimulated a major debate about the state and public policy. Globalization has not only affected state but also influenced the public policy to a great extent. It has challenged the nature of public policy by summoning a series of non-negotiable, external and largely economic imperatives that must be appeased in a technically proficient manner if good economic performance is to be maintained, at the cost of democratic accountability. Globalization necessitates a certain privatization and technicization of public policy rendering it publicly less accountable. Public character of public policy is potentially seen as a casualty of globalization. The neo-liberal economy has further compounded the unevenness and inequality in society. In the light of these changes, we need to rethink about these aspects of public policy. There are three actors, whose major role on formulation of public policy. These are; state, society and market. In contemporary context role of state is regulate and insured the implementation of public policy, for this purpose some agencies of state is working as a controlling agency i.e., IRDA, TRAI, CCI and other agency. In time turbulence in developing countries and as well as India, policy paralysis word has been emerged in debates. The roles of some agencies are increased due to this situation; these are national advisory committee, CAG, Supreme Court and other similar bodies.

The process of globalization has brought forth several challenges before public administration, as a result of which many new concepts like e-governance, good governance, minimal government, reinventing government and private-public partnership, have developed. These new concepts have presented public administration in a new form, due to which a condition of new discussion on state and public policy has emerged. Fed Riggs gives the advice that "in order to meet the challenges of globalization state governments has to focus on the correct formation of public policies" (Riggs W., 2012). Centralized policy process, lake of political support, political integration, lake of public involvement and poor coordination are also big factor in policy process (Sapru R.K., 2011).

In any decision-making process and policy-formulation, there is always a need for a detailed working out of strategic programs and suitable administrative organizations and operational steps. "Administrative planning begins where economic planning ends. It is conveyor system without a dichotomy between planning and implementation, but there is always feedback from implementation to make planning much more purposeful. From time to time bureaucracy had indeed risen to deliver the goals in time of crises. It is, thus responsibility of the bureaucracy to ensure that the policies are conceived so as to be relevant to prevailing conditions and implemented with patience and conviction" (Haldipur R.N., 2006).

De-bureaucratization means decreasing the form of bureaucracy, i.e., reduction of employed staff in government organizations and ease in simplification of legal and managerial activities. This argument is given for developing a small form of government organizations so that a small public organization process can be formed that will be more appropriate and flexible for the fast changing world. The concept of a reduced form of organizations has emerged from private organizations. In these organizations more stress is laid on greater output from minimal resources. As a result of this idea it is also expected from public administration that they provide better services and assistance to the public in a limited time and with limited resources.

Governments have expanded after the emergence of the concept of a public welfare state. In this context the argument of new reformists is that in the sector of the public the number of posts has increased which is causing greater expenditure on the public budget of the government. That is why at present, it is very important to reduce them and to bring them within normal limits. As a by-product of globalization the idea of new public management shows that in different public activities and unskilled process which in reality causes harm to the implementation of policies and that is why it is important to minimize it. The beginning of advanced technology was production and distribution of information and services, flexible supervision process and control process etc, through which the public sector can be made more efficient and accountable.

Contemporary Reforms

After liberalization and globalization the new concepts that have emerged like minimal government advocate new flexible, regulated, and good governance working processes in place of the existing strict bureaucratic regime, which is more democratic, accountable and competitive. At present the main challenges in front of bureaucracy is to change itself in favour of the expectations of the citizen. For this it is very important to bring about administrative reforms in the contemporary context. The concepts of e-governance and right to information in reality were brought in after globalization, through which have increased the need of governments to go for contemporary administrative reforms.

1. Improvement of working process
2. Role of the state in policy formation
3. Intervention of constitutional bodies
4. The emerging strong condition of advisory institutes and bodies
5. Contribution of research on policies
6. Contribution of the public on public policy
7. Impact of global institutions on public policy

The concept of a global village and the competition between various sector of public enterprises that have emerged from globalization have forced public administration to think on three lines. These are 3E i.e., efficiency, effectiveness and economy. A new concept called Public Private Partnership (PPP) has emerged before the government and private sector under which mutual agreement and understanding have come into existence. This reform is being emphasized as a work culture in European countries.

"Decentralization is basically distribution of authority with responsibility in the various lower levels. In the administrative sector decentralization implies deciding different levels of decision making" (Chouhan A.P.S. & Gupta Kamlesh, 2009). In general the process of decentralization gives impetus to an environment of competition since the officers and staff of all these levels have more authority to work with responsibility. However in general in public organizations the nature of political intervention and centralization is found. In developing countries intervention of government is found at all levels. Thus in the era of globalization decentralization in the decision making process and policy formation level in public organizations is a major challenge.

"Important to this has been emergence of the new public management (NPM). NPM allows private bodies to take greater responsibility for the delivery of services through privatization, contracting out and market testing. These ideas have been taken out most enthusiastically in New Zealand, UK, USA, and Scandinavia" (Heywood Andrew, 2010). In his book Vikert focus that challenges of NPM includes different branches of industrial management process are:

1. In general capable manger is who trend in business, should be employed and they should be made accountable.
2. NPM emphasis on citizens should be given recognition as consumers. This implies that for providing better facilities to the citizens emphasis should be given to more flexible managerial process.
3. NPM lays more emphasis on the need to implement flexibility in the functioning of government organizations along with priority and accepting new techniques. Through this there will be development of good organizational environment, decentralized leadership, and team spirit. The NPM wants to implement this concept in the government sector. For implementing it NPM considers training an important method.

In the public sector for increasing work efficiency and producing better facility has to give more attention to work evaluation. Under this public organizations have to remove their attention from resources and processes and focus it on results and evaluation so that improved human facilities can be obtained. In this age of competition challenges related to evaluation of public organizations is very important. For this the process of fixing of goals and obtaining results by focusing on efficient reforms has to be developed.

Privatization is in reality considered to be the harbinger of the new managerial revolution. Through privatization the public organizations can be transformed, which will help in the move of public organizations from their centralized nature to decentralization (from policy level to lower level). This includes decreasing government participation in public organizations (Disinvestment) and developing an environment of competition with private organizations. The special features of privatization are inherent in NPM.

Concluding Remarks

Through in process of privatization the work culture of government bureaucracy can be decreased, number of staff can be reduced and the nature of de-bureaucratization can be emphasized. The government will only have to organize essential services through public organizations. Thus, privatization tries to convert the state into the form of a regulated and minimal rights state. Due to globalization the notion of e-governance was spread in order to make the government more efficient and functional. There are also efforts to bring about openness, transparency, and accountability. There is also emphasis on granting power to the process of emerging due to recent trends in decentralization. As a result of the impact of globalization the governments of the state are slowly converting their important policies likes; organizational structure and personnel policies, which can help them to compete in the era of globalization.

"With regard to India the effect of globalization in reality has came effort in a mixed form, but the results in the sectors of social development and poverty seem to be negative" (Bhattacharya, 2006). Thus in the contemporary context there is need for the state to transform itself in order to obtain its goals in the case of developing public policies and in order to meet the challenges of globalization, it is important to transform itself by adopting new ideas so that in this era the state and public policies can present themselves in a strengthened form and the positive effects of the globalization can fall on these organizations. Thus, in the end in short it can be said that globalization has affected the state and various sectors of the public administration but has not been able to form a new system in place of the state and public administration. Globalization has given a tough challenge to the democratic system in developing countries along with various other countries of the world and has also affected their independence and the right to form decisions (Farzmand A., 2001). Globalization has tried to establish the state as a regulated state and is trying to establish the hegemony of privatization and capitalistic system all over the world.

In a welfare state, services like education, health and justice should be provided either free or at subsidized rates to the citizens of the country and the government should take appropriate steps in this direction. If India is seriously interested in establishing itself strongly among the other developed countries then it has to empower itself in the field of policy concern & implementation. For this purpose the reforms should be implemented within a stipulated period of time. The government should also try to develop and maintain a creative balance between the private and government sector under government control for the better public policy initiatives. Proper step taken by the government for reforming the public policies of the country are not being done, which should be done as soon as possible. For this purpose it is necessary that the policies formed by the government with support of other actors like; society and market and alongside there should be an effective system for controlling these institutions at both the national and the state level. After the discussing challenges, we offer a few suggestions for policy concern: Promote empowerment and decentralization through policy initiatives; Effective formulation and implementation; Positive role of the constitutional bodies; To develop coordination between government, market and other agencies; and To need of Evaluation and Control Board.

Endnotes & References

Bhanbari C.P. (1996), Globalisatioon, Liberlasation and welfare State, Indian Journal of Public Administration, Joly-Sept. 1996, Vol. 40(II) No. 3.

Bhattacharya Mohit (2006), write up on Reconstruction of Public Administration, Jawahar Publication, New Delhi.

Bislon Seven (2004), Globalisation State Transformation and Public Security, International Political Science Review, July 2004, Vol. 25.

Chouhan A.P.S. & Gupta Kamlesh (2009,), Recent Trend in Decentralisation, associated publication, Agra.

Dhameja Alka (2004), Contemporary Debate on Public Administration, P.H.I. Leening.

Farzmand A. (1999), Globalisation and Public Administration, Public Administration Review, Vol. 59, No.6, December 1999.

Farzmand A. (2001), Globalisation State and Public Administration: A Theoritical Analysis with policy Implication for Developmental State, Public Administration Review, Vol.1, No. 4, December 2001.

Ferel Heddy (1996), Comparative and International Public Administration : building of Technical Bridge, Public administration Review, vol. 58(1).

Haldipur R.N., Bureaucracy's Response to New Challenges, in SC Dubey (ed.), Public Service and Social Responsibility, New Delhi, Vikas Publication..

Hantigton Semuel (1996), The case of Civilisation and A Remaking World Order, Simon and Structure Publication, New York.

Heywood Andrew (2010), Politics, Palgrave Macmillan, New York.

Indian Constitution, Central Law Agency, Allahabad, 2010.

Kothari Rajni (1996), Under the Globalisation Bill Nation State Hold, EPW, July, 1996.

Mohanana B. (2000), from Eco Globalisation to Post Globalisation Societies Order and India State, IDSA Journal, July-Sept. 2000.

Moren M., Pein M. and Goodin R.E. (2006), The Oxford Handbook of Public Policy, Oxford University Press, New York.

Nayar Baldev Raj (2009), the Myth of srinking state: Globalisation and state of India, Oxford University Press.

Riggs F.W., Globalisation and Public Administration access on http://www.2huwai.edu/n glop.htm on dated14/06/12

Sapru R.K. (2011), Public Policy: Art and craft of policy analysis, PHI Publication New Delhi.

Scoolt J.K. Global Capitalism and the State, International Affairs, Vol. 73, No.3.

Stebar James (1988), The End of Public Administration, Transition Publication, New York.

Stigilor Joshef E. (2010), Freefall America free Market and Srinking of the world Economy, W.W. Northen and Co.

World Bank Report, 2012.

3

Public Policy and Globalization: An Emerging Framework of Global Public Policy

Abhishek Pratap Singh

The concept of state occupies central place in Political Science. No discussion on political theory is complete without reference to the word 'state'. The functioning of state, indeed affects various aspect of human life, and this is why it has very rightly captured the attention of political philosophers. In addition to this, with the evolution of modern-nation state of renaissance period in sixteen century, its nature has changed from a early non-interventionist state of industrial revolution era to the welfare state model of twenty century. In post-Cold War era there has been a structural transformation in the nature of functioning and conception of state from welfare oriented to ensure enabling environment for individual and communities to play larger role in process of its functioning. In this context, the role of public policy has also changed and acquired new meaning. The objectives and public policy priorities have changed in the era of globalisation. Also, the importance of public policy and its impact in general has been reshaped. There are certain limitations with newly emerging framework for operation of public policy. Whether public policy is a viable option in contemporary global era or its role has changed with emerging challenges is the question that this paper will attempt to answer.

Understanding Public Policy and its Origin

The Public Policy is defined as a system of "courses of action, regulatory measures, laws, and funding priorities concerning a given topic promulgated by a governmental entity or its representatives" (John W., 1995). The definition given primarily covers all the areas of public policies but it resembles to public policy being an area of public domain. In the United States, this concept refers not only to the result of policies, but more broadly to the decision-making process and analysis of governmental decisions. It underlies public policy as a state centric affair that includes government policy formulations and its further execution. In general public policy is the principled guide to action taken by the administrative and executive branches of the state with regard to various numbers of issues in a manner consistent with law and institutional customs.

Public policy is a purposive and consistent course of action produced as a response to a perceived problem of a constituency, formulated by a specific political process, and adopted, implemented, and enforced by a public agency. It is largely characterized as a dynamic, complex, and interactive system through which public problems are identified and addressed by formulating appropriate policy. In public policy making, numerous individuals and interest groups compete and collaborate to influence policymakers to act in a particular way. It is noticeable that public policy is commonly backed by constitutions, legislative acts, and judicial decisions. This is because the formulation and supervision of public policy is state affair in practice. It necessitates that public policy to be *adopted, implemented,* and *enforced* by a governmental body, is meant to emphasize that the policy, as such stated, must be put into practice in a manner consistent with the formal and stated legislative sanctions.

The concept of public policy has its origin in the discipline of public administration. In 1960 John Kennedy was elected President of the United States and was concerned with the reform in domestic policy administration in United States of America (USA) and due to the lapses in implementing New-Deal programme. In staffing his administration, Kennedy sought the "best and the brightest". Taking into account the highly specialized skills required to develop and oversee the Policy Planning Budgeting System (PPBS), which applied a cost-benefit analysis framework. And to meet this demand, major US universities responded by establishing programmes and projects, training students in understanding, formulating and executing public policy. This move was aimed to promote academic analysis on public policy and its importance for administration.

Between 1967 and 1971, graduate programs at the master's or doctoral level in public policy were created at: the Institute of Public Policy Studies, University of Michigan; the Kennedy School at Harvard; the Graduate School of Public Policy, University of California, Berkeley; the School of Urban and Public Affairs, Carnegie Mellon University; the RAND Graduate School; the Department of Public Policy and Management, University of Pennsylvania; the School of Public Affairs, University of Minnesota; the Lyndon B. Johnson School of Public Affairs, University of Texas; and the Institute of Policy Science and Public Affairs, Duke University (Graham Allison, 2008).

Over the following five years, the Ford Foundation provided multi-million dollar general support grants to eight grantee programs that were developing a concentration on graduate training in public policy. The Foundation's initial seed money proved crucial in nurturing the incipient development of a new field in an era marked by deep distrust of government (Miles, R.E., 1967). A key innovation within these programmes was a shift in focus from public administration to public policy. Emphasizing public policy, these institutes addressed emerging areas related to public policy re-orientation in the light of contemporary situation. This refocus required a greater understanding of the complex social and political environment within which policy is shaped and implemented. It also required training policy analysts, and not simply public administrators, who could inform decision makers about the consequences of alternative policy choices. The insights involved budgetary cost and efficacy, but also issues of social equity, civil rights, and quality of life.

In the United States this concept refers not only to the result of policies, but more broadly to the decision-making and analysis of governmental decisions. As an academic discipline, public policy has emerged as a cornerstone of contemporary curriculum of political science. Shaping public policy is a complex and multifaceted process that involves the interplay of numerous individuals and interest groups competing and collaborating to influence policymakers to act in a particular way. As an academic discipline, public policy brings in elements of many social science fields and concepts, including economics, sociology, political economy, program evaluation, policy analysis, and public management, all as applied to problems of governmental administration, management, and operations. At the same time, the study of public policy is distinct from humanities, in its focus on the application of theory to practice.

Early Debates on Public Policy

The evolution of public policy and its orientation in the realm of policy affairs also went through academic debate between scholars. The academic debate was largely focused on the issues related to the understanding and scope of public policy, involved stakeholders, functional units, organizational structure and policy feed backs. The early debates on public policy discourse were occupied with the questions related to the extent to which public policy intended to train individuals to participate effectively in the governmental process as policy makers as well as policy analysts; and if so, how individuals trained to be policy analysts, or policy makers and claimed to be useful in revealing the social or public value of governmental action, would relate to the political processes that were an inevitable part of policy making in a democratic society (Moran, M. 2002).

At the same time, scholars on public policy wanted to distinguish themselves from the schools of public administration that had focused on the narrow questions of efficient administration of public policies established elsewhere by others. The Association for Public Policy Analysis and Management (APPAM) was formed in 1979 to support academic institutions training students for distinctive professional careers as policy analysts. In 1981, APPAM merged two journals, Policy Analysis and Public Policy, into the Journal of Policy Analysis and Management, which served as an outlet for multidisciplinary research into public policy issues, and as a sounding board for shifts in the profession. This was pivotal for the development of public policy discourse at global scale.

The influence of liberal democratic model which became popular theme in post war politics was also overt on public policy discourse. More importantly, after third wave of democracy and with increased enfranchisement of masses and social awareness it was being emphasized that, one of the key function of representative democracy is to provide a mechanism through which public opinion, and public policy are regularly connected. On one hand, there should be policy representation; public preferences for policy should be reflected in policy itself. And on the other hand, there should be public responsiveness; public preferences should be informed and should react to public policy (Stuart and Christopher, 2010). Policy representation is important in everyday politics. Failure of adequate policy representation may result on disaffection of the public for the government.

Globalisation and Public Policy

Virtually no topic in contemporary public policy is more contested or more potentially consequential than the impact of globalization. The concept of public policy has been subject to revision in its characteristics under the impact of globalization. In particular, globalisation is seem to challenge the public nature of domestic public policy by summoning a series of non negotiable, external, and largely economic imperatives that must be appeased in a technically proficient manner if good economic performance is to be maintained, whatever the cost in terms of democratic accountability. Similarly, globalization is seen as the enemy of policy, public or otherwise, in the sense that it is seen to dictate policy choices whilst itself being beyond the capacity of domestic political actors to control. Although if globalization is seen as antithetical to public policy, then it is only antithetical to public policy at the domestic level; arguably it merely reinforces the need for effective and democratic public policy at the transnational level. In most conventional treatments, globalization and public policy are counterposed. Globalization is seen to intensify the competitive struggle amongst nations for global market share, driving states to subordinate public policy considerations to economic imperatives, thereby exposing their public sectors to an effective competitive audit.

The impact of globalization has led to change in the orientation and goals of public policy. This characteristic change leads to paradigm shift in the process of public policy formulation. And this can be seen at four distinct levels.

Firstly, globalization is held to necessitate a certain privatization and technicization of public policy, rendering it less publicly accountable. It is distinctly the public character of public policy that is potentially seen as a casualty of globalization. By virtue of "time space compression" and the complex interdependencies that follow the order, globalization is seen to render policy deliberations so technical and involved as to necessitate significant changes in the conduct—and notably the legitimization—of public policy (Ayres and Braithwaite, 1992). Globalization, and its interdependent complexities which are seen to characterize it, are here associated with powerful tendencies to depoliticization, privatization, and technicization of public policy formulation and regulation (Sheri and Kathleen, 1999).

Secondly, globalization is seen to necessitate internalization and preference of capital and an associated squeezing of the fiscal space for public policy. This is perhaps the most conventional sense in which globalization is seen to be antithetical to public policy. Globalization is treated as synonymous with the mobility of capital. In order to retain high levels of investment, on which economic growth and high levels of employment are predicated, states must increasingly provide an investment climate conducive to profit maximization or more to the point, conducive to the anticipation by potential investors of profit maximization (Behn, R.D., 1978). They must, in short, internalize the preferences of capital. Such preferences are conventionally assumed to be for a lightly regulated marketplace relatively free from public policy interventions and characterized by low levels of taxation. The mobility of capital is seen both directly and indirectly, to exert strong downward pressures on public policy.

Thirdly, globalization is seen to diminish the policy making capacity and autonomy of the nation state, resulting in a displacement of functions from public to quasi public bodies (such as independent central banks) and from national to transnational institutions such as those associated with the process of European integration and more obviously global institutions such as the International Monetary Fund (IMF), World Trade Organisation (WTO) and World Bank (WB). This is a third sense in which globalization and public policy making capacity at the national level are seen to be antithetical.

Lastly, globalization is seen as driving a process of convergence, thereby diminishing both variations between states in public policy and the significance of variations in public policy as variables in the explanation of comparative performance. Questions of convergence, divergence, or continued diversity have provided a key focus for public policy analysis in an era of globalization, provoking considerable controversy. In its more subtle, differentiated, and increasingly influential perspective globalization heavily circumscribes public policy makers' autonomy (Hay Colin, 2008). In liberal market economies, for instance, it essentially imposes on them market conforming policies, raising questions again about the extent to which public policy can be held publicly or democratically accountably.

Conclusion

In this context, it is perhaps hardly surprising that commentators like *David Marquand* have point to the notion of "decline of public" in public policy making (Marquand David, 2004). Yet before rushing to endorse such a pessimistic conclusion, it is important to acknowledge that most of the issues discussed above rest on strong assumptions as to the nature, extent, and consequences of globalization on public policy. Whether acknowledged as such, these are unavoidably empirical claims and, moreover, empirical claims that do not always stand up to a close consideration of the available evidence. Indeed, although the contemporary period is invariably referred to as one of globalization, and although globalization is invariably seen as placing stringent constraints on the size of the public sector, in aggregate terms states consume a larger share of global Gross Domestic Output (GDP) than at any previous point in their history.

In addition, the scope and nature of public policy has widened as the new framework of global public policy has come to acquire larger space in global political and economic discourse including non-state actors as well. In this context the understanding of public versus private becomes complicated when we move to transnational global policy-making. In the realm of policy-making, now a potentially large and rather heterogeneous number of non-state actors are involved also. The policy problems and their solutions now are transboundary in nature necessitating supraterritorial efforts on a global scale. The policy problem arises independently in a number of different places in the world but cannot be systematically addressed without acting on a global scale. Thus, it may not be end of public policy as concept, rather an opportunity for the emergence of global public policy framework with more convergence of interests and actions.

Endnotes & References

Ayres, I. and Braithwaite, J. (1992), *Responsive Regulation*, Oxford: Oxford University Press.

Behn, R. D. (1978), 'How to terminate a public policy', *Policy Analysis* 4: 393-414.

Graham Allison (2008), Emergence of Schools of Public Policy: Reflections by a Founding Dean.

Hay Colin (2008), "Globalization and Public Policy" The Oxford Handbook on Public Policy.

Kingdon, John W. (1995), *Agenda, Alternatives and Public Policy*, Harper Collins, New York.

Marquand David (2004), Decline of Public: The Hollowing Out of Citizenship, Polity Press.

Michael Moran, Martin Rein, Robert E. Goodin ed., *The Oxford Handbook on Public Policy*.

Miles, R.E. Jr (1967), The Search for Identity of Graduate Schools of Public Affairs, *Public Administration Review*, 27 (4).

Moran, M. (2002), 'Understanding the regulatory state', *British Journal of Political Science* Volume 32:

Sheri Berman, Kathleen R McNamara, (1999), Bank on Democracy: Why Central Banks Need Public Oversight, *Foreign Affairs*, Volume 1.

Soroka and Christopher Wlezien (2010), "*Public Opinion and Public Policy*", The Oxford Publication.

4

Globalization of State Policy Agenda's

R.K. Sapru

Policies, be they public or private, are everywhere being conditioned by the global environment as well. They are interlocked with global issues. It is impossible to separate the external environmental factors as they invariable influence the political processes and policy comes. It may be noted that the notion of the world politics was central to Horold Lasswell's conception of the policy sciences. In 1951 Laswell argued that policy sciences should take account of world trends and forces when considering the context of policy problems. He maintained, "Indeed, one of the major tasks of the policy sciences today is to follow in detail the processes of social invention, diffusion, and restriction throughout the globe for the sake of estimating the significance of specific events". (Harold Lasswell, 1951). Writing in 1968, Lass well also maintained: "As the globe shrinks into interdependence, relying more fully on science and technology, the policy sciences gain significance ... Interdependence implies that every participant and every item in the social process is affected by the context in which it occurs." (Harold Lasswell, 1951).

Similarly Etzioni in 1968 also observed that there was a rising interdependence between nations and economics. But he also felt: "Surprisingly, many social scientists tend to overplay the nation-state as the unit of societal analysis and underplay supranational bonds and controls, above all they tend to take the nationalistic moral community as the community of values." (Atzeoni, 1968).

As has been already maintained that the country's 'political system' also functions within the 'world system' and the boundaries of the political system are no longer impermeable to outside pressures and influences. The world has become a single social system as a result of growing ties of interdependence. The point is that there is a new kind of interplay between transnational companies and national and world economics. To Giddens (Anthoni & Giddens, 1869 & 1990), transnational corporations, growing economic integration, and the globalization of communications and media are major factors that make for globalism.

Globalization as a tern has gained wide attention and recognition. To Albrow. 'Globalization' refers to 'all those processes by which peoples of the world are incorporated into a single world society, global society." (Albro & King, 1990). He further says that "globalism is one the forces which assist in the development of globalization". The implications of the notion of globalization are that policy makers must consider agenda formation and problem definition within a global context. The "policy makers in each country share a policy context formed by the international economic cycle of prosperity, recession, depression and recovery (Haroop, 1992), in a global environment, it is possible to speak of the convergence of concerns for which global strategies may be formulated. As such in a global context more and more issues will be structured by larger forces outside the nation's constitutional framework of public policy making.

Global Expansion Impact

We are nearly in the midst of a global expansion and consequently national policies are being altered and updated in tune with international requirements. The boundaries of the political system are no longer impermeable to outside pressures and influences. Public policy now takes place in a world system as well as in national political systems. The international environment has an added role to play in influencing the national policies. The mass media and international conferences ease the process of policy diffusion. Harrop notes: "The international environment forms much of the context of national policy making. Policy makers in each country share a policy context formed by the international economic cycle of prosperity, recession, depression and recovery ... International organizations such as the EC also from an increasingly important part of the context of national policy making. The policy agenda is also becoming international". (Haroop, 1992).

As international organizations and multinational corporations come to exercise a great degree of influence, so the capacity of national policy making to frame their own agenda is reduced. National policy agenda in a developing country like India is now exposed to developed countries. With globalization there is a greater scope of interaction between a nation state and other countries. A nation state has now come to exercise less control on policy agenda than it was in the second half of the twentieth century. From the national perspective this means that the policy agenda may be global but the policy making and implementation remain national. Thus there is a new kind of inter-play between transnational companies and the national and world economies. Global politics has an added role to play in the determination of national policies, specially of developing nations. Global issues interact with national issues. For example, previously, most developing countries treated pharmaceutical innovations as non patentable or at best offered only minimal protection for new manufacturing processes. Today, as a result of bilateral pressure and membership requirements of the World Trade Organization, developing countries are implementing new patent laws that look very similar to those in Europe and the United States, granting full protection to all invention in this area.

In the European context a new policy level has developed in terms of an Europeification of national policy making. (Anderson & Elison, 1993). Europe's currency (Euro notes and coins issued by the European Central bank from 1 January 2002) has opened the way to a closer political union among European nations. Similarly most developing countries undertook significant liberalization of their trade regimes during the late 1980s and the 1990s, slashing tariffs, redacting non-tariff barriers to trade and privatizing public enterprises under the pressures of the World Bank and European countries.

Globalization positions that national and international layers are becoming ever more interactive and permeable and that a new policy is emerging. But most developing countries are vulnerable to global events and actions and have come to depend heavily on the international community for financial and technical assistance. Consequently, national politics are interlocked with global issues. "Because poor countries generally have fragile politics and weak systems of accountability, with few autonomous institutions and little power to offset that exercised by the central government, external agencies are potentially key political players, capable of exerting considerable influence." (World Bank Proceeding, 1991).

Police Agenda in a Global Context

International agencies including those of the United Nations have been playing a vital role in promoting peace and development. They contribute to policy making through guidance, technical and financial assistance and support. It is important for policy makers at the international level to take account of global issues when considering the context of policy problems in a national setting.

Environment

Pollution of the air and water, destruction of forests, and loss of fertile soil and becoming critical problem with serious consequences for health, food production, productivity, and perhaps even the ability of the earth to support human life. Protection and improvement of the quality of the environment has become a global issue since the 1980s. For Gareth Porter and Janet Brown (1991), the environment issue is increasingly penetrating policy issues such as international security, North-South relations and world trade. Their study shows how the issue has involved the development of new levels of interactions among states to form a 'global environmental regime'. Because of a growing global environmental stress there is a sustained pressure on national policy makers to change or modify their policy positions.

Looking at the gravity of the environmental problems, the World Commission on Environment and Development (WCED) observed: "The traditional forms of national sovereignty are increasingly challenged by the realities of ecological and economic interdependence. Nowhere is this more true than in the shared ecosystems and in the global commons' – those parts of the planet that fall outside national jurisdictions". (WCED, 1987).

Industrial growth places pressures on policy makers to prevent and control pollution. International agreements on ways to control pollution and close ties between environmentalists have provided and exchange of information that shapes the policy agenda. (Sapru, 1998). The United National Conference on Environment and Development in Brazil in June 1992 produced treaties to control global warming and preserve the diversity of species. The meeting issued the Rio Declaration, setting forth broad principles of environmental protection and sustainable development, and Agenda 21, a detailed plan for combating various environmental problems. In such sectors as land, fresh water, forests, biodiversity and climate change, the 1997 UN assessment found that conditions either were no better than in 1992 or had worsened.

Furthermore, such issues as, climate change and ozone layer depletion require international co-operation. The UNDP assists to improve capacity to manage these challenges at all levels in society. It also searches for and shares knowledge on best practices, provides policy advice, and links partners through pilot projects in this area.

India has been fully engaged in the global discussions on sustainable development and climate change including proactive participation in the formation of positions and negotiations at the meetings of the UN Framework convention on Climate Change and its Kyoto Protocol given the critical implication that these can have for India's growth and development. The involvement in climate change issues has also included interactions with key countries and in India's participation in partnerships for clean technologies.

AT the summit in Brussels on 12 December, 2008, the European Union leaders reached a unanimous agreement on an ambitious climate change package. The EU's climate-energy package, the "20-20-20" deal, seeks to decrease greenhouse gas emissions by 20 percent by 2020, make 20 per cent energy savings and bring renewable energy sources up to 20 per cent of total energy use. (Tribune, 2008).

Poverty and Population Explosion

Developing countries face increasingly serious population growth and poverty problems. Despite lower poverty rates, the number of poor people has increased in large part because of population growth in developing countries, as well as uneven development, and increasing concentration of wealth.

Almost half the world's people (some 3 billion) live on less than $ 2 a day, and a fifth (some 1.2 billion) live on less than $ 1 a day. This horrific level of poverty persists despite unprecedented increase in global wealth in the past century. As the 21st begins, growing numbers of people and rising levels of consumption per capita and depleting natural resources, and in developing countries increasing the dimensions of poverty.

Poverty and population growth have now become global issues. The World Bank (WB) new strategy proposes, for example, an approach to fighting poverty. The three—pronged approach of the WB focuses on increasing opportunities for people, facilitating their empowerment, and enhancing their security. (WBPR, 2000-2001). Policy makers and environmentalists now largely agree that efforts to reduce poverty and population growth and to achieve better living standards can be closely linked and are mutually reinforcing. The policy agenda at the global level is now on slowing the increase in population and attacking poverty.

Most countries, specially developing ones have come out with national health policies which are global in context. Health for All by 2000 AD, for example, for India was drawn as a policy measure in the wake of Alma-Ata Declaration. (Sapru, 1997). As diseases have no barriers, there is the need for international cooperation and national political action by turning statements of principle into specific policies and action throughout the world.

Family planning is seen as a strategy to reducing population growth. The 1994 International Conference on Population and Development (ICPD) Programme of Action states that "the aim of family planning programmes must be to enable couples and individuals to decide freely and responsibly the number and spacing of their children" with a view to reducing population size. (UNP, 1995). Governments of nations that sign international documents of principles make a commitment to act on these principles.

India's National Population Policy (2000) provides a policy framework for advancing goals and prioritizing strategies during the next decade, to meet he reproductive and child health needs of the people of India, and no achieve net replacement levels (TFR) by 2010.

HIV/AIDS Issue

AIDS as a communicable disease has become a serious concern to the international community. AIDS has already killed more than 30 million people, and today 50 million people are living with HIV/AIDS (PLWHA)—30 million of them alone in Africa. Everyday another 15000 people are infected. India's HIV/AIDS population in about 5.8 million. According to the UNAIDS report, India is the home to the highest number of HIV positive people in the world. The fact is that only some 5 percent of people who are HIV positive have access to life-prolonging patented anti-retroviral drugs. The 95 per cent who do not are among the 2 billion poor people in the world who live on less than $ 2 a day.

UNDP works as a partner to prevent the spread of HIV/AIDS, and reduce its impact by mobilizing all levels of government and civil society; advocating the placement of HIV/AIDS at the centre of planning and budgeting; assisting in building national capacity to mange initiatives in institutions and fields; traditionally considered outside the field of health; and encouraging a decentralized approach that supports community-level action. The UNDP assists national efforts by providing knowledge and resources, including best practices in dealing with the HIV/AIDS issue.

In UNDP Regional Programme on HIV and Development, the UNVs are working to create regional platform and strengthen the voice of people living with HIV/AIDS (PLWHA) for advocacy and developing the capacity of PLWHA groups to influenced HIV/AIDS policy development, prevention and care and support responses. In this manner, they are involved in planning., implementation, monitoring and evaluation and also in upscaling of this initiative.

The UN Volunteer (UNVs) are working especially on Greater Involvement of People living with HIV/AIDS (GIPA) in India. A project has been formulated by the UNAIDS co-sponsors in India as a joint UN system response to reduce the risk of HIV infection among the vulnerable section of Indian society, especially adolescent girls. The co-ordinated HIV/AIDS/STI Response through Capacity Building and Awareness. CHARCA project was developed in collaboration with the UN Foundation and the World Economic Forum with assistance from the Netherlands government. It is an attempt to develop a model for public private partnership between the government, NGOs, and the UN system. The project is being implemented in six districts, that is, Guntur (Andhra Pradesh), Kishanganj (Bihar), Ballery (Karnataka), Aizwal (Manipur), Udaipur (Rajasthan) and Kanpur (UP). It aims to equip women, especially young girls, to protect themselves against HIV/AIDS and realize their rights, by reducing their vulnerability. The CHARCA also aims to build leadership, support networks and an enabling environment.

Since it is a global issue, the policy analyst must find a global solution involving a coordinated international cooperation and national political action. Johnathan Mann, the Director of the WHO's AIDS programme stressed that AIDS is bringing about a 'new paradigm of health' because of four factors: 'It is a global problem; it is understood and spoken as a global problem; and it is known worldwide; and AIDS is combated at a truly global level.' (Flaming, 1998).

Further, the global prevalence of the dreaded disease, kala azar, is estimated to be 2.5 million cases per year. The incidence of the infectious disease in India is among the highest in the world and diseases like Leishmaniasis and HIV co-infection are on rise and pose a diagnostic and therapeutic challenge. There is the need for international collaboration to fight infectious diseases.

Drugs

The use of drugs has become an equally global concern. Earlier it was regarded as a social problem and the focus was on seeking a national policy. However, since 1980s drug use has posed a serious menace to the international community and it requires a global cooperation and action. The international concern has addressed the supply and transportation of drugs from the producer nations such as Thailand, Pakistan, Columbia, Peru and Bolivia.

In India the Ministry of Social Justice and Empowerment is implementing a project on 'Developing Community Drug Rehabilitation and Work place Prevention Programme' in collaboration with the UN Office on Drugs and Crime (UNODC) and International Labour Organization (ILO). Its objective is to sensitise and train voluntary organizations on prevention of alcoholism and substance abuse at the workplace.

Terrorism

Terrorism is another global problem which is spreading like a cancer. In India, for example, People's War Group in Andhra Pradesh, the Maoist Communist Centre in Bihar, Jharkhand and Orissa, Lashkar-e-Taiba, Hizb-ul-Mujahidden, Jaish-e-Mohammed and Jamaat-ud-Dawa in Jammu and Kashmir and many parts of India are operating as terrorist organizations. Sri Lanka is wrecked by Tamil extremist organizations like LTTE, which have developed a formidable network spanning South-East Asia, Europe and North America. Attacks on the World Trade Centre and Pentagon in the United States on 11 September, 2001, attack on India's Parliament on 13 December in 2001 and the terrorist attacks on Mumbai on 26 November 2008 are three important dates that made the whole world realize that terrorism had challenged the world community.

Further, the Akshardham incident in Gujarat, on New Delhi's Red Fort, Mumbai serial train blasts followed by countless bomb blasts in various parts of the country including those in Bangalore, Hyderabad, Jaipur, Guwahati and on Mumbai's Chhatrapati Shivaji Terminus Railway Station, Taj Mahal Hotel, Oberoi Trident and Nariman House on 26 November 2008, all show the extent of terrorist menace in this country.

Sabharwal observed: "Our main enemy in the twenty-first century will be terrorism. Terrorist Organizations or countries using them as a front, could explode a stray unclear warhead or carry out biological or chemical attacks which in turn could cause a chain reaction and bring the world to the brink of destruction". (Sabharwal, 2002).

Addressing the UN's anti-corruption campaign members before the International Anti-corruption Day (9 December), the UN Secretary General Ban Ki-moon has also said in no unclear terms that corruption allowed terrorists to finance their nefarious operations. (Tribune, 2008).

There were several wars in the last century including two World Wars, but the first year of this century saw a radically different scenario highly motivated groups of people launching attacks on nation-states. The shadowy figure of the terrorist has loomed large in the homes and outside, menacingly. The sub-continent, specially, is in turmoil with conflicts emerging sharply in India, Afghanistan, Bangladesh, Sri Lanka and Nepal.

Now, there is the need for global cooperation for fighting global terrorism. The United States, the United Kingdom and the European Union issued demarches to Pakistan in the wake of terrorist attacks on Mumbai on 26 November 2008. The United Nations Security Council panel declared Jamaat-ud-Dawa a terrorist group and banned it on 10 December 2008.

Similarly, in a tough message to Pakistan, the US official "insisted that they had enough evidence to prove that Lashkar-e-Taiba and Jamaat-ud-Dawa were involved in the Mumbai attacks and they wanted concrete action against all such groups". (Tribune, 2008). India's External Affairs Minister Pranab Mukherjee asserted that "the terrorist infrastructure in Pakistan was the greatest danger to peace and security of the entire civilized world". (Tribune, 2008).

Earlier, setting aside difference among its members, the SAARC standing committee on 1 January 2000 resolved to implement the UN Security Council anti-terrorist resolution 1373 in totality.

While welcoming the adoption of a Counter-Terrorism Strategy by the UNGA is September 2006, India continued to pursue the important issue of expeditious finalization of a Comprehensive Convention on International Terrorism for which it has presented a draft as far back as in 1996. India is also a signatory to International Convention on Suppression for Acts of Nuclear Terrorism on 24 July 2006 reflecting India's responsible attitude as well as its commitment to contributing to the objective of global peace and security.

In a swift response to terrorists' audacious assault on Mumbai, the Parliament of India passed: (i) the National Investigative Agency, and (ii) Unlawful Activities (Prevention) Amendment Bills (2008) in ensuring speedy and efficient investigation and deterrent punishment to those involved in terrorist activities. (Tribune, 2008).

Trade and Industry

Changes have occurred in industry as a consequence of global changes and shifts. The major sources of global shift are transnational corporations which organize production on a world-wide scale, the policies pursued by national governments, and the enabling technologies of transport, communication and production. This has largely weakened the ability of national government to make policies independently of those changes. Dicken observes: "... the well-being of nations, regions, cities and other communities depends increasingly not merely on events in their own backyards but on what happens at a much larger geographical scale.... We need a global perspective". (Dicken, 1988).

Yet nearly 80 countries containing a third of the world's population are being increasingly marginalized, and over the past 30 years developing countries' share of global trade fell from 0.8 to 0.4 per cent. (Karlson, 2001). The fact is that 3 billion people live on less than $ 2 a day, and 1.2 billion live on less than $ 1 a day. In this way international development cannot be achieved.

In his message to the world on 7 December (9 December is the day for observance 'fight against corruption'), the UN Secretary-General expressed "...Yet another, silent financial crisis afflicting the world's poorest people attracts far less attention. Every year across the developing world, billions of dollars that are badly needed for health care, schools, clean water and infrastructure are stolen or lost through bribes and other misdeeds". (Tribune, 2008).

Beginning of 2008 a recession has been declared. Companies like, General Motors, Fannie Mae and Freddie Mac, AIG, Merrill Lynch and Citibank each with assets running into hundreds of billions or trillions of dollars have failed since August 2008 and has been bailed out by the US government or bought over by the other companies.

China cut interest rates for the fifth time in three months to support the world's economy after trade growth collapsed because of recessions in the US, Europe and Japan. (Business Standard, 2008).

Japan's exports plunged at a record annual pace in November 2008 with shipments to Asia dropping the most since 1986 as a global economic slump and a surging yen slashed demand for everything from autos to electronics. (Tribune, 2008).

Following the global financial meltdown, India's exports for the first time after a gap of seven years dipped by over 12 per cent in October 2008. India has been facing the ripple effects of the global financial turmoil, which has resulted in slowdown of country's exports. Several developed markets including the US, the UK, Japan and other countries in the Euro zone, which are India's major export destinations, are officially in recession. (Tribune, 2008).

Expressing concern at the fall in the industrial production to a 15 year-low registering a negative growth in October 2008, the government attributed in partly to the impact of global meltdown that had choked up the financial system.

Governments the world over are pumping in trillions of dollars to shore up their economies. Britain, China, Germany, Japan, etc. have also offered their own packages each running into hundreds of billions of dollars. The Reserved Bank of India at the direction of Government of India had injected Rs. 1.60 lakh crore as liquidity into the Indian market to tide over the financial crunch faced by the business fraternity. Thus, the total amount committed world over has swelled to above $ 10 trillion (eleven times India's national income). "For a world economy of # 65 trillion, this is a staggering amount of money and most of it is committed since September 2008. Yet, things seem out of control even though the pace of the collapse may be slower compared to two months back." (Kumar, 2008). And then financial frauds are reported in the private industries also. In the first week of January 2009, it was surfaced that the chairman of the Satyam Computer Services (India) committed financial fraud of Rs. 7000 crore and the central government had to appoint three musketeers to steer the IT giant out from the crisis. (Tribune, 2008).

Industrial output shrank by 0.4 per cent in October 2008 for the first time in 15 years after recording a whopping 12.2 per cent growth a year ago. The RBI came out with recent measures, including cutting short terms policy rates by 100 basis points and announcing other sector-specific steps, and the government announced fiscal package. With a view to overcoming these crises, Arun Kumar notes: 'Remedy requires that controls over resources be reworked, monopolies need to be split up and their control over resources and political power and the resulting increase in disparities all need overhaul."

However, national policy makers have the task of formulating policies which help create business climate. The global industrial environment interacts with the national political processes, and consequently national policies are increasingly influenced by activities and events happening well away from the national contexts. So the capacity of the national policy makers to frame their own agendas is considerably reduced.

Privatization

The beginning of 1990s witnessed a marked trend towards privatization. Instead of government control, these has been a renewed emphasis on privatization and competition throughout the world. Governments of most countries, both developed and developing, 1 have adopted policies of (i) transferring governments-controlled enterprises to the private sector, and (ii) opening up a large number of industries to the private sector to encourage competitions. (Sapru, 2002). Privatization is now fashionable in European community, South and North America. Australia, Asia, Africa and is gaining popularity in Eastern Europe and the rest of the world.

The concept of privatization is ambiguous, as it may imply severs reductions in the size of the public sector and a drastic shrinkage of public ownership of key industries. (Lane, 2000). Privatization is being driven by the shift of important economic sectors to operation on a global scale. National policy agendas are being shaped by the forces of global economic restructuring.

Since August 2008 the US, European zone, japan, Taiwan, etc. have been declared to be in recession. Chinese economy has slowed down considerably since mid-2008 and so has the Indian economy (whatever be the government's claims of healthy growth). Demand is plummeting everywhere and companies are laying off people many of whom were anyway losing their houses in the US due to foreclosures. Temporary employees are losing jobs and the permanent workers are working fewer hours because of plant closures. Failure of bank and companies is rising in the USA. This is spreading to other countries including China and India.

In the case of China, for example, Demick notes: "Now demand has plunged because of the recession in the United States and the flurry of scandals over tainted foods and dangerous toys produced in China." (Demick, 2008).

To offset the global increase in demand for money that is being transmitted to India, the Mid-Year Review of the economy presented to Parliament said: "An aggressive monetary policy may be necessary if the global economic depression continues to adversely affect manufacturing." (Business Standard, 2008).

Investment is falling everywhere since companies are facing a collapse in consumer demand. Exports have collapsed as demand has fallen and nations are buying less from others. Thus, all the major components of demand—consumption, investment and exports—have declines drastically. This is the reason that the various economies are headed into deep recession and possibly a depression. (Kumar, 2008). Nationalization and government intervention have suddenly become acceptable. Minimum government is no more the desirable state of affairs.

Other Global Issues

It may be added that the world is becoming reluctantly internationalist, recognizing that diversity of domestic social and economic issues (social welfare, trade, industry, agriculture, health, terror, security, education, human rights, famine, etc.) are items on the national political agenda which are tied up with global issues. This has been accompanied by growing regionalization and internationalization. The global environment forms much of the context of national policy making.

Conclusion

It is largely felt that in developing democratic countries, policy agendas are driven by global forces. Problems arise in a context in which economic and social conditions play a major role in shaping opinions and political strategies. For example, the economies that stuck with the planning model experienced slow growth, stagnation, or worse; the collapse of the socialist economies was but "the final nail in the planning coffin". By the 1990s countries around the world were actively engaged in privatizing public enterprises.

Now since August 2008 most economies of the world are in the grip of recession. The nature of the crisis being faced today is different from the ones in the last 75 years. Hence analysts are groping for answers and specially those in policy making who led the world into this crisis. The nationalization/ government takeover of major institutions and the introduction of regulation in the hitherto unregulated parts of the financial structures is itself changing the economy in fundamental ways but even this maybe mere tinkering and more basic change maybe required. When those entities that were thought of as "too big to fail" actually fail, it signifies the failure of the system of which they are a part. (Kumar, 2008).

But the power of decision or policy and the capacity to implement it remains largely within the nation states. There is therefore a tension between the spillover, which may be said to be taking place at the global level and the reality of the maintenance of national sovereignty. Against the pressure of global agendas the fat remains that at times of crisis "governments are prone to with draw from intergovernmental cooperation and supranational policy making rather than move positively into closer collaboration" (Metcafe & Rechards, 1987). Common issues and problems within a global context may be increasingly identified in international terms, but policy making and implementation still remain largely within nation states. The global socio-economic framework interacts with the political processes and policies pursued by governments of nation states. The success of nation states in policy performance will diverge notwithstanding the convergence of the global policy concerns.

As the globe shrinks into interdependence, policy making at the national level is affected by the global environment and also affects the global environmental regime. On the one hand, there is a global change which impacts on every participant; on the other, the need to address the problems in a manner which goes the national policy making structures.

Endnotes & References

Albrow M. and King E. (eds.) (1990), Globalization, Knowledge and Society. Readings from International Sociology, Sage, London

Andersen S.S. and Eliassen K.A. (1992), Making Policy in Europe : The Europeification of National Policy Making, Sage, London.

Business Standard (Chandigarh), 23-24 December 2008.

Demick Barbara (2008), "In China anger rises as economy goes down," *The Tribune* (Chandigarh), 15 December 2008.

Dicken Peter (1988), Global Shift: Industrial Change in Turbulent World, Paul Chapman, London.

Ell-Mills Pierre-land and Seraglio Is mail (1992), "Governance and the external factor", World Bank, Proceedings of the World Bank Annual Conference on Development Economics, 1991, WB, Washington.

Etzioni A. (1968), The Active Society: A Theory of Societal and Political Processes, Free Press, New York.

Fleming A.F. (1988) et. al. (eds.), The Global Impact of AIDS, Alan R. Liss, New York.

Giddens Anthony (1989), Sociology, Polity Press, Oxford

Giddens Anthony (1990), The Consequences of Modernity, Polity Press, Cambridge

Harrop M. (ed.), (1992), Power and Policy in Liberal Democracies, CUP, Cambridge.

Karlsson Mats (2000), "Opening address", Annual World Bank Conference on Development Economics, World Bank, Washington

Kumar Arun (2008), "Sign of systemic crisis", The Tribune, 13 December 2008

Lane Jan-Erik (2000), The Public Sector, 3rd ed., Sage Publications, London.

Lasswell H.D. (1991), "The policy orientation", in D. Lerner and H.D. Lasswell (eds.). The Policy Sciences, Stanford University Press, Stanford

Lasswell H.D(1968), "The policy sciences". in The Encyclopedia of the Social Science, Macmillan, New York

Metcalfe L and Richards S (1987), "Evolving public management cultures", in J. Kooiman and K.A. Eliassen (eds.), Managing Public Organizations, Sage, London

Porter Gareth and Brown Janet (1990), Global Environmental Politic, West view Press, Boulder

Sabharwal O.P. (2002), The Killer Instinct, Rupa Publication, New Delhi.

Sapru R.K (1998)., "Environmental policy and politics in India", in Uday Desai (ed.), Ecological Policy and Politics in Developing Countries, State University of N.Y. Press, New York.

Sapru R.K (1997), "Health care policy and administration in India", Indian Journal of Public Administration, vol. 43, no. 3 July–September 1997

Sapru R.K. (2002), Development Administration, 2nd ed., Sterling, New Delhi.

The Tribune, 1 January 2009

The Tribune, 13 December 2008.

The Tribune, 8, 12, 14, 22, 23, 19 Dec. 2008.

United Nations, Programme of Action of the International Conference on Population and Development (1995), UN, Cairo.

World Bank Policy and Research Bulletin, Vols. 11 and 12, October–December 2000 and January–March 2001.

World Commission on Environment and Development, Our Common Future (1987), OUIP, Oxford.

5

A Borderless Internal Federal Space? Reorganization of States in India

Mahendra Prasad Singh

The purpose of this paper is to take a synoptic view of internal boundaries of India in periods of subcontinental states in history, and closely examine the issue of reorganization of States in independent India. The major hypotheses of this paper are that (i) the historical internal boundaries are more a reflection of accidents of war and conquest than physical and cultural and regional geography and demography; (ii) the reorganization of States in independent India suffers from hangovers of history and ad hoc decisions of the Centre under regional protests and passions of the moment than any comprehensive deliberative design of redrawing of internal boundaries; and (iii) the Constituent Assembly of India missed the opportunity of making a comprehensive reorganization in conformity to cultural, administrative, and fiscal rationales that may have been feasible at the constituent defining moment in the life of the Indian nation-state. That opportunity having been missed by a beleaguered and fatigued nationalist political elites, the only conceivable conditions under which a comprehensive perspective plan for internal territorial reorganization can be imagined is under conditions of unsustainable fiscal overload or further political fragmentation crippling governability and politico-economic management of India. Given the foregoing, the foresight of the article 3 of the constitution leaving the final authority of reorganization with the Parliament of India with the obligation to only "consult" the States concerned is a pragmatic feature of the Indian federal experiment, even though it is generally supposed to be an unfederal feature by scholars like K.C. Wheare (1964). However, as B.R. Ambedkar, the chairman of the drafting committee of the Constituent Assembly subsequently explained: "Article 3 of the Constitution gives power to Parliament to create new states. This was done because there was no time to reorganize the states on linguistic basis for which there was a great demand".[1]

Pre-Independence Internal Boundaries

Independence, accompanied by the Partition in 1947 was, of course, the politically constitutive defining moment in India negotiated interdependently by the modern historical forces of nationalism and colonialism. "Partition was", observes Bidyut Chakrabarty (2004:10), "not forced upon the subcontinent, but it emerged as the best possible alternative at a particular historical conjuncture. Even the Congress that never accepted the two-nation theory was forced to swallow its outcome, possibly to avoid a further bloodbath in the name of protecting communal pride and interests". This dramatic imperial demarcation of India's external boundaries glosses over several significant moments, both before and after Independence, when internal boundaries of colonial and post-colonial India were drawn and redrawn. The process, indeed, goes back to medieval and ancient times. While the focus of this paper is limited to modern India, especially to India since 1947, we may at least take three historical snapshots at the internal boundaries of Mauryan India (c.322-185 B.C.), Mughal India (c.1526-1858 A.D.), and British India (1757-1947). Ashoka's India was divided into four provinces, besides of course the centre with its capital at Pataliputra (Patna): (a) the eastern province (capital city Toshali, Orissa today); (b) the western province (capital city Ujjain in Madhya Pradesh today); (c) the northern province (capital city Taxila, in west Punjab in Pakistan today), and (d) the southern province (capital city Suvarṇagir Brahamagiri somewhere in the south) (Romila Thapar, 1997:100-1). Akbar's India was divided into 15 "*subas* or Governments" (H.S. Jarrett's preface to *The Ain-I-Akbari*, Vol. II: viii): Bengal, Orissa, Bihar, Allahabad, Oudh, Agra, Malva, Khandesh, Berar, Gujarat, Ajmer, Delhi, Lahor, Multan, and Kabul (Abul-Fazl Allami, 1981:129-404). "The empire... stretched from Afghanistan up to the head of the Gulf of Bengal, from the Himalaya up to the Deccan" (Jarrett, 1989: viii)[2].

As in Mauryan and Mughal India, internal provincial divisions in British India were products more of incidents of war and annexation than anything else. The period of extension and consolidation of British rule in India was fairly long. There was, for example, a gap of nearly a century between the onset of the preliminary British conquest of Bengal in the trail of the Battle of Plassey in 1757 and the annexation of Punjab in 1846. By the time the British Parliament enacted the feebly federal scheme of provincial autonomy under the Government of India Act, 1935, and held elections to provincial legislatures early in 1937, there were eleven provinces in British India (besides the native princely states linked in subsidiary alliances with the British Raj under the paramountacy of the Crown of the United Kingdom): Madras, United Provinces of Oudh and Agra, Bihar, Central Provinces and Berar, Bombay, Assam, North-West Frontier Province, Bengal, Punjab, and Sind (M.V. Pylee, 1984: 99-100).

The three cross-sectional points in time telescopically selected above for fleeting glimpses of internal territorial divisions of India are separated by millenniums and centuries: the Mauryan centuries fell in the last millennium B.C., the Mughal centuries in the mid-second millennium A.D., and the British centuries ran from the latter half of the eighteenth to the first half of the twentieth. Mauryan India was civilizationally Brahmano-Buddhistic in its worldview and geopolitically pulled eastward. Mughal India was civilizationally Indo-Islamic and geopolitically pulled westward. British India, without abandoning its subcontinental cultural heritage, joined the orbit of European Enlightenment and was pulled into global geopolitical equations for the first time. The Mauryan state was thus autocthonic in terms of political culture with its centre of political gravity in Magadh located in modern Bihar, the Mughals came to India from Central Asia through the perennial northwestern mountain passes by which foreign travelers, traders, migrants, and aggressors had poured into India since times immemorial. The European explorers and traders came to India from the sea route, among whom the British finally established their political ascendancy and gradually moved into the hinterland from coastal British outposts of Bengal, Bombay, and Madras Presidencies and finally moved the capital from Calcutta to New Delhi in 1911-1912.

The internal boundaries in pre-modern India, after the emergence of state-based socio-political formation at the end of the Age of the Buddha in the sixth century B.C., were a product of *realpolitik* and annexations predicated on royal matrimonial alliances and conquests. The first redrawing of boundaries in response to popular mass pressures occurred in the early twentieth century British India following Lord Curzon's imperial partition of Bengal on religious-communal lines in 1905. The move was aimed at breaking the back of newly emergent spirit of Indian nationalism in the English-educated Bengali middle class *(bhadralok).* The decision stirred up a strong popular protest in the form of the *swadeshi* movement which ultimately forced the British rulers to annul the partition of Bengal in 1911. This popular movement in Bengali-speaking part of the Bengal Presidency was subsequently to be emulated by the Hindi-speaking Biharis and, after some time, by the Oriya-speaking people in the Bengal Presidency. The British decided to shift the capital to Delhi in 1911, created a new province of Bihar and Orissa the same year, and held a huge assemblage of native rulers at the Delhi Durbar in 1912 coinciding with the royal visit of George V to India. Several years later, at the earliest manifestation of the popular demand for a separate Oriya-speaking province, the British rulers bifurcated Orissa out of the province of Bihar and Orissa in 1936.

These province-creating drivers were animated by the undercurrent of three forces at work then in British India. The hornets' nest was stirred, as briefly alluded to above, by the attempt of the British colonial rulers to weaken the force of proto-pan-Indian nationalism beginning to be championed by the English-educated Bengali *bhadralok* in the last quarter of the nineteenth century mingled with Hindu revivalism (with other religious rivivalistic tendencies waiting in the wings) by the beginning of the twentieth century. With this objective in view the British portioned Bengali linguistic region of the larger Bengal Presidency Province on religious Hindu–Muslim line in 1905. In reaction to it the *swadeshi* nationalist movement sprung up, which ultimately succeeded in forcing the British to annul the partition. The *swadeshi* movement in Bengal engendered similar linguistic provincialist fervour in Hindi–speaking and later Oriya-speaking parts of Bengal Presidency—Bihar and Orissa. Demand for separate province-formation in Bihar in all appearances was less strongly linked with indigenous linguistic identity and more with prospects of greater employment, middle class professional earnings, and freedom from domination by Bengalis (Rajendra Prasad, 1992: 55; Girish Mishra and B.K. Pandey, 1996: 28-38).

The situation in Orissa was probably not all that different from Bihar. Thus began the modern historical process of nationality-formation in India. The major landmarks of this development were the acceptance of the federal idea by the Lucknow conference of the Indian National Congress in 1916, acceptance of the idea of linguistic provinces by the 1920 Congress held in Nagpur, submission of memoranda in large numbers to the British

Government of India and the India Office in London for recognition of nationalities of Oriyas, Kannadas, Andhras, Tamils, Bengalis, and Jharkhandis and creation of linguistic states for them. The 1942 "Quit India" Resolution of the Congress pledged "the largest measure of autonomy for the federating units". Things moved into different gears in 1946 when memoranda were submitted to the British Cabinet Mission visiting India by the Dravid Kazagham for a sovereign state of Dravidastan and by the Communist Party of India for "17 sovereign National Constituent Assemblies based on national homelands of various Indian peoples" and advocated "a voluntary union of national states" (Suniti Kumar Ghosh, 1996, quoted in Himanshu Roy, 1996:23).

Post-Independence Reorganization of States

With transfer of power to the Indian National Congress under the Government of India Act, 1947, and lapse of paramountacy of the British Crown over native Indian states in 1947, the Government of India combined consensual diplomacy and 'police action' (Hyderabad) and defensive intervention-on-invitation (Jammu & Kashmir) to effectuate the integration of these states with the Indian Union in the process of being crafted by the Constituent Assembly doubling as the provisional Parliament. The Constitution of India created, to begin with, three categories of states out of the British Indian provinces and the native states in response to the variety and varying stages of integration with India that marked the federating and federated units. The States and categories of states created by the Constituent Assembly are given in Table 1.

Table 1: The States of the Union: Crafted by Constituent Assembly

	PART I: STATES
1.	Assam
2.	Bengal
3.	Bihar
4.	Bombay
5.	Koshal-Vidarbha/Madhya Pradesh
6.	Madras
7.	Orissa
8.	Punjab
9.	United Provinces/Uttar Pradesh
	PART II: STATES
1.	Bhopal
2.	Bilaspur

3. Coach Behar
4. Himachal Pradesh
5. Kutch
6. Manipur
7. Rampur
8. Tripura

PART III: STATES

1. Hyderabad
2. Jammu & Kashmir
3. Madhya Bharat
4. Mysore
5. Patiala & East Punjab States Union
6. Rajasthan
7. Saurashtra
8. Travancore-Cochin
9. Vindhya Pradesh

Source: B. Shiva Rao *et al* (eds.), *The Framing of India's Constitution: A Study/Select Documents,* Vol. V (New Delhi: Indian Institute of Public Administration, 1968): 543-545. In the text of the Constitution the three categories of states were finally called I, II, and III category states.

Part I states listed above largely corresponded with British Indian provinces administered by a Governor under a central Governor General overseen by the authority of the Parliament of Great Britain. Part II states were also administered likewise before the commencement of the Constitution but, instead of being placed under a Governor, they were put under a Chief Commissioner. Part III states were former native states ruled by Indian kings under the paramountacy of the British Crown, deputized in India by the Viceroy who doubled as the Governor General of the British Indian Provinces.

If the reorganization of provinces in the Bengal presidency by the British rulers around the first decade of the twentieth century in response to popular demands and movements may be said to be the first wave of 'democratic' reorganization of territories in modern India, such democratic waves were soon to follow with almost seasonal frequency following the 'constitutionalization' of democracy with commencement of the Constitution in 1950 and the holding of the first general elections in 1952 on universal adult sufferage. The nationalist leaders during the freedom struggle had kept adopting a variety of strategies of deepening the sociological foundations of India nationalism. Besides using territorial patriotism[3] as the bedrock of civic nationalism by Congress Moderates, Congress Extremists leaned on Hinduism, and Gandhi on Indian languages in search of "cultural" nationalism with ethnic undercurrents. As early as the early 1920s Gandhi advocated the reorganization of the Indian National Congress along linguistic lines instead of the British administrative provincial boundaries. Gandhi's proposal was adopted by the Congress at its Nagpur session in 1920. However, Gandhi`s demand for a directly elected constituent assembly for future and independent India made in 1922 was never conceded by the British rulers.

Shortly after Independence movements for linguistic reorganization of states appeared in several states. The central Congress leadership as well as the States Reorganization Commission (SRC) Report (1956) largely accepted the linguistic principle in some cases but preferred, unless pushed to the wall, the maintenance of multilingual states for cultural homogenization. The reorganization of states as proposed by the SRC is given in Table 2.

The SRC Report took pains to point out some "obvious limitations to the realization of unilingualism at the state level" due to the following "limiting factors": "(i) not all the language groups are so placed that they can be grouped into separate states; (ii) there are a large number of bilingual belts between different linguistic zones; and (iii) there exist areas with a mixed population even within unilingual areas" (Report of the State Reorganization Commission Report, 1955:205). The SRC recommended the reorganization of the states as listed in Table 2

Table 2: The Reorganization of States as Recommended by SRC, 1955

S. No.	*States*	*Area (in Sq. Miles)*	*Population (in Millions)*
1.	Madras	50,170	30.00
2.	Kerala	14,980	13.60
3.	Karnatak	72,730	19.00
4.	Hyderabad	45,300	11.30
5.	Andhra	64,950	20.90
6.	Bombay	151,360,	40.20
7.	Vidarbha	36,880	7.60
8.	Madhya Pradesh	171,200	26.10
9.	Rajasthan	132,300	16.00
10.	Punjab	58,140	17.20
11.	Uttar Pradesh	133,410	63.20
12.	Bihar	66,520	38.50
13.	West Bengal	34,590	26.50
14.	Assam	89,040	9.70
15.	Orissa	60,140	14.60
16.	Jammu & Kashmir	92,780	4.40

Source: *Report of the State Reorganization Commission* (1955:203-4.).

Soon after the submission of the SRC Report, B.R. Ambedkar (1989 b, preface date 23 December, 1955) presented a critique of it mainly on the ground that the proposed reorganization would result in great imbalance among the states on account of disparities of population: eight states with populations between one and two crores each, four states with populations between two and four crores, and two states with populations of above four and six crores each. In his opinion "It will be impossible for the small States to bear the weight of the big States" (Ambedkar, 1989 b:18), especially because the Constitution of India, as pointed out by K.M. Panniker in his note of dissent to the SRC Report, had not incorporated the principles of equality of states qua states in the federal second chamber, and popular and the federal chambers were endowed with disparity of size and powers (Ambedkar, 1989 b: 19). This disparity in Ambedkar's view boiled down to a serious North-South divide:

> The North is Hindi-speaking. The South is non-Hindi speaking. Most people do not know what is the size of the Hindi-speaking population. It is as much as 48 per cent of the total population of India. Fixing one's eye on this fact one cannot fail to say that the Commission's effort will result in the consolidation of the North and the balkanization of the South (Ambedkar, 1989 b: 20).[4]

As a solution to this problem, Ambedkar proposed a scheme for division of four Northern states of Uttar Pradesh, Bihar, Madhya Pradesh, and Maharashtra, into smaller states. U.P. could be trifurcated into Western, Central and Eastern U.P. (with capitals in Meerut, Kanpur, and Allahabad, Bihar into North and South, Bihar (with capitals in Patna and Ranchi respectively); Madhya Pradesh into Northern and Southern M.P.; and Maharashtra into the city-state of Bombay, Western, Central and Eastern Maharashtra. He summarized the principles governing his scheme of reorganizing Northern India into smaller states into the following points: (1) All mixed states must be replaced by unilingual states; (2) "The formula of one State, one language, must not be confused with the formula of one language, one state"; (3) People speaking one language may be divided into more than one state, depending on (a) administrative rationality, (b) developmental needs/backwardness, (c) popular sentiments, and (d) a rational proportion between the majority and minority. Smaller states were advocated by Ambedkar especially to avoid what he called the "tyranny of the communal majority" (The term "communal" for him here subsumed religious as well as linguistic and caste majorities.) The remedies against this phenomenon suggested by him were mainly two: (a) "not to have too large a State", and

(b) "to have plural member constituencies (of two or three) with cumulative voting" (specifically rejecting reserved seats as well as separate electorates) (Ambedkar, 1989 b: Chapters 6-10). Finally, taking into account considerations of history and climate, culture, convenience, and strategic defence in war, Ambedkar recommended two capitals for India – Delhi and Hyderabad (1989 b: Chapter 11).

The seventh amendment to the Constitution supplemented by the States Reorganization Act (both enacted in 1956) created the following states with effect from 1 November 1956, eliminating the distinction between Part A, B, and C states (see Table 3):

Table 3: Reorganized States in 1956

1. Andhra Pradesh (merging Andhra and Telangana region of the erstwhile Hyderabad state)
2. Assam
3. Bihar
4. Bombay (enlarged by the addition of Saurashtra and Kutch and Marathi-speaking districts of Nagpur Division. Southernmost districts of Bombay were transferred to Mysore state)
5. Jammu & Kashmir
6. Kerala (merging Travancore-Cochin state with the Malabar district of Madras state)
7. Madhya Pradesh (merging Madhya Bharat, Vindhya Pradesh, and Bhopal: Marathi-speaking districts of Nagpur Division were transferred to Bombay state)
8. Madras
9. Mysore (enlarged by the addition of the Coorg state and the Kannada-speaking districts from southern Bombay state and western Hyderabad state)
10. Orissa
11. Punjab (enlarged by the merger of Patiala & East Punjab States Union, PEPSU)
12. Rajasthan (Rajputana was renamed Rajasthan and enlarged by adding Ajmer-Marwar state)
13. Uttar Pradesh
14. West Bengal

Sources: The Seventh Constitutional Amendment and SRC Act, both 1956.

Thus the Union government in 1956 conceded to the demand for unilingual states only in case of Andhra Pradesh, where the agitation had culminated into the self-immolation of a popular Telugu leader. Milder agitations for linguistically mixed rump states of Madras after bifurcation of Andhra, Bombay, Mysore, Punjab, and elsewhere were ignored. However, the popular linguistic movements did not die down.

As it happened, under the pressure and persistence of linguistic, religious, and tribal movements, the central government yielded, creating Andhra Pradesh (Telugu-speaking), Tamil Nadu (Tamil-speaking), Karnataka (Kanada-speaking), Gujarat (Gujarati-speaking), Maharashtra (Marathi-speaking), Punjab (Punjabi-speaking with a Sikh majority), Haryana (Hindi-speaking), and Himachal Pradesh (Hindi-speaking) in the 1950s or 1960s. This process of territorial reorganization extended to the northeast in the 1960s or 1970s. Beginning with the bifurcation of Nagaland out of Assam (1962), the process culminated in the emergence of the so-called 'seven sisters'—states or the union territories—in the region. (see Table 4).

Table 4: States and Union Territories in India Today

	STATES
1.	Andhra Pradesh (1953, 1956, 1959)
2.	Assam (1951, 1962, 1971)
3.	Bihar (1950, 1956, 1968, 2000)
4.	Gujarat (1960)
5.	Kerala (1956)
6.	Madhya Pradesh (1950, 1956, 2000)
7.	Tamil Nadu (1950, 1953, 1959)
8.	Maharashtra (1950, 1960)
9.	Karnataka (1950, 1956, 1968)
10.	Orissa (1950, 1960)
11.	Punjab (1950, 1956, 1960, 1966)
12.	Rajasthan (1950, 1956, 1959)
13.	Uttar Pradesh (1950, 1968, 1979, 2000)
14.	West Bengal (1950, 1954, 1956)
15.	Jammu & Kashmir (1950)
16.	Nagaland (1962)
17.	Haryana (1966, 1979)
18.	Himachal Pradesh (1966)
19.	Manipur (1971)
20.	Tripura (1950)
21.	Meghalaya (1971)
22.	Sikkim (1975)
23.	Mizoram (1971)
24.	Arunachal Pradesh (1971)
25.	Goa (1987)
26.	Uttaranchal (2000)
27.	Jharkhand (2000)
28.	Chhattisgarh (2000)
	UNION TERRITORIES
1.	National Capital Territory of Delhi (1950, 1956)
2.	Andaman and Nicobar (1950, 1956)
3.	Lakshadweep (1956)
4.	Dadra & Nagar Haveli (1961)
5.	Daman & Diu (1987)
6.	Pondicherry (1962)
7.	Chandigarh (1966)

Note: The years in the parentheses denote the dates of creation of the units as states or union territories or changes in their states by constitutional amendments.

Source: The Rajeev Dhavan Typescript on the State of the Federal Union (early 2000s) revised and used by Rekha Saxena (2006:114) and further revised by the present author.

Sub-state movements based on tribal or ethnic identities acquired salience in several states in the 1980s such as Gurkha National Liberation Front in the Darjeeling hill district of West Bengal, Bodoland agitation in Assam, and Jharkhand Mukti-Morcha in the Chhotnagpur region mainly in Bihar but marginally also in the adjoining states of West Bengal, Orissa, and Madhya Pradesh. To meet these sub-state demands, a new proto-federal innovation of autonomous Regional Development Councils was set up in Jharkhand, Darjeeling, Bodo, and Ladakh areas of Bihar, West Bengal, Assam, and Jammu & Kashmir respectively.

The three new states created in the Indian Union in 2000 were Jharkhand (replacing the Jharkhand Regional Development Council), Uttaranchal, and Chhattisgarh bifurcating the states of Bihar, U.P., and M.P. in the year 2000. These three new states were made also in response to some popular demand, backed by mass movements in descending order of intensity in the more backward regions of these three backward Hindi-speaking states. The element of novelty in their case is that they are the first clear-cut category of states created more on considerations of economic backwardness and step-motherly treatment by the political elites of the respective parent states than on considerations predominantly linguistic, religious, or tribal. Uttaranchal is hardly distinguishable in these ethnic terms from U.P., except in terms of regional economic disparities. Jharkhand and Chhattisgarh do have disproportionately larger tribal populations than their parent states. However, over the years, the tribal majority in the former is said to have been reduced to a minority by migration into the area from Bihar plains and other parts of India. It is another matter that the migrants too joined the movement for creating a new state initiated by the tribals. Chhattisgarh region never really mounted a regional movement of any agitational magnitude. In both Jharkhand and Chhattisgarh the tribal population is around one-third of the total population of the newly created states concerned. The creation of these new states is understandable more by looking at a new federal coalitional governing framework in New Delhi. More than any other reason what really prompted the BJP-led National Democratic Alliance (NDA) Government to give a new lease of life to forces of regionalism and elevate them to statehood appears to be the desperate need of the BJP to bolster its electoral strength by winning new vote blocs or new regional parties in coalition in New Delhi and the states.

The latest state in India was created in 2013-14 by the Congress-led United Progressive Alliance (UPA) Government. The demand for bifurcation of Telangana from Andhra Pradesh has a rather long history. The movement first came to ahead in 1969 when nearly 400 people lost their lives in police firing. The Indira Gandhi Congress Government intermediated a settlement with an agreement for greater regional autonomy for Telangana within the united Andhra Pradesh, including a central University of Hyderabad and preferential public employment for Telangana 'Mulkis'. The movement intermittently kept surfacing on lack of sincere implementation of the regional accord despite the incumbency of some political leaders from Telangana holding the office of the Chief Minister. However, as in the case of the three new states of Jharkhand, Chhattisgarh, and Uttarakhand, so also Telangana the new state formation actually took place when the Congress-led UPA suddenly brought out a dormant issue out of the closet in December 2009 by announcing its intention of initiating the process of carving out Telangana from Andhra Pradesh. This was prompted by partisan interests of the Congress party in the state politics. Congress first unscrupulously and instrumentally dealt with the Telangana Rashtra Samithi (TRS) in coalition government formation and maintenance and was driven to take the precipitate action on division of the state when faced with a fast unto death by the TRS political entrepreneur called Chandrasekhar Rao. This immediately flared up intense violent agitations for and against the move in the Telangana and Seemandhra regions in a vicious competitive cycle. This was the first instance where the decision to divide a state was so determinedly opposed by both sides to the dispute. In face of this dilemma the Union government belatedly appointed a judicial committee chaired by Justice Srikrishna to study and report on the problem, which recommended that the best step forward was the maintenance of status quo. But the government proceeded in its bind pursuit of party-political interests. For by now the Congress then ruling in Andhra Pradesh had suffered a grievous loss in the accidental death of Chief Minister Y.S. Rajasekkhar Reddy and, on denial of the dynastic right of succession to the office to YSR's son Jaganmohan Reddy, a major split in the formation of a separate regional party, YSR Congress. Thus Congress appeared all set to lose Andhra Pradesh electorally in reaction to the division of united Andhra. To compensate the loss, the high command of the drowning Congress clutched at the straw of Telangana at least in the flow of events getting out of its control. As it happened, the promised merger of TRS after the creation of the new state also eluded the Congress in poetic justice, so to say. This was the first time that the Centre divided a state in blatant disregard of the resolution of the State Legislature rejecting the Parliament`s proposal to do so. Moreover, whereas Andhra Pradesh was the first Telugu-speaking linguistic state to be created in independent India in 1953, Telangana ironically turned out to an instance of the division of that unilingual state on the basis of the step-motherly treatment to its backward southern landlocked region.

The latest round of state formations in India must cause a rethinking on Articles 3 and 4 of the Constitution granting unilateral power to the Parliament in the matter of creation of new states, in *consultation* (not necessarily *concurrence*) with the affected state(s). This unfederal provision is uniquely Indian aberration in comparative federal theory and practice. The makers of the Indian Constitution presumably decided to grant this absolute power to the Parliament as they realized that the internal boundaries of India were accidents of historical conquests and colonial convenience. And they did not have time to open this question right in the Constituent Assembly and in the midst of the greatly unsettled conditions of the partition, communal holocaust, and war-time economic crisis. But perhaps they grossly erred in their estimation of our future Honourable Members of Parliament and governments in making trustees of the national/federal interest. In any case, this onerous power must now be made subject to special majority required for constitutional amendment (scrapping the simple majority clause) and must be *federalized* by requiring the Parliament to solicit the consent of the state concerned for any such move.

The foregoing discussion suggests that the reorganization of Indian Union since Independence has mostly been done in ad hoc ways in response to political passions of the time. Interestingly, a regional geographer has made out "a case for constituting the federal structure on the basis of smaller units [of] most preferable cultural regions, with a regional capital acting as a powerful economic node". C.D. Deshpande envisages four categories of federating units and subunits "having regional identity and consciousness of their home environment and socio-economic problems" plus "practicability of territorial changes and adjustments" (Deshpande, 1992: 309). The Deshpande plan advocates nineteen federating states, two devolutionary states, nineteen regional development authorities within the federating states, and six substates with special responsibilities cast upon the Union government. A closer scrutiny of the proposed scheme suggests that Deshpande's major first-order reorganizing principle is, by and large, the linguistic basis, with departure from this principle made only in the case of the Hindi-speaking region. The two devolutionary states of Deshpande appear mainly guided by constraints of size and prohibitive fiscal costs of separate federal statehood. One of these, Himachal Pradesh, falls in the Hindi-speaking region, and the other,

Purvanchal Pradesh, is the mixed bag of tribal areas in the northeastern region and northern Bengal. The sub-state regional development authorities attached to various linguistic federating states are based on physical-cultural factors and fiscal viability and metropolitan character. Finally, the Union territories directly attached to the federal government appear to be carved out by Deshpande on considerations of characteristics such as national metropolitan capital location, Indo-Portuguese exotic cultural traits, hilly or islandic socio-cultural distinctiveness, and fiscal viability. (see Table 5).

Table 5: The Deshpande Scheme for Reorganization of States of the Union, 1992

	STATES
1.	Jammu and Kashmir
2.	Punjab
3.	Haryana
4.	Western Uttar Pradesh
5.	Eastern Uttar Pradesh (Avadh-Bhojpur)
6.	Bihar (Mithila-Magadha)
7.	West Bengal
8.	Assam
9.	Rajasthan
10.	Gwalior-Bundelkhand-Baghelkhand. (Parts of Madhya Pradesh and Uttar Pradesh)
11.	Malwa (Western Madhya Pradesh)
12.	Mahakoshal (Part of Madhya Pradesh)
13.	Gujarat
14.	Maharashtra
15.	Orissa
16.	Andhra Pradesh
17.	Karnataka
18.	Tamil Nadu
19.	Kerala
	STATES UNDER THE UNION GOVERNMENT WITH DEVOLVED POWERS;
20.	Himachal Pradesh
21.	Purvanchal Pradesh (Sub-states of Sikkim, Darjilling Region (North-Bengal), Arunachal Pradesh, Meghalaya, Nagaland, Manipur, Mizoram, Tripura.
	SUB-STATES AND REGIONAL DEVELOPMENT AUTHORITIES (R.D.A.) IN THE STATES (NUMBERED ACCORDING TO THE STATES IN WHICH THEY ARE LOCATED)
6.1	Jharkhand (Bihar) Sub-State
6.2	Santhal Paraganas (R.D.A., W. Bengal)
7.1	Calcutta Metropolitan Region (W. Bengal) Sub-State
9.1	Mewar Hills (R.D.A., Rajasthan)
13.1	Kutch (R.D.A., Gujarat)
13.2	Eastern Hill Areas of Gujarat (R.D.A.)
14.1	Konkan (R.D.A., Maharashtra)
14.2	Marathwada (R.D.A., Maharashtra)

14.3 Vidarabha (R.D.A., Maharashtra)
14.4 Bombay (Metropolitan Region) Sub-State
14.5. Western Ghats comples (R.D.A., Maharashtra)
15.1 Baudh Khondmals and Highlands (R.D.A., Orissa)
16.1 Telangana (R.D.A., Andhra Pradesh)
16.2 Rayalaseema (R.D.A., Andhra Pradesh)
16.3 Eastern Ghats Region (R.D.A., Andhra Pradesh)
17.1 Malnad or Western Ghats Complex (R.D.A., Karnataka)
18.1 Madras Metropolitan Region (Tamil Nadu) Sub-State
18.2 Nilgiris and other Tribal Hills (R.D.A., Tamil Nadu)
19.1 Western Ghats Complex (R.D.A., Kerala)

SUB-STATES UNDER THE UNION TERRITORIES WITH SPECIAL RESPONSIBILITIES:

1.1 Ladakh (J & K)
4.1 Uttarkhand (Hill Region of Uttar Pradesh)
22. Delhi Metropolitan Region
23. Goa
5. Andaman and Nicobar Islands
6. Lakshadweep Islands

Source: Deshpande, 1992: 309/311.

I find at least some features of the Deshpande proposal questionable. First, it is not clear why Bhojpuri areas are attached to Avadhi areas in Eastern Uttar Pradesh and not with Mithila-Mgadha in Bihar. To me Magahi, Maithili, and Bhojpuri dialects have mainly coexisted in Bihar and would also make Bihar territorially and fiscally more viable than it is today. Second, I find it indefensible why Gwalior, Malwa, and Mahokoshal in the present state of Madhya Pradesh should form three separate states and Sikkim, Darjiling, Arunachal, Meghalaya, Nagaland, Manipur, Mizoram, and Tripura should be jumbled up in a new devolutionary state called Purvanchal Pradesh. This is specially so when there has been no popular demand for separate statehood in Gwalior/Malva/Mahakoshal, while the northeastern states have had stronger regional identity movements, some verging on separatism. Third, Deshpande does not pause to ponder whether some existing full-fledged states would agree to be reduced to the status not only of devolutionary states but also to substate regional development authorities. In any case, the centralized political authority that is needed to execute the plan of reorganization suggested by Deshpande is simply not available right now. The only moment when this scheme could have been implemented was at the historic defining moment of the making of the Constitution in the wake of the Independence. It is debatable whether the Indira Gandhi regime could have effectuated it. Yet a rethinking of the kind suggested by Deshpande could begin when the sheer fiscal costs of the present political mentality of a termite colony visible in

India today becomes too prohibitive and crippling. The Deshpande proposal deserves deliberation in view of the fact that even after the latest reorganization giving birth to three new states, there are still many more pending demands for new federal statehood within the Union (Ajay Kumar Singh, 2003). Incidentally none of the newly created states, with the exception of Chhattisgarh, deserved federal statehood in Deshpande's reckoning. In my understanding, even Chhattisgarh is a doubtful case. Jharkhand ought to have been at most a devolutionary state, and Uttaranchal and Chhattisgarh substates with special Union responsibilities.

Prospect

Crystal-gazing into the future one can identify the following major problems on the agenda of reorganization of states in India in the decades ahead. First, the North-South divide that preoccupied the mind of Ambedkar so intensely in the 1950s is at least partly moderated by division of some bigger North Indian states since then. However, another dimension of this problem has surfaced due to postponement of the delimitation of electoral constituencies following a decennial headcount since the 1971 census. After being held in abeyance earlier until 2000, the process has now been frozen until 2026 by the eighty-fourth amendment (2001). It has aheady resulted in a potentially explosive question on the North-South axis, as disproportionate increase of population in the two mega macro-regions has produced distressing representational disparities in the Parliament. The northern region has considerably larger populations and proportionately fewer seats in the Parliament. This disparity is likely to be further magnified by the time the question of delimitation of constituencies is reopened after 2026. (Ashish Bose, 2000: 1698-1700).

Secondly, rise of fragmented ethnic identities and strong micro-regionalism have forced the short-sighted Union governments to create new states, often in blind disregard of administrative rationality and financial viability. In the new political economy of neo-liberalism, privatization, and globalization, when even the more resourceful central and richer provincial states are facing growing and chronic deficits, how long the older and new poorer states can sustain their statehood is a big question-mark. Most of these new states have been created in an ad hoc political manner without the benefit of recommendations of a States Reorganization Commission like the one appointed by the Nehru government in the mid-1950s. The problem has become messier by the year since. A second states reorganization commission would appear to be called for.

Thirdly, the asymmetrical federal relations of Jammu & Kashmir and Nagaland with the Indian Union are still not satisfactorily resolved. The problems are particularly complicated due to insurgencies in these states aggravated by external forces by neighbours and others. The existing special status enjoyed by these states under the constitution are basically sound. What is needed is to give these formal constitutional provisions greater democratic substance and federal autonomy in practice. The moderates and hard-liners in these states need to be seriously engaged in a democratic dialogue for meaningful alternatives in power-sharing, security of life and property for the citizens, and economic development.

Fourthly, even after creation of numerous new states before and since Independence, the Union of India is still a complex mosaic of religious, linguistic, caste and tribal minorities within and across the existing internal boundaries. Given the compact geographical template of the subcontinent and the endowment of complex demographic but an overarching civilizational unity-in-diverstiy, no reorganization of states can produce internally homogeneous and administratively and financially viable set states in all cases. Hence endless fragmentation of the Indian nation-state is not a solution but a part of a problematic package of ungovernability and international instability. There is a strong tendency of clinging to majority-minority straight-jacket of Hindu-Muslim communalism of the period around the bloody imperial partition of 1947. Commmunal violence in India today has become radically transformed. It is a far more complex and messier affair right now. It would be an ostritch-like self-imposed blindness to gloss over the massacre of Dalits and upper castes in Bihar and of tribal elsewhere as less serious and heinous than the slaughter of Muslims in Gujarat and elsewhere and of Hindus and Sikhs in Punjab, Jammu & Kashmir and Delhi. The bland view that minority communalism in less of an evil than majority communalism is not only unethical but it has also proved to be destructive of civic community and Indian citizenship. By now both Hindus and Muslims have come to suffer, for this reason and others, by what may be called "minority" syndrome or psychosis. India is now face to face with hydra-headed communalism involving not only Hindus and Muslims, but also other ethnic communities of whatever kinds we have. We are challenged by the problem of guaranteeing the rights and securities of 'internal minorities' i.e. minorities within minorities, 'discrepant majorities' i.e. majorities that may be nationally so called but are provincial minorities or vice versa. Federal solution has historically been predicated on the grant of statehood to provincial majorities within a composite federal union. Federal theory and practice is yet to adequately address to the problem I have posed above. To come to grips with this problem, federal theory must self-consciously engage more thoroughly than in the past with the theories of constitutionalism and the rule of law, consociationalism, and multiculturalism.[5]

Finally, if South Asia has exit from the history of internecine feudal and colonial feuding and warfare, it must become internally democratic and move ahead to embrace the processes of regional and global integration like other supranational regions of the world. It must make a concerted effort to emulate what David Held (1994:316) called "the cosmopolitan model of democracy". This model envisages a global and regional order comprising multiple and overlapping networks of political, economic, and social power and clusters of individual autonomy and rights "within and across each network of power" spanning states, civil societies, and regional and global organizations. These developments would give birth to "an empowering legal order—a 'democratic international law'." The emergent legal principles would "delimit the form and scope of individual and collective action within the organizations and associations of state *and* civil society. Certain standards are specified for the treatment of all, which no political regime or civil association can legitimately violate" (Held 1994: 319). This cosmopolitan model of democracy in the core and peripheral nation of South Asia alone can ensure simultaneous pursuit of democracy and development and an escape from the vicious cycle of war and poverty. There is no other way.

Endnotes & References

1. In a memorandum on the safeguards for the Scheduled Castes submitted to the Constituent Assembly on behalf of the All India Scheduled Castes. Federation, Ambedkar had earlier incidentally dealt with the question of federating provinces and centrally administered areas of the British Indian states and the native Indian states. He had then evinced a more federal approach as also a more complex approach to the problem. The incorporated territories were to be divided into "Qualified States" and "disqualified states" and in a phased manner they were to be reorganized into a Union of qualified states. "A state shall not be deemed to be Qualified State unless it is proved it is of a standard size prescribed by the Union Legislature and is endowed with natural resources capable of supporting a decent standard of living for its people and can, by reason of its revenue and population function as an autonomous State, protect itself against external aggression, maintain Law and Order against internal disturbance and guarantee to its subjects minimum standards of administration and welfare which are expected of a modern State." Such qualified states would also be in

a way indestructible as much as they could not tampered with, without their "Consent", by the Union Legislature. (Ambedkar, 1989 a: 11-12).

2. Jarrett's Preface gives 16 *subas* but the text of the *Aim* only 15.
3. Such territorial patriotisms in various regions of India served as the prelude to Indian nationalism. See C.A. Bayly, 1998.
4. Ambedkar (1989 B) also quoted the view of C. Rajagopalachari expressed to the former in an interview when the latter was the Head of the state in the interim government and Ambedkar was law minister: "You are committing a great mistake. One federation for the whole of India... will not work. In such a federation the Prime Minister and President of India will always be from the Hindi-speaking area. You should have two federations, one Federation of the North and a Confederation of the North and the South with three subjects for the confederation to legislate upon and equal representation for both the federations" (Ambedkar 1989 b: 22). To get back to Ambedkar's comment about lack of data about Hindi-speaking people in India, the 1991 census offers some clues. Hindi-speakers then constituted 40.22 percent of India's population. Grammatically and lexically in the form Gandhi called Hindustani the closest cognate language of Hindi is Urdu. It is reported to be spoken by 5.18 percent. North Indian languages originating from Sanskrit, a member of the Indo-European linguistic family, together amount to 74.37 percent. And South Indian languages belonging to the Dravidian linguistic family add up to 21.72 percent. Registrar General and Census Commissioner of India, Series 1-India, 1999, C-7 Part C-1: 203-205.
5. On constitutionalism and rule of law, see the two classics that continue to be eminently relevant today, i.e., Albert V. Dicey, (1974); Carl J. Friedrich, (1974). On consociationalism, see Arend Leijphart. On multiculturalism, the best contemporary theoretical statement is Will Kymlicka, (2002). The implications of these theoretical interfaces, especially in the Indian context, are yet to be thoughtfully worked out. Preliminary attempts may be sampled in the writings of Bhikhu Parekh (2003); Gurpreet Mahajan, 2002; and M.P. Singh, 1994, 1996.

References

Ambedkar, B.R. *States and Minorities* (Aligarh: Anand Sahitya Sadan, 1989 a, Preface dated 15.3.1947).

Ambedkar, B.R. *Thoughts on Linguistic States* (Aligarh: Anand Sahitya Sadan, 1989 b, Preface dated 23.12.1955).

Baley, C.A. *Origins of Nationality in South Asia: Patriotism and Ethical Government in the Making of Modern India* (Delhi: Oxford University Press, 1998).

Bose, Ashish "North-South Divide in India's Demographic Seene", *Economic and Political Weekly* (Mumbai), Vol. XXXV, No. 20, 13-19 May 2000.

Chakrabarty, Bidyut. *The Partition of Bengal and Assam 1932-47: Contour of Freedom* (London: Routledge. 2004).

Deshpande, C.D. *India: A Regional Interpretation* (New Delhi: Indian Council of Social Science Research and Northern Book Centre, 1992).

Dicey, Albert V. *Introduction to the Study of the Law of the Constitution* (with a new Introduction to the 10th ed. By E.C.S. Wade) (Delhi: Universal Book Traders, 1974; first published 1885).

Dua, B.D. & M.P. Singh (eds.), *Indian Federalism in the New Millennium* (New Delhi: Manohar, 2003).

Fazl Allami, Abul. *The Ain-i-Akbari,* Trans. Into English by Colonel H.S. Jarrett, corrected and further corrected by Sir Jadu Nath Sarkar (Delhi: Low Price Publications, reprint in 1989 of the 1st ed. Of 1927-1949).

Friedrich, Carl J. *Constitutional Government and Democracy: Theory and Practice in Europe and America* (New Delhi: Oxford & IBH Publishing Co., 1974, reprint of the 4th ed. Of 1968).

Ghosh, Suniti Kumar. *India's Nationality Problem and Ruling Classes* (Calcutta: the author, Calcutta, 1996).

Government of India (Republic). *Report of the States Reorganization Commission Report* (New Delhi: Ministry of Home Affairs, 1955) (Chair Fazal Ali).

Held, David. "Democracy: From City-states to a Cosmopolitan Order? in *The Polity Reader in Social Theory* (Cambridge, the U.K. : Polity Press, 1994)."

Kymlicka, Will. *Contemporary Philosophy: An Introduction* (New Delhi: Oxford University Press, 2002, 2nd ed.).

Mahajan, Gurpreet. *The Multicultural Path: Issues of Diversity and Discrimination in Democracy* (New Delhi: Sage Publications, 2002).

Mishra, Girish and B.K. Pandey. *Sociology and Economics of Casteism in India* (Delhi: Pragati Publications, 1996).

Parekh, Bhikhu. *Re-imagining India,* The Sixth D.T. Lakdawala Memorial Lecture, 28 March 2003 (New Delhi: Institute of Social Sciences, 2003).

Prasad, Rajendra. *Atmakatha* (Autobiography) (New Delhi: Allied Publishers Ltd., 1992, first published 1947).

Pylee, M.V. *Constitutional History of India 1600-1950* (New Delhi: S. Chand & Co. Ltd., 1984 rev. 3rd ed.)

Pylee, M.V. "Seventh Amendment" (Text) in his edited compilation *Constitutional Amendments in India* (Delhi: Universal Law Publishing Co. Pvt. Ltd., 2003).

Rao, B. Shiva *et. al.* (eds.) *The Framing of India's Constitution: A Study/Select Documents, vol. V* (New Delhi: Indian Institution of Public Administration, 1968).

Roy, Himanshu "Facets of Nationality Question in India", *Frontier* (Calcutta), Nos. 11-14, October 19-November 9, 1996.

Saxena, Rekha. *Situating Federalism: Mechanisms of Inter-governmental Relations in Canada and India* (New Delhi: Manohar, 2006).

Singh, Ajay Kumar. "Federalism and State Formation: An Appraisal of Indian Practice" in B.D. Dua and M.P. Singh (eds.), *Indian Federalism in the New Millennium* (New Delhi: Manohar, 2006)

Singh, M.P. "India: The Constitution and Consensus" in J.S. Grewal and Hugh Johnston (eds.), *The Indo-Canada Relationship: Exploring the Political, Economic and Cultural Dimensions* (New Delhi: Sage Publications, 1994).

Singh, M.P. & Rekha Saxena, "Lok Sabha Elections 2004: Change with Continuity," *Think India Quarterly,* Vol. 8, No. 1, January-March 2005.

Thapar, Romila. *Asoka and the Decline of the Mauryas* (Delhi: Oxford University Press, 1997 rev. 2nd ed.).

Wheare, K.C. *Federal Government* (New York: Oxford University Press, 1964, 4th ed.).

6

States' Paradiplomacy in India: Prospects and Pitfalls

Prakash Chandra Jha

Literature on International Relations or Foreign Policy is still dominated by state-centric approach. The Paper argues that the traditional state-centric approach cannot adequately explain sub-national role in foreign economic policy. Sub-national activism in foreign policy with a view to promote their interests is referred as 'paradiplomacy', i.e., 'parallel diplomacy'.[1] Subnational paradiplomacy especially in economic sphere has become a worldwide phenomenon in recent time. As the global trend shows, central government often tries to accommodate the transnational economic interests of its constituent units. India is a federal system where states enjoy considerable autonomy. The economic globalisation and regionalisation have made it possible for constituent units of India to interact with their respective investors in foreign countries in *de facto* sense if not in *de jure* sense (Jha, 2004, 159). Compared to other countries, including some of our neighbours subnational paradiplomacy in India is still at an incipient stage. However, paradiplomatic initiatives by states, of late, have begun gathering momentum. States' high profile investment-promotion activities abroad are testimony to the fact. Such activities have indeed helped some states in their economic development and reduced their economic dependency on centre. Regionalisation of political parties and coalition rule at centre do not adequately explain the subnational paradiplomacy. Earlier in pre-liberalisation period existed two routes, i.e., partisan route and bureaucratic routes to engage in paradiplomatic activities. With centre donning the role of facilitator of states' transnational economic activities, these channels are becoming ineffective now. This has led to symmetrical horizontal competition among states to pursue paradiplomacy. In this states' capacity to engage in economic paradiplomacy depends more on subnational-business linkage, promotional strategies, public relations exercises, creating pro-business environment etc.

States in India so far have adopted a host of instruments which fall under paradiplomacy. They include putting pressure on central government to sign or not to sign or to have a say in an international treaty affecting their region/interest, trade negotiation with external bodies, negotiating loan directly with World Bank, showcasing states' achievement abroad, providing incentives to attract foreign investments, participating in international forum such as World Economic Forum, visiting abroad for trade prospects, hosting foreign diplomats, foreign ministers and even head of states and organising annual meet, conference and seminar and wooing NRIs using their diasporas, setting up sister cities and twin cities, border *haats*, among others. Aside from economic gains, states' paradiplomatic activities can arguably also be useful for the purpose of addressing some of the long-standing problems with our neighbouring countries such as water-sharing, terrorism, and illegal cross-border migration, environmental protection, among others. Further, it can also be used by the centre as soft diplomacy that can complement the national foreign policy. Nevertheless, Paradiplomacy presents challenges too. Given the increasing subnational international activities there is hardly any debate or discussion either in academia or government over the need for the greater role of states in India's foreign policy. The study examines the factors responsible for the development of paradiplomacy in India. It also focuses on responses of the centre towards subnational diplomacy. Further, it also underlines the potential gains not only in economic terms but also in political and cultural terms from paradiplomacy. Furthermore, the study also highlights challenges to national foreign policy on account of states' international activism.

Factors Responsible for the States Activism in Foreign Economic Policy

Federalism

The studies on subnational paradiplomacy began in the 1970s in the form of case study on the external activities of constituent units of the federal countries such as Canada, USA and Australia. Theoretical works on paradiplomacy were undertaken by scholars who predominantly had an academic background in federalism. Therefore, the most of them understands the subnational governments' diplomacy first of all as a result and attribute of the vast transformations that are taking place within federalism and intergovernmental relations. Thus they primarily studied the impact of paradiplomacy on federalism and intergovernmental relations rather than to study the paradiplomacy as a new political phenomenon. Notwithstanding the fact subnational paradiplomacy takes place also in non-federal countries, until today this federalist dimension plays a leading role in studies on paradiplomacy (Duchacek, Latouche and Stevenson, 1988; Kincaid, 2002; Hocking, 1993; Cornago, 2010; Aguirre, 1999; Michelmann, 2009). It is imperative to examine the following questions: Does being part of federal system help the sub-national governments to engage in paradiplomacy? In other word, does federalism as an institution help subnational governments in their quest for paradiplomacy?

Indeed, federalism helps because it constitutionally divides power between central government and its constituent units. But not necessarily subnational governments only in federal country participate in foreign policy (Cornago, 2010: 17). Even in federal countries, foreign policy is normally one of very few areas, along with defence and monetary/fiscal policy that does not come under the jurisdiction of subnational governments. In federal system state enjoys autonomy in several areas well-protected by the constitution. Thus, federalism as an institution may help the constituent units of a country to influence/participate in foreign economic policy (Kincaid, 2002; Hocking, 1993). Constitutionally speaking, however, states and local governments are not legitimate international actors in most of federal countries in the world.

Despite the adoption of India's new economic policy (NEP) in 1990s with some state governments playing important role in foreign policy in form of paradiplomatic activities, however, states' role appears to be quite limited compared to other countries. Let aside countries with federal set up (Australia, Canada, USA, Brazil etc.) Indian states are playing weaker role in this regard than provincial/subnational governments in even unitary countries such China, UK, Japan among others. It can however be argued that subnational international activism is gaining momentum in India and India's federal structure would, in fact, prove to be an asset in this regard in helping the constituent units in developing paradiplomatic activities.

Globalisation and Regionalisation

Aside from federalism, globalisation and regionalism remain important factors behind the state's paradiplomacy in India. First once coalition governments became dominant at the central level in India, the influence of the states in national government became pronounced. Second, adoption of economic liberalisation in the early 1990s has given the Indian states unforeseen opportunities to engage in paradiplomacy.[2] The quest for trade and investment has forced them to look across the border. Rise of regional parties and coalition formation at national level led to empowerment of states at the expense of centre. Rudolph and Rudolph have posited that economic liberalisation combined with coalition politics led to emergence of powerful Chief Ministers like Chandra Babu Naidu who was in position to engage in paradiplomacy via partisan route. Thus regionalisation led some forward looking states to further their interest. Mention must be made here of other factors such as great efforts made by Naidu in image makeover in order to make Hyderabad a global city and Andhra Pradesh a forward looking investment friendly state. Through use of IT, public relation exercises, creation of pro-business environment he created a high tech and global image for AP to suit the time (Rudolph and Rudolph, 2000).

During pre-liberalisation era, industrial development in the states was determined by central government often in partisan manner. Sarkaria Commission, that was constituted to examine the centre-state relations in 1980s, observed that this was major complaint of states. Karnataka, a state not governed by Congress party when Commission was making its inquiries, cited instances of industries not being located in Karnataka for political considerations. The location of public-sector unit was not only influenced by political considerations, but Karnataka government also noted that private sector corporations, such as Glaxo, the Tata Electric Locomotive Company, and Tractors India wanted to set up industries in Karnataka and were asked by the centre (led by the Congress Party) to locate plans elsewhere. Kerala government argued that no objective criteria had been followed in deciding where investment by centre in public sector would occur (Chhibber and Kollman: 2004, 139-140). Sinha has noted that in the primary mode of regional competition was vertical through the national state. In order to get things done through centre, until recent past, states followed mainly two routes: some states followed through bureaucratic channels, while others deploy partisan and political routes, shaped by coalition patterns. Gujarat, for example has followed a more *bureaucratic route* that relies on intra-bureaucracy lobbying and monitoring, while Tamil Nadu, West Bengal, and Andhra Pradesh pursue a *partisan route* that attempts to deploy their political and party influence at the centre for greater economic rewards (Sinha, 2005).

Regionalisation of parties, coalition at centre and globalisation remain important factors but they do not adequately explain subnational paradiplomacy. The formation of business and commercial classes in many states and a regional bourgeoisie, apart from national capitalist classes also helped some states in their quest for paradiplomacy.[3] Some states (Gujarat and Maharashtra) also attempted to create new entrepreneurs through the Entrepreneurial Development Program, contributing to the growth of indigenous subnational entrepreneurs. Thus business-politics linkage has yielded rich dividends in these states and helped them in paradiplomatic pursuits.[4] Rudolf and Rudolph (2001) have argued that in people's perception of the business men as "a symbol of greed and of anti-social gain" has undergone a sea change; they have rather become persons to be respected and emulated.

Public relation exercises have become important driving force for attracting foreign FDIs.[5] Media has become an important tool to showcase the achievements of states. Chief Ministers, consciously seek out the media to advertise their industrial policies and achievements, and explicitly compare themselves with their competitor states. There is much greater emphasis on conferences, meetings, exhibitions, road shows, and press conferences. States make presentations at conferences, utilizing the latest technology, video-conferencing, and computers. The promotional literature handed out by states is usually crafted by private advertisement agencies tasked with selling the state. The struggle over perception and image building has become intense. After the Enron controversy, Maharashtra spent a considerable amount of money on a public relations exercise in partnership with the Indian Engineering Trade Fair in New Delhi in a bid to promote itself as a good investment destination (Sinha, 2005). Recently Haryana appears to be doing the same after Maruti-Suzuki controversy. Speaking at World economic Forum hosted by his state recently, Haryana CM also boasted of performance by players on Haryana in London Olympics 2012 where they bagged four out of six medal won by India. Education and health were other two areas he highlighted as potential sectors for the private sector to invest.[6]

Growing Subnational Paradiplomacy and Centre as Facilitator

Historically some states in India—implicitly or explicitly— influenced the foreign policy making of central government occasionally. Recently, there is a growing tendency to involve relevant state governments in diplomatic discussions, which were previously conducted mostly between the central government and the country in question. The centre has now realised that regional leaders can help to provide greater understanding because of common cultural ties between their states and the people across the border. On his trip to Bangladesh the Indian PM was accompanied by a number of Chief Ministers of Northeast regions. Recently in International Labour Meet at Geneva, Labour Minister of India was also accompanied by his state counterparts from Bihar, Haryana and Andhra Pradesh (*Time of India*, May 27, 2012).

Centre has facilitated states' direct lending negotiations with the overseas bank. The World Bank President claimed that the Bank was directly dealing with some Indian states, which is a major departure from the established norm (Sridharan, 2003). Centre has established India Trade Promotion Organisation (ITPO) and it has also encouraged states to set up regional trade promotion centre in state capital and major cities. This has led to the intensification of paradiplomatic relations at vertical level, anchored in bilateral agreement, between Indian states and foreign countries. Union government have advised all the state governments/union territories to set up WTO cells and appoint nodal officers to effectively coordinate various WTO related matters. A number of states have established WTO cells. The objective of the cells is to carry out research and provide inputs to the state government for taking up state specific issues with the government of India to be negotiated with WTO.

In short, the central government has recognised and to some extent favoured this increasing international activism of states in economic sphere. These can be seen as an act of legitimisation of subnational paradiplomacy by the central government. As a result, subnational paradiplomacy appears to have become symmetrical. There exists horizontal competitive federalism as far as states' engagement in transnational activities is concerned. This paradigm shift in centre-state relations has led some states to adopt aggressive promotional strategies that have yielded positive result.

Aggressive Promotion Strategies at Subnational Level

When it comes to aggressive promotion of state both nationally as well as globally, Gujarat has perhaps no parallel in India. CM Narendra Modi's promotional strategies resemble those of Chandra Babu Naidu. A glance at the Gujarat government's website (www.vibrantgujarat.com) which is daily updated shows how aggressively state is promoting itself as the best FDI destination in the world.[7] Diplomatic delegations from several other countries, including the UK, USA, Australia and Singapore, have already visited the state in the run-up to the event and expressed interest in inter-governmental and business partnerships.

A number of states are taking leaf from the book Chief Minister Narendra Modi in promoting pro-business atmosphere and showcasing their states' achievement. Recently Chief Minister of Madhya Pradesh had gone on three nation's tour of Japan, South Korea and Singapore for attracting industrial investment and export from states. Till recently, Bihar, Madhya Pradesh, Rajasthan and Uttar Pradesh were known as the "Bimaru" states. But these states are trying hard to leave this image far behind by seeking external investment. They compete with each other in providing the potential investors with numerous incentives such as Special Economic Zone (SEZ), some guaranteed return on investment, and reimbursement of Value Added Tax etc.

Aggressive promotion of states for seeking investment was perhaps nowhere more visible than at Pravasi Bharatiya meet. One newspaper reported that "the third Pravasi Bhartiya Divas congregation in Mumbai would be remembered more for chief ministers than NRIs". The chief ministers from Uttar Pradesh, Rajasthan, Punjab, Gujarat, Chhattisgarh, Maharashtra, Kerala and Karnataka had literally queued up to woo prospective investors to their states (*The Economic Times*, January 10, 2005).[8] States chief Ministers are aggressively pitching their states not just nationally but also globally for the sole purpose of attracting more and more investment and intensifying states' export. Several forward looking states are organising global business Summit to promote their achievement.[9] Kerala, of late, has floated the idea of having its own airlines.

CMs of Bihar and Gujarat visited China to explore trade and investment opportunities.[10] Their visits attracted huge media attentions in India. Chief Minister of Gujarat was received at the Great Hall of People, where normally head of the national governments is received and accorded such honour. As per media report Gujarat CM was not only invited by Japan but also treated him almost at par with head of the nation.

What is noteworthy is that states are also learning from each other. In fact during their interaction at world Economic Forum India Conference in Mumbai in November 2011, Chief Ministers of Maharashtra, Kerala and

Madhya Pradesh also backed the idea of institutionalizing an innovation centre to help states share best practices.

Use of International Forum by States

Use of international forum to showcase their achievement and potential are becoming norms almost for every state. Maharashtra CM, Chavan recently headed a high-level delegation to attend the World Economic Forum's annual event at Davos. In November 2010, Chief Minister Prem Kumar Dhumal of Himachal Pradesh has been invited by the Governor of California, Arnold Schwarzenegger, for participation in "Governors' Global Summit on Climate Change" (3 November, *Tribune* 2010).

In the World Economic Forum's 'India Economic Summit' hosted by Maharashtra in November 2011, Chief Ministers of Maharashtra, Kerala, Madhya Pradesh and Premier of the British Columbia a Canadian Province discussed a host of issues concerning subnational paradiplomacy.[11]

India's marginalized north-eastern region is also trying to catch up with other states. Mizoram has recently organised its first ever industry summit to harness the resources of the state in a bid to woo investors to set up projects in the industry-starved northeast state.[12] Chief Minister Nabam Tuki has once again made a strong case for Arunachal Pradesh as the "next investment destination of India" by highlighting its potential areas for investment and also its impressive growth rates recorded in past two years.[13]

Together these developments indicate parallel diplomacy, in which states have become additional players in a sphere that is usually the preserve of the central government.

Foreign Trade Offices in India

Increasingly, there is realisation among the investors that the states in India are becoming autonomous players in crafting foreign economic policies suited to their own needs, and that the old way of approaching the central government to pursue trade relations at the state level cannot be useful. Not surprisingly therefore, various state capitals have witnessed opening of number of foreign trade offices such as Mumbai, Delhi, Bangalore, Ahmadabad, Hyderabad, Chennai, etc. Several sub-national governments of foreign countries are also setting up foreign trade offices in India. Taiwan has a trade office in New Delhi rather than a full-fledged embassy. Some year ago it has sought permission from Ministry of External Affairs (MEA) to open a subsidiary office or consulate in Chennai since Taiwanese companies have substantial investments in Tamil Nadu. Worried about the reaction of Beijing, MEA dithered. Finally Taiwanese asked the then DMK government in Chennai to use its political clout with UPA (The Asian Age, 30 July 2012).

City Twinning and Sister Town

Sister town and twin cities are recently evolved concept. It is when two cities are considered to be in an agreement to promote culture and commercial ties. Allahabad Bangalore, Jaipur, Delhi, Mumbai, Chennai, Lucknow, Hyderabad etc. have sisters/twin abroad. Government of India is encouraging India cities to develop twinning link with other cities.[14] City twinning supports exchanges between the cities be they business, culture or education. Under this agreement both sides agreed to carry out, promote and support exchanges and cooperation in a wide range of areas of common interest in the public, private, voluntary and community sectors aimed at deepening links between local people in the two cities in the field of education, training, culture, leisure, economy, science youth and women's issues, voluntary and grassroots developments and civic management.

Prospects of State Paradiplomacy

The implication of paradiplomacy on economy of some states such as Gujarat, Maharashtra, Tamil Nadu, Andhra Pradesh, Haryana, Delhi, Karnataka, among others has been unquestionably huge. With increasing volumes of FDIs these states have registered phenomenal growth in recent times. Various industries in these states have grown, developed and also expanded. Success stories of some of these states have been globally acclaimed. States are competing with each other in attracting investment. In their competitive horizontal federalism, they are adopting a number of strategies such organising global summit, making foreign trip, showcasing their growth story to their potential investors, providing number of incentives. These strategies have helped states such as Maharashtra, Karnataka, Andhra Pradesh, Gujarat, Tamil Nadu etc. tremendously. Other states such as Bengal Bihar, Orissa, Kerala, Madhya Pradesh, Haryana, UP etc. are also resorting to these paradiplomatic activities to woo foreign investors (Srivastava, 2012). FDI giants like Maharashtra is facing stiff competition from several states that are vying each other to attract investments.[15] States are busy formulating a new industrial and investment policy. A number of states have set up a single-window clearance system. They are trying to upgrade infrastructure of their less developed regions that can attract investments.

Tourism is one of the biggest industries in the world with the capacity to employ 200 million people worldwide. Projection of tourist inflow around the world will be in the range of 1.6 billion spending US$ 5 billion a day by 2020. It goes without saying that India has immense tourism potential that has not been exploited so far. States' paradiplomacy in this regard can play a significant role. Subnational paradiplomacy can help FDI laggard state such as Bihar and north-eastern region to realise their tourism potential.

Border States and Paradiplomacy

India shares a border with Pakistan in Kashmir, Punjab, Rajasthan and Gujarat in the north and west. It shares border with China and Nepal in the north-central states of Uttar Pradesh and Bihar. With Bangladesh it further shares boundary in the eastern state of West Bengal and the small north-eastern states to the east of Bangladesh and with Sri Lanka in Tamil Nadu in the south (a littoral border) (Dossani and Vijaykumar, 2005). Due to commonalities in ethnicity, religion, and stages of economic development, Border States have great incentive to undertake paradiplomatic activities.

Northeast India shares 98 percent of its border with Myanmar, Bangladesh, China and Bhutan. Thus building transport and trading corridors at various border points can make essential subsistence items much cheaper in this region. It has been observed that due to higher transport costs people in the region pay very high price for goods coming from the industrial metros like Delhi, Mumbai and Kolkata. The opening of transport connectivity and trading routes within the Forum of Bangladesh, China, India and Myanmar (BCIM) neighbourhood can substantially relieve the burden in the frontiers of northeast India, whose market turnover is estimated at US$ 50 billion. India's willingness to closer trade and economic ties with its eastern neighbours has opened possibilities for northeast states to engage in paradiplomacy. India can take lessons from China which has taken full advantage of Yunnan's geographical location and its cultural affinities with China's neighbours in its efforts to strengthen ties with Southeast Asia. Baruwa (2005) has critiqued the central government role of not facilitating northeast region for regional diplomacy:

It was in Yunnan's capital Kunming where experts, scholars and business people from China, India, Myanmar and Bangladesh got together to initiate the BCIM Forum. Yunnan's provincial government plays a far more active role in attracting foreign investments to the province than Northeast Indian states. It plays a role in institutions of the Greater Mekong sub-region. But there is little room for India's Northeastern states in the Mekong Ganga Cooperation forum or in BIMST-EC (Bangladesh, India, Myanmar, Sri Lanka, Thailand Economic Cooperation). The difference is quite ironic given that China's political system is centralized and authoritarian while ours is democratic and federal.

There is growing awareness that India can take advantage of the northeast's history and culture, and their shared cultural ties with Southeast Asia as a soft power resource. It has long been recognised that subnational paradiplomacy has huge potential to address some of the long-standing problems from water sharing to terrorism, and illegal migration to environmental protection that exist between India and its neighbours such as Afghanistan, Pakistan, Sri Lanka, Bangladesh, Myanmar and China.

There is demand for closer economic interaction between Tibet and India's Ladakh regions of Jammu and Kashmir and of China's Yuan province with north-eastern states. Horizontal paradiplomacy between subnational governments India and China will help in a great deal of good will in reducing tension between two countries. In Arunachal Pradesh there exist several traditional routes for trade that could not be reopened on the account of security considerations. In Tripura many projects irrigation, flood control and embankment building have been stopped since 2007 following objection from Bangladesh. These are some areas where states paradiplomacy can be successful given the failure of national diplomacy to sort out the differences.

Myanmar is considered significant part of India's Look East Policy for the simple reason that it is the only South East Asian nation with which India shares a land border. Four of our sensitive north-eastern states (Arunachal Pradesh, Nagaland, Manipur and Mizoram) share 16,00 KM land border with Myanmar. Cross-border ethnic link with Naga and Mizo tribes' inhabitating both sides of India-Myanmar border can be asset for paradiplomacy.[16] Similarly, two Punjabs can benefit immensely from cross-border trade (Maini, 2013).

Bangladesh which at present has a negative trade balance vis-a-vis India is seeking for 726.6 MW of power from ONGC Tripura Power Company (OTPC) amidst acute power crisis faced by the north eastern part of Bangladesh. This demand is strongly supported by Tripura Chief Minister

Manik Sarkar for the simple reason that Bangladesh allowed transportation of heavy power gears from its territory to Tripura (Maini, 2013).

Opening of Border *haats* (local marketing centre) between India's border states and Bangladesh has been quite successful. There is proposal to establish more border *haats.* (*Business Line*, 8 January 2012). *Haats* would permit people to sell locally-produced vegetables, fruits, spices, fish, poultry, minor forest produce, produce of local cottage industry, small agricultural household implements, second-hand garments, melamine products and processed food items. According to Commerce Minister of India "an estimated $20 million worth trade will take place annually between India and Bangladesh through the 'Border *Haats*'" (*Business Line*, 21 July 2012).[17] Chief Minister of Arunachal Pradesh played a crucial role in persuading the centre to have Indo-Myanmar Border haat at Pangsau Pass in Changlang district.

In short, there is growing awareness that subnational governments' engagement in paradiplomacy can also contribute to an enhanced regional security and eliminating trust deficit between hostile neighbours.

New Trend in States' Paradiplomacy

Subnational paradiplomacy can take place both vertically and horizontally. Indian states are new to this (horizontal) inter-subnational cross-border trade. Sub-national governments across the border have begun establishing trade offices in India's developed states. Visit of states/provinces delegation led by their governor/premier to states' capital in India are becoming a regular affair in recent time. Last year, 12-member delegation from the Gansu province of China visited Bihar in order to explore trade and other opportunities.

States in India are, however, not allowed to open trade office abroad. But given the global trend in this direction days are not far when states in India will also have trade offices abroad. States are, however, permitted to host representative of subnational/national government from foreign countries.

States are becoming part of bilateral state-to-state negotiations, making the relationship a multilateral one. For example, Chief minister of Bihar after his return from the four-day official visit of Bhutan in 2011 put a proposal before the centre to make the state a partner in the hydel power projects of Bhutan and give permission to take equity stake in them so that the power-starved state can get assured power from the neighbouring country.

More recently, Bihar CM was on a week-long visit to the Pakistan on the invitation of not just the federal government but also the provincial governments of Sindh and Punjab. This engagement at the 'sub-national level' was encouraged by the Prime Minister's Office and the External Affairs Ministry as it builds on the initiative taken by Manmohan Singh to build peace with Pakistan.[18] These developments are indications that Indian states in future would engage in inter-provincial diplomacy abroad. A number of countries in the world including USA, Brazil, Australia, China and Japan have taken full advantage of states' paradiplomacy in their efforts to strengthen ties with other countries.

Pitfalls of State's Paradiplomacy

It is often argued that states lack the skills to exercise responsible foreign policy especially in political sphere given the fact that states do not have trained diplomats. Then there are other concerns in form of most of India's neighbours being hostile neighbour. Thus states' paradiplomacy is likely to pose threat to the country's sovereignty and integrity from forces of terrorism, insurgency and separatism often supported by some of India's hostile neighbours. How to reconcile the demands of a globalising economy that relies on greater opening with security concerns is a policy dilemma we face today?

States' paradiplomacy especially in political sphere can affect the national foreign policy negatively. On both *teestha* river treaty and US-led resolution on UN General Assembly, national interest was subordinated to regional interest and the centre abdicated its national responsibility by keeping its alliance partner happy. Bhambari (2012) maintains: "India is likely to pay a very heavy price if it makes foreign policy a football game where 'regionalists' begin to dictate and decide the directions of policy". Centre can do great disservice to the nation by allowing it to be dominated by parochial regional interests. Thus states' political paradiplomacy has evoked negative reactions. Singh and Mishra (2012) argue that it is important that demands of states on foreign policy fronts should be seen in a larger perspective. They argued:

> ...when West Bengal demands that the Central government cannot conclude an agreement on the issue of waters of a river that flows through the state to Bangladesh, it also needs to consider the implications on other states and related security issues. The North Eastern States could have benefitted with more river water transport from the north eastern region of India to Bangladesh, opening the gates for more commerce. Bangladesh has proactively cooperated in controlling militant activities in North East, particularly Assam, which now gets compromised over the rift on Teesta waters.

Paradiplomatic activities motivated by nationalism can inflict great harm to our national interest. As some policy analysts have stated: "There are regions and subnationalities in the country that have not yet fully accepted the unity of the country. Under such circumstances, it might be rash to grant constituent units such freedoms". (Mattoo and Jacob: 2009, 185).

While there is euphoria and media hype over FDI induced development there are also concerns that it is resulting into uneven development. Gujarat here is the case in point where despite the impressive growth, state has failed to reduce malnourishment level while Uttar Pradesh and Bihar, among the most backward in the country, have done better in improving the lot of their marginalised Dalits and tribals. Like Gujarat Karnataka is other state.[19]

State engagement in political paradiplomacy in the garb of economic paradiplomacy appears to be questionable. For example, during his visit to China, Gujarat CM raised a few controversial issues such as the presence of Chinese troops in Pakistan Occupied Kashmir during his talks with Communist Party leaders in Beijing. He also took up the case of speedy trial in the diamond smuggling case involving 22 Gujarati diamond merchants. It is ironic that there is hardly any discussion over the implication of this on national foreign policy in Media

Summary and Conclusions

In this paper, I have argued that paradiplomacy is a multifaceted phenomenon; it can both complement and conflict our national foreign policy. Paradiplomacy has indeed made some states especially developed states in India economically more independent. Border region especially northeast would arguably gain as their economies benefit more from the economies across their borders. Subnational paradiplomacy can also be useful for addressing some of problems with our neighbouring countries such as water-sharing, terrorism, and illegal cross-border migration, environmental protection among others.

Indian states have adopted a quite distinct form of subnational paradiplomacy. Instead of states' overseas representation and mission around the world, states' paradiplomacy has been largely the result of a variety of informal economic schemes which have helped rich states (Mattoo and Jacob, 2009: 185)[20].

Subnational economic paradiplomacy is often facilitated and supported by centre leading thereby to symmetrical horizontal competition among states to engage in their paradiplomatic pursuits. States' political paradiplomacy has however evoked different kind of reactions from centre as well as academia. While international economic activities of states have increased of late, potential for paradiplomacy of border regions especially northeast regions remains unused.

On the one hand there is euphoria over investment-driven growth on the other hand there are also concerns that FDI-induced economic growth has not been inclusive. Increasing urban-rural divide and gap between rich and poor in some of India's developed states are testimony to this fact. This paper makes a strong case for states' involvement in paradiplomacy through institutional mechanisms. There are two ways wherein states' economic paradiplomacy can be institutionalised. First constitutional amendment can be made in order to incorporate states' role in foreign economic policy making. This is not very practical approach as very few countries in the world have done it. Second, delegation of power to states as in China, UK, Japan, Brazil etc., and establishment of institutions meant for cooperating and coordinating with states in their paradiplomacy. The Centre could invent a system where safeguards can be placed so that any untoward happening in name of paradiplomacy affecting national interest could be checked. States should be made agents and partners of national government in foreign policy. Subnational paradiplomacy has great potential as soft-diplomacy resources that can be used by centre to resolve some of major cross-border problems. China has, since long time, been using its provinces to have inter-provincial relationship with their counterparts in other countries.[21] It has shown a great deal of interest in the internationalization of the vast majority of its provinces, not only through market integration, or the establishment of informal relations across the border, but also by authorizing its governors to sign international agreements and to receive and send international missions all over the world (Zhimin, Junbob and Diyuc, 2010).

Centre in India can delegate to states a number of foreign economic policy making powers and responsibilities which states can undertake with their own resources. This in turn can also reduce Delhi's workload. Trade and investment promotion activities of states and transnational economic engagement would deepen India's relations with foreign nations. A systematic study of paradiplomatic activities of states in India is overdue. What is required is a more thorough examination of subnational paradiplomacy. There is felt need in India to stimulate debates and discussions over challenges and opportunities of subnational engagement in foreign policy.

Endnotes & References

1. The term "paradiplomacy" was introduced by the Canadian scholar Panavotis Soldatos. The American author Ivo D. Duchacek further developed it. Duchacek, Latouche and Stevenson, 1988); Michelmann and Soldatos 1990); Paradiplomacia.org is an online magazine designed to promote the international projection of provincial and local governments. It seeks to enhance the international relations of local governments in order to connect cities, towns and regions for an enriching and sustainable trade. Available at http://www.paradiplomacia.org/institucional.php?lang=en&seccion=2; The term paradiplomacy is not used until recently in India. See Indian Express, *Modi's Parallel Diplomacy*, 4 January 2012; there is no consensus in academia on which term is more convenient for defining the subnational governments' external activities. Paradiplomacy, state diplomacy, constituent diplomacy, subnational diplomacy, regional diplomacy, subnational foreign policy etc. are used synonyms for the involvement of subnational government in foreign policy. I prefer use of paradiplomacy in this article for it has become very popular term.
2. The second reason for the paradiplomacy is because of adoption the New Economic Policy (NEP) in 1991. NEP opened new vistas for creative and innovative activities by the sub-national governments (Chelliah, 1996, 19).
3. Baru has argued: "The process of agrarian change in many part parts of the country has laid the foundations for capitalist development in the non-farm sector. This process has allowed a new generation of agrarian capitalists or other middle class professionals to make transition to capitalist entrepreneurs...the latter seek political and material support from state governments and regional political parties. It is not surprising the regional political parties...have been active in states where regional business groups have been more dynamic and assertive". (Baru 2000: 226; as cited in Sinha 2010; 463).
4. A 50-strong contingent of senior management officials from industrial houses like Reliance Industries Limited, Adani Group, Essar Group, Zydus Cadila, Suzlon, Torrent Group, Rasna Industries, Tata Group companies, Mamta Group, Cadila Pharmaceuticals would promote Gujarat as investment destination to the potential investors in different countries as a run up to Vibrant Gujarat Global Summit 2013 (Economic Times 21 June 2012).
5. An NRI, Mahendra Khari, the president of the International Punjabi Chamber for Service Industry (IPCSI), pointed that unlike other states like Gujarat, the Punjab government was not efficient in propagating polices or taking initiatives to attract foreign investment. "In Punjab, they (Punjab government) do not have much public relations exercise like Gujarat... I have not seen much support from state functionaries like NRI help centres, professional support, etc.. It (support) is at a personal level (rather) than any other level," rued Khari, who is based in the UK, see Business Standard, 8 November 2012.
6. Haryana CM pointed out that average annual growth rate of 9.4 percent in the past seven years and contributes roughly 3.4% to the country's GDP. Referring to a recent Assocham report, he said, 87% of the total investments received in Haryana are from the private sector. An earlier report, according to CM, said Haryana achieved 81 per cent implementation rate of the pledged investments, ahead of States like Gujarat, Maharashtra, Tamil Nadu and Karnataka, see Business Standard, 8 November 2012.
7. The Gujarat government is trying hard to tell its success story to external investors through "Vibrant Gujarat Global Investors' Summit". Slated in January 2013, state government has already started posting advertisements on the websites of international publications like Washington Post and Wall Street Journal. The state government is also using social media

websites like Facebook, and search engines like MSN, Yahoo and for promoting Vibrant Gujarat advertisement campaigns. US-India Business Council in Washington and Australia-India Business Council based in Sydney are the official partner organisations while Japan and Canada are the official partner countries of the summit.

8. Mulayam Singh Yadav, who was CM at that time, announced the setting up of an investment commission headed by himself in order to bring all government departments under one umbrella to provide a single-window clearance for investors. He invited NRIs to participate in the development of Kanha Kunj in Brindavan and build international convention centres at Agra and Varanasi. Rajasthan CM Vasundhara Raje Scindia requested NRIs to contribute to the state's development through adoption of monuments, villages and schools. She also intended to make Rajasthan a year-long tourist destination. Kerala surprised the audience with its plans to start a budget airline to the Gulf region. According to chief minister Oomen Chandy, the state is in the process of seeking Centre's permission for starting it. With about 15 lakh Keralites in the region, the cash-strapped Kerala government hopes the airline will be a profitable venture. See *The Economic Times*, January 10, 2012.
9. Kerala has organised "Emerging Kerala 2012", the flagship global connect programme of the state government held at Kochi from Sep 12 to 14, 2012. Other states who have/are organised/organising State Summit this year to promote states globally include Bihar, MP, Maharashtra, Karnataka, Haryana, among others. This year Gurgaon, national Capital region of Haryana is going to host annual World Economic Forum meet. See www.weforum/events/word-economic-forum-india; The first-ever "Goa Investment Forum 2012", to attract industries to Goa, was held in Panaji on June 30, 2012.
10. The Government of the People's Republic of China and the ruling Community Party of China (CPC) accorded unprecedented importance and highest level of protocol to the Chief Minister going beyond the established norms.
11. Since the last 26 years World Economic Forum India Summit was being in held in India's Capital Delhi. Maharashtra became the first state to host the summit in 2011. In 2012 Haryana is hosting WEF India summit. The shift from national capital to state capital clearly mentioned on website of WEF: "Last year's summit in the state Maharashtra validated our model going forward to corporate the important role which states are playing in shaping India's political and economic landscape".
12. Addressing the summit, state Industries Minister S. Hiato said, "Mizoram, one of the most peaceful states in northeastern India, is blessed with natural resources which are still under-utilised. According to an official document of the Mizoram government, the northeastern state has a potential to generate 3,500 MW hydel power from its rivers. ". http://www.northeasttoday.in/our-states/arunachal-pradesh/arunachal-cm-continues-to-woo-foreign-investors/
13. "The advantages that Arunachal can offer are unique...No other region can match these," asserted Tuki while Tuki was speaking at the inauguration of the Brand India Expo 2012 in Ottawa. He stated that the travel icons—Lonely Planet—had recently selected Arunachal Pradesh as the fourth best place to travel in the world terming it as "the last of the great Shangri-las". http://www.northeasttoday.in/our-states/arunachal-pradesh/arunachal-cm-continues-to-woo-foreign-investors/
14. See in details guideline for Twinning of cities in India available at urbanindia.nic.in/programme/lsg/Twinning_Guidelines.pdf
15. Even when Maharashtra succeeded in attracting an investment of Rs 1 lakh-crore since April last year till date, it lost big-ticket investments—including Maruti and Peugeot—to

neighbouring Gujarat. Even smaller states such as Chhattisgarh and Uttrakhand besides Orissa are giving a run to Maharashtra (Business standard, January 14, 2012).

16. Dean (2005) gives the example of a community known as Kachin in Upper Myanmar, Singpho in Assam and Arunachal Pradesh and Jingpo in Yunnan, China. According to her the community has 'creatively adjusted to the dominating international system of the states' by incorporating into their self-definition references to the three 'host' states of China, Myanmar and India. Despite being citizens of three different states they are 'united through a tight unique kinship lineage network of various spatial trajectories and social bonds, a commonly recognized *lingua franca* and a variety of tangible ethnic features.
17. The Chief Ministers of Meghalaya, Arunachal Pradesh, Minister for Industry and Commerce of Tripura and Minister for Public Health Engineering of Assam along with delegation members paid separate calls on Foreign Minister of Bangladesh Dr. Dipu Moni and discussed about means to enhance cooperation in trade, border management and other areas of mutual benefit.
18. Bending protocol, the President of Pakistan organised special dinner for Bihar CM on the occasion of Deepawali (a festival of light) see, The Hindu, November, 10, 2012; November 13, 2012.
19. These are some of the conclusion of India's human development report. "Human Development Indicators: Gujarat worst", see, *Indian Express*, 21 October, 2011.
20. However, there is some silver-lining as some poor states are also trying to catch up with developed states.
21. Chinese provinces have developed a sophisticated provincial foreign affairs management system. It is usually led by a small leading group on foreign affairs, headed by either the governor or the provincial party secretary. Under provincial leadership, the provincial Foreign Affairs Office (FAO) and the Foreign Trade and Economic Cooperation Commission (FTEC) are the two major bureaucratic organs dealing with provincial foreign relations. FAO, which is under the dual leadership of provincial leaders and the Ministry of Foreign Affairs in Beijing, deals with political affairs at a subnational level and coordinates overall provincial foreign relations. FAO has responsibility for implementing the national foreign policy locally; arranging for the reception of foreign VIPs and for the overseas visits of provincial leaders; administering passport and visa matters for provincial official business travel abroad; organizing and promoting activities with sister cities and provinces of other countries; administering consular affairs and foreign media affairs; and guiding foreign affairs-related work of other local government departments, etc. See Shanghai FAO website, http://www.shfao.gov.cn/.

PART II

GOVERNMENTAL POLICIES AND EXPERIENCES

7

Regional Disparities of Public Policy in India

Manoj Sinha

It would be agreeable to argue that while democracy having struck deep roots in the country can be termed as India's highest achievement, Rampat structural inequality and regional disparities are our gravest failures. It would be prudent to recall here, that though Indian thinkers and political leaders were always aware of the high levels of inequality and regional disparities in the country, yet their view-point differed in regard to concern for these. Eight industrialists of the country in January 1944 prepared a plan for the development of the country known as Bombay Plan. They observed that the gross inequality was undesirable, but they did envisage that total abolition of inequalities, three months after the Bombay Plan in April, 1944, M.N. Roy emphatically argued for reduction of inequality in People's Plan.

The Indian struggle of independence was fought with high ideals of patriotism, freedom, and equality. After independence, the Constitution of India provided equality and equal opportunity as fundamental rights of the people, with special safeguard for women, children, Scheduled Castes and Scheduled Tribes, and the weaker sections of the society. Despite these statutory provisions the maladies of inequality and regional disparities continue to be all-pervasive and equitable distributions of gains of development are still a distant dream even in the second decade of the twenty first century. This fact was corroborated in the Approach Paper to Eight Plan (1990-95) as follows: "...the kinds of development we have had has led to growing disparities and inequalities, a felt sense of injustice and oppression", and that "a shift in investment allocations should be accompanied by more direct measures to bring about a more even distribution of income". This concern for inequalities and regional disparities was strengthened further when National Front Government decided to observe 1990-91 as the year for equality and social justice.

These facts raise a number of questions, such as: What has been wrong with strategy pursued for the development and removal of regional disparities? Why has the idea of regional balance, though all along with us, failed to work? What strategy would be effective in removal of regional disparities and for acceleration of overall process of development? This paper would try to find answers to some of these questions.

Public Policy Making in India

Public policy making is necessarily shaped within the frame work of a country's constitutional system of which three features stand out most prominently in the case of India: the parliamentary form of government, federalism and a broad band of social, economic and political philosophy articulated in the preamble, the directive principles of state policy and the fundamental rights.

India has adopted the parliamentary form of government along with federalism as its ordering constitutional frame-work, but of the two features parliamentarism is the one more solidly entrenched. Broadly patterned after the Westminster mode, the political executive is composed of members of parliament and is accountable to the latter, the Parliament being the front of executive power, subject only to the Constitution. This mentioned here because of the important role Parliament has in public policy making. The five year plans of the country acquire finality only after Parliament has accorded its approval. Similarly, Parliament has over a period of time passed a number of policy resolutions such as the Industrial Policy Resolution, Policy Resolution on Science and Technology, Resolution on National Education Policy etc. and these policies have since come to acquire sanctity of the highest level.

Legislatures everywhere are on the decline, and Indian Parliament is no exception. Today, the legislative leadership has undisguisedly shifted into hands of the Executive and this process has been further reinforced and strengthened in India by the long continuing single party dominance system of the country, and arguably, particularly by the Congress culture of functioning. The subservience has become much more deeply marked since 1984 under the prime minister-ship of Rajiv Gandhi. The passage of the Muslim (protection of rights on Divorce) Act, 1986 by the Parliament in the face of stiff nationwide opposition in an evidence of the Executive firmly moving elsewhere-notably in the direction of the Prime Minister's House.

Policy-making process in India has equally to contend with the federal form of the country's polity. Indian federalism, which has evolved out of extreme unitraism, is marked by some unique features. While the Constitution attempts a division of functions between the two levels of government all "line" or substantive functions remain entrusted with the state government. Most subjects, which constitute the ingredients of development administration are, constitutionally within the states direct jurisdiction: Agriculture, Education, Housing, Industries, public health and sanitation, family planning, water-supply, animal husbandry, minor irrigation, forests, fisheries and local government. While many others like electricity, labour, economic and social planning etc, are in the concurrent list, subject to state as well as central jurisdiction with the centre exercising over-riding power but effective one nonetheless remaining with the states. Because the financial resources are concentrated in the Central Government the state have necessarily to look to the Centre for funds. It is axiomatic, according to the Centre's mode of thinking, that one who provides money also exercises control, and the states are thus made to look the Centre more and more, especially since the adoption of social-economic planning in the fifties.

Changes in Regulatory Reform

Government regulations have been important policy tools for policy makers to manage the development of a market economic system, to protect the interest of the general public, and to promote new values of the modern society. The oppression of a market economic system requires the appropriate intervention by governments to assure the role of fair competition among companies and industries. Intervention is important for governments to protect public interests because of the· issue of market failures and absence. The improvement in economic condition and quality of life has promoted new values (e.g. individual rights and social equity) in the society. To achieve these values social and citizen groups have also asked for the involvement of governments to develop new regulatory policies and institutions. The expansion of regulatory policies and the increasing requirements of regulatory programs have resulted in difficult problems or burdens for businesses and citizens. These problems refer to the increase of regulatory inflation and the growth of regulatory costs. The negative effects of regulatory burdens include the direct cost to government and businesses in terms of rising administration and compliance expenses as well as the indirect costs to the economy and the society in terms of reducing competition and productivity.

To resolve the negative problems and burdens, policy makers in many nations have promoted different types of regulatory reforms since the late 1970s. These reforms are designed to achieve two purposes:

1. Improving the current system by reducing the unnecessary programs and increasing the efficiency of the operation, and
2. Developing a new system by considering alternative approaches and encouraging flexibility and competition.

The development of regulatory policies and programs in the 20th Century was necessary for governments to deal with many public issues occurring in the modern industrialized society. Regulatory policies have contributed to the normal operations of a market economic system on the one hand and to the protection of public interest and social values on the other hand.

Public Policy and the Corporations

"Did you ever expect a corporation to have a conscience, when it has no soul to be damned, and nobody to be kicked? (Edward, First Baron Thurlow)."

Despite the modern and rather fanciful conception of the 'soulful' corporation, economists by and large continue to regard corporations, or firms, as operating on behalf of their owners and responding in a somewhat mechanistic fashion to changes in the economic environment. Perhaps economists might be allowed to invoke the decree of Pope Innocent IV who forbade the excommunication of corporations on the grounds that the latter, in contrast to the former, having neither minds nor souls, could' not sin. Yet politicians often condemn corporations as being amongst the greatest of sinners, partly no doubt because, in modem capitalist societies, the corporation can lay claim to be the most important economic institution outside government.

The same politicians have been busy devising new policies to encourage firms to move in certain directions, while at the same time trying to restrain their worst excesses. Also the growth in the power and importance of large corporations has attracted a great deal of attentions in the professional literature, with the focus of this discussion being mainly concentrated 'on the alleged separation of ownership and control and the increase in the industrial concentration. Only relatively recently, however, the more advanced and rigorous techniques of economists have been brought to bear on the study of corporate behaviour. Within the last 20 years we have witnessed burgeoning of work on, for example, the investment and financing decisions of firms, but there still remains a great many unsolved questions. This is an attempt to explore some of the theoretical and empirical issues raised by an analysis of the impact of public policy on the behaviour of corporations and in particular the responses of companies to changes in the tax' structures.

Corporations now dominate economic activity 111 most advanced industrial countries, especially in manufacturing industry, and large corporations in particular,—are growing in importance. The growth and development of the corporate form of enterprise and especially the rise of the large corporation, might suggest that a revolution has occurred in both the position of the corporation and perception of its role by economists. In fact, concerned over the potential power of corporation has been expressed in various ways over a long period of time. When the modern corporation acquires power over markets, power in the community, power over the states, power over belief, it is a political instrument, different in form and degree but not in kind from the state itself.

Nevertheless, although the viewpoints are similar, giant corporations occupy a dominant position in the economy, especially in manufacturing industry and he evolution of this strength has increased public skepticism of the virtues of unreined private enterprise and of the simple identification of the interests of the firms and the community in America, as expressed in the words of Charles Wilson in 1952:

> "What is good for the country is good for General Motors, and what's good for General Motors is good for the country".

The classic statement of the position that the power and influence of large corporations has grown enormously is the book by Berle and Means, published in 1932. They identified 3 factors which both they and subsequent writers have stressed as being of importance for the understanding of the modern capitalist system:

1. They pointed to increasing industrial concentration. This phenomenon has been documented in much greater detail since.
2. They stressed the separation of the ownership from control with an accompanying centralisation of economic power 111 the hands of a relatively small group of managers.

3. One of the consequences of this divorce of ownership from control is that major changes have taken place in the pattern of corporate behaviour.

Clearly, especially since *Glasnost* and *Perestroika,* institutional developments of this kind will play an important role both in determining the nature of the "optimal" public policy towards corporations, and in fashioning the response of companies to changes in those policies; for the theoretical models used to analyse the effects of different policies must make some basic assumptions about the institutional framework within which companies operate. Although the idea that the separation of ownership from control has transformed the modern corporations has been widely canvassed, this line of thought has not, unfortunately, produced a satisfactory theoretical successor to the profit:" maximising entrepreneur of Marshall.

Realistic Alternative: Decentralized Public Policy

The majority of the masses who are deprived of participation in the decision-making process of public policy would prefer a process that is decentralised, mass-communicative and participatory. Is such an alternative possible or will it simply remains as a Utopian idea?

Small is not only beautiful, but effective and satisfactory too. We shall start boom this premise. Democracy and public policy in industrialised capitalism and state-capitalised socialism have been structured in such a way that the relationship between the whole and the pans has become one of dominance and dependence. The part seems to be the dependent subsidiaries of the dominant centre. Therefore they are not expected to exile any effective influence on the whole structure or system. The centrally structured public policy does not leave much scope for its constituent peripheries to build up their own intra-peripheral public policy, because the centralised dominant structure is afraid of the co-operation of local public policies which in the long run may cause qualitative change in the centrally structured public policy. That is why the constituent states of a federal structure in industrially developed capitalism, socialism and in the 'Third World have grievances against the dominant centralized power structure and the public policy. Here the parts are bonded to the centre. Decentralization or peripheralization of the public policy and its implementation at the local peripheral level can be regarded as the best solution for our complex modern social structure. The cry of the day is to let the people take part in and decide on their own policy matters in their own localities or communes, and they can solve their own problems through their own action. It means, in essence, the decentralization of public policy.

Most of the global population's problems which relate to fundamental human and social needs should constitute the basic elements of a local public policy and so be dealt with at the local communal or peripheral level if the most appropriate, democratic and effective solution is to be found. Can all the public problems of a certain locality be solved at the level of that locality? Maybe, except for those which enter areas of vital national interest or which are beyond the capacity and resources of the locality concerned? Most of the problems related to the fundamental human and social needs of a given place may be solved' at that level, with policy measures made by local people and implemented in their own interest. Micro-level planning and problem-solving is, the best and most effective approach, and has been proved to be so in recent experiments and experiences. Though China tried at the People's Commune level and India has been trying at the village Panchayat (administration) level to adopt policies and solve the problems of their people locally, they have failed because of the high-handedness of the centrally structured power-base-the Bureaucracy.

The relationship of the central public policy with its constituent spheres is one of strength versus weakness. Public interest at the peripheral level involves the following major items:

Economic: full employment, job security and normal wages to meet the· employee's basic needs.

Social: classless society in which the interests of the society as a whole can best be promoted by avoiding the dominance-dependence relationship.

Political: mobilization and participation.

Cultural: promotion of the people's culture through avoidance of hegemony of one or a few cultures over the rest.

Military: safety of all members of society through guaranteed peace with the help of conventional security and defence, avoiding the armament process, the modernization of arms, nuclearisation and the militarization of the public.

These public interests, as component parts of the whole, are not properly and proportionately integrated in the central public policy, because the functions and roles of the component parts are dominated from the centre.

Again, there is little or no interaction between the peripheral spheres which could provide co-operation, adjustment, communication, settlements and decisions regarding their role in the overall public policy.

The establishment of inter-territorial and peripheral interaction and the adoption of a decentralised democratic public policy, acceptable to and accepted by as great a pall of the public as possible, is the effective alternative to the existent centralized public policy. But how can this be done? The transfer of power to the masses to enable them to decide their own policy measures and implement them to their own advantage is not something for the centre to be afraid of. With appropriate measures, through proper stages and processes, public policy can be popularly decentralised.

Conclusion

The foregoing analysis of the public policy and its impact on regional and structural disparities leads to certain conclusions which have high policy implications. These are: (1) In the pre-colonial days the question of regional disparities was insignificant. Certainly there was regional variation which was mostly the product of natural factors. (2) The regional and structural inequalities became very wide and stiff due to British political, administrative and investment policies. The independent India inherited inequality and regional disparities as colonial legacy. In post-independence period, Indian planning and development evolved with reference to and in the context of national needs and requirements.

An ardent national feeling and sacrifice for the national building overshadowed the necessity of balanced regional development. Economic euphoria was the guiding principal and the role of charismatic leaderships at the Centre was important in keeping regional feelings in bound.

After 1960's suppressed regional disparities surfaced. A number of people are area-oriented programmes were initiated and positive discrimination in devolution of development funds started. But still existing gaps between developed and under-developed areas are too wide. Therefore, centralised planning, though most effective for diverting development funds from developed to backward regions, would not be advisable and effective. It is argued, in the context of contemporary development scenario of the country, that no state would be called developed. Thus so called developed states are developed only in relative terms. Hence, it is not possible to divert sufficient amount of funds from these states to poor states.

The plausible solution, therefore, would not be that each depressed region should seek solution within itself. Each backward region is unique. As such, a uniform strategy for the development of different backward regions, contemplated at the Centre, would not provide suitable answers at the grassroots level. Hence the area specific strategy for the development is the first necessity. What Centre can do is to provide each region with sufficient opportunity to develop its own potential.

Endnotes & References

Aberbach, J.D., R.D. Putnam, and B.A. Rockman, 1981, *Bureaucrats and Politicians In Western Europe,* Harvard University Press, Cambridge.

Albrow, M. and E. King (Eds.), 1990, *Globalization, Knowledge and Society Readings from International Sociology,* Sage, London.

Anderson, James E., 1975. *Public.: Policy-making,* Praeger, New York.

Baijal, Pradip, "*A much quieter privatisation of Hindustan Zinc*". *HT2Business & World,* July 2013.

Baijal, Pradip, "*Commercial Feature on Karnataka's Fiscal Reforms*", Business Standard, October 19, 2002.

Baijal, Pradip. "*Disinvestment: Why Strategic Sales Worked*", Business Standard, December 12, 2002.

Chandler, Ralph C. and Jack C. Plano, 1982, *The Public Administration Dictionary.* John Wiley, New York.

Cobbe, R.W., and C.D. Elder, 1972, *Participation in American Politics: The Dynamics of Agenda-Building,* Johns Hopkins University Press, Baltimore.

Dhameja, Nand, 2003, "*Disinvestment of Central and State Enterprises: Analysis and Way Ahead*", Indian Journal of Public Administration, Vol. XLIX, No.2, April-June.

Dhameja, Nand, 2006, "*PSU Disinvestment in India: Process and Policy—Changing Scenario*", Vision, Jan.-March.

Dhameja, Nand and K.S. Sastry, 1998, *Privatization: Theory and Practice,* Wheeler Publication, New Delhi.

Dhameja, Nand and K.S. Sastry (Eds.), 2002, *Public Sector Restructuring and Privatisation Including Urban Infrastructure and Public Service Finance,* Kanishka Publication, New Delhi.

Dicken, Peter, 1988, *Global Shift: Industrial Change in a Turbulent World,* Paul Chapman, London.

Dror, Y., 1968, *Public Policy Making Re-examined.* Scranton, Pennsylvania.

Dye, T.R., 1976, *What Government Do. Why They do it, What Difference it Makes,* University of Alabama, Alabama.

Dye, Thomas R., 1978, *Understanding Public Policy,* Prentice Hall, Englewood Cliffs.

Easton. David, 1957, "*An approach to the analysis of political Systems*", *world Politics,* Vol. 9, No. April.

Easton. David, 1965, A *System Analysis of Political Life.* Wiley, New York. Friedrich. Carl J., *1963, Man and His Government,* McGraw-Hill, New York.

Ghosh, Arun. 2000, "*Disinvestment in PSUs and the IPCL Conundrum*", Mainstream, May 20.

Gormley, W.T., 1983, *The Politics* of *Public Utility Regulation.* University of Pittsburgh Press, Pittsburgh.

Government of India, 1993, *Report of the Comptroller and Auditor General (C&AG) of India on Disinvestment of Government Shareholding in Selected Public Sector Enterprises during* 1991-92, No. 14.

Hogwood, B.W. and L.A. Gunn. 1984, *Policy Analysis for the Real World,* Oxford University Press, London.

Hogwood, B.W., 1987, *From Crises to Complacency. Shaping Public Policy in Britain,* Oxford University Press. London.

Heidenheimer, A. et al., 990. *Comparative Public Policy,* St. Martin's Press, New York. Kirlin, J.J., *"A Political Perspective",* T.C. Miller (Ed.), 1984, *Public Sector Performance: A Conceptual Turning Point,* Johns Hopkins University Press, Baltimore.

Lasswell, Harold, 1970, *"The Emerging Conception 0/ the Policy Sciences",* Policy Sciences, Vol. 1.

Lasswell, Harold, 1948, *Power and Personality,* W.W. Norton, New York.

Lineberry, Robert L., 1977, *American Public Policy, What Government Does and What Difference It Makes,* Harper & Row. New York.

Lowi, T.L., 1972, *"Four Systems of policy, politics and choice",* Public Administrative Review, Vol. 32, No.4.

Massey A., 1993, *Managing the Public Sector,* Edward Elgar, Aldershot. Mueller, D., 1989, *Public Choice,* CUP, Cambridge.

"Overall Development: Objectives and Strategies" (U.N.) 1977, *Journal of Development Planning* No. 11.

Parsons. W., 1995, *Public Policy' An Introduction 10 the Theory Clnd Practice of Policy Analysis, Edward Elgar Cheltenham.*

Ramamurti, Ravi and Vernon Raymond (Ed.), 1991, *"Privatisation and Control of State-Owned Enterprises",* EDI, Development Studies, The World Bank, Washington DC.

Robin, Jack (Ed.), *2005, Encyclopedia of Public Administration and Public Policy,* Taylor & Francis, London.

Sapru, R.K., *"Environmental Policy and Politics in India".* .Uday Csai (Ed.), 1998, *Ecological Policy and Politics in Developing Countries.* State University NY Press, New York.

Sapru. R.K., 1994, *Public Policy, Formulation, Implementation and Evaluation,* Sterling Publishers, New Delhi.

Schattschneider E., 1961, *The Semisovereign People,* Rinehart and Winston, New York. World *Bank Policy and Research Bulletin,* Vol. 11 and Vol. 12, No. 4 and No 1, October-December 2000, and January-March 2001.

Self Peter, 1972, *Administrative Theories and Politics: An Inquiry into the Structure and Processes of Modern Government,* George Allen & Unwin. London.

"Survey of India", *The Economist,* London, January 21-27. 1995.

"Survey of India" 2001, *The Economist,* London, June 2.

'Teitz, Michael, 1968, *"Towards a theory of Urban Public Facility Location",* Papers of *the* Regional Science Association, No. 21.

Vaidya. Rajindra R. *"Disinvestment of Public Sector Enterprise. Mid-year Review of the Economy.* 1994-95, Media International Centre, New Delhi.

Vickers, Sir Geoffrey, 1965, *The Art of Judgment,* Chapman & Hall, London

World Commission on Environment and Development 1987, *Our Conzmon Future,* OUP, Oxford.

World Development Report, 1991. Oxford University Press. New York.

8

The Systemic Sources of India's Nuclear Policy

Abhay Kumar

The purpose of this article is to understand, describe and analyse the transformation of India's nuclear policy since the end of the Cold War. The shift in the nuclear behaviour of India can be seen as a transformation from moral principles based on global nuclear disarmament and sovereign equality of all states, to a completely different approach of declaring itself a nuclear weapon state. The purpose of the article is to explain the shift of the India's nuclear policy from deliberate ambivalence to measured participation. The focus of this article is to discuss the influence of the systemic factors on the transformation of India's nuclear policy. For this purpose the introductory part of the article focuses on the ambiguous nature of the India's nuclear policy, since independence, though briefly. It analyses various reasons responsible for the nuclear tests and tries to explain why nuclear option was always retained by India. The second part of the article provides a brief outline of the theories in International Relations which deal with the question of proliferation of the nuclear weapons. Thereafter, the ensuing section provides a brief analysis of various systemic factors responsible for the outbreak of nuclear explosion in 1998. The conclusion part of the article sums up the observations.

Introduction

After a gap of almost 24 years, India shocked the world by exploding nuclear explosive device in early May 1998. It was the time when the international community had solemnly expressed a desire, through the Comprehensive Test Ban Treaty (CTBT), to refrain from the field testing of nuclear explosives. On May 11, 1998, India abruptly announced that New Delhi had conducted three nuclear tests, one of which involved the detonation of a thermonuclear device. The global community before responding to this development, saw India announcing two days later that it had conducted two more detonations that purportedly "completed the planned series of underground tests" (2000: 1). These developments, among many others, moved one of India's leading strategic commentators to reflect on the momentous events of May 1998 in the following terms,

> The world knew for quite some time that both India and Pakistan have been in possession of atomic weapons, although they were not formally recognized as nuclear weapon powers. The great powers have hoped that the anomalous nuclear standing of India and Pakistan in the international nuclear system could be fudged. They have striven hard to keep the Indian and Pakistani nuclear capabilities under wraps forever. But the hot summer of 1998 has finally vapourised [sic] the veil of nuclear ambiguity in the Indian subcontinent. As a consequence, the security situation in the subcontinent and the global nuclear order are unlikely to be the same ever again (Mohan: 1998).

In the same time frame, another prominent Indian analyst concluded that the nuclear tests had allowed India to become "a willing and active player in the international nuclear arms control regime," but with a difference: "the difference now is that India seeks to play that game as a nuclear weapons power. This is the end of ambiguity and hypocrisy" (Gupta: 1998).

The history of the Indian nuclear program began with the country's independence in 1947. The attitudes of India's leadership towards nuclear weaponry evolved gradually over the years. Strong opposition to nuclear weapons was most visible during the 1950s, when India, having recently emerged from the colonial era, sought to put forth a brand of politics that emphasised economic development and, the harnessing of atomic energy for peaceful purposes (Ganguly 1983: 30).

India's approach toward nuclear power during this period was the use of nuclear energy as a cost effective solution to its vast developmental problems. This opposition to nuclear weapons and to nuclear weaponry per se as instruments of high politics, changed during the 1960s when India became aware of the Chinese threat and of China's nuclear power, following its defeat in the Sino-Indian border war of 1962. Indian strategic circles thought of the possibility of extending civilian nuclear technology to defense applications (Tellis 2001:10-11).

This attempt to exploit the civilian nuclear energy and research infrastructure for strategic purposes reached its peak in 1974, when India carried out its first atomic test and dubbed it as a "peaceful nuclear explosion", while simultaneously reiterating its opposition to nuclear weaponry (Jaipal 1977: 44-51).

The ambiguity that arose from India's demonstrated ability to make nuclear weapons, continued throughout the 1980s and well into the 1990s. Finally the end of the Cold War transformed international politics and tilted the axis in favour of United States. The rise of China and continued strains with Pakistan made the 1980s and 1990s a greatly troubling period for India. The nuclear non-proliferation treaty (NPT) was extended indefinitely and unconditionally in 1995, perpetuating the existence of nuclear weapons in the hands of five countries busily modernizing their nuclear arsenals. In 1996, after they had conducted over 2,000 tests, a Comprehensive Test Ban Treaty (CTBT) was opened for signature, following two and a half years of negotiations in which India participated actively. This treaty was neither comprehensive nor related to disarmament but rather devoted to ratifying the nuclear *status quo.* India's options had narrowed critically (Singh 1998: 41).

India's strategic environment grew both more complex and dangerous after 1990, the medium range political calculations seemed to have made it easier to go nuclear, and there was a general movement away from opposition to nuclear weapon *per se* and growth of militant nuclearisation. Nuclearisation now seemed capable of solving a wide range of national, cultural and strategic problems. These created an environment in which the decision to go nuclear was domestically permissible and perhaps politically essential for those on the Indian right (Cohen 2001: 177). Indian nuclear policy for much of the Cold War period and thereafter focused on attaining two sets of objectives. The first set of objectives consisted of promoting the global abolition of nuclear weaponry and, secondly towards sustaining India's capability to produce fissile materials for nuclear weapons (Tellis 2001: 13).

Theoretical Analysis

The concept of nuclear proliferation has not been adequately defined by the contemporary approaches, making a rigorous approach more difficult.

Furthermore an elaborate definition of the word 'nuclear puzzle' has not been given. Different theories have explained their own perception about nuclear proliferation.

Classical realism is perhaps oldest of theories to be applied to the proliferation puzzle. Classical realist explanations of international politics are based on the assumption that states are unitary actors that seek to maximize their power. Political realism believes that politics, like society in general, is governed by objective laws that have their roots in human nature. It's main emphasis is on how statesman think and act in interest defined in terms of power. In order to improve society it is first necessary to understand the laws by which society lives. The main signpost that helps political realism to find its way through the landscape of international politics is the concept of interest defined in terms of power. It sets politics as an autonomous sphere of action and understanding apart from other spheres, such as economics understood in terms of interest defined as wealth, ethics, aesthetics, or religion (Morgenthau 1978: 4-15).

It explains how nuclear weapon plays a peculiar tool to acquire power in the adverse circumstances in post-Cold War years. Classical realist tends to explain some extent that during the 1990's era India main interest was to maximize its power. Therefore development of nuclear weapon was regarded as an apparent solution for it.

Kenneth Waltz uses rational deterrence theory to explain the slow spread of nuclear weapons and their impact on the international system. According to this theory, once more than one state has acquired a second-strike nuclear capability, war between the nuclear armed states is unlikely to occur, due to the fact that mutual destruction is virtually assured (Waltz 1990: 734). This creates an incentive for many states to acquire nuclear capabilities to guard against war and to ensure their survival. It follows from this argument that nuclear weapons will inevitably spread, and that the more they spread the better it will be for international stability. Waltz's is of the opinion, however, that when faced with explaining the complex dynamics of nuclear proliferation, rational deterrence theory alone is not suited to the task (Waltz 1990: 737).

Zachary S. Davis developed broader approaches to explain nuclear weapons proliferation, which remain in the classical realist mould, but provide a more convincing explanation of proliferation dynamics. He claims that "Classical realism provides a complete explanation for the causes of nuclear proliferation and international responses to it non-proliferation. Davis argues that states are driven to acquire nuclear weapons only if they feel that they will contribute in some way to their national security. In many cases, states will decide that their security will actually be threatened by the presence of nuclear weapons, and this is their incentive to cooperate with other states in the non-proliferation regime (Davis 1993: 79).

The theory of neorealism has also been used to explain the dynamics of nuclear proliferation and has provided some controversial explanations of the phenomenon. It is based on the same assumptions as classical realism, buts adds an extra dimension to it: based on the idea that the structure of the international system (whether unipolar, bipolar, or multipolar) influences international politics and can explain international outcomes. Waltz originally developed the theory to explain why the world enjoyed such a long period of peace between the great powers during the Cold War, concluding that the bipolar structure of the international system caused this peace. However, he made it clear at the time that the theory was developed to explain how states are constrained by the structure of the international system and not to explain the more complex problems of how states would react to these constraints (Waltz 1979: 72-73).

The international system constrains the states within the system to behave in a particular way so as to ensure their own security and in turn, of the other states within the system. It dubs international system as being anarchic which asks for cooperation among the states for mutual survival. He admits that both unit level and external factors would need to be taken into account to explain behaviour of this kind, and that neo realism as not developed for this task (Keohane 1986: 343). Structural realist explains India's nuclear tests purely on strategic constraints. The deteriorating security environment and discriminatory nuclear non proliferation treaties were structural constraints which pushed India towards nuclear tests.

Benjamin Frankel believes that neorealism is an "explicit and accessible theory of nuclear weapons proliferation" (Frankel 1993: 37). He argues that the shift from bipolarity to multi polarity since the end of the Cold War is the most important incentive for intensified proliferation as states attempt to ensure their survival after the removal or loosening of superpower "overlay" (ibid: 38).

Barry Buzan, Charles Jones, and Richard Little have attempted to rectify some of the problems of traditional neorealism by bringing the state back in (Buzan, Jones, and Little 1993: 9). They began their work in response to Waltz's brand of neo-realism, which could not explain the dramatic system change that occurred with the disintegration of the Soviet Union. This version of what they term "structural realism" argues that ultimately, unit level characteristics must be brought back into neo-realist theory to explain the shift from the bipolar structure of the international system during the Cold War to the multi polar structure of the post-Cold War world. As a result they have developed a more complex form of neorealist theory that allows for functional differentiation among states, accepts that states do not necessarily imitate each other in their battle for survival, and shows the system to be more dynamic and more difficult to predict than traditional neorealists had claimed (Buzan 1993: 11-13).

Thus it may be argued that if policymakers accept the arguments of the realist school, it leads to nuclear proliferation being regarded purely as a security issue determined by external pressures. Thus logically the policy recommendations will tend to focus on external constraints such as arms control, security assurances, and security environment in the immediate neighbourhood of country, global nuclear regimes and search for a greater role in the world politics. After explaining various theories of nuclear non proliferation it will be discussed how these theories fit into the case of India's acquisition of nuclear weapons.

Strategic Factors of Pokhran II

From the above discussion it follows that three factors may be identified to explain the shift in the India's nuclear policy in the post-Cold War era. Among them, the systemic influences had a great bearing on the policy together with the changes in the immediate security environment which India had to face in that era. Further, India's desire to achieve responsibility as a global power strengthened it resolve to bring about a deliberate shift in the ways it's looked at the nuclear weapons both in the normative as well as realistic sense. All of them need a separate discussion out here for a better and clear understanding. First will be the explanation of the concept of system approach by Robert Jervis and sub-systematic by William R. Thomson. Secondly the three systemic factors will be elaborated in detail.

Robert Jervis identified three characteristics of a systemic approach. First, outcomes may not be due to the attributes of actors, because a system can produce consequences that are not necessarily what the actors intended. Second, units are interconnected, that is, changes in some parts of the system produce changes in other parts. And third, relations between any two actors are conditioned in part by the relations between each of them and other actors in the international system (Jervis 1997: 212-244).

The term "sub-systemic" is used for interactions limited to a specific regional system. A systemic approach would explain the security behaviour of a state in terms of its position in the international system and how this position is affected by the interactions between it and the major power actors. A sub-systemic analysis would focus on interactions and power relationships among the most prominent actors within a region (Thompson 1973: 89-117).

Therefore a systemic approach is based on the assumption that states placed differently in the international system will have different security concerns and interests. Great powers tend to have global interests, while the security concerns and interests of most middle powers and small powers are concentrated in a given region. Aspiring great powers also perceive their security as being tied to the larger balance-of-power processes occurring in the international system, involving other established powers. India perceived the then prevailing world order as being discriminatory and negating India its legitimate position within the International system which stemmed from the continued opposition of several countries most of them the great powers, against induction of India in the United Nations Security Council as a permanent member. This pressure on India only strengthened the resolve of New Delhi to shed off it's earlier normative considerations regarding the use of the nuclear physics and to embark upon a new thinking on the issue of nuclear energy.

China-Pakistan-United States Triangle

The regional security apprehension deterred India to renounce it military option to strive for its survival and security. The nuclear activities of China and Pakistan, the United States and its allies have solidified their position on the non proliferation regime. Therefore it is evident for India to act on its self help which could only be fulfilled by acquisition of nuclear weapons. The circumstances which leaded to US Pakistan China axis clearly determined the path for nuclear proliferation.

Ehsan Aharari argues that India wanted to become a nuclear power for three reasons. First, because China had detonated its own nuclear device in 1964 only two years after it had humiliated India's armed forces in a limited border war. Second, because Pakistan's closeted nuclear program constantly drove India's own fear of getting caught off-guard (Ahrari 2004: 210).

The end of the Cold War saw India's close ally and a friend for several decades the former Soviet Union disintegration and thus losing its power and influence in the international system. With the collapse of the Soviet Union India had no one to fall back on in case of a nuclear attack on it. The post-Cold War developments gave rise to new world order where the United States as the sole super power dominated the world. Moreover, because non-alignment was a response to Cold War rivalry, it lost much of its meaning as a policy posture when the Cold War ended. India's regional rival, China, has become accepted as a major power despite initial opposition by the West. India thus feels more isolated than ever (Paul 1998: 2).

China and India have been rivals in South Asia and world affairs. Territorial issues namely boundary dispute in the Himalayas and Chinese possession of a part of Kashmir along with China's refusal to acknowledge Indian sovereignty in Sikkim and Arunachal Pradesh intensified the rivalry (Kapur 2001: 181-182).

This rivalry ended in a military conflict in the 1962 India-China war. Following India's humiliating defeat in the war, India became embroiled a wide-ranging debate on the need to develop nuclear weapons. This was exacerbated the public declaration by the Chinese in 1964 of their intention develop atomic weapons. Homi Bhabha, the founder India's atomic energy program, stated that it would be difficult to follow policy of restraint with introduction of nuclear weapons in the neighbourhood. Soon after the Chinese, thermonuclear test in 1967, a scientific effort began to study the design of nuclear explosives (Ollapally 2001: 929).

The China factor impacted India's strategic psyche from two other directions. Beginning in the early 1980s, China developed its diplomatic, economic, and military links with Myanmar. Secondly, Chinese naval personnel were active in developing radar and low frequency communication facilities in the Bay of Bengal, which were close to Indian naval facilities. In short, this period revealed China's increasing encirclement of India by diplomatic and military means, and by the build-up of a China-US-Pakistan coalition-with support from the international community (Kapur 2001: 89).

After discussing China the next sub systemic constraints which posed threat to India was Pakistan. The origins of the India-Pakistan conflict have been traced to many sources: the cupidity of British in their failed management of the partition; the deeply rooted antagonisms between the Subcontinent's major religious communities, Hindu and Muslims; the struggle for control over Kashmir; Kashmir's importance to the national identities of both states;

and the greed or personal short-sightedness of leaders on both sides of the border (Cohen 2001: 198).

If there is anything constant in the relations between the two, it has been that they have never been constant. Several ups and downs have marked the relations between the two over six decades. These two have fought four wars in 1947, 1965, and 1971 and recently in 1999. Bilateral disputes created a deep trust deficit in the relations between the two ever since they came in to existence. India does in fact face a nuclear threat of some magnitude from Pakistan. India's civilian leadership has clearly accepted and affirmed the emergence of Pakistan's evolving nuclear capabilities even if many uncertainties remain about what that implies in terms of the balance of power vis-a-vis India. Pakistan's nuclear potential, as exemplified both by its weaponry and by the plethora of delivery systems it is developing or has already acquired is certainly problematic in that for the first time in India's post independence history (Tellis 2001: 45).

If Pakistan perceives its nuclear capabilities as providing, among other things, the requisite strategic cover with which to immunize it against any military counteraction in the context of some ongoing unconventional conflict with India, New Delhi will face strong pressure to shift its overall nuclear posture to cope with the challenges of nuclear coercion. Overall end of the cold war clearly carved out the strong position of United States.

Geography is the great determinant of potentially good or bad relations between a great power and a would-be great power. The farther away a great power is the more diluted its interests in any particular region, and the more diffused its stake, the less likely it is that there will be a clash of interest, or that such clash will be resolved by the use of force. With India and the United States on virtually the opposite sides of the earth and keeping in the mind the global nature of American interests, the only serious differences between them can emerge, as they did during the Cold War, on the basis of conflicting ideology and or geopolitical alliance (Karnad 2002: 541).

Pakistan is important to the US both for its connection with Afghanistan and Central Asia, and for its long-standing relationship with Saudi Arabia. The latter link in very well with the paramount importance the US attaches to strategic control of Middle East. Here, it is informal US-dominated nexus pertaining to its influence and control over three states that is of vital significance-Saudi Arabia, Egypt and Israel. Moreover, Pakistan, unlike India, is more pliable and reliable strategic ally for future and it has proved to so in the past (Bidwai and Vanaik 1999: 229).

Thus US has no reason whatsoever to interpret the India-US relationship in the way that India's own strategic community understands or interprets it, or to draw the same corollaries concerning the necessary 'rearrangement' or 'adjust' attendant upon consolidating such a strategic link between the two countries. For this reason alone, tensions have continued to persist throughout the nineties in the post-Cold War era despite the new opportunities and inclinations that have arisen for forgoing a closer Indo-US relationship (ibid: 230). Thus individually India foreign policies in respect to these countries were not smooth. So post-Cold War when India was isolated in the world the alliances among three countries provoked India to seek for its own self help.

The Sino-Pakistani connection, which has steadily strengthened since the early 1980s, is seen this context as placing Islamabad at an additional advantage. According to authoritative sources in the West, China has been involved in significant degree of nuclear cooperation with Pakistan (Tellis 2001: 46)

China has also helped Pakistan acquire reasonably efficient missile delivery systems-weapons that Islamabad had always desired because of the high degree of assured penetrability they represented in the face of India's relatively superior air defense network Indeed, Chinese assistance is suspected even in the development of Pakistan's first indigenous missiles, the Hatf-1 and Hatf-2, both of which derived from the sounding rocket technologies imported from France by Pakistan's Space and Upper Atmosphere Research Organisation in 1992 or thereabouts, when Beijing sold 34 M-11 ballistic missile to Islamabad (Tellis 2001: 47).

With active support from China, Pakistan was emboldened to almost openly support the uprising in Kashmir. Further, the collusion of China with Pakistan and the active support to Pakistan's nuclear ambitions by China called for a rethink on the India's nuclear policy. In regard to both China and Pakistan, India's attachment to nuclear weapons therefore remains strong in the new political environment. Nevertheless, the security benefits that India gains from them seem increasingly open to question (Mirchandani 1968: 39).

In 1997 more evidence surfaced on the proliferation between China and Pakistan and about US permissiveness on this issue. During Chinese President Jiang Zemin's recent visit to Washington, the US insisted on a separate agreement with Zemin on Chinese proliferation to Iran and Pakistan which china signed instead of professing their innocence. Both the US unease and the Chinese signature attest Chinese proliferation as a threat to security. After all these assurances, continued to pass missile technology and components to Pakistan. Despite this, the Clinton administration was still willing to certify that China was not proliferating or even worse for India—that the US was either unable or unwilling to restrain China. As the range of options for India narrowed, so, too, did the difficulties of taking corrective action (Singh 1998: 46).

US on the other side too supplied aid package which included F-16 fighting aircraft. It was viewed that F-16 would fundamentally change the conventional balance of power (Kux 1992: 383). In addition Indian was worried of the fact US-Pakistan alliance and China-Pak alliance would eventually lead to Washington Beijing and Islamabad axis. It would dramatically change India's strategic environment.

In short, this period revealed China's increasing encirclement of India by diplomatic and military means, and by the build up of a China-US-Pakistan coalition with support from the international community. As before the aim was to corner was India in sub-continental as well as in global affairs.

"Nuclear weapons may have psychological value for India as it contemplates China's development in years ahead, but it is becoming harder to see how India could use them to influence Chinese behaviour in any substantial way. And in the context of relations with Pakistan, nuclear weapons have, if anything, blunted the advantage that India undoubtedly possesses in the field of conventional warfare" (Walker 1996: 64).

Non-Proliferation Efforts and the Question of India

Since independence from Britain in 1947, India became a strong proponent of nuclear disarmament. In the word of the first Indian Prime Minister, Jawaharlal Nehru: "The objective of India is disarmament and we regard arms control as a means to achieve it. It is a step in that direction. It is important to seek agreement, on arms control measures especially when we have a situation in which disarmament has become a complex problem" (Jain 1974: 2-4). But he reiterated that "arms control is not disarmament and to make it an objective is to abandon the hope for disarmament" (Jain 1974: 5-6).

With China's nuclear test in 1964, the Indian position on nuclear weapons changed dramatically. Although China was acquiring nuclear weapons to obtain major power status and to prevent nuclear coercion by the United States or the Soviet Union, the Chinese action nonetheless altered India's immediate strategic environment profoundly. Following the nuclear tests by

China the world leaders particularly the great powers started negotiations regarding a non-proliferation treaty.

The Nuclear Proliferation Treaty (NPT) of 1967 was the logical outcome of the efforts. The NPT was opened for signatures in 1968 and presently about 189 countries are signatories to the treaty except India, Pakistan and Israel. North-Korea signed the treaty, ratified it and later withdrew. India favoured the conclusion of a non-discriminatory treaty, but later became a strong opponent of the NPT, believing that the nuclear powers wished to maintain their monopoly and that the treaty was primarily aimed at curtailing the nuclear aspirations of non-nuclear weapon states.

The NPT and associated arrangements in the non-proliferation regime were openly discriminatory. The Treaty validated the legality of five nuclear weapons states and it legitimized their right to bear nuclear arms; conversely, it de-legitimised the sovereign rights of others to use all military measures nuclear weapon for self-defense. The NPT was politically discriminatory because it created two different sets of obligations and rights. The non-nuclear weapon states have an obligation to disarm as well as never to seek nuclear arms except when supreme interests require a renunciation of NPT obligation with three months notice. On the other hand nuclear weapons states have their rights; but their obligation to move towards nuclear disarmament was vague as it lacked a time frame, and contrary to the declared military doctrines and the national interests of the five nuclear powers (Kapur 2001: 187).

The NPT calls upon the signatory nuclear weapons states not to transfer induce or, assist the non nuclear weapon states to acquire nuclear weapons or nuclear devices. It recognizes only five nuclear weapons states that have tested a device before 1967 (Mirchandani 1968: 123).

Initially India was favourable to the conclusion of a non-discriminatory treaty, but later became a strong opponent of the NPT, realising that the nuclear powers wanted to curb the legitimate right of the non-nuclear weapon states, that is, the right to peaceful uses of nuclear energy. During the negotiations leading to the treaty, the Indian leaders vehemently opposed it. The major irritant was that the treaty created two classes of states: those that had tested a nuclear device before January 1967 and those that had not done so by that date. The treaty would not only legitimise the nuclear capabilities of the five states that had conducted such tests, including China, but would prevent India from developing a nuclear weapon capability, even if a major threat arose (Rai 2009: 214).

In the second half of the 1990s, two events that were related to then non proliferation regime further aggravated the Indian sense of grievance against the world nuclear order. The first was the indefinite extension of the NPT in May 1995, largely as a result of pressures exerted by the United States and its allies. Some non-aligned signatories of the treaty sought rolling extensions for 25-year periods, with further renewals sub subject to progress in nuclear disarmament, but they did not carry the day. This treaty outcome gave every indication to India that the nuclear weapon states were keen to maintain their monopoly rights for a long time. From the Indian point of view, "disarming the unarmed" had become the main value of the NPT, rather than genuine global nuclear disarmament (Rauf and Johnson 1995: 28-41).

The indefinite expansion of NPT after 1995, largely as a result of the pressure from the United States, further aggravated the concerns of India. The Indian government thought that US would fail to cobble together a coalition that would unconditionally and indefinitely extend the treaty. Such expectations were belied as able and relentless American diplomacy ensured the achievement of the US goal (Dunn 1995: 3-9).

The indefinite extension of NPT in 1995 was premised on the belief that a genuine Comprehensive Test Ban Treaty (CTBT) by the end of 1996 would be the next logical step. As a consequence, goal nuclear disarmament was seen ideally by most countries as the final goal of extension and review conference.

In India's case, there was no opposition to a test ban *per se*, but the nuclear establishment strongly opposed any treaty that threatened the nuclear option. Its members knew that the 1974 test was not a success, and fresh tests were required (Cohen 2001: 173).

Unsurprisingly, the debate within India over the CTBT was framed by the Indian pro-bomb lobby in such a way that opposing the CTBT was taken to be a blow for Indian autonomy and a blow against American hegemonism. The anti-CTBT position thus encompassed right-wing and conservative militants, a traditional left-wing anti-American faction, and advocates of nonalignment (ibid: 174).

India, during the CTBT negotiations, was more concerned that the treaty that would emerge would effectively prevent proliferation and would ensure the process of disarmament. This approach epitomized in the language and the spirit committee—primarily concerned with the drafting of the treaty but final treaty that emerged did not do justice to this negotiating mandate as it lacked a definitive commitment to nuclear disarmament (Mattoo. 1999: 341).

As Bidwai wrote, "Whatever the weakness of the present CTBT, it is indisputably a normative measure favouring nuclear arms reduction and disarmament, and a commitment not to conduct nuclear test explosion. This commitment is the least that India can demand of the world, and above all, of itself" (Perkovich 2000: 381).

It has been argued that this posture of 'strategic ambiguity' helped India to harmonise its national security imperatives with its disarmament objective. First, because of its very opaqueness and uncertainty, it offered an existential deterrent against China. Second, it pre-empted Pakistan from overtly seeking countervailing nuclear capability. Third, it implicitly avoided any direct confrontation with global non-proliferation regime led by the nuclear powers. Lastly, this ambiguity helped India to continue with efforts towards nuclear disarmament (Mattoo 1996: 41-57).

By summer 1995, it become clear to Indian negotiators that the scope of the proposed treaty was basically a P-5 bargain, just as the NPT's scope was basically a US-USSR bargain. It also became clear to them that the CTBT was being projected by all the P-5 countries, and especially by UK, as a non-proliferation measure and not ads a disarmament one. The Indian concern was shared by many third world participants but they were not able to effectively challenge the authority of the P-5 powers (Kapur 2001: 206).

The defining moment in the Indian debate came on June 20, 1996 when the United Front government in India authorised Arundhati Ghose to publicly stated in the Geneva negotiations over the CTBT, that as far as India is concerned," security interests were a consideration and would be compromised by signing the treaty (cited in Cohen 2001: 174).

"We cannot accept that it is legitimate for some countries to possess nuclear weapons while denying this right to others. Under such circumstances it is natural that our national security considerations become a key factor in our decision making... Countries around us continue their programmes either openly or in a clandestine manner. In such an environment India cannot accept any restrained on its capability, if other countries remain unwilling to accept obligation to eliminate their nuclear weapons", the Indian representative Arudhati Ghose said. "The present CTBT is shaped more by technical preferences of nuclear weapon states rather than by imperatives of disarmament. This cannot be the CTBT India can be expected to accept" (Statement by Ghose cited in Singh 1998: 242).

Finally India rejected the Treaty on three grounds:

> First, the nuclear weapon states failed to give a commitment to eliminate their nuclear weapons in a reasonable and negotiated finite span of time. India felt that in the absence of such a commitment, The Treaty would become an unequal treaty retaining the present discriminatory nuclear regime and sanctioning, in effect, the possession of nuclear weapons by some countries for their security, while ignoring the security concern of other States (Mattoo 1999: 339).
>
> Second, the CTBT failed to effectively contribute to nuclear non-proliferation in all aspects. It banned only explosive testing. As the Treaty text does not ban qualitative development, it cannot be considered an integral first step of a nuclear disarmament process (ibid: 340).
>
> Third, the Treaty includes the EIF (Entry into Force) clause: Article 14 of the CTBT concerns the requirements for EIF. The EIF clause requires that 44 states, including all P-5 nuclear powers, as well as Israel, India and Pakistan must sign and ratify the treaty before it comes into force. The United Kingdom, Russia, China, Egypt and Pakistan insisted on EIF. Russia would not agree to the CTBT unless the People Republic of China (PRC) did, and the PRC would not agree until India did, and so on. The United States initially did not insist on this particular formula for EIF, but it faced a dilemma, and it agreed eventually with the formula as it was finally adopted (Rai 2009: 234).

These three major criticisms indicate that the critics of the treaty see it as way to co-opt India into the non-proliferation regime. It is a control mechanism for those who are not members of the NPT. India's hardened its stances against the treaty during 1995-96 and the eventual refusal to agree to the consensus at the Disarmament Conference in Geneva in June 1996.

According to Ashok Kapur the main constraints in the CTBT were: Firstly according to India Article I was not comprehensive. It allowed weapons development and testing in laboratory condition. It created a technological discrimination in favour of the technologically advanced states. It permitted nuclear weapon states especially the USA to maintain their technological advantage in nuclear sphere. At the same time, this article capped other states that are lower on the technological curve by eliminating their right and opportunity to test and to manage the gap with the states higher on the technological curve. Secondly it was an offspring of NPT as it was projected by the permanent countries e.g., US, Russia, China, France and United Kingdom as a non-proliferation measure and not as disarmament measure. Thirdly there is no time bound scheduled for nuclear disarmament in the CTBT. Fourthly it affected Indian security because it choked the test route to the development of nuclear explosive technology and it narrowed the window of opportunity to the development of non-explosive technology under laboratory conditions. Lastly, the other objections concerned the harassment potential and EIF (Entry into Force) requirement that placed India on a collision course with USA and China. In rejecting the CTBT in 1996, the Gujral government emphasised the importance of national security and the Indian nuclear option in the Indian decision on the CTBT (Kapur 2001: 239).

Thus there were three major contextual elements in the 1990's that shaped the CTBT and India's reaction to it; there loomed nuclear clouds over Sino-India and Indo-Pak relations, there was a subtle redistribution of powers and authority within Indian political system and, adherence of France and China to NPT indicated the emergence of strategic bargain that solidified the discriminatory regime (Rai 2009: 229).

It seemed that the Indian position on CTBT had come a full circle after it conducted tests in 1998. India declared a moratorium on further nuclear tests and simultaneously indicated it would convert this *defacto* commitment to *de jure* status. India's accession to the CTBT had been one of the main issues that were being negotiated in the Indo-US talks in 2000. The Indian prime minister, Atal Bihari Vajpayee too, in his address to the UN General Assembly in 1999 had indicated that India was prepared to bring the discussion on CTBT to successful conclusion (Rai 2009: 234).

Although the Indian government has expressed it willingness to sign the CTBT in the past, the political uncertainty in India and an intense opposition to this move had made it difficult for it to make its position clear on these vexed issues. The decision to sign the CTBT had generated an intense political controversy and it had emerged as one of the most debated issues in the Indian strategic circles. Till date no consensus seems to have emerged in India on the issue of CTBT. The preceding discussion makes it clear that there has been a gradual change in India's position with regard to CTBT over time, thereby representing a historic opportunity for international community to complete the global nuclear architecture. Despite some security implications from India signing the CTBT, It has tried hard to reconcile it security interests with the global arms control norms, highlighting the significance of nuclear arms control for international stability. The CTBT emerged as the key vehicle for redefining India's arms control position after its nuclear tests and coming to terms with global nuclear order that India had long considered inequitable.

Accordingly India went nuclear to enhance its prestige and status. It was found that the NPT and the CTBT were measures to target India and to bring it under the purview of non proliferation regimes. Therefore, in order to maintain a stable and powerful position and disapprove the discriminatory non proliferation treaties India exploded nuclear devices on May 1998. The nuclear tests reflected the credibility of India as a strong and powerful state.

Richard K. Betts argues that the incentive for India to go nuclear had more to do with the prestige element. He argues that "India is the dominant power in the region and one of the principal 'emerging middle powers' in the world. On a prima facie basis, this suggests that prestige incentives for nuclear weapons would be higher for India than they would be for Brazil" (Betts 1979: 1053-1072).

The essence of the nuclear arms race is power-military, political, and economic, argues William Epstein. He is of the opinion that "the incentives and disincentives for countries to go nuclear comprise a combination of military, political, and economic concerns and motivations. These vary over time for different countries" (Epstein 1977: 16).

He further adds that it has become obvious to all countries that the acquisition of nuclear weapons and the technology for making them enhance a nation's prestige and status in the world, not just in military terms, but also in other ways. States possessing these arms are given greater weight in the entire range of foreign policy matters. They are brought into more top level international discussions of all kinds, and their views are treated with greater respect (ibid: 21).

In Search of a New Role

India's foreign policy during the early decades after independence was based on a global role centred on non-alignment and leadership in the developing world. It relied heavily on India's standing as the largest democracy in the world, and on articulate Indian leaders who appealed to justice and idealism. Its hallmarks included resistance to the then prevailing division of the world into East and West and a push for economic aid and redistribution. As the world and India's role in it evolve, India's military power and economic success are key building blocks for the role it aspires to have.

India seeks greater standing in global affairs and institutions as they are now organised, but it also would like to see a different global organisation emerge, one in which power is distributed more evenly, among a larger number of important powers, including itself. Almost all nations want to enhance their power and thus improve their positions in the world and increase their influence over the behaviour of other nations. At the very least, many wish to diminish their dependence on other states and to increase their freedom of action-outcomes which again may depend on their accumulation of power. The particular forms that this quest for power will take may vary from country to country. Some of them see nuclear weapons as promoting their security, enhancing their prestige, augmenting their influence, and improving their economic conditions. Whether, and to what extent, a given state will act on these views depends in part on its leaders' perceptions of the international environment and on their assessments of the best ways to achieve national objectives in that environment.

Scott Sagan argues that one ambition which guides states to acquire nuclear weapons is their perception that nuclear weapons enhance their prestige within the international system. Nuclear weapons acquisition, seeing nuclear decisions as serving important symbolic functions-both shaping and reflecting a state's identity According to this perspective, state behaviour is determined not by leaders' cold calculations about the national security interests or their parochial bureaucratic interests, but rather by deeper norms and shared beliefs about what actions are legitimate and appropriate in international relations (Sagan 1997: 73).

The 1998 nuclear tests were one way of stating India's ambition to be taken seriously as a major power (Cohen 2000: 46). Since the Nehru era, Indians have seen the world as unjust and dangerous. Nehru pursued a wide-ranging foreign policy with two major aims. The first was to speed up decolonization in Asia and Africa, the second to reduce the threat of nuclear war.

The fact of the matter is that India was hardly a middle power during the Cold War years. As a result, because it remained vocal in its moralistic rhetoric in a number of world forums, such as the Nonaligned Movement, India, rightly or wrongly, was depicted as a moralistic loudmouth, with no economic or military power to back up its apparent dignity (Ahrari 2004: 2009).

India changed from implicit to explicit to nuclear weapon status with its nuclear tests in 1998. The sanctions India faced from most of the world's industrialised countries after the tests had a modest effect on India's economy. India has worked with four aspirants to permanent seats (Germany, Japan and Brazil) to craft an approach that can command substantial global support. Whether it succeeds or not in the current round of UN reforms, India will continue to work on this as a long term effort (Schaffer 2005: 14).

C. Raja Mohan describes India's decision to become a nuclear power in 1998 as a decision to redefine its 'approach to the question of power' and an effort to temper the idealism in its foreign policy with a strong dose of realism' (Mohan 2003: 15). In George Perkovich's words, which the authors quote approvingly, India exploded its own nuclear device 'for reasons of international prestige' (Perkovich 2000: 200).

Acquiring global status is however not just about a seat at the table. It requires a clear strategic direction, and military capabilities sufficient for projecting power beyond own region. Measured against this, India's military modernization program is indicative of a rather prudent approach towards acquiring global power status.

Conclusion

The initial phase of India's strategic vision was shaped by the following factors. First, the Cold War influenced India's security discourse and subsequently its vision. External threats were seen as being the primary sources of insecurity. Military security became synonymous with national security; building a strong and powerful military apparatus was seen as essential to safeguard India's security interests. Nuclear weapons were seen as a symbol of power and providing a security guarantee. Second, as mentioned above, the security policies and strategic vision of India were determined more by its charismatic political leaders, rather than by institutions including the Parliament, cabinet and concerned ministries. It was only in 1999 that the National Security Council was born.

Hence India's strategic vision, from the beginning, has been shaped by the historical and geopolitical situation in which it has been placed and how it has perceived its own security. From independence until the 1990s, one can trace a pattern in which India had been responding to the regional and international geopolitical situation, based on its own security perceptions. Ever since, India achieved independence in 1947; it has always remained within the strategic calculations of the great powers owing to its vast size and resources, both human and natural. Past experience and future prospects were certainly a motivating force behind the decision. To a large extent, India's nuclear tests in 1998 acted as a catalyst in reorganizing its security perceptions and, in the process, its strategic vision as well. These factors had a great bearing on the transformation of the Indian nuclear policy.

Endnotes & References

Ahrari, Ehsan (2004), "India's Great Leap Forward", *Security Dialogue,* 35: 207-215.

Betts, Richard (1979), "Incentives for Nuclear Weapons: India, Pakistan, Iran", *Asian Survey,* 19 (11):1053-1072.

Bidwai, Praful and Achin, Vinaik (1999), *South Asia on a Short Fuse: Nuclear Politics and the Future of Global Disarmament,* New Delhi: Oxford University Press.

Buzan, B. et al (1993), *The Logic of Anarchy: Neo-realism to Structural Realism,* New York: Columbia University Press.

Cohen, P. Stephen (2000), "India Rising", *The Wilson Quarterly,* 24(3): 32-53.

Cohen, P. Stephen (2001), *Emerging Power,* Oxford: Oxford University Press.

Dunn, A. Lewis (1995), "High Noon for the NPT," *Arms Control Today,* 25(6): 3-9

Davis, Zachary S. (1993) "The Realist Nuclear Regime," Security Studies 2: 79.

Epstein, William (1977), "Why States Go and Don't Go Nuclear", *Annals of the American Academy of Political and Social Science,* 430 (3): 16-28.

Frankel, Benjamin (1993), "The Brooding Shadow: Systemic Incentives and Nuclear Weapons Proliferation," *Security Studies* 2 (3/4): 37-65.

Ganguly, Sumit (1983), "Why India Joined the Nuclear Club," *Bulletin of the Atomic scientists,* 39(4): 30.

Gupta, Shekhar (1998), "Road to Resurgence," *Indian Express,* Delhi 12 May, 1998.

Jaipal, Rikhi (1997), The Indian Nuclear Explosion, *International Security,* 1(4): 44-51.

Jain, P.J. (1974), *India and Disarmament Vol.1 (The Nehru Era: An Analytical Study),* New Delhi: Radiant Publisher.

Jain, P.J. (1974), *Nuclear India, Vols. 1 and 2,* New Delhi: Radiant Publications.

Jervis, Robert (1979), "Systems Theories and Diplomatic History," in Paul Gordon Lauren, (eds.), *Diplomacy,* New York: Free Press.

Karnad, Bharat (2002), *Nuclear Weapon and Indian Security: The Realist Foundations of Strategy,* New Delhi: Macmilan India Ltd.

Kapur, Ashok (2001), *Pokhran and Beyond: India's Nuclear Behaviour,* New Delhi: Oxford University Press.

Keohane, Robert O. (1986), ed., Neo-Realism and Its Critics, New York: Columbia University Press.

Kux, Dennis (1992), *India and the United States Estranged Democracies,* Washington D.C.: National Defence University Press.

Mattoo, Amitabh (1996), "India Nuclear Status Quo", *Survival* 38: 41-57.

Mattoo, Amitabh (1999), *Indian's Nuclear Deterrent Pokhran II and Beyond,* New Delhi: Har-Anand Publications Pvt. Ltd.

Mirchandani, G.G (1968), *India Nuclear Dilemma,* New Delhi: Popular Book Services.

Mohan, Raja C. (1998), "Living in a Nuclear South Asia," *The Hindu,* Delhi, 28 May 1998.

Morgenthau, J. Hans (1978), *Politics Among Nations: The Struggle for Power and Peace,* New York: Alfred A. Knopf.

Ollapaly, M. Deepa (2001), "Mixed Motives in India's Search for nuclear Status", *Asian Survey,* 41(6): 925-942.

Paul, T.V. (1998), "The Systemic Bases of India's Challenge to the Global Nuclear Order", *The Nonproliferation Review*, 6(1): 1-11.

Perkovich, George (2000), *India's Nuclear Bomb*, Berkeley: University of California Press.

Rai, Ajai (2009), *India Nuclear Diplomacy After Pokhran II,* Delhi: Pearson Kindessley.

Rauf, Tariq and Rebecca Johnson (1995), "After the NPT's Indefinite Extension: The Future of the Global Non-proliferation Regime," *The Non-proliferation Review,* 3(1):28-41.

Sagan, Scott D. (1997), "Why Do States Build Nuclear Weapons? Three Models in Search of a Bomb", *International Security*, 21(3) 54-86.

Schaffer, Teresita C. (2005), "Pramit Mitra, Deutsche Bank Research", December 16, 2005, India Special, [Online: web] Accessed 04 April 2010, URL:www.dbresearch.com.

Singh, Jasjit (1998), "Why Nuclear Weapons?" in Jasjit Singh (ed) *Nuclear India,* New Delhi: KW Publishers Pvt. Ltd.

Singh, Jaswant (1998), "Against Nuclear Apartheid", *Foreign Affairs,* 77 (5): 41-57

Singh, Jaswant (1999), *Defending India*, New Delhi: Macmillan India.

Tellis, J. Ashley (2001), *India's Emerging Nuclear Posture,* Oxford: Oxford University Press.

Thompson, R. William (1973), "The Regional Sub-System: A Conceptual Explication and a Propositional Inventory," *International Studies Quarterly* 17: 89-117.

Walker, William (1996), "India Nuclear Labyrinth", The Non-proliferation Review, 4 (1): 61-77.

Waltz, N. Kenneth (1979), *Theory of International Politics,* New York: McGraw-Hills.

Waltz, N. Kenneth (1990), "Nuclear Myths and Political Realities," *American Political Science Review* 84.

9

Indian Nuclear Strategy: Pokhran II and Beyond

Minu Jha

India detonated its first nuclear device on May 18, 1974 and the then Prime Minister, Mrs. Indira Gandhi deliberated to convince the world of India's stature of being a responsible state, terming it as a "Peaceful Nuclear Explosion" where India would refrain from surging on the path of nuclearisation. The obvious fallout of such a nomenclature was visible on India's nuclear strategy post Pokhran-I in the way of a resistance by future Prime Minister's on the scientists and engineers not to eye on any future explosions. This resulted in treading on a path of covert nuclear weapon programme. Despite this, an attempt was made during Prime Minister Narashima Rao's tenure to go ahead with the nuclear explosion. But substantial evidence unveiled India's testing attempt of 1995 which was made futile by the US satellites that detected them and hence under United States pressure the Rao Government jettisoned the nuclear explosion plan. Therefore, Perkovich rightly observes that "Moral doubts, political turmoil and the censure of the United States and the international community put the break on their plans (Perkovich George, 1999)."

The advent of the Bhartiya Janata Party on the Indian political scene marked a historic turning point in the entire nuclear policy of India. The BJP attempted to test in its very first term in the office but failed as the government did not succeed in achieving a majority in the parliament. The

Indian nuclear ambiguity finally was silenced on May 11 1998 when the Indian state, under a new coalition government, the National Democratic Alliance led by the Bhartiya Janata Party that came in power at the centre in March 1998, exploded three nuclear devices followed by two more explosions on 13 May. Though it was the BJP Government that gave the decisive push for the actual tests, but in fact the nuclear tests of 1998 were the culmination of a programme started long back, under Congress regime. This event however marked a critical shift, for now India emerged as a nuclear weapon state from its earlier position as a nuclear-capable state. For 24 years India neither closed nor overtly exercised the nuclear option personifying ambiguity. During this period the military related nuclear policy and programmes too remained shrouded in a veil of ambiguity and uncertainty. There had been no official pronouncement on the exact state of India's nuclear programme since 18 May 1974. According to Kripa Sridharan domestic level determinants and elite perceptions were far more important in charting a different course of action. In that sense, the macro-level external factors set the scene while the micro-level factors provided the incentives for policy alteration (Sridharan Kripa, 2006). More or less, he adds this holds good for changes both in the nuclear policy and Indo-US relations. Thus on 11 May 1998, the veil was finally lifted (Mattoo Amitabh, 1998). Air Commodore Jasjit Singh expressed in his statement about a great shift that was marked in the wake of India's nuclear explosion, post-Pokhran II. He stated: "On May 11, 1998, the world, a 970 million Indians sat up to take note of India's nuclear status when the nation successfully tested three nuclear devices.... The decision to finally shake off a quarter of a century old self-imposed restraint on exercising the nuclear option was indeed a momentous one ..." (Singh Jasjit, 1998)

It was therefore being widely held that in India's nuclear realm, three particular factors were vivid. The first, India's idea of a coercive framework of international non-proliferation regimes that was being pulled up by the major powers, particularly the United States, and New Delhi's profound dissatisfaction with it (Ayoob Mohamed, 1999); second, the internal political developments which saw the rise of BJP to power, a party that had always justified revisiting and reformulating country's nuclear policy in the direction of acquiring a nuclear capability and third, according to Raja Mohan, a strategic analyst:

> For good or bad, and whether the world liked it or not, India decided to cross the nuclear Rubicon. Fifty years after independence, India now wanted to become a normal nation—placing considerations of realpolitik and

> national security above it until recently dominant focus on liberal internationalism, morality and normative approaches to international politics (Gupta, 1997).

The nuclear action of India however surprised both the world and the Indian public. In the wake of the tests a number of questions haunted the minds of Indian and the foreign analysts. The questions concerned India's thinking about nuclear weapons, its future planning regarding nuclear force deployment, the situations under which India shall exercise its nuclear option, will India depart from the path of disarmament, will New Delhi sign the Comprehensive Test Ban Treaty (CTBT) and adhere to the FMCT guidelines. The chapter under discussion is an attempt at understanding the government's response to these questions as well as taking an account of the opinions of the non-official brigade. As far as the Indian Government is concerned it was rather quick in responding to these questions merely a couple of months after the tests. The government issued a number of detailed accounts on the background of the test and the future of its nuclear policy (Statement of Prime Minister in Parliament). Prime Minister Vajpayee, in his statement of December 15, 1998 in the Rajya Sabha indicated that the main features of weaponizing nuclear policy were as follows: (a) India will deploy its nuclear deterrent; (b) India's nuclear doctrine includes a policy of 'No-First-Use' and 'Non-use against non-nuclear weapons states'; (c) a policy of 'No-First-Use' with a minimum nuclear deterrent implies "deployment of assets in a manner that ensures survivability and capacity of an adequate response," in other words the development and deployment of a deterrent with a second-strike capability; (d) by way of meeting the concerns of the United States and its allies, India was willing to join the Comprehensive Test Ban Treaty (CTBT) and the Fissile Material Cutoff Treaty (FMCT)-to-come and to make its export control laws relating to "sensitive technologies" more stringent; and (e) India will continue its missile development programme and not accept "any restraints on the development of India's R&D capabilities" (Ram N, 1999).

Rejecting Nuclear Ambiguity

In May 1998, India departed from a self-induced restraint, and tested five nuclear devices at Pokhran in the desert of Rajasthan. Undoubtedly, its reverberations took everyone by surprise, sending shock waves all across the globe and particularly among the non-proliferation regimes. The economic sanctions that followed were well anticipated by India. Then, one wonders that despite expected economic penalties why India decided to go nuclear?

What compelled India to abandon its policy of nuclear restraint pursued since 1974? It would be apt to discuss about some of the most pragmatic and rational factors that led India on the path of overt weaponization and to analyze how both domestic and the international events unfolded to push India towards Pokhran II.

Ostensibly it has been debated ever since that a series of events coupled with some immediate factors resulted in the Pokhran II nuclear explosion. From the beginning of the 1990, the Indian political and economic scenario underwent a change. The period marked the beginning of the coalition era, concomitant with the liberalization of the economy. There were serious internal strife (domestic) in Punjab, northeast and the Kashmir. This increased New Delhi's security anxiety as the coalition era was the one of increasing political instability. With the changing domestic scenario there was also emerging threat from the neighbouring Pakistan and china. The end of cold war seemingly added more ballast to India's emerging challenges. Soviet Union, a long time ally had disintegrated and India had by this time not developed any substantial closeness with the United States and was constantly looking for a strategic engagement with her. With the end of bipolarity, the non-aligned movement too collapsed as it rendered meaningless. Behind such domestic constraints and fast changing international scenario, India had no option but compelled by circumstances had to answer her own security concerns, which it eventually found in the path of weaponisation. Security concerns hence became one of the contending issues which were extensively cited by the BJP for their decision to test. The BJP led NDA Government made an announcement on the eve of assuming charge in 1998, that the government would 'exercise all options including nuclear options' to safeguard the country's security and sovereignty (INWP, 1998). They felt that no one owed India a living, and a self-help approach to security was the only option. The leadership also was prepared to ride out the negative reactions from its bold move, calculating that, after the dust had settled, the fact of a nuclear India would have to be acknowledged by the international community. In the meantime, it would do its best to bear the cost of any sanctions. Post test analysis however has also brought to the front a fact that internal policies of the BJP and positive support of the nuclear scientists were responsible for the decision. As it is evident from the fact the decision was taken precisely by a small group that consisted of a couple of top level political leaders and the country's nuclear establishment. However as I proceed, it will become explicitly evident that in case of India's Pokhran II blast, domestic considerations took precedence over international determinants, though their presence cannot be dismissed, as has already been discussed above. Theoretically speaking James Rosenau talks about this very preponderance of domestic variables on an issue of foreign policy decision making, in his exposition of 'Linkage Politics', and states that: "Domestic factors may be of considerable significance, even if they are not primary sources of foreign policy and on some issues they may be well dominant" (Rosenau, 1967).

The BJP Government's realization that the idealist orientation of Nehruvian foreign policy was inadequate was based on the assessment that it had hitherto failed to answer the security concerns of India and should be discarded in favour of a more robust national security strategy. Highlighting the shortcomings of the Indian foreign policy, Foreign Minister Jaswant Singh, said strategically, Nehruvian foreign policy did not leave a legacy of a stable security environment, or even secure frontiers; what it did confer as a legacy was ambivalence, ambiguities and an uncertain apprehension-filled future. During 1998 election campaign the BJP's foreign policy spokesman, Brajesh Mishra, stated that if his party was elected to power, it would make the bomb. The point was reiterated by him as Principal Secretary in Vajpayee's Government in favour of "nuclear option" (Cherian John, 1998). Further reiterating their departure from earlier ambiguous posture of India, Prime Minister Atal Behari Vajpayee clearly spelled out that "you will have noted that neither my statement of 11 May nor the longer official text released later that day has characterized the nuclear tests as "peaceful nuclear tests" (Khanna, V.N., 2002). He further noted that 'our intentions were, are, and will always be peaceful but we do not want to cover our action with a veil of needless ambiguity. India is now a nuclear weapon state (Khanna, V.N., 2002)."

The internal pressures had started to mount within the BJP in view of the fact that due to coalition compulsions the party was forced to mellow down on policies which it had promised in election manifesto such as the Ayodhya temple construction, a uniform civil code and the status of Jammu & Kashmir (J&K), and hence the party was in no mood to shelve the only one of its agenda that was left, which was revisiting nuclear policy. The party's election manifestoes of 1996 and 1998 supported the concept of a nuclear weapons-free world but reiterated its concern "to re-evaluate the country's nuclear policy and exercise the option to induct nuclear weapons." There are others like Stephen Solarz, who extend the argument that it was the pressure emanating from within the Bhartiya Janata Party and also from its ideological partners such as the Sangh Parivar (the Rashtriya Swayamsevak Sangh) that the BJP exercised the nuclear option to prove that they were capable of fulfilling at least one of the major agenda (Cohen, 2000) which they had talked about in their election manifesto though covertly. Apart from these factors the mood of the public in India too favoured the government which is evident from the mass euphoria that had generated over the tests. In an opinion poll conducted within less than 24 hours after the tests, 91% of those polled in six metropolitan cities approved of the tests, 7% opposed it, while 2% had no opinion to offer. However, at the same time if one goes by the result of the subsequent assembly elections, where the opposition fared far better than parties in the ruling coalition this logic holds no good (The Hindu, 1998). Another reason for the decision to test nuclear devices was to bolster regime stability. It has been argued that a party heading a weak coalition government might have been tempted to use the nuclear card to bolster its survival (Mehta, 1998).

Another viewpoint that is espoused to explain the reason of Pokhran II is the desire and quest of India to be able to hold a place of high prestige and status in the international arena. Stephen Cohen and Babbage too have interpreted India's recent policies as indicative of her ambitions for great power status (Cohen, 2001). The advocates of the viewpoint claim that India wished to have a status in the global order that ultimately led to the nuclear tests. India thought that the possession of nuclear weapons would give her the required power to have an international standing. The Bhartiya Janata Party wished to show the world about their power being no less than other if not equal and this they thought was possible only by flexing nuclear muscle (Ganguly, 2000). It was argued that technological advancement would make the world more audible to India's concerns and priorities than otherwise. As John W. Garver opines that the acquisition of nuclear capability was perceived by Indians as an assertion of their place in the world, much as China had done four decades ago to announce its arrival on the world scene and win the attention of United States (Garver, 2001). These argument holds true to a great extent because despite sanctions and initial criticisms, the subsequent action by United States in the form of lifting of sanctions, support to the Kargil war of 1999 followed by US President Clinton's visit in March 2000—first by an American president in 22 years and finally the last feather in the cap being the civil-nuclear accord shows that India started to figure more keenly in their calculations.

George Perkovich and other likeminded scholars have put forth the argument that the politicians cannot be solely held responsible for the nuclear adventure of 1998 (Perkovich, 1999). The responsibility should equally be shared by the nuclear hawks within the bureaucratic-scientists/technologists community who were driven by the quest of making a nuclear weapon state. It was this community that accelerated the process of development of nuclear weapon capabilities and pressurized the political leaders to follow suit. This influence that was visible during 1974 Pokhran blast, peaked up the momentum again in 1995-1998 period, leading to the test of thermo nuclear device (Perkovich, 1999). The nuclear scientists comprising the Atomic Energy Commission and the Defence Research and Development Organization (DRDO) had held since long strong desire for nuclear tests (Chari, 1999). Given the proclivities of the NDA elite, they did not need too much persuasion from this quarter to alter the country's nuclear policy. As Ashok Kapur opines, adding to the views of decision-makers inside the government was the influence of the Indian nuclear establishment in persuading the government to change its policy (Kapur, 2001). Hence, the nuclear establishment's yearning and the aspirations of the political leadership neatly fitted, in the words of Kripa Sridharan, like 'sword and sheath' (Sridharan, 2006).

Looking at the external environment, the Indian Government expressed its antipathy at the indifferent treatment meted out to its global disarmament and non-proliferation proposals. This was the reason India distanced itself from NPT and ultimately CTBT. The consistent pressure emanating from the United States on indefinite extension of NPT and subsequently over signing of CTBT was being seen by India as their effort to keep the 'nuclear apartheid' intact. Finally the nuclear non-proliferation treaty was extended indefinitely in 1995, perpetuating the possessions of nuclear weapons by the United States, Russia, Britain, France and China for the indefinite future while denying the rest of the world these weapons (Perkovich, 1999). This development outraged the Indian specialists, coaxing them to rethink on their nuclear strategy. Both the election manifestoes of the BJP (1996 & 1998) therefore emphasized the party's proposition to the Comprehensive Test Ban Treaty (CTBT), the Fissile Material Control Regime (FMCR) and the Missile Technology Control Regime (MTCR) which they said, were discriminatory. On the other hand the nuclear hawks of India cashed on the occasion by accelerating the process of turning the nuclear tide in their favour, to which they succeeded to a great extent. This also made India realize that, unless it soon exercised the nuclear option, it may have to permanently accept a non-nuclear status (Jaswant Singh, 1998). Justifying India's Pokhran II blasts, Indian National Security Advisor Brajesh Mishra's, statement reflects an alarming concern over the ineffectiveness of these non-proliferation regimes, which failed to contain even its member China from consistent proliferation designs;

> The tests undertaken by India in May, 1998, were in response to the failure of international non-proliferation regime in addressing India's security concerns. Nuclear proliferation in our neighbourhood, including by NPT members, was well established, with missile proliferation adding a more dangerous dimension (Mishra, 2006).

Besides, the Ghauri test conducted by Pakistan was seen as another important and immediate reason to conduct nuclear test as it threatened the security of the nation, along with the persistent transfer of sensitive nuclear technology transfer to Pakistan by China. Finally, as the government was over with its nuclear adventure, it got down to its pro-active diplomacy to check the damage by reiterating its continued commitment to global nuclear disarmament. Projecting itself as a responsible nuclear power, India immediately after the May 1998 blasts of five nuclear devices, announced unilateral moratorium on further test, informing the world community of no further tests. Making it strikingly clear that it was still committed to total nuclear disarmament but decided to go nuclear to claim the status of a 'nuclear weapon state' exclusively for its security urgencies. The Bharatiya Janata Party to silence its international critique put forth the argument that since India was not a CTBT signatory, it did not violate any of the international commitments.

Nuclear Strategy: Post-Pokhran II

Abandoning the period of nuclear restraint and nuclear ambiguity, India in 1998 decided to move on by exercising the nuclear option and thereby jettisoning the period of restraint. The world bemoaned at India's move and subjected it to heavy penalties by imposing sanctions (economic) on India. US, France, Britain etc were the countries who overtly denigrated the Indian action. In May 1998 there were eight rounds of talks between US Deputy Secretary of State, Strobe Talbott and Indian Minister of External Affairs, Jaswant Singh. One point repeatedly stressed by Talbott was the need for India to define its doctrine of minimal nuclear deterrence. During his visit to Islamabad, in early February 1999, Mr. Talbott said: "It was more important now that both (India and Pakistan) define conceptually and operationally a credible minimum deterrence in a way that will be recognized by each other and the world (Times of India, 1999)." Therefore the need was being spelt out by the United States that India must conceptualize its strategic policy based on the doctrine of minimum nuclear deterrence. Therefore Immediately after the blasts India realized that it was no longer possible to keep the world guessing about their future nuclear policies and hence under this backdrop the Government of India constituted a National Security Advisory Board (NSAB) that was given the charge of drafting the broad framework of India's Nuclear Doctrine thereby signaling out its strategies so as to calm the international pressures/sanctions/outrage mounting on it in the wake of the Pokhran II adventure.

The draft was released by the National Security Advisor, Brajesh Mishra, on August 17, 1999 for the purpose of public debate. From August 1999 until January 2003 when the doctrine was pronounced by India's national security advisor, the document had not been put before any parliamentary committees or been given a formal title. It was not clear whether the doctrine as presented was a set of recommendations or just simply a set of formulations based on reasoned judgment made by a select group of India's leading academics, bureaucrats, diplomats mostly based in the New Delhi's power corridor (Alam, 2002). The draft was reflective of the coherence in general between the statements by the Government of India and particularly the Prime Minister, Atal Behari Vajpayee as well as the writings of the strategic analysts. There were disagreements but restricted to the community outside the government. Those who were critical of government policy were not irrelevant, but their numbers and role remained limited (Bajpai Kanti, 2000). Indian official statement on the nuclear posture of India based on the nuclear doctrine has seven broad guidelines.

Indian Official Pronouncement after Pokhran II

The Government of India took an official stand with respect to describing its main tenets of nuclear posture. Minimum Nuclear Deterrence was supposedly the basic premise that guided the rest of the features of the India's nuclear posture. Therefore scholar like P.M. Kamath has given to the draft the nomenclature of the MIND, i.e. Minimal Nuclear Deterrence (Kamath, 1999). These features of the draft are:

- The pledge for minimum deterrence
- Commitment to the principle of "No First Use" and non-use of nuclear weapons against non-nuclear state
- A comprehensive programme of missile testing

- Voluntary declaration on adhering to moratorium on further nuclear testing and acceding to the Comprehensive Test Ban Treaty (CTBT)
- Negotiating a Fissile Material Cut-off Treaty (FMCT)
- Exercising export control
- Continue to emphasize on global nuclear disarmament

It needs to be mentioned here that despite India putting forth the nuclear doctrine for the world to make its nuclear position clear, it simultaneously was engaging United States in high level arms-control negotiations in an attempt to define the broad contours of the India-United States relationship post-Pokhran-II (Pant, 2002).

An official announcement in January 2003 was made in which the essence of the draft was adopted as official policy paralleled with the announcement of a formal nuclear command structure under civilian control (Pant, 2007). India's nuclear doctrine emerged after a great deal of debate and discussion. In fact it is believed that ever since 1974 peaceful nuclear explosion, India's strategic and political elite were engrossed in arriving at a broad consensus on the nature and scope of India's nuclear programme (Pant, 2007). Hence, in 1998 India ended the ambiguity by declaring itself a nuclear weapon state and the first attempt to convert this fiesta into reality occurred in January 2003 when the nuclear draft doctrine for the first time was officially incorporated as a final set of political principles and administrative arrangements to manage its arsenal of nuclear weapons (CCS Review). The main elements of the Indian nuclear doctrine that was adopted as official policy after almost five years of recommendations put forth by the NSAB are:

- Building and maintaining a credible minimum deterrent;
- A posture of No-First-Use;
- Retaliatory attacks to be authorized by the civilian political leadership through the Nuclear Command Authority (NCA) only;
- Non-use of nuclear weapons against non-nuclear-weapons states;
- India's retention of the option or Indian forces anywhere, by biological or chemical weapons; and
- A continuance of controls on export of nuclear and missile-related materials and technologies, participation in the FMCT negotiations, observance of the moratorium on nuclear tests, and working toward the goal of universal nuclear disarmament (Pant, 2007).

Credibility of "Minimum Credible Deterrence"

When the draft document was released, it included statements within the purview of deterrence by stating that India would not conduct more nuclear tests, join the Comprehensive Test Ban Treaty with some modifications, and enter negotiations to stop fissile materials production without conditions. It was also proclaimed by India's official spokesperson of pursuing a 'no-first use' policy vis-à-vis non-nuclear weapon states and to finally establish a 'credible, minimum nuclear deterrent (Alam, 2002).'

What does a Nuclear Deterrence mean and why is it needed; it is believed to be a rather subjective concept. The question is how many weapons are enough to ensure deterrence? Is deterrence achievable? If yes, how to maintain deterrence? Another important question is how crucial does a country's technical details about its nuclear arsenals play such as the size, configuration and readiness towards the aim of attaining deterrence. It has been observed that the answers to these questions vary across recent history and across geographic areas (Lewis, 2006). The phrase 'minimum deterrence was first coined in the late 1950s in the United States during the debate over the sanctioning of the inter-continental range ballistic missiles carrying nuclear-powered submarines.

A further probe into the western concept and understanding of deterrence suggests that deterrence can be achieved only through difficult choices, sustained with intelligent effort, and depend very much on the technical details. This view has been expressed in Albert Wohlstetter's 1958 Rand Monograph. The delicate balance will be deterred by the prospect of a counterattack, even if it consists of only a few nuclear weapons. Beyond that minimum threshold, nuclear weapons provide little additional deterrent benefit. Mathew Evangelista in "Unarmed Forces: The Transnational Movement to End the Cold War reflects on a rather noteworthy remarks by Soviet Premier Nikita Khrushchev and President Dwight D Eisenhower where both saw nuclear weapons in terms of minimum deterrence. "Missiles are not cucumbers", Khrushchev said, "one cannot eat them, and one does not require more than a certain number in order to ward off an attack". Eisenhower was more precise about that "certain number". We should develop few of these missiles as a threat but not 1000 or more," Eisenhower said (Lewis, 2006). However, it is absurd to debate over the technical details of a country's nuclear arsenal in determining the extent of deterrence as the balance of terror is a very delicate matter. An enemy, who can be deterred, shall be deterred even at a prospect of a counterattack, even though the stockpile is only of a few nuclear weapons. Beyond that minimum threshold, nuclear weapons provide little additional deterrent benefit.

Indian position on minimum deterrence was officially accepted when India overtly weaponized itself in the May of 1998, when it declared a no-first use posture to subside the growing international reaction on its nuclear tests. There are some observers who suggest that minimal deterrence is a default posture for India as well as for China. And the arguments they put forth in support is that both the countries lack the economic and technical resources for any other posture and also rebuffs the Indian thinkers for not understanding the deterrence theory. George Pekovich too points out that when the Indian scientists used their manipulation on the policy makers they did so solely to give shape to their national ideas of greatness more than military exigencies (Lewis, 2006).

India officially accepted the notion of "Credible Minimum Deterrence" which was reiterated by the prime minister—"Just as our conventional defence capability has been employed in order to safeguard the territorial integrity and sovereignty of India against any use or threat of force, the adoption of our nuclear deterrent posture has also followed the same logic. We have announced our intention to maintain a minimum nuclear deterrent, but one that is credible ('PM's Statement in Parliament)." In one of the other statement in the parliament, Prime Minister Vajpayee echoed "India does not intend to use these weapons for aggression or for making threats against any country; these are weapons of self-defence, to ensure that India is not subjected to nuclear threats or coercion. (Tellis, 2001)" Minimum credible nuclear deterrence therefore need to be looked into from the Indian perspectives whereby India wishes that it should be viewed by its enemies in a manner of being capable of inflicting such damage upon their country, that they would be deterred to use nuclear weapons against India. The basic premise of this argument is that the enemy country should be well aware of India's position as well as its ability to strike back with the available means that according to India is both credible as well as militarily effective. This basic strategy of India's nuclear doctrine of 'minimum deterrence' that has been argued in the preceding paragraphs finds an echo in Dipankar Banerjee's views. He states: "Deterrence has been a fundamental part of military doctrine through the ages. It has relied essentially on two basic principles: one is through the threat of punishment. This is borne out of a belief that if other nation carries out a hostile act, it will be visited by a sure and devastating response. Offensive forces held in reserve are meant to enforce this threat. The other is through dissuasion or denial. This implies that the action a hostile nation plans to take would be so difficult and certain to be defeated, that it would not be worth the effort." Hence, what India tries to convince the world through its assertion on the 'credible minimum deterrence' is being dealt here in Dipankar Bannerjee's second principle of the deterrence whereby the weapon shall be used as to deter the enemy from actual use by convincing it that the repercussions of using the weapon would mean its confirmed defeat. It is this which will keep the hostile nation away from the first strike and therefore avert a situation of actual war.

Minimum deterrence can therefore be understood as possessing the minimum number of deliverable nuclear weapons that can be considered as enough to keep out an adversary from carrying out a nuclear strike against India. As V.K. Nair sums up: "It assumes an opposing nation's political leadership will act according to the logic of national self-interest, although this self-interest will be viewed through the dictates of given situations.' He further adds, 'The deterrence strategy must be clearly limited to retaliatory action and any military response to aggression must be delimited to objectives within the nuclear threshold which could trigger a nuclear strike (Nair, 1998).' The Government of India though has been reluctant in indicating the number of nuclear weapons it intends to possess but, has officially stated that it is not interested in entering into any form of nuclear arms race and that in no way is India interested in matching up with the stock of Chinese arsenal (Perkovich, 1999). India maintained that the idea of minimum deterrence cannot be itched in stone for ever and that no numerical details of the minimum deterrence can be proffered. Minimum deterrence is rather a way of looking at nuclear issues and not a set of fixed numbers (*The Hindu*, 1998). Though India tried to explain its doctrine of minimum deterrence but United States appeared to be least satisfied with India's posture and stressed on defining the term "minimum". The Prime Minister was very categorical in his reply to such interferences by the United States and in one of his speeches to the parliament he commented: "matters related to the defence postures are sovereign functions, not subject to negotiations. In fact our talks are based on the fundamental premise that India will define its own requirements, for its nuclear deterrent, on its own assessment of the security environment (PM's Statement in Parliament, 1998)." K Subrahmanyam rather gave a more categorical explanation regarding the number politics on the minimum deterrence issue. He very categorically states: "Those against India being a nuclear weapon state and those conditioned by US nuclear strategic theology both raise the question of what minimum nuclear deterrent the Indian Government has adopted as its declaratory policy. It is an aerate question and cannot be answered in precise numerical terms .... The very idea that there must be a precise numerical value to the deterrent arsenal is part of the sedulously fostered nuclear theology of former US Defence Secretary, Robert McNamara (Subrahmanyam, 1998)."

However, post Fukushima meltdown of March 2011 has once again alarmed the world at the extent of nuclear disaster that can occur owing to the possession of nuclear weapons. This has thrown open a debate that possession of nuclear arsenal for deterrence that has occupied security discourse of the 20th century needs to be revisited. After all such nuclear catastrophes brings the deterrence to ground zero. Hence, recent debates on deterrence call for an immediate end to our dependence on nuclear weapons, which needs to change. Dipankar Banerjee focuses on two such reasons, for why nuclear deterrence discourse be re-assessed. He states:

> First, the nature of threats has fundamentally changed and is both non-military as well as conventional force-related. From cyber attacks to possible climate wars, to terrorist strikes, there are several others. Nuclear weapons are inadequate means to deter these threats, yet their availability and presence makes their possible use likely. Second, the character of adversaries and the nature of war too have changed. Instead of sovereign nation states opposing each other, accountable to international law and lending their arsenals capable of being under careful state control, one or more opposing forces today may be a terrorist group owning up to no nationality or shadowy groups owing indirect allegiance to several. The latter's chosen method of conflict is sudden unprovoked attacks through clandestine means symbolized by the suicide bomber. The ultimate threat in today's world is that such a group could acquire a nuclear capability (Banerjee, 2011).

India too has become very conscious of such catastrophes and has been taking the safety measures to be instituted at the nuclear plants quite seriously. Fukushima alarmed the people and numerous civil society members participated to protest against the construction of nuclear plants in India, such as the one witnessed in the Koodakulam nuclear power plant even though these plants are for civilian purpose and not military. What is bothering people is the hazardous impact the nuclear emission has on their health today and for generations to come as had been witnessed in the Bhopal gas tragedy.

No-First-Use and No Use against Non-Nuclear Powers

India is firmly committed to the principle of no-first-use and it has also on number of occasions shown its intentions of signing treaties with Pakistan, China or with any other country to give a solid premise to this ideology. Immediately after the blasts India cleared its stand in the parliament on this issue whereby the Prime Minister reiterated India's earlier stand—"In 1994, we had proposed that India and Pakistan jointly undertake not to be the first to use their nuclear capability against each other. The government on this occasion reiterates its readiness to discuss a 'no first use' agreement with that country, as also with other countries bilaterally, or in a collective forum (Bajpai, 2000)." Pakistan has out rightly rejected for being a party to such a treaty as it views nuclear weapons as a credible deterrence. China in the past have not given any indication of being interested in such an arrangement though in the days of the Cold War politics it together with the Soviet Union were committed to the principle of no-first-use but at present its posture on the issue only projects an ambiguity. However, India continues to urge other nuclear countries to sign in a no-first-use multilateral convention. India on other hand stands by its commitment of exercising nuclear restraint by moving on the principle of no-fist-use. India has however tried to clear that it is totally against any form of misuse of nuclear weapon to be used to coerce or deter other countries.

India also underlined its policy of resorting to non-use of nuclear weapons against states which do not possess nuclear weapons or are not aligned. This was in keeping with adherence to the concept of possessing nuclear weapons solely for self-defence rather than for entering into any form of arms race or being an aggressor country. On August 4, 1998, the Prime Minister clarified that India would in addition adhere to a no use policy with respect to non-nuclear states: "Having stated that we shall not be the first to use nuclear weapons, there remains no basis for their use against countries which do not have nuclear weapons (Kunadi Savitri statement)." This was to assert that India will not use its nuclear weapons in conventional war, and even in a nuclear war it will not use the weapons till India is attacked first by a nuclear weapon. India will hence, use nuclear weapons in a second strike to retaliate and to inflict damage unacceptable to the aggressor. India's point of argument however differs in essence from the similar commitments by the NATO countries for no-first-use of nuclear weapons. Explaining this noted analyst K Subrahmanyam posits: "The policy implicit in Mr. Vajpayee's declaration is different from the NATO doctrine of using the nuclear weapon as the last resort of defence. That (NATO Doctrine) implies use of nuclear weapons even against a conventional attack if the situation turns unfavourable..." he further added "The present declaration of Indian Government would commit this country not be the first to use the nuclear weapons unless they are used first against this country. The weapons will be used only for retaliation and to deter the use and threat of use against India (*The Times of India*, 1998)". But the important point to be noted here is that the credibility of such deterrence will depend upon the sufficient number of available nuclear weapons at the disposal of the country concerned. In February 1999, K. Subrahmanyam further gave an enunciation on the Indian approach to the doctrine of no-first-use: He said, "The Indian no-first-use doctrine is not just a declaratory policy unrelated to deployment and command control. It is rooted in the perception that the core of deterrence lies in the uncertainty about the adversary's likely capability to cause unacceptable damage to oneself after the initial use of nuclear weapons against him. The survivability of the assets to strike back in retaliation constitutes deterrence and not the provocative forward and risky deployment as was carried out by the nuclear weapon powers (Balachandran, 1998)." G. Balachandran described Subrahmanyam's explanation as subject to a high degree of uncertainty.

- It would require an estimate of the amount of damage likely to be considered unacceptable by adversary likely to initiate a nuclear exchange.
- Having an idea of the level of damage required to be caused, it is necessary to estimate the optimum number of warheads needed, at the point of impact, to cause such damage. From, this one should estimate the number of warheads needed at the point of impact.
- Since India will use nuclear weapons only after experiencing a first strike by the adversary, it will be necessary to estimate the damage to the Indian nuclear strike force as a result of the first strike. In turn, this would require the estimate of the adversary's nuclear force in order to arrive at a conservative estimate of the loss that will have to be borne in the first instance.
- In view of the above, it will be necessary to consider various options for the disposal of the nuclear force to minimize the loss of the nuclear assets.
- Once we have assured ourselves that the remaining nuclear assets will be sufficient to cause unacceptable damage to the adversary, it would be necessary to develop suitable signals to remove any doubt the adversary may have about the uncertainty of a response from India.

Balachandran further adds that "it is obvious that all aspects are not capable of being quantified. For example, an adversary's estimate of the certainty of an Indian reprisal depends much on factors that cannot be given numerical values, such as the political will to use nuclear weapons (Balachandran, 1998)." Despite much hyped rhetoric about India's pledge of no-first-use principle there are some skeptics who still question the viability of such a pledge. For instance Kanti Bajpai comments "How seriously India itself takes the no-first-use is not clear. In the aftermath of the May tests, the affirmation of no first use helped propagate an image of strategic restraint. Whether no-first-use can have any real operational meaning remains controversial at best, though clearly some Indian security analysts, such as K. Subrahmanyam, in particular, believe it can (Bajpai, 2000).

Missiles for Deterrence

There's no denying the fact that for India to tread on the path of 'credible minimum deterrence' it must keep its missile artillery in order as deterrence would prove to be futile without an appropriate delivery vehicles. There are different kinds of missiles that have been developed by India and continuously strive to improve their sophistication by meeting up with the advancement in technologies. The role of the missiles are to carry and deliver nuclear warheads, launch attacks on enemy tanks from a distance on the ground as well to target enemy aircraft. After the Pokhran II, Dr. A.P.J. Abdul Kalam announced that by 2000 the country will be capable of manufacturing all missiles of tactical and strategic importance. He also was of the opinion that India will be far ahead in missile technology by the turn of the century and induction of these missiles will definitely boost the capability to deter enemies. The Indian Air Force's Mirage 2000s, Jaguars, and newly acquired Sukhoi 30s are being viewed as the most effective means of delivering a nuclear strike in the years to come. India at present possesses 250-Kilometer range nuclear-capable Prithvi ballistic missile, and this can be used to carry a small Hiroshima-type nuclear device. The Prithvi missile however could be used only to hit targets upto the range of Pakistan and China could not be struck by it as it could reach only upto Tibet. Therefore the credible minimum deterrence of India seemed to be far from being achieved. The need was hence felt for a long range missile for which India endeavoured continuously on developing an extended range of Agni Intermediate Range Ballistic Missile (IRBM). On the importance of these missiles for India, Air Com. Jasjit Singh (Retd.), Director, Institute of Defence Studies and Analysis stated that the truth is that "we could manage without a test explosion. But there can be no credibility or reliability in our strategic deterrent posture without adequately testing and developing a long-range ballistic missile (Singh Jasjit, 1996)." He further added that "Ballistic missile development and their induction into operational service is critical to India's security (Singh Jasjit, 1996)." Prime Minister Vajpayee on December 15, 1998, briefed the parliament on India's plans for missile tests which addresses the concerns raised by Air Com Jasjit Singh. He said: "We have announced that a new version of the Agni, will be conducted fully in accordance with established international practice (PM's Statement in Parliament, 1998)." The Agni II was successfully test fired in April 1999, with the capacity to carry nuclear warheads up to a distance of 2000 Kilometers. India realized that for an effective deterrent capability it must develop a long-range surface-to-air missile and a sea-launched ballistic missile for a submarine force. India is building the Trishul and Akash ground-to-air missiles. The four kilometer range tank-busting missile Nag is also under development (*The Hindu,* 1998).

Agni II was developed and demonstrated at the Republic Day Function in 1996 but it was finally test fired in April 1999, barely a year after the Pokhran II. This was seen as a major breakthrough in India's missile technology and was believed to have filled in the strategic gap in India's minimum nuclear deterrent profile. The then Defence Minister with the Government of India, Mr. George Fernandes commented: "The Agni test has added a new dimension to our defence capabilities which have reached a point when no one from anywhere will dare to threaten us (*The Hindu,* 1999)." While Pokhran II provided India the know-how to design all types of atomic warheads but the mechanism to deliver them rested with the development of missile technology and therefore the charged euphoria was witnessed in India on the successful test fire of Agni II.

India, informed the nuclear establishments of Pakistan about their plans to test fire Agni II and this was done in accordance with the Lahore Declaration of February 1999, even though the convention of the declaration had not been negotiated. Pakistan responded by giving a prior information about Ghauri II. All these developments goaded United States which did not hesitate in showing its apprehension for Agni II and Ghauri II missile tests. Such anxieties about escalating tensions in the sub-continent between India and Pakistan and mitigating the rapprochement that had been reached during the Lahore Declaration of 1999 were unwarranted. This was so because there were no qualms in Pakistan over India's Agni II test. If we go by

K. Subrahmanyam's analysis, he said that Pakistan though can be said to have retaliated with Ghauri II but that was in accordance with the 'equality syndrome' whereas India's Agni II was directed at maintaining effective and credible minimum deterrence, as per Raja Mohan's analysis. K Subrahmanyam wrote: "When Agni II test was conducted, I was in Pakistan and had an opportunity to interact with their strategic community. They all accepted that Agni II is not Pakistan-oriented and it did not have much relevance for the Pakistan security calculus since Prithvi 250 and Indian aircrafts can cover all of Pakistan. At the same time they pointed out that Pakistan was conditioned to matching India move to move.... *(The Times of India,* 1999)" Commenting on US apprehension Raja Mohan wrote: "For years now, the Western nations have seen India's nuclear and missile policy through the prism of Indo-Pak relations. Although India has always insisted that its nuclear concerns extend beyond Pakistan, it has been convenient for the great powers to argue that the sub-continent is a nuclear flash-point *(The Hindu,* 1999). On the other hand the Agni III with a strike range of 3500km to 5000km is an intermediate-range ballistic missile which has been inducted into the armed forces and is under production. India has successfully test-launched its over 5,000 km Agni-V missile, which can carry a nuclear warhead in the east as far as all of China and in the west all over Europe. The development of Agni-5 began in 2009 according to DRDO it will now be rolled into production mode with and induction likely in 2015 (NDTV.com). India has also successfully test-fired its second-most ambitious nuclear missile in the making, the new-generation Agni-IV with a strike range of 4,000 km, and promptly declared it was ready for induction. Both the missiles are geared towards providing the country with some much-needed credible strategic deterrence against China, which can target any Indian city with its intercontinental ballistic missiles (ICBMs) like the 11,200 km range Dong Feng-31A (Pandit Rajat, 2014).

India's nuclear doctrine speaks of a triad, which comprises of air, land and sea-based nuclear weapons, where sea-based weapons have been kept in the backburner. But if we go by the analysis of W.P.S. Sindhu, an Indian Defence Analyst at the Cooperative Monitoring Centre, Albuquerque, New Mexico than 'sea-based-deterrence' would be an ideal nuclear deterrence for India. It is considered as the most stable and having assured second strike capability. On the other hand the land-based and the air-based system are considered most vulnerable to the first strike. If we go by the record of the United States stocks, it is believed that half of them consist of submarine-launched-ballistic missiles (SLBMs) and that US intends to increase its stock of SLBMs and will cut on land and air based missiles. Hence, if we further go by Sindhu's analysis then the future of nuclear weapons will find the dominance of sea-based nuclear weapons. India therefore must bring together its efforts for future more credible sea deterrence with induction of adequate numbers of SLBMs. Meanwhile the induction of the Dhanush sea-based, surface-launched ballistic missile (SLBM, a naval variant of Prithvi) is expected to ensure a sea-based deterrent. Another SLBM under development is Sagarika/K-15.

Moratorium on Nuclear Testing and Signing the CTBT

Immediately after the tests, the Vajpayee Government was quick enough to make an announcement about observing moratorium on further nuclear tests (Bajpai, 2000). The Government of India confirmed that the tests were successful and that there was no requirement for further tests. Prime minister in his speech to the parliament on May 27, 1998 informed the world that tests "had achieved their stated objective" of maintaining the skills of the younger generation of scientists and engineers and building on the work of the earlier generations. He further said, "In terms of technical capability, our scientists and engineers have the requisite resources to ensure a credible deterrent (Bajpai, 2000)." The Joint Statement by Department of Atomic Energy and Defence Research and Development Organisation issued on May 17, 1998 and noted that the tests:

> "have provided critical data for the validation of our [India's] capability in the design of nuclear weapons of different yield for different applications and different delivery systems. These tests have significantly enhanced our capability in computer simulation of new designs and taken us to the stage of sub-critical experiments in the future, if considered necessary (Statement by DAE & DRDO)."

India began giving an indication to the United States about its willingness to sign the CTBT but on its own conditions. The BJP Government was attacked severely by the left and the Rashtriya Swayamsevak Sangh (RSS) about going soft on its foreign policy agenda. Mr. Brajesh Mishra Principal Secretary to the Prime Minister announced, on May 11 1998, a willingness to consider accepting in parts the CTBT provided that there would be reciprocity on part of the US and the other permanent members of the UN. On the other hand the Prime Minister too indicated at India's interest in signing the Treaty. While addressing the Fifty-third UN General Assembly in September 1998, he said: "We are prepared to bring these discussions [with key interlocutors in the international community] to a successful conclusion, so that the entry into force of the CTBT is not delayed beyond September 1999 (PM speech, 1998)." India's soft posture is quite explicitly reflective in the conditions listed by US in the Strobe Talbott-Jaswant Singh talks. These are to sign and ratify the CTBT without conditions, and to do so quickly; halt all production of fissile material; participate in the Committee on Disarmament on Fissban; exercise restraint in the development, flight testing, storage, basing, and deployment of missiles and aircraft, that is, in all delivery systems; define Indian security requirements at the lowest possible level and clarify the meaning or requirements of India's quest for a 'minimum, credible nuclear deterrent'; tighten export controls and bring them up to international standards; develop the Indo-Pakistani dialogue *(Times of India,* 1998).

Fissile Material Cutoff Treaty

India showed its willingness to join the talks in Geneva at the Conference on Disarmament (CD) on the fissile material cutoff or the "fisban." The cut-off would stop any further production of weapon grade fissile material in a verifiable manner. In the May paper tabled in Parliament, the Indian Government notes that it had "indicated its readiness to participate in negotiations in the Conference on Disarmament in Geneva on Fissile Material Cut-off Treaty (Bajpai Kanti, 2000)." The paper further adds that India's participation in the negotiations would be in "the full confidence of the adequacy and credibility of the nation's weaponised nuclear deterrent (Bajpai Kanti, 2000)." As stated in the preceding paragraph, Joint Statement between Strobe Talbott and Jaswant Singh too very clearly mentions the direction given to India by the United States with respect to the FMCT negotiations. Vajpayee too in his speech at the 53rd UN General Assembly in September vociferously admitted its inclination to join the negotiations in the CD on a fisban and added that India was conscious that this is a partial step" and that it would not "eliminate existing nuclear arsenals (PM speech, 1998)." India would however join the negotiations to show its solidarity and commitment as a responsible nation and also that India wanted to ensure that the treaty would not be discriminatory and would meet India's security needs (PM speech, 1998). However, India made it a point to mention that India in no way was committed to moratorium on fissile material production (PM's Statement in Parliament, 1998), thereby rejecting US demand for a unilateral moratorium on fissile material production. The Indian point of view on the issue of FMCT has been that it should only cover prospective or future production of fissile material and not existing stockpiles and that the outcome of the negotiations should be in the nature of a "universal and non-discriminatory treaty, backed by an effective verification mechanism (Bajpai Kanti, 2000)." India on the other hand also expects from Washington a better access to dual-use and high technologies in view of India's impeccable record of stringent control over sensitive technologies. Despite all these assurances the future of FMCT and the resultant fisban is uncertain. India does not want to get fisban applicable on existing stockpiles with the intention of maintaining minimum deterrent, in such scenario the future of fisban remains undecided.

Tightening Export Controls

India also significantly stated through its nuclear draft doctrine of strengthening and tightening its export control laws implied on nuclear, missile and dual-use technologies to bring them in commensurate with global norms. Prime Minister's statement at the General Assembly categorically declared that India had a much better record than many other members of the global non-proliferation regime who were in fact the members of the Non-Proliferation Treaty (NPT), the Nuclear Suppliers Group (NSG), and the Missile Technology Control Regime (MTCR). In fact, India is already observing the provisions under the MTCR by refusing to export missile or any missile technology to any third country. Prime Minister stated in the UN that: "we have an effective system of export controls and shall make it more stringent where necessary, including by expanding control lists of equipment and technology to make them more contemporary and effective in the context of a nuclear India (Bajpai Kanti, 2000)." The matter related to the export control had also figured in the Strobe Talbott and Jaswant Singh's Joint Statement. While it continues to agree and abide by stringent norms on export control India also put forth its reservations on the issue. The Prime Minister of India stated on the issue both in the Parliament as well as in the UN General Assembly (Bajpai Kanti, 2000) that first, India will continue to move on its nuclear programmes and missile programmes and any interference will be deemed unacceptable; second, India will continue its cooperation with other countries on nuclear technology in accordance with international norms and third, all the discriminatory technology control against it should be withdrawn. However export control initiative of the Government of India reached a new height with the passage of the more stringent laws immediately after signing of the Joint Statement and before the conclusion of the Indo-

US nuclear deal as the United States repeatedly stressed on this point as a major prerequisite towards the final deal.

Global Nuclear Disarmament

India silenced its critiques skeptical about India's commitment to global nuclear disarmament Post Pokhran II by once again asserting its adherence to the global nuclear disarmament and rather affirmed that now it can speak more authoritatively on the issue of nuclear disarmament. It was in fact in the very first announcement after the Pokhran II that the Prime Minister re-authenticated India's continued commitment to nuclear disarmament. India categorically asserted that weaponization would not result in nuclear proliferation. Prime Minister stated in the Rajya Sabha that India was "committed to initiatives that can open negotiations for a global convention for the elimination of all nuclear weapons (Bajpai Kanti, 2000)." Prime Minister was of the opinion that abolition of nuclear weapons was in the interest of the security concerns of all the nations. This fact was asserted by him in his address to the Parliament with respect to the dialogue with the United States, he said: India will stand by its 'undiluted' commitment to nuclear disarmament and at the same time added that a nuclear weapons free world would "enhance not only our security but the security of all nations (Bajpai Kanti, 2000)." In one of his statements Vajpayee emphasized on India's continuance on its earlier stand on disarmament and while addressing 53rd UN General Assembly Prime Minister made reference to Rajiv Gandhi Action Plan and said that India still adheres to its principles of time-bound elimination of nuclear arsenals. At another forum i.e. in his statement on the evolution of India's nuclear policy, he said: "India remains committed to the basic tenet of our foreign policy—a conviction that global elimination of nuclear weapons will enhance its security as well as that of the rest of the world. It will continue to urge countries, particularly other nuclear weapon states to adopt measures that would contribute meaningfully to such an objective (Bajpai Kanti, 2000)."

Command-and-Control Structure

After declaring the world about itself being a nuclear power, India largely felt the need to correct its command-and-control structure which in the past had not been given primary importance. There was already a loosely knit structure in operation, but the need for formalizing it and making it public had become apparent to India (Pant, 2007). Hence after understanding the significance of a sound command-and-control system India decided to place its nuclear arsenal under the control of a formal command chain. A two-layered structure, the Nuclear Command Authority (NCA), will have the overall control of nuclear weapons. The NCA is composed of a political council headed by the prime minister and an executive council presided over by the national security advisor. The details regarding the actual composition of the NCA has not been made explicit by the government at its political and executive level but as per the reports taking round in the media, the political council includes the members of the Cabinet Committee on Security (CCS) and the national security advisor, while the executive council is composed of the chairman of the Chiefs of Staff Committee (COSC) of the three services, heads of the intelligence agencies and members of the scientific community associated with the nuclear program (John Cherian, 2003).

The Prime Minister will be the sole authority to issue orders to release the use of nuclear weapons in the event of a nuclear war. The national security advisor, who chairs the executive council of the NCA, would execute the directives of the political council. It is the job of the security advisor and the executive council to assist the political council, headed by the Prime Minister, in making the decision on the use of nukes and then ensuring that the orders are carried out (Pant, 2007). A triservice command called the Strategic Forces Command (SFC) will be NCA's operational arm, having its own commander-in-chief reporting to the chairman of the Joint Chiefs of Staff, and it will control all of India's nuclear warheads and delivery systems. Further the Indian Government also has "approved the arrangement for alternate chains of command for retaliatory nuclear strikes in all eventualities." In its first formal meeting in September 2003, the state of the Indian nuclear arsenal was reviewed and the establishment of the nuclear command post in concrete, underground bunkers at "secure locations" was the highlight of the meeting (Pant, 2007).

India's formal declaration of its nuclear doctrine and creation of the NCA brought into effect a long-standing requirement, thereby formalizing what was essentially a set of unstructured arrangements among senior members of the politico-military-scientific establishment (Pant, 2007 & Perkovich, 1999). It was India's attempt to set at rest some doubts about nuclear issues while reiterating the promises it made to the international community (Pant, 2007). The new framework accords the necessary doctrinal underpinning to India's evolving nuclear posture and the sanctity of government approval for the use of nuclear weapons (Pant, 2007). Hence, maximum restraint in the use of nuclear force, absolute political control of decision making, and an attempt to evolve an effective interface between civilian and military leaders in the administration of its nuclear arsenal have emerged as the basic tenets of India's nuclear weapons policy (Pant, 2007). India's declaration of its nuclear doctrine and the NCA marked a significant step in the nation's plan to develop effective and robust command-and-control and indications-and-warning systems and infrastructure for its strategic nuclear forces commensurate with its strategic requirements (Pant, 2007). Nevertheless, an effective command-and-control arrangement still remains a challenge since it requires an integration of the Indian military with the civilian authorities for the management of the nation's nuclear arsenal (Pant, 2007).

The Debate after Pokhran II

The precise timing of the release of the DND (Draft Nuclear Doctrine) raised eyebrows due to the fact that, in August 1999, the Vajpayee Government was in a caretaker capacity having lost its majority in the lower house of parliament. A new election had already been called for October 1999. Some have argued that the draft doctrine was released to the media to bolster Bharatiya Janata Party's electoral advantage. It has also been suggested that the nuclear doctrine was formulated only to formalize BJP's nuclear policy declared after the nuclear tests conducted in May 1998. Yet, another view is that it was done to legitimize India's nuclear weapons through the formulation of DND arising out of "the reciprocal fear of surprise attack" on the part of political leaders, military planners and strategic analysts in India. Perhaps a succinct view was put forth this way. "The bomb has many fathers. The Congress conceived it, the United Front nurtured it, The BJP delivered. Let us not give the obstetrician any more credit than is due (Prakash, A.S., 1998)."

The heated debate that would follow post-Pokhran II was anybody's guess, but that the opinions will be profoundly fragmented and narrow among the Indian scientific, intellectual circle and the political circle was not presumed to be so. The Indian debate divided the reactionary groups into two lobbies the pro-bomb lobby and anti-bomb lobby. Praful Bidwai, Achin Vanaik, N Ram and the Left were the ones who advocated unilateral Indian nuclear disarmament and therefore did not form the part of the bomb euphoria. Among the Pro-bomb lobby the prominent figures included K. Subrahmanyam, Jasjit Sigh, Amitab Mattoo, Muchkund Dubey, Brigadier Vijay Nair, Bharat Karnad etc who favoured India's nuclear posture. However it is interesting to note that within India's pro-bomb strategic community, three viewpoints on nuclear policy are contending for dominance. These may be called *rejectionism, pragmatism* and *maximalism* (Bajpai Kanti, 2000). All the three seems to be in unanimity on one thing and that is the vitality of nuclear weapons for India's security. Apart from this they disagree on most of the nuclear decisions from deterrence to the issue of global disarmament (Bajpai Kanti, 2000).

To conclude it is important to recognize the role that the strategic culture ultimately plays in deciding on virtually all aspects of the decision making process. The Pokhran II too is a product of its strategic culture as different strategic cultures yield different kinds of nuclear doctrines and arsenals. Having said this, India after maintaining twenty four years of nuclear ambiguity, decided to come out of the closet by exercising its nuclear option and covertly declaring to the world of its nuclear status. India immediately after the tests projected a responsible posture and the prime minister was quick to announce unilateral moratorium on further testing. The Government of India later on constituted a National Security Advisory Board (NSAB) that was given the charge of drafting the broad framework of India's Nuclear Doctrine thereby signaling out its strategies so as to calm the international pressures/sanctions/ outrage mounting on it in the wake of the Pokhran II adventure.

It is equally pertinent to take cognizance of the fact that the basic aspects of the Indian Nuclear doctrine had already been enunciated by the Indian Government after it conducted its nuclear tests in May 1998. India decided to adopt a no-first-use policy and also that it will never use nuclear weapons against a non-nuclear state. India also announced that it will continue to tread on its earlier path of nuclear disarmament and that the nuclear test was not meant to start an arms race in the subcontinent. She also started participating in the high-level arms-control negotiations with the United States in order to shape up the India-United States relationship that had to an extent been derailed in the wake of India's nuclear tests. India also was indicative about its readiness to comply with the negotiations on CTBT and FMCT as well as strengthening export controls though with certain strings attached to them.

What can be viewed as a rather significant move was that the 1998 test marked a major shift in India's foreign policy. "This shift was as significant as the 1991 shift in economic policies, which had already presaged new directions in India's foreign policies. By 1999, India had at least a draft nuclear doctrine, which, inter alia, determined India's need for only a credible minimum deterrent and a posture of 'no first use'. In foreign policy these developments had a long lasting impact (Ghose Arundhati), 2009." The foreign relations after the tests, which had been adversely affected started to come on track with India taking initiatives in establishing bilateral talks with most of the European countries in general and United States in particular, on various issues particularly the one's related to security issues. India thus succeeded in downplaying the impact of various sanctions that had been imposed on it as a reaction to its Pokhran tests by extensively working towards bridging up the gaps.

ENDNOTES & REFERENCES

'Address of the Prime Minister of India to the 53rd UN General Assembly', 1998, reprinted in *Strategic Digest*, November, p.1801.

Alam Mohammad B, 2002, 'India's Nuclear Doctrine: Context and Constraints', *South Asian and Comparative Politics,* Heidelberg, 11 October.

Bajpai Kanti, 2000, 'India's Nuclear Posture After Pokhran II', *International Studies,* vol. 37, no 4, New Delhi, Oct-Dec.

Balachandran G, 1999, 'India's Nuclear Doctrine', *The Hindu*, 15 February.

Banerjee Dipankar, 2011, 'Seeking Alternatives to Nuclear Deterrence in India'. See for details http://www.ipcs.org/article/india/seeking-alternatives-to-nuclear-deterrence-in-india-3419.html, accessed on 31.03.2012.

Chari P.R., 1999, 'Indo-US relations: Nonproliferation Concerns', in Gary K. Bertsch, et al. (eds.), 1999, *Engaging India: US Strategic Relations with the World's Largest Democracy*, New York: Routledge.

Cherian John, 1998, *The BJP and the Bomb*, Frontline, vol.15, no.8, 11-24 April.

Cherian John, 2003, 'The Nuclear Button', *Frontline,* vol. 20, no. 2, January 31.

Cohen Stephen P, 2001. *India: Emerging Power,* Oxford: Oxford University Press. Babbage, Ross and Sandy Gordon, (eds.) 1992. *India's Strategic Future: Regional State or Global Power?* New Delhi: Oxford University Press.

Cohen Stephen P., 2000, 'Why India Go Nuclear', in Raju G C Thomas and Amit Gupta, (ed.), *India's Nuclear Security,* New Delhi: Vistaar Publications.

Ganguly Sumit, 2000, 'Explaining the Indian Nuclear Tests of 1998' in Raju G C Thomas and Amit Gupta, (eds.), *India's Nuclear Security,* Vistaar Publications, New Delhi.

Garver John W, 2001, *Protracted Conflict: Sino-Indian Rivalry in the Twentieth Century*, Seattle, WA: University of Washington Press.

Ghose Arundhati, 2009, 'Nuclear Weapons, Non-proliferation and Nuclear Disarmament: Evolving Policy Challenges', *India Quarterly*, Sage, vol.65, no.

Gupta Bhabani Sen, 1997, 'India in the Twenty First Century', *International Affairs,* vol. 73, no.2, pp. 308-10 and also Kripa Sridharan, n.2.

India felt that its 'options had narrowed critically'. See Jaswant Singh, 1998, 'Against nuclear apartheid', *Foreign Affairs*, vol. 77, September–October.

India's Nuclear Weapons Programme, Operation Shakti 1998, URL: http://nuclearweaponarchive.org/India/IndiaShakti.html, also cited in Kripa Sridharan, n.2.

Joint Statement by Department of Atomic Energy and Defence Research and Development Organisation, issued on May 17, 1998, New Delhi. URL: http://www.meadev.gov.in/govt/drdo.htm,

Kamath P M, 1999, 'Indian National Security Policy: Minimal Nuclear Deterrence', *Strategic Analysis*, November.

Kapur Ashok, 2001, *Pokhran and Beyond*, New Delhi: Oxford University Press.

Khanna V N, 2002, 'Nuclear Option Exercised', *India's Nuclear Doctrine*, New Delhi: Samskriti Publications.

Lewis Jeffrey, 2006, Minimum Deterrence, *Bulletin of the Atomic Scientists*, vol. 64, no.3.

Mattoo Amitabh, (ed.) 1998, 'India's Nuclear Policy in an Anarchic World' in *India's Nuclear Deterrent*, New Delhi: Har-Anand,

Mehta Pratap Bhanu, 1998, 'India: the nuclear politics of self-esteem', *Current History*, vol. 97, no. 623,December.

Mishra Brajesh, 2006, 'Global Security: An Indian Perspective', cited in Kripa Sridharan.

Mohamed Ayoob, 1999, 'Nuclear India and Indian-American Relations', *Orbis*, vol. 43, no.1.

Nair Vijay K, 1998, 'The Structure of Indian Nuclear Deterrent' in Amitabh Mattoo, ed., *India's Nuclear Deterrent: Pokhran II and Beyond*, New Delhi: Har-Anand.

Pandit Rajat, 'Agni IV Test Successful, Ready for Induction', *The Times of India*, January 21, 2014.

Pant Harsh V, 2002, 'Indian and Nuclear Arms Control: A Study of the CTBT', *Comparative Study*, vol.21, no.2, April.

Pant Harsh V, 2007, 'India's Nuclear Doctrine and Command Structure: Implications for Civil-Military Relations in India', *Armed Forces and Society*.

Perkovich George, 1999, *India's Nuclear Bomb*, New Delhi: Oxford University Press.

PM's Statement in Parliament on 'Bilateral Talks with United States', December 15, 1998. URL: http://www.meadev.gov.in/speeches/part115dec.htm,

PM's Statement in Parliament on 'Bilateral Talks with United States,'" December 15, 1998, http://www.meadev.gov.in/speeches/part115dec.htm.

PM's Statement in Parliament on 'Bilateral Talks with United States'

Prakash A S, 1998, 'All were Party to the nuclear gatecrash', *The Pioneer*, Chandigarh, 25 May.

Prime Minister's key responses include: May 27 statement, the September 24 statement before the United Nations General Assembly, and the December 15 Statement in Parliament on the India-US dialogue.

Prime Minister's Statement in Rajya Sabha regarding U N Security Resolution on 8 June, 1998.

Ram N, 1999, 'Dreaming India's Nuclear Future', *Frontline*, vol. 16, no.18, Aug 28-Sep 10.

Rosenau, James N, 1967, 'Foreign Policy as an Issue Area', in James N Rosenau (ed.), *Domestic Sources of Foreign Policy*, New York: Free Press.

Singh Jasjit, 1996, 'Extinguishing the Agni', *The Indian Express*, 12 December.

Singh Jasjit, 1998, 'Nuclear India', *Knowledge World*, in association with IDSA', New Delh..

Sridharan Kripa, 2006, 'Explaining the Phenomenon of Change in Indian Foreign Policy Under the National Democratic Alliance Government', *Contemporary South Asia*, vol. 15, no. 1.

Statement by Ambassador Savitri Kunadi in the Plenary Meeting of the Conference on Disarmament in Geneva, August 6, 1998'. URL: http://www.meadev.gov.in/speeches/part115dec.htm.

Subrahmanyam K, 1998, *The Times of India*, 7 December.

Tellis Ashley J, 2001, *India's Emerging Nuclear Posture: Recessed Deterrent and Ready Arsenal*, New Delhi: Oxford University Press.

The Cabinet Committee on Security Reviews Operationalisation of India's Nuclear Doctrine'. URL: http://meaindia.nic.in//prhome.htm.

The Hindu, 1998, 'Losing the Authority to Govern', International Edition, 5 December.

The Hindu, 1998, 10 December.

The Hindu, 1998, 7 December.

The Hindu, 1998, International Edition, 23 May.

The Hindu, 1999, 12 April.

The Hindu, 1999, 14 April.

The one's who were critical of the Government's decision to test are N. Ram, and Praful Bidwai and Achin Vanaik, Also see Praful Bidwai and Achin Vanaik, 1999, *South Asia on* a *Short Fuse: Nuclear Politics and Future of Global Disarmament,* New Delhi: Oxford University Press.

The Times of India, 1998, 'US Looks to India's Emergence as a Global Power', 13 November.

The Times of India, 1998, 28 May, New Delhi.

The Times of India, 1998, 5 August.

The Times of India, 1999, 14 April.

Times of India, 1999, 4 February.

URL: http://www.ndtv.com/article/india/agni-5-india-s-most-potent-nuclear-capable-ballistic-missile-launched-successfully-418800Accessed on 04.07.14.

URL:http://afs.sagepub.com/content/33/2/238.

10

Globalization and Tribal Development in India

Krishan Gopal

The World Bank—a financial institution designed to cater to the needs of the international community, which provides technical assistance within the highly volatile fiscal world, to enable developing countries to address important infrastructural requirements. World Bank funds target development programs to reduce poverty. It is the largest public development institution in the world. In existence for over 60 years, the Bank has expanded from a single institution—the International Bank for Reconstruction and Development (IBRD) to five institutions, each dealing with a particular area of operations. These include financing and other supports for relief and rehabilitation, physical and institutional infrastructure in sectors such as energy, transportation, extractive industry and telecommunications, restructuring of key sectors such as health, education, water and agriculture to make them private sector and market friendly, private sector development, and mitigating investment-associated risks for private companies. Corporate influence is manifested in and through the Bank in several ways. Most obvious are the supports extended to private corporations through three of its specialised institutions: the International Finance Corporation (IFC), Multilateral Investment Guarantee Agency (MIGA) and International Centre for the Settlement of Investment Disputes (ICSID). Every year, the World Bank channels more than US$ 25 billion to developing countries in the form of loans and grants with the ostensible aim of reducing poverty and promoting economic growth. A significant amount goes directly to the private sector, especially large corporations, in the form of loans, technical assistance and mitigation of investment risks.

The World Bank in India

India was among the 17 original participants of the 1944 Bretton Woods Conference which conceived the idea of the International Bank for Reconstruction and Development (IBRD)—more commonly known today as the "World Bank". In fact, it was the India delegation which first suggested the name IBRD. The Bank's New Delhi office, established in 1957, is the oldest continuously functioning World Bank country office.

The World Bank does not operate alone. In India, the Bank works with multiple development partners: the government, other bilateral and multilateral donor organizations, nongovernmental organizations (NGOs) and the most important the private sector. The Bank's method of operation is not to implement "World Bank projects," but to provide financing and advice for projects. The World Bank has developed an action plan known as the India Country Strategy (CAS) which describes what kind of support and how much could be provided to the country over a period of around four years. The CAS directly supports the government's five-year plan and focuses on strengthening the enabling environment for development and sustainable growth and supporting critical interventions of special benefit to the poor and disadvantaged.

Since 1991, the so called inception of liberalization period India is blindly following every policy direction in all spheres of economic activities. Gradually it remains the Bank's largest single borrower. WBs lending to the India touched $2.9 billion in FY 2005—more than double the amount lent a year earlier. Interestingly, the bulk of new lending has gone to infrastructure and human development projects, reflecting the potential for corporate interests. Another symbol of the wasted interest is India's HIV/AIDS control programme of which WB is the largest financers of India's National Aids Control Program (NACP) with US$275 million credits, ignoring other major health sector requirements of nation. Gradually the WB is encroaching India's sovereignty as nation state and direct extending its credit to state governments. A key focus of its credit to state government has been fiscal reforms of state governments.

The World Bank's Country Strategy (CAS) for India for 2009-2012 focuses on fast-track development of infrastructure. It is said that the strategy is closely aligned with the Government of India's own development priorities expressed in the Eleventh Five Year Plan i.e. ensuring participation of private sector. Under the strategy, the Bank will use lending, dialogue, analytical work, all with engagement of the private sector to achieve its goals.

World Bank suggests that for India's rapid and sustained growth, major investments in power, transport, water, and urban development are important. Inadequate power supply remains a critical constraint to growth; while GDP grew at an average of about 8% a year over the past five years, electricity generation only grew at an average of 4.9% per year. The national and state highway networks have not kept pace with the tremendous growth in demand for road transport: only about 30% of state highways are two-lane and more than 50% are in poor condition. Inadequate urban infrastructure is hampering the expansion of growth centers. While the Eleventh Plan foresees a major role for private sector involvement in infrastructure development through public private partnerships, these may not materialize to the extent hoped for in the aftermath of the global financial crisis, therefore the World Bank specially focuses on infrastructure investment in its new strategy, including on strengthening the capacity of government agencies to design and manage public-private partnerships (PPPs). In other words only public-private partnerships (PPPs) are the answer of all development troubles.

Agriculture is another sector having vast potential for this PPP model. Low agricultural productivity is keeping some 60 percent of India's population behind. Shortages of basic rural infrastructure—from roads to electrification—are hindering the growth of off-farm activities. According to bank, sustaining this level of performance over the longer term will be difficult without addressing several policy and structural constraints, including a myriad of restrictions, subsidies, support prices, sector governance issues, as well as the tiny size of landholdings and years of underinvestment. In this radiance the World Bank to places special emphasis on agricultural development in its new strategy. This practice is extending to other natural resources. The WB suggest that India is highly vulnerable to climate change; cyclones, floods and droughts are happening with increasing frequency, and the Himalayan glaciers that feed India's largest rivers show clear signs of retreat. Further, most environmental indicators suggest that growth is extracting an increasing toll on the country's natural resources—water, land, forests, soils and biodiversity—and leaving a larger pollution footprint. Indeed, climate change will impact India first and foremost through its water resources. Therefore, India will need to better manage these resources (particularly water).

India's seven low-income states—Bihar, Chhattisgarh, Jharkhand, Madhya Pradesh, Orissa, Rajasthan, and Uttar Pradesh—which are home to more than half of India's population, are softest target of WB reform policies. The new strategy devotes more resources (read more guided credit and loans) to engaging in these states. Intensive technical assistance will be provided to help these states develop their administrative capacity. Technical and advisory services are the major part of bank lending to these states.

The assistance to other states such as Andhra Pradesh; Karnataka, Punjab, Tamil Nadu, Haryana, Gujarat, and Maharashtra is costlier, where bank is helping to forge the institutions needed in these middle income states. Lending to these states are in the form of comparatively high priced IBRD loans, with the International Finance Corporation (IFC)—the Bank's private sector arm—providing support for private sector clients.

Through the IBRD and IDA, the WB offer two basic types of loans and credits: investment operations and development policy operations. Countries use investment operations for goods, works and services in support of economic and social development projects in a broad range of economic and social sectors. Development policy operations (formerly known as adjustment loans) provide quick-disbursing financing to support a country's policy and institutional reforms. Each borrower's project proposal is assessed to ensure that the project is economically, financially, socially and environmentally sound. During loan negotiations, the Bank and borrower agree on the development objectives, outputs, performance indicators and implementation plan, as well as a loan disbursement schedule.

IDA grants-which are either funded directly or managed through partnerships-have been used to:

- Relieve the debt burden of heavily indebted poor countries
- Improve sanitation and water supplies
- Support vaccination and immunization programs to reduce the incidence of communicable diseases like malaria
- Combat the HIV/AIDS pandemic
- Support civil society organizations
- Create initiatives to cut the emission of greenhouse gases

Interestingly and incidentally these are the areas where private corporate has strong interests.

India is one of the major clients of WB. As mentioned earlier that the

World Bank offers two basic types of loans: investment loans and adjustment loans to support policy and institutional reforms. A large amount of loan to India is granted as Development Program Landings (DPL). DPL lending is aimed at helping states to increase their development spending on basic social services such as education and health, safety nets for the poor, as well as for building critical investments in basic infrastructure. Lend to states in India that are relatively poor or otherwise disadvantaged. These states often have large fiscal burdens and need to create greater fiscal space for more effective spending on development programs. To be eligible for

DPL financing, state governments need to have effective policies and programs in place to meet their development priorities. They must also demonstrate their ability to address issues of inclusive growth by improving their basic systems of governance with greater transparency and accountability to their people. DPLs support state governments in India to generate greater employment opportunities for their people. State governments frequently find that the biggest obstacle to generating new jobs is the regulatory burden imposed on private enterprises which hinders new investment. These regulations mostly end up hurting small businesses and farmers and implicitly supporting larger businesses that can cope more easily with the costs of such burdensome regulations. DPLs therefore support state governments in their efforts to encourage more open and competitive environments and polices, such as those that remove local monopolistic practices which hurt farmers and small producers.

Where relevant, DPLs support state governments in the development of policies and programs that encourage greater inclusion and protect the environment. State governments may seek to address these issues in different ways, such as through regulations that: strengthen indigenous peoples' rights, conserve forestry resources, provide for more equitable property rights, and those that strengthen environmental protection and benefits to local residents affected by mining, hydropower or other issues. DPLs follow the guidelines of the Government of India, especially to ensure that state governments' policies and programs are able to return them to a path of medium-term fiscal sustainability.

But in fact, the DPL reduce government spending on development programs and priorities. Advocate or support any form of forced privatizations and lay-offs of public sector employees, since these are counter-productive. Instead, they support programs and policies that arrive at ways of protecting workers and jobs, and those that generate more jobs by promoting new avenues of growth in the rural, agricultural and urban sectors.

The World Bank clearly state that it believes that development needs and priorities vary widely between countries depending on a variety of factors, and that there is no one-size-fits-all model of development. Privatization is only best options available. India today, like many developing countries, is facing a large and growing shortfall in the provision of electricity, water, transportation, schools, hospitals, etc. To meet the rapidly growing needs of the people, the World Bank believes that the private sectors have important roles to play.

Apparently the World Bank's program in India is guided by the country's own development agenda, however country's development agenda itself is govern by World Bank's agenda. Within this broad agenda, the World Bank focuses on areas where it can contribute the most. These include primary schooling, healthcare, basic infrastructure, rural livelihoods, water supply and sanitation.

The World Bank believes that there is no single approach that can improve basic services as varied as water, power, health, and education.

In case of education the World Bank does not believe that primary schooling should be privatized, because it may be a huge burden on private sector to reach in rural areas. Therefore it suggests that "at the secondary level (Grades 9-12) where the financing and provision of schooling for all children is not the government's sole responsibility, the Bank is of the view that both the public and private sectors need to expand to absorb the increasing numbers of students, and improve the access, equity and quality of education provided. The same is true for vocational and higher education".

In Health Care services the bank's report suggests that given the already large private sector service delivery taking place in India the World Bank believes that well designed policies to selectively engage private providers can expand the coverage and quality of basic health services for the people, especially the poor because public financing has been shown be an essential element in providing health care to the poor. But governments across the world are often constrained in reaching widely dispersed poor populations with good quality health services. As a result, India's health sector is already highly privatized; most health care services are delivered by private providers, and more than 3/4 of all health expenditure comes from private sources. Most of this spending goes to private providers.

In case of electricity, the World Bank believes that it is neither desirable nor possible to have a single solution for improving the delivery of electricity services.

As it does for other urban services, the World Bank recommends that water supply utilities be run in a professional manner, are financially sustainable, and ensure affordable supply for those who cannot pay. It recognizes that the public sector must retain primary responsibility for ensuring reliable, affordable and safe water supply to India's citizens. For this reason, the World Bank recommends that the government retains ownership of water supply infrastructure and regulates water resources.

The World Bank's support for rural services in India has gone through an important evolution over the last decade. Gradually the WB is directly interfering in all sphere of economic activities. While implementing these projects in India and elsewhere, the Bank has increasingly recognized that local governments play a critical role in scaling-up and sustaining the delivery of services. Drawing on these lessons, the Bank has increasingly focused on the linkages between service delivery and Panchayati Raj Institutions (PRIs). For example, in the rural water and sanitation sector, the Bank has adopted a set of rules for sectoral investments that strengthen ties with PRIs.

The World Bank's current Country Strategy goes a step further and proposes direct support to Panchayats rather than relying on indirect links through sectoral delivery systems. If livelihood projects can strengthen the ability of communities to organize themselves around the delivery of private goods, the direct strengthening of local governments increases PRI's capacity to respond to the demand by communities for local public goods. It also strengthens the ability of PRIs to support existing sectoral programs in water and sanitation, rural roads, health and education. The predicament in this idea is that direct involvement with PRIs makes them unaccountable to state government of which WB itself a proactive advocate. The Karnataka Panchayat Strengthening Project is the first of this new generation of projects that directly focuses on strengthening the PRI system. The Bank is now looking at adopting this approach in other States.

Another important aspects of WB projects are displacement of peoples. In principle World Bank projects have social safeguard policies on Involuntary Resettlement and on Indigenous Peoples. The first lays down principles and processes to safeguard the interests of those adversely affected by land acquisition and displacement on account of Bank projects. The second requires free, prior, and informed consultation with tribal populations to ensure that

Bank projects deliver social and economic benefits that are culturally appropriate and inclusive. It also ensures that potentially adverse impacts are either avoided, or when avoidance is not feasible, that such effects are minimized and mitigated.

The Bank's social safeguard policies define higher standards than those found in most countries, including India, in terms of compensation for land acquisition (at replacement value) resettlement (livelihood restoration), and for citizen participation. In the preparation of Bank financed projects, assessments are made of the borrower's policies, and measures are put in place to fill gaps between the Bank's policy requirements and the borrower's policies. Specific implementation plans as well as institutional and monitoring arrangements are put in place based on these policy frameworks. The policy frameworks and specific implementation plans (e.g. a Resettlement Plan or an Tribal Peoples' Development Plan) are legally binding on the borrower who is responsible for the preparation, implementation, and monitoring of specific plans. The Bank's role is that of reviewing policy frameworks and plans to ensure that they conform with the Bank's Safeguard Policies.

World Bank projects are designed to ensure that Indigenous Peoples receive social and economic benefits that are culturally appropriate, and gender and intergenerationally inclusive. In the Indian context, a Tribal Peoples' Development Plan is prepared in consultation with the scheduled tribes inhabiting the project area in accordance with the requirements of the Indigenous Peoples' policy. Tribal and other vulnerable communities are engaged in micro-level planning along with other members of the village. Specific Tribal Peoples' Development Plans are prepared to address the specific needs of tribals and other vulnerable groups. These are costed and monitored separately. But in practice merely there are any example in which case banks has followed these policies to avoid the distress of indigenous peoples.

Tribal Development in India

The Constitution of India contains a number of provisions for safeguard of interests of STs and their protection, notably Articles 15(4), 1 6(4), 46, 243M, 243 ZC, 244, first and second provisos to 275(1), 334, 335, 338A, 339(1), the Fifth and the Sixth Schedules. Besides, a battery of laws has been enacted by the Central Government (like the Protection of Civil Rights Act, 1955, the Scheduled Castes and Scheduled Tribes (Prevention of Atrocities) Act, 1989, the Provisions of the Panchayats (Extension to Scheduled Areas) Act,

1996, the Scheduled Tribes and Other Traditional Forest Dwellers (Recognition of Forest Rights) Act, 2006) as well as by the state governments (particularly those relating to prevention of alienation and restoration of tribal land, money-lending, reservations, etc.). The Centre has been given the authority of giving directions to the State Governments (Article 339(2), Para 3 of the Fifth Schedule) in the interest of tribes people. Further, a National Tribal Policy is on the Central anvil. It is a unique dispensation.

The Present Scenario

Notwithstanding the overall policy frame in force spelt out hereinbefore, as well as the pledges made from time-to-time: (a) exploitation has continued through land alienation, exchange transactions, money-lending, bondage, atrocities, and (b) economically they have been suffering due to subsistence level from the beginning, low productivity and production, continual attrition of economic means, displacement on account of expropriation of their land for location of development projects, dispossession of other natural resources like water, minerals, forests, CPR and low success rate among them of the planned development process.

Evidently, the policies and actions followed so far have not yielded the expected results. Planned development has benefited some sections but left the tribal mass more or less marginalised, mangled and brutalised despite the formidable array of promotive-cum-protective constitutional provisions, a battery of legal instruments, large-scale investment in terms of plans, personnel and finance during the preceding ten Five-Year Plans as well as the concern of the right-thinking people in the society. Resultantly, Naxalism and Maoism have gripped a considerable part of tribal areas, bearing ominous portents, threat to the development process being the immediate repercussion.

Three contemporary antithetical dynamics-factors appear to aggravate the scenario and posit the tribal communities on a confrontational course.

First, the anachronous juxtaposition of the present state policies to privatise, energise and speedily industrialise versus the largely pre-industrial, in some cases pre-agricultural, laid-back socio-economic tribal milieu.

Second, the widening gulf between the rapidly globalising, modernising and prospering mainstream upper strata of the Indian people and the distant, marginalised, aloof, backward, impoverishing tribes people.

Third, the jagged interface between the aggressive domestic and multinational corporate sector avidly set to exploit the country's mineral, forest, water, etc. resources and the ST communities' quiescent berth over these resources since aeons, now threatened abrupt ouster there from.

Tribal Development Efforts and Outcomes

The Tribal sub-Plan (TSP) was launched in the Fifth Five Year Plan period 1974-79. It is conceived to be a holistic plan, combining regulatory and development components. The TSP aims at projectised thrusts for raising tribal standards in economic, educational, health, drinking water and other social sector spheres with the aid of financial resources pooled from state plans, Central ministries plans, Centrally sponsored schemes, Special Central Assistance of the Ministry of Tribal Affairs and institutional finance. Special administrative structure has been created for conveying the benefits to STs through integrated services delivery. It aims, in the first instance, at promoting and upgrading the STs' existing economic activities and livelihood patterns as also consonating new programmes and schemes with the ethos of the tribal communities that inhabit the project area.

As per a paper of the Planning Commission, during the Ninth Plan period, the total allocation to the TSP from the state plans was Rs. 22,314.22 crore i.e. 9.45 per cent and from the Central Ministries Rs. 6,462 crore i.e., 5.9 per cent. During the Tenth Plan period, flows from state plans amounted to Rs. 17,317.83 crore, while the figure for allocation from Central ministries has been left blank. If we persist with 5.9 per cent as the percentage of allocation from the Central ministries, it would mean roughly Rs. 10,358 crore. Thus, during the Ninth Plan and Tenth Plans periods, flows from state plans and Central plans added respectively to Rs. 28,776 crore and Rs. 27,678 crore, totalling roughly Rs. 56,000 crore.

Taking into consideration the contributions of Special Central Assistance of the Ministry of Tribal Affairs and grants under Article 275(1) of the Constitution, the aggregate may work out to more than Rs. 65,000 crore for the two Plan periods. Further, if investments during the Fifth, Sixth, Seventh and Eighth Plans periods are reckoned, the total outlay may well-nigh touch one lakh crore. The same paper estimates an expenditure of not more than 50 per cent of the outlay, which means that a maximum of Rs. 50,000 crore were spent during these six Plan periods. Assuming that half of this amount was directed towards infrastructure development, Rs. 25,000 crore would have been available for family-oriented schemes. No document either of the Planning Commission or of the Ministry of Tribal Affairs educates us as to the manner in which the quality, either in macro or micro scale, of tribal life improved with the help of this huge investment.

Indeed, no balance sheet is available showing financial investments made and physical and social benefits accruing. The monitoring and evaluation framework has been, to say the least, weak, but what we do know is that, as per the computations in the Planning Commission, in 1999-2000, 45.86 per cent of STs in rural areas lived below the poverty line as against 27.11 per cent all-India.

There are two important issues that need to be considered further in the light of experience so far. A small number of states have made a success of the tribal sub-plan so far. It looks that the pressure for improvement of tribal life has so far emanated mostly from the Centre. First, the state governments should implement the PESA Act in letter and spirit, bolstering the four-tier panchayat structure with adequate infrastructural support as well as financial devolutions. Having done so, their performance needs to be graded in parameters that can be worked out.

Secondly, the time has come for considering whether the Centre should wield the power of giving directions to states in the interest of welfare of STs and administration of scheduled areas in the state, under Article 339(2) and para 3 of the Fifth Schedule of the Constitution. The spirit, impulses and instincts of a democratic order may run counter to coercion. But should circumstances compel and it becomes essential, the issue of directions should not be ruled out altogether.

A draft National Tribal Policy has been on the anvil in the Ministry of Tribal Affairs. The draft has been a distillate of the observations of well-known milestones reports like those of Dhebar Commission (1961), Elwin Committee (1950), Shilu Ao Team (1969), Bhuria Commission (2004) and experience of life-long empathising experts. It should be finalised and operationalised.

In projects involving displacement of STs, the primary principle should be "no displacement" or minimum displacement in case of imperative, carefully selected projects. A priori, the principle of land for land should be followed in case of unavoidable displacement. The National Policy on Resettlement and Rehabilitation of Project Affected Families 2003 should include, among others, provisions for creating legal obligation to ensure resettlement and rehabilitation of project-affected families, inclusion of justiciable clauses as redressal mechanism in case PATF's rights are ignored and ensuring a better quality of life in rehabilitation sites than the PATFs were accustomed to.

However, despite the overabundance of development plans, programmes and activities initiated in the tribal areas, the majority of tribal people still continue to be backward. Many of the tribal problems are because of the fact that they predominantly inhabit in forest areas. According to the Forest Survey of India Report 2003, about 60% of the forests cover of the country and 63% of the dense forests lie in 187 tribal districts, i.e districts covered by the Fifth and Sixth Schedules of the Constitution. The inhospitable terrain of the forests restricts the reach of administration. But in spite of these difficulties the tribal people have to be reached and their backwardness has to be removed.

"The development paradigm pursued since independence has aggravated the prevailing discontent among marginalised sections of society. This is because the development paradigm as conceived by the policy makers has always been imposed on these communities, and therefore it has remained insensitive to their needs and concerns, causing irreparable damage to these sections. The benefits of this paradigm of development have been disproportionately cornered by the dominant sections at the expense of the poor, who have borne most of the costs. Development which is insensitive to the needs of these communities has invariably caused displacement and reduced them to a sub-human existence. In the case of tribes in particular it has ended up in destroying their social organisation, cultural identity, and resource base and generated multiple conflicts, undermining their communal solidarity, which cumulatively make them increasingly vulnerable to exploitation". Tribal development is a very complicated process comprising many delicate issues. While the development of the tribal people is attempted proper care has to be taken as the tribal people are sensitive and they value their distinctiveness. No general model of development can be applied to develop all the tribes in the country. However, tribal development should be effected without any imposition on the tribal communities and the tribal people should be allowed to develop along lines of their own genius and tradition. Besides safeguarding their interests and protecting their culture efforts must be made to bring them into the mainstream of the country's socio-economic-political process. But when deciding and implementing tribal development programmes the most vital fact to remember is to judge result not by statistics nor by the amount of money spent but by the quality of human character that has evolved.

11

Population Policy of India: A Critique

Archana Srivastva

By 'policy' is generally meant an official formal declaration or statement of some programme of action purported to be in public interest and to be adopted by an organisation, including a government. Before discussing population policy of India let us first of all define as to what is understood by population policy. The UNO considers a population policy to be inclusive of the measures and programmes designed to contribute to the achievement of economic, social, demographic, political and other collective goals through affecting critical demographic variables, namely, the size and growth of population, its geographic distribution and its characteristics. (Mishra: 2012, p.33). G. Myrdal (1968) has said that a population policy can be nothing less than a social policy at large. In his opinion a population programme must work itself into the whole fabric of social life. Under it are covered programmes and policies relating to increase and decrease of death and birth rates, increase in population growth rate and distribution of population, etc. J.J. Spengler (1966) says that under a national population policy are covered all such population problems which influence either quality or distribution of population. Population policy can be both explicit or implicit. Under explicit policy, population problems are solved directly whereas under the implicit policy, population problems are solved under some economic, social or political policy. The population policy, according to him, can be formulated with immediate as well as long term objectives. The objects of such a policy can also be quantitative, qualitative as well as spatial. Frank W. Notestein

(1964) considers the main objective of national population policy to be to ensure that there is reasonable gap between death and birth rates.

It is agreed that national population policy should consist of norms as well as methodology. The norm should be that birth of children should be well planned, and whether a child should or should not be born be also planned and be optional. The policy should make it possible to give them proper education and maintain good health for them; it should help in keeping population growth at a reasonable level. In methodology, he suggested that there should be improvement in production, increased availability of food supplies, sufficient storage of food, late marriages, tax on producing more children, etc. According to R.K. Mukerjee (1976): "A democratic population policy will accent the increased supply, but it will neglect the possibility of reducing demands. Anti-democratic population policies have opportunistically followed lines of action suggested in both groups." But D.V. Glass (1968) has rather appropriately said that it is wrong to believe that there can be a national population policy. In fact, there can be no universal national policy and even a nation cannot pursue a national policy for all times to come. It will have to change it with changing times.

Population policy is thus a very comprehensive term which includes all efforts which are made by any government to control and change a population structure. UNESCO Population Commission Report of the Adhoc Consultative Group of Experts of Population Policy, 23rd March, 1972 includes measures and programmes which contribute to the achievements of economic, social, demographic, political and other collective goals through critical demographic variables e.g. size and growth of population and its geographical distribution. If population policy is taken in its broadest sense, it will include birth, death and growth rates, internal and international migrations, and social, ethical, economic and biological factors which effect populations. Briefly speaking these are:

> There can, however, be a negative population policy, that is, a policy under which every effort is made to keep death rate high so that population could be controlled. In the past, people were concerned and worried about population growth, and accordingly population was kept low by such deliberate methods as infanticide and abortion. Then the old and infirm or the infected people were also killed. There are thinkers like Gerald F. Winfield (1948) and William Vogt Winfield (1963) who believe that in the under-developed countries, as long as birth rate is not controlled, death rate should be kept high, so that their population is controlled to some

Variables of Population Policy

Demographic	*Economic*	*Political*	*Social*
Fertility Rate, Death Rate, Migration Rate ;	Gross national income; per capita income ;	System of government, system of administration;	Status of women in society; status of women in family;
(i) National to international;	Income Distribution;	Extent of independence;	
(ii) Urban to Urban	Economic Welfare standard of living;	International realtions;	Social customs ;
(iii) Urban to Rural	Capital investment	Personnel of the Government;	Hold of religion on society;
(iv) Rural to Rural	Labour force,	Political party in power;	Rural urban population ratio;
(v) Rural to urban	Employment opportunities	Nature of government (coalition, non coalition)	Rituals of society
(vi) One state to the other	Natural resources; their exploitation and availability		Nature of society (orthodox or progressive)

extent. But their viewpoint has, however, not been appreciated due to its inherent inhumanitarianism.

A population policy can be a fertility-influenced policy, which may be either pro-natalist or anti-natalist. It can be both direct as well as indirect. Under pro-natalist policy, efforts are made for achieving high fertility. In societies marked by control of religion over population, it is believed that fertility is a matter of divine will and should not be checked. In such countries as Sweden, Japan and France, this policy is being followed. The anti-natalist policy aims to reduce child birth rate and fertility. Here the stress is on quality rather than on quantity. The direct methods of anti-natalist policies consist of using contraceptives and other birth-control devices, whereas indirect methods include disincentives for high birth rates and big-family size.

Population Policy: The Indian Context

In India family planning programme drew the attention of the leadership long back because it was felt that the main reason of India's poverty was its rapidly growing population which was increasing uncontrollably in proportion to food supplies, and that if this growth rate was not checked, the problem could become very serious. H.N. Kaul (1971) had said that reduction in fertility would make the process of modernisation a success. Drawing attention of the nation to the gravity of the problem, S. Chandrasekhar (1950) had said, "We are in great hurry. You cannot wait for a night. One exposure lasting 6 minutes leads to a baby and every year India adds one Australia to its population. During the decade 1961-71, 12.5 crore persons were added India's population. The below-poverty line ones and crores of other persons are unemployed, and thousands and thousands all over the country have no proper dwelling houses. As early as in 1968, about 10 crore persons were in reproductive age group and out of that only 8% were using family-planning methods. Keeping in view this magnitude of the problem, Gandhi, Rabindra Nath Tagore, Rajendra Prasad, Jawahar Lal Nehru among other leaders had raised their voice in favour of family planning programme in India.

It was as early as in 1925 that Dr. R.D. Karve opened a family planning clinic in Bombay in face of all opposition. Thereafter, at the official level, in 1930 the Mysore Government opened a family planning clinic in the state. In 1932 the Madras Government opened family planning clinics in the state. In December, 1935 Society for the Study and Promotion of Family Hygiene was founded with Lady Cowsaji Jehangir as its first President. The Indian

National Congress appointed a National Planning Committee under the Chairmanship of Jawahar Lal Nehru in the same year. The committee too strongly supported the family-planning programme, and in 1936 the first women family-planning centre was opened. In the same year Dr. A.P. Pillai conducted a family-planning course. In 1937, family planning clinics were opened both in U.P. and M.P. and in 1940, Sir P.N. Sapru successfully moved a resolution in the Council of States for the establishment of birth-control clinics throughout the country. In 1946, Bhore Committee in its report also made very strong recommendations in favour of opening birth control clinics. In 1949, the Family Planning Institute was set up in Bombay which is still working for population planning programme in India. In 1949, Jawahar Lal Nehru made the nation realise the need and necessity of family planning programme through the Planning Commission. Since then India has been constantly endeavouring for controlling population in the country.

In India family planning programme was formally adopted in 1952 and that continued till 1961. But more importance to this programme was given to it during the five-year plan when it was realised that birth rate was increasing faster than the anticipated rate. The clinical approach was then supplemented by the extension approach. In 1966, a full-fledged department of family-planning was created. It was during the fourth five-year plan that the programme was accorded a high priority and which still continues. Some of the guiding principles of the policy and the programme even today are as follows:

1. People should be properly educated about the need and necessity of using family planning services, so that they use them as and when these are provided.
2. The number of children which a family should have should be left to the care of the parents.
3. People should be persuaded and approached through leaders whom they respect.
4. Only such media should be used which is acceptable to the people.
5. Efforts should be made to provide services at the door steps.
6. These services should be made an integral part of the medical and public health services.

The whole programme was aimed at reducing the annual birth-rate from about 39 per thousand in 1969 to 30 by the end of third plan and 25 by 1983-84. The policy planners had then agreed that there was considerable need and necessity for population control in India. They felt that first of all, the people should be made to realise the need and necessity of controlling population alongwith having scientific analysis of causes of increasing population in the country. The likely hindrances in the process and the appropriate methods for their removal were also pondered over. The programme was made an integral part of health services and that in the hospitals, doctors were to be persuaded to convince the couples of reproductive age to adopt the programme. The people were to be educated in a manner suited to educational level of the masses.

In order to implement these ideas in 1953, the family planning research and programme committee was set up. A year later in 1954 Family Planning Grants Commission was set up. Though during the first five year plan, a provision was made for an expenditure of Rs. 65 lakhs out of which only 14.51 lakhs were actually utilised i.e. 77.7% remained unutilised. In fact, the states did not show much interest in the implementation of the programme. During the period of the plan, 147 family planning clinics were opened, out of which only 21 were in the rural areas. In addition to this, 205 privately-run clinics were financially assisted.

From all available evidence of its implementation, the policy has not led to desired results so far. Though during the emergency period in the country (June 25, 1975 to December 28, 1976) its persuasive character was forsaken to be replaced by compulsory sterilization, yet it proved to be only a drop in the ocean. Many authors and experts of India's population policy, particularly Bose (1996; 2001) and Banerjee (1971), have all noted the failure of the country's population policy.

The magnitude of the problem is gigantic as compared with that of other countries of the world. The problem becomes still more serious because India is a developing country; its seriousness can be imagined from the fact that one Australia is added to the population annually. In India at any point of the time, there are about 13.5 crore couples of reproductive age spread all over the country. These are spread in 5,60,000 villages, 3000 towns and cities covering over 1.23 million sq. miles of area. The couples are both literate as well as illiterate. In addition to this, there are areas where there are no adequate means of transportation and communication, and there are people who are traditionally opposed to the whole concept of family planning.

The policy in the rural areas is implemented through Primary Health Centres as well as Sub-Centres. In the urban areas there are urban family welfare planning clinics and centres, and each such centre caters to 50,000 population. At the district level there is district family welfare Bureau which forms part of the district medical and health organisation. It is headed by the District Family Welfare Officer. At the state level there is State Bureau, which is headed by State Family Welfare Officer. A full-fledged Department of Family Welfare exists both at the centre and at the state levels, which is responsible for guiding and directing all family welfare programmes for the whole nation. Both in the centre as well as in the states there are Cabinet Committees. The chief policy making body is the Central Family Welfare Council which is headed by the Union Minister of Health and Family Welfare.

The British reluctance in framing a clear population policy for India was pointed out by Chandrasekhar (1950) in the following words: "Till the early twenties, the British measured the prosperity of their rule, to some extent, by the magnitude of the net addition to India's population. The degree of satisfaction over and the justification of the British rule in India was directly in proportion to the substantial increase in the population that the censuses revealed every decade" (p. 28). Their reluctance was partly due to the controversy over birth control in Britain and partly to the policy of not interfering in a local matter, particularly of social or cultural nature. During the two world wars, the Indian elite had showed concern about the fast growth of the country's population, but a controversy was created doubting India being over populated, although the Neo-Malthusians were sure about it with appropriate statistics at their command. Even as early as in 1916, P. K. Wattal had supported the family planning movement through his book *The Population Problem in India.* As noted earlier, the first birth control centre in Bombay was opened by R.D. Karve in 1925, and that Rabindra Nath Tagore had strongly supported the then prevailing family planning movement.

It has been pointed out that despite the determination to vigorously implement the family planning measures, including those adopted during the emergency, not much success could be achieved. The prevailing policy was therefore reviewed in the year 2000, according to which the population growth was intended to be curbed such as not to exceed 110 crores by 2010. However, the census report for the relevant decade found it to have far exceeded the said target and stood at about 121 crores. The 2000 population policy further envisages the country's population to stabilise by 2040-45, but many projections have come out with grim prospects and disappointing results, predicting yet another failure of the so-called new population policy as it appears to be only carrots and no sticks to contain the phenomenon of population explosion.

On April, 16, 1976 (i.e. during the emergency period), the government of India outlined several approaches to the improvement of family planning programme. It provided for freezing of representation in the Lok Sabha and the state legislatures on the basis of 1971 census until the year 2001. Eight per cent of the central assistance to state plans was to be earmarked against the performance of family welfare programmes. It also proposed raising of age at marriage for girls to 18 years and for boys to 21 years. Any violation was to be treated as cognisable offence. The policy statement provided for a system of graded monetary compensation based on the number of living children at the time of sterilisation. The contribution of voluntary organisations was recognised and provision was made for the legitimisation of such bodies. It also recognised that family planning was a multi-facted problem and should be tackled on that basis. It promised government support to research in reproductive biology and contraceptive technology. The statement proposed legislation of compulsory sterilisation of a couple after they had certain number of children.

Impediments on the Way of Family Planning

It is universally believed that birth rate should be kept as low as possible, but in spite of all this, in most of the countries population is rapidly increasing. It is because there are certain impediments and hindrances on the path of family planning programme, which do not make the programme a success. One such great hindrance is the attitude of the old religious people and many of our religious leaders. According to them, both family planning programme as well as abortion are sins. Even today Roman Catholic Church does not favour family planning programme to a large measure. Similarly in India there are many religious leaders who have openly opposed family planning programme. Of course Hinduism does not oppose family planning, yet producing children is considered a religious duty of every Hindu. In rural India even today the child is thought to be a gift of God and abortion a sin. So is the case with many other religions, which though might not oppose the programme as such, yet they believe that producing of children is religious duty of the people belonging to their community. Some of the social reformers also oppose family planning programme as, according to them, such a programme encourages immorality and creates many social problems. Even the intellectuals also oppose this programme in some cases. The lack of proper education, costly availability of advice for family planning and non-availability of easy methods of checking births aggravate the problem further.

But, by and large, it is accepted that family planning is essential under present conditions. Even the poor are realising its need and necessity. Many people wish to have sexual satisfaction but do not wish to have children. Similarly, people are by and large realising that family planning helps in maintaining good health and reducing tensions in the family. It is wrong to think that the people cannot afford to have contraceptives etc., because most of the people all over the world are spending on unnecessary items. Thus, many impediments are cracking and many religious leaders are adjusting themselves to new environments.

All developing countries including India are very much in need of making the programme of family planning a success. Some suggestions for it may be as follows:

1. The state should provide employment guarantee for a small-sized family.
2. The people should be made more conscious about making the programme a success. For this they should be properly educated and the needed money and technical knowledge should be provided to them. It will be better if in every village a family welfare clinic is set up.
3. Adequate number of doctors, health visitors and other field staff should be commissioned into service. They should be made to feel that they are meeting a national need and as such they should work with a missionary spirit. Those who perform their duty successfully should be honoured and rewarded.
4. Latest family planning material should be supplied free of cost to the people and their use be demonstrated in a commonly accepted way, particularly through the visual media.
5. Mobile vans with contraceptives, etc., should be commissioned into service, particularly in the rural areas.
6. Only the first two children should be given a share in the ancestral property.
7. Family planning material should be supplied at cheap rates, if it is not possible to supply it free of cost.
8. The people should be properly educated through the media as to how they can enjoy a sexual life without producing children.
9. The people should be made to realise the need and necessity of spacing the birth of children, both for the health of the children as well as for that of the mother.

10. Family planning facilities should be provided not only in big hospitals but also in big industries, factories, etc.
11. After two children no free medical aid should be provided to those who are entitled to receive free or subsidised medical aid.
12. In promotions in services and allotting of houses and quotas, big family size should be treated as a disqualification.
13. The diseased couples should be discouraged from producing children.
14. Co-operation and assistance of both religious and social reformers and leaders should be obtained.
15. The people should be given population education and even in the school, this education should be given to children, though somewhat discretely.
16. Sometimes people increase their family size in order to have a son who is considered a guarantee for social security. This attitude must be discouraged by promoting consciousness of gender equality.
17. After every few years, a year should be declared as year of the childless.
18. Political parties should not allot tickets at the time of election to those who have big families.
19. A uniform code for family planning for all communities should be prepared and strictly enforced for which there has to be a strong political will.
20. Keeping in view the seriousness of the problems, it should not be politicised.

Conclusion

It seems best to us to conclude this discussion by referring to certain observations made by the Planning Commission of India as far back as in 1991, yet still relevant, as follows: "The population explosion which is undermining all our efforts towards socio-economic development of the country is perhaps the singlemost distressing problem faced by it. The 1991 census has revealed that while there has been a marginal decline in the rate of growth of population (from 2.22% in 1971-81 decade to 2.11% in 1981-91 decade), still the growth rate of about 2% per annum is very high. If the population growth continues as at present, the country will have about 100 crores people by the turn of the century and the population will double to about 170 crores by 2024 A.D. Such a large population would be vertically unmanageable and despite best efforts, it would not be possible to provide even the basic necessities of life to people at large. It is therefore imperative that the highest priority is accorded to population control." Though the speed of family planning and family welfare is slow, yet it is a matter of hope that the people of India will realise the need and importance of restricting the family size.

ENDNOTES & REFERENCES:

Myrdal, G. (1968), Asian Drama: An Enquiry into the Poverty of Nations, Vol. 3, California: Allen Lane, The Penguin Press.

Notestein, F.W. (1964), Population Growth and Economic Development, Colombo: Reprinted in Population and Development Review, No. 9 (1983): pp. 345-360.

Spengler, J.J. (1966), The Economist and the Population Question, American Economic Review, Vol. 56, No. 1 and 2, pp. 1-24.

Glass, D.V. (1968), 'Population Growth and Population Policy' in M.C. Sheps and J.C. Ridley, Public Health and Population Change: Current Issues, Pitsburgh: University of Pittsburgh Press.

UNESCO, Population Commission Report on Population Policy, March 1972.

United Nations (1973), Determinants and Consequences of Population Trends, Vol. I, New York.

Winfield, G.F. (1948), China: The Land and People, New York: William Sloane Associates.

Winfield, W.V.C. (1963), The Road to Survival, New York: William Morrow and Co.

Planning Commission of India (Dec. 1991), Population Control: Challenges and Strategies, New Delhi: Government of India.

Kaul, H.N. (1971), Population Control, Delhi-6: Atma Ram And Sons, p. 2.

Chandrasekhar, S. (1950), India's Population: Fact and Policy, Chidambaram: Indian Institute for Population Studies, Annamalai University.

Mukherjee, R.K. (1976), Family and Planning in India, Calcutta: Orient Longman.

Bose, A. (1996), Meeting India's Best Needs: The Human Development Index, Delhi: Government of India.

Ibid. (2001), Population of India, 2001 Census Results and Methodology, Delhi: B.R. Publishing Corporation.

Banerjee, D. (1971), Family Planning in India: A Critique and a Perspective, New Delhi: People's Publishing House.

Mishra, J.P. (2012), Demography, Agra: Sahitya Bhavan Publications, p. 331.

PART III

PUBLIC POLICY, DECENTRALIZATION AND DEVELOPMENT

12

Governance, Public Policy and Peace-Building in India: Exemplifying Status of Decentralization Policy in J&K State

Ashish Saxena

Scholars had only begun to analyze the beginnings of the "third wave" of democratization in the early 1980s, and the term peace-building only gained currency in the 1990s. By the early twenty-first century, the study of democracy and democratization had firmly become a subfield of political and sociological inquiry. Consequently, peace-building enjoyed a rapid rise, especially in policy circles, without the same degree of institutionalization. Specialists only recently began to pay more rigorous attention to the relationship between peace-building and political governance and, more specifically, the extensive research on democratization. Interestingly, democratization theory has also addressed the question of centralization versus decentralization in transitions. Peace implementation, therefore, often seems to require empowering a central authority to exercise control over all legitimate means of violence. Yet decentralization is often seen as necessary to remove the excessive and often abusive power concentrated in a central government, granting voice and power to local and marginalized populations.

The de-centring and the pluralisation of the state into a number of levels are considered to be a welcome development for several reasons. For one, governance promises an exit from bureaucratic, hierarchical and overloaded structures of decision-making, which are inept because they are unable to act either quickly or efficiently. The pluralisation of the state enables a multiplicity of agencies—which are free from rigid and tiresome bureaucratic constraints—to respond immediately to problems and issues that require swift resolution. Governance may make for efficiency and flexibility in the making of decisions. This is incontrovertible. But a word of warning may be in order here—that practices of governance may also aggravate a specific tendency that we find governing political imaginations today: that of technocratic management of politics.

Actually at first glance the new orthodoxy of governance seems to bear a deep resemblance to the old and by now discredited pluralist model, which had perceptibly shifted the balance of power from state to society. But when we take a hard look at the literature available to us today, we find at least two major differences between pluralism and governance. Firstly, despite the fact that pluralism recognized that society is constituted by a number of dense associations, it assumed that these organizations pursued their own distinctive, different, and separable interests and goals. They therefore competed with each other. And this was a distinct good, for competition between different groups achieved a rough and ready balance of power in and for society. Secondly, the pluralists had demoted the state to being just another, and not necessarily the most consequential institution among a variety of other associations. But in the ultimate instance, when social transactions broke down, the state was expected to perform the role of arbitrator and regulator. Theories of governance on the other hand assume that distinct institutions pursue overlapping ends, even if they track different paths to the same goal. Thirdly theories of governance are more ambivalent as far as the state is concerned. The state may or may not define the regulatory mechanisms that lay down the ground rules for net-working. It may turn out that the state is just one and not necessarily the most important institution in governance. The role of the state in governance in other words is contextual as well as contingent.

Contextually, conflict and violence is the intentional generation of chaos and crisis for the purpose of destabilizing established regime. As a regulating and remedial mechanism to the forms of dysfunctionalities, the role of State and its specific form of governance becomes an issue of primary concern. Contemporary issues of good governance reflects that the governance is considered good when the state retrenches, becomes less powerful, assumes a low profile, and operates in a network with private interests and groups, each of which is as powerful as the other. Apparently, decentralization is the essence of federalism, having a system of multi-level government and multi-level planning. Its execution may enable efficient allocation of resources, improve governance, accelerate economic growth, achieve a gender balance and empower weaker sections of society. After Independence, the statutory recognition of the third tier of fiscal structure and evolution of formal three-tier federalism subsequent to the 73rd and 74th Constitutional amendment in 1993 is evident. It was comprehended that local government in democratic polities are likely to be more effective in providing certain goods and services than are national and provincial governments. Thus, there is an urgent need of debating the successes of third-tier in delivering public services in different States and to examine extent of sub-State decentralization in different States. It is to be emphasized that decentralization must proceed with sensitivity to the specific context, only in functional areas and in societies where decentralization is likely to foster participation and peace. The usual question that is asked in this context is the following—has the state disappeared? Keeping in view the general understanding of governance and nation-state in the conflicting situation, the paper humbly addresses such issues pertaining to conditions of governance in Jammu and Kashmir State (J&K). It is to be emphasized that the said state had a contentious history and allied disturbances, especially conflicting issues and terrorism at large, owing to its strategic location and conflicting ethnic diversities. The paper analyzes the progression of local government and implementation of three-tier federal framework in India, with special reference to Jammu and Kashmir (J&K) State.

Poor-Governance in J&K State: Glaring Antecedent

Signifiers of good governance are—participatory democracy, accountable, transparent, responsive, effective, equitable and inclusive, rule of law, legitimate and acceptable to the people, promote gender balance, strengthens indigenous mechanisms, efficient and effective in the use of resources, service oriented, able to develop the resources and methods of governance, tolerates and accepts diverse perspectives, etc. these features are very important when government functions in conflicts zone. But deficit of theses features in J&K has enhanced frequent conflicts in the state. In a generic sense 'governance' refers to the task of running a Government or any other entity. An important distinction between government and governance is the notion of the civil society. Governance transcends the state to include civil society organizations and the private sector, which is significantly missing in J&K state.

According to Chandran (2009; 20), there are two sets of conflicts relating to Jammu and Kashmir—the conflict in Kashmir and the conflict of Kashmir. The conflict of Kashmir is primarily linked to the larger Indo-Pak conflict and its actor includes India, Pakistan, and Kashmiris. The conflict in Kashmir refers to the relations between New Delhi and various communities and their aspirations in Jammu, Kashmir and Ladakh regions. For example, people of Ladakh have been demanding a Union Territory status within India, while the people of Jammu region have been demanding a separate state, again within India. A major section within Kashmir Valley demands complete independence from India, while another section demands more autonomy in terms of federal-provincial relations. Political manipulation, bad governance and corruption have been major issues for all three regions. In the context of Kashmir, the political, bureaucratic and corporate governance is hostage not to two decade but the six-decade old conflict. Historically speaking, governance has always carried a big question mark in the J&K State.

Unfortunately, India perceived both the 'conflict in' and 'conflict of' J&K mainly through the prism of terrorism. Internally, the absence of militant attacks is seen as the presence of peace and political stability in Kashmir. Problems of governance are seen as an offshoot of militancy; hence, the government has believed that once the latter is brought under control, there would be better governance. Issues such as corruption and bad governance are carpeted under militancy. Counterinsurgency operations have assumed more significance, without understanding that militancy has been the product of certain political and that once these political questions are addressed, the militancy would automatically die down. These political questions raised by the Kashmiris may be real or imaginary or both; but it is the duty of the government to address them politically (Chandran; 2009: 21).

The center's authority in Kashmir has always been tenuous, and Kashmiri support for full integration uncertain. The ruling National Conference government ran a patronage-based, one-party system heavily beholden to political leaders in Delhi. Yet despite corruption, mis-governance, curtailed freedoms of speech, and inordinate dependence on central largesse, the National Conference enjoyed a high degree of legitimacy and little popular opposition (Meyerle; 2005). Commenting upon the issue of insurgency in Kashmir, Siddharth Prakash (2000) is of the view that militancy in Kashmir has been motivated solely by political considerations. It has unearthed the economic roots of the imbroglio by assessing factors that shaped the agricultural and industrial policies of the state. Additionally, this study has demonstrated that even supposedly benevolent decisions, such as equitable land ownership, can be debilitating to production.

Surprisingly, the 2002 elections in Jammu and Kashmir, which were held in four phases, were fair. But it was not necessarily free, particularly for those who have seen and lived with violence for the last 12 years. For the people of Kashmir life has been and is a fight against terror. It did not change during the elections; in fact, it only worsened. The militants had threatened to disrupt the polls forcing the government to deploy the largest-ever security forces to help in the conduct of the polls. The state, in any case, is known for its centralized structure of power and despite persistent regional discontent, the successive state governments have resisted all demands for devolution of power. Even, the state has still to bring its Panchayat Raj Act of 1989 at par with the 73rd Amendment Act of the Constitution of India.

Year 2010 witnessed the controversial act—Armed Forces Special Powers Act (AFSPA), which generated huge conflict and distrust in the state. Needless to mention, this people's movement was altogether different from the 1990's armed revolt against Indian army. Searching for a democracy out of the barrel of a gun and coercion resulted into stone pelting as a new form of gunless terrorism. Contextually, its healing demanded reducing security presence and delivering genuine democracy.

The connotation local self governance has been defined in terms of enjoying functional, financial and administrative autonomy in their functioning at different levels. However, the Paradox is, even though the 73rd Amendment Act has been uniformly passed to regularize self-governance but the corresponding State Acts have been amended time-to-time to either rationalize or invalidate the existence of PRI's (Panchayati Raj Institution) as model of grassroot democracy. It is realized that the PRI's normally suffered from lack of motivated leaders, shortage of staff, lack of financial resources as well as autonomy in decision-making. Planning from below remained only in theory as all the terms and conditions of the various rural development schemes were decided at the central or state government levels. Though, the J&K state enjoys the special status of special category state with center aided funding, the prevailing local self-governance in J&K State is the evidence of such undemocratic practice.

Decentralization in J&K State: The Ethical Problem

The J&K State has seen more radical social reform than in many other States in the country. It can be judged through the historical document called "The Naya Kashmir", which became the inspiring source of National Conference policies and Programmes. The implementation of Land Reforms (1948-1953) is one radical attempt in this direction.

Execution of Article 370, a perfect sign of decentralization and State autonomy, demand for State Trifurcation for better regional power sharing, plea for Self-rule by regional parties etc. are glaring examples for decentralization practices operating in the state. Envisaging this background, it is encouraging that J&K State is a congenial setting for the successful democratic decentralization and social transformation. This is also evident from the fact that the idea of democratic decentralization in J&K was initiated as early as during Maharaja Hari Singh's reign in 1935, since then the metamorphosis of Panchayati system is taking place to justify the prevalence of local governance in the State, it was followed by the agenda of the New Kashmir Manifesto of 1940's and ultimately the J&K Panchayati Raj Act, 1989 which emphasized the implementation of local self government and grass root democracy in the State. It may make anyone to presume that these dedicated attempts in different phases of history might have led to the efficacy of Panchayati Raj Institution in the State, which could not be actually comprehended till date.

At this juncture it is to be emphasized that the decentralization measure ensuring people's participation in the affairs of the State can pull the State out of the political turmoil and can proliferate order and stability in the State, unfortunately it has found itself of late. It is further hypothesized that achieving greater democracy at the local level must be a crucial component not only in achieving quality democracy but also in combating alienation among the people against nation-state and also insurgency and terrorism in the state.

Trajectory of Public Policy on Participatory Democracy in J&K State

This section critically reviews the salient features of the various Acts pertaining to local governance in the state and the possible gaps.

Village Panchayat Act of 1935

The introduction of local self-government in J&K State commences with the promulgation of J&K Village Panchayat Regulation Number 1 by the Maharaja of the State in 1935. The preamble of the Act laid: "Whereas it is expedient to establish in J&K State the village Panchayats to assist in the administration of civil and criminal justice and also to manage the sanitation and other common concerns of the village". A Department of Panchayats and Rural development affiliated to the Revenue Department was establishment in 1936. The department organized "Dehat-Sudhar Committees" to advice panchayats. These committees laid more emphasis on voluntary work (*Halshari*) in the villages. The member of this committee included non-panch also or others who were not in any way connected with panchayats or rural development. It is emphasized by me that the "dehat-sudhar" committee should be revived and empowered in the contemporary local governance to act a watchdog and a pressure group for the existing panchayat functioning.

J&K Village Panchayat Act of 1958

After the coming of Balwant Mehta Committee in 1957, which made a strong plea for devolution of power to lower level through Panchayat, the State was first to take lead by passing a new J&K Panchayat Act of 1958. In a bid to express solidarity with the ruling elite at the Centre, rather than developing any genuine concern for implementing Panchayati Raj, The State government passed the J&K Village Panchayat Act, 1958. In this Act, any 'panch,' 'sarpanch' or 'Naibsarpanch' could be removed from office in case his conduct in office was 'undesirable'. The Panchayats in the State continued to remain dormant even after the Indira Gandhi-Sheikh Abdullah Accord of 1975.

The popular government of 1977 (Sheikh Abdullah) introduces the *Single Line Administration* with the objective of securing a mechanism for developing the planning process at the district level and to take complete account of resource endowment. The Single Line Administration has assured the participation of the people in the developmental process and paved the way for decentralization and delegation of authority. It is unfortunate that due to some political upheavals in the State, these institutions remained dormant for some time. The Act provided for establishment of Panchayat Adalats to decentralize the administration of justice (ISS: 90).

J&K Panchayati Raj Act 1989

The panchayats as the local institutions of self-government are lying moribund for a very long time especially from 1982. Prior to this, the panchayat institutions existed only at the grassroot level and there was no linkage with any other institutional framework at the block or district Level.

The preamble of the Act states: "Whereas it is expedient to promote and develop Panchayati Raj in the State as an instrument of vigorous local self government to secure effective participation of the people in the decision making process and for over-seeking implementation of development programmes".

Existing Three Tier Model

i) ***Halqa Panchayat:*** There shall be Halqa Panchayats for every halqa[3] (area comprising a village or such contiguous number of villages as determined by the government), consisting of 7-11 panches including Sarpanch and Naib-Sarpanch, with village level worker (VLW) as the Panchayat Secretary.

ii) ***Block Development Council:*** It is at the block level and *consists* of Chairperson, all sarpanch of halqa panchayat and chairpersons of marketing societies within the jurisdiction of the Block. Here BDO act as the secretary of BDC.

iii) ***District Planning and Development Board:*** It is at the district level with Chairmen of BDC, M.P. of the area, Member of State legislature of area, Chairperson of Town Area committee at the district level.

Panchayat Adalat: There shall be a Panchayat Adalat for every Halqa and consist of five members nominated by prescribed authority. The term of member will be five years and three members from the quorum. Further all cases pending before a Panchayat adalat constituted under J&K village Panchayat Act 1958, for matters within the jurisdiction of a Panchayat Adalat shall be transferred to the concerned Panchayat Adalat. Adalat can only go with limited criminal jurisdiction as referred in the code of Criminal procedure, Samvat 1989.

Looking to the Panchayat Election-2001 of Jammu division, it reveals the fact that there were few vacant post of Sarpanch and Panch lying in various districts, especially Doda, where the post were yet to be notified by the government also. Surprisingly, Table 2 reveals that the percentage voting in Jammu division was quiet satisfactory except Doda again. However, interesting fact is that out of total contest 9.95% of the Sarpanch were elected unopposed however 37.39% of the panch were elected unopposed. This is yet a researchable question that why there significant proportion of unopposed elected representatives. Either it lacks the democratic character or the people are not interested for contest.

Probable Constraints in Empowering PRI in J&K

- Lack of periodic panchayat elections (held after 23 years) in the State might have really de-motivated the spirit of true grass root leadership among the rural masses. Only a small proportion would have been exposed to leadership qualities. Thus on one hand the panchayat leadership included the first generation Sarpanch and Panches lacking even basic skills for public speaking or conducting a meeting. They would have to enter the hitherto unknown but daunting world of governance, unequipped with the requisite training and skills.
- Lack of implementation of 73rd amendment in true spirit discouraged the marginalized categories to share and exercise their rights pertaining to rural power structure. However, now it has been materialized by the state in 2003. It is assumed that the next elections will follow the strict norms of 73rd Amendment Act to make the next election and the PRI system more effective in terms of real decentralization and participation of marginalized grass root masses.
- Overall, the lack of implementation of 3-tier system, lack of awareness, proper training and orientation about the rights and duties of PRI's by the government to the elected members made the prevailing local self governance defunct in the state.
- Jammu and Kashmir will have around 1600 new Panchayats as the Shahwaz Commission for Delimitation of Panchayats has submitted final report to the Government for its approval. With Government approving fresh delimitation of Panchayats after objections, number of Panchayats in Jammu and Kashmir has gone up from 2600 to 4200. Next Panchayat elections, due from July last year but delayed due to delimitation, will be held on 4200 Panchayats. **Tentatively, in Jammu division, the number of Panchayats is going to increase 59 percent after delimitation while in Kashmir Division, the increase is 46 percent.**

Suggestions for Enhancing Peace-Building and Empowering PRI in J&K

- The first steps what government can do as part of the good governance is that they can invite people from different conflicts zone to understand the conflicts and make conflicts studies of certain areas. But government has not taken serious steps by involving civil society group and hence conflicts have not stooped in the region. The presence of Arms Forces Special Power Act of 1958 clearly shows how a draconian law still exists in a democratic country. Good governance means repealing such acts which are not pro people. As one of the chief demands of the stone-throwing pro-azadi protesters has been the withdrawal of the controversial Armed Forces Special Powers Act (AFSPA). The Act which has been in force in J&K since 1990. The partial withdrawal of AFSPA will be the first step in initiating this long-delayed political process.

- Governance deficit in J&K is directly linked to the absence of political institutions at the grassroots, which has led to a concentration of state power in Srinagar and Delhi. Strengthening of local bodies could empower people at the grassroots and unable better use of public funds.
- The violent response of the state to the violence of the extremists has failed to bring peace and has exacerbated the cult of violence. The situation could conceivably be salvaged only by vesting all powers of governance—regulatory and developmental—in the elected Panchayati Raj Institutes at the village, block and district levels. The zila (district) parishad (ZP) should be the representative district government, subsuming under it all existing line departments including the police. Being more representative, the ZP would be responsive to the urges and aspirations of the people below. True local self-government will bring effective governance implying accountability, transparency, participation, openness and the rule of law between State, Bureaucrats and masses. By adopting these ethics it can play crucial role in overall societal transformation. Thus, implementation of 73rd amendment will lead to wider participation of the extreme marginal like SC/ST/ Women in the State affairs, leading to higher integration of socially alienated masses. This may make them to be part of participatory democracy in true sense. Establishment of effective local governance will ultimately lead to better all round interlinkage between State, bureaucrats and masses. These '*Halqa panchayats*' may act as check post against anti-State elements in their local areas and can play a crucial role in combating militancy in the State. The panchayat members should be given extra powers to monitor the criminal activities of their area and they should be accountable for any mishappiness in their jurisdiction. This will also expand the hands of

security forces for better control and surveillance of state's territory (Saxena, 2008).

- The possible approach by the government, policy-planners, politicians and civil society should not be 'elite-level' integration i.e. favouring elitist ideology, elite politics or elitist development but they should also pacify and incorporate 'All' (sub-regional and peripheral masses) in the mega-project of restructuration and re-conciliation (Saxena, 2007).

Regarding the issue of democratic decentralization following issues need attention:

- Effective governance implies accountability, transparency, participation, openness and the rule of law between State, Bureaucrats and masses. By adopting these ethics, J&K state can come out of political trauma and will promote effective decentralization through local self-governance, which at its front can play crucial role in societal transformation.
- Gram Sabha (*Halqa majlis*) is really a cornerstone of the entire scheme of decentralization as within this arrangement only the face-to-face community interaction exist and which makes the system more transparent and accountable. If the members and masses don't realize the relevance of '*Halqa majlis*', the PRIs will only remain as agencies of development in rural areas. Thus there is a need of timely '*halqa majlis*' with effective quorum for better results of PRI's.
- Keeping the constraints like prolonged implementation of PRI in the state and now the newly implemented 73rd amendment in the State, requires rigorous support and training, for the future nominated/ elected representatives of PRI's especially at *halqa* level and that too for the SC/ST/women, who are new entrants and probably participating in electoral politics for the first time. Most of them may not have had experience of participating in public life, supervising delivery of services, designing developmental plan or party politics earlier. Obviously, these functionaries would have no clear vision of their role and its evolving nature. It is necessary that they be trained to develop potential as well as appreciate limits of their position to enable them to discharge their functions properly. Here the training implies genuine and effective efforts and the official formalities. It should mean re-socialization of the elected representatives for the new

world. However one such effort has been initiated in the state by ISS, New Delhi on "Strengthening of good governance".

- Finally, the crucial suggestion-cum-potentiality in establishment of effective local governance is, it will lead to better interlinkage between State, bureaucrats and masses. It is also felt that achieving greater democracy at the local level must be a crucial component not only in achieving quality democracy but also in combating alienation among the people against nation-state and also insurgency and terrorism in the state. Thus, apart from viewing one practical aspect of 'answering bullets with ballot', the other practical possibility can be, empowering each *halqa* panchayats about their alliance with security forces for accountability of their respective area regarding incidence owing to terrorism and other security threats. This may include the constitutional provision of maintaining security and vigilance of their respective '*halqas*'. In nutshell, these measures can play a crucial role in combating militancy in the State.

Endnotes & References

Aslam, M. (1999) 'Panchayati Raj in J&K-Retrospects and Prospects', in J.Roy (eds.) *Restoration of Panchayats in J&K,* New Delhi: ISS.

Chandran, Suba. 2009. J&K: India's objective and strategies, Epilogue, Vol. 3, issue 7, July 1, 2009, Jammu

Prakash, Siddhartha, 2000; 'The political economy of Kashmir since 1947', Contemporary South Asia, 9:3, pp. 331 To link to this article: DOI: 10.1080/713658753 URL: http://dx.doi.org/10.1080/713658753

Nisar, Sabiha (2001) *Development of local self-government in J&K 1846-1947—A historical background,* Srinagar: Gulshan publisher.

Parthasarthy, G and Radha Kumar (2006): *Frameworks for a Kashmir settlement,* A Delhi Policy Group Publication, New Delhi.

Saxena, Ashish (2002): *Women's representation in Panchayati Raj—A study of Halqa Panchayat in Jammu region* in N.A. Mir (eds) "Panchayati Raj—Why and How", J&K State Resource Centre, Srinagar.

Saxena, Ashish (2007). 'Democratic Decentralization: A way out for Peace-Building process in Jammu and Kashmir' in Journal of '*Security & Society*', Vo. 3, No. 2, winter.

Saxena, Ashish (2008). 'Pragmatism of implementation of Panchayati Raj in J&K: A Critical Appraisal' in *Indian Journal of Federal Studies,* No. 2.

Task force on Panchayati Raj (2000) *Panchayati Raj in India—Status report 1999,* New Delhi: Rajiv Gandhi Foundation.

13

Minority Policies in India: The Post Sachar Scenario

Muneer Illath

Debates and deliberations over the intensity, success and failures of policies aimed at the reversal of historical disadvantages and discriminations of marginalized communities in India have dominated the scholarship in social science for the past few years (Kohli 2001, Hasan 2009, Sheth 2010, Basant and Shariff 2010). However, many recent studies have been apprehensive about the differential policies and approaches to disadvantages within the diverse socially unprivileged sections in Indian Society (Galenter 1984, Hasan 2009). In the case of India's largest religious minorities, i.e., the Muslims, policy interventions at national and state level remained highly controversial due to the historical location of the community as well as the heterogeneous nature of their social, economic and political status.

This paper attempts to investigate the actions and responses from multiple stakeholders in the policies aimed at addressing the socio-economic grievances of Muslims in India with a special focus on the policies and programs initiated after the publication of the Prime Minister's High level Committee Report headed by Justice Rajinder Sachar in 2006. Investigating government's response to Sachar Committee recommendations, Harsh Mander (2011) observes that solution to any problem begins with an acknowledgment that it exists and this public realization echoed in Sachar Committee report would have to be actualized through inclusive development, mainstreaming of community while respecting diversity as the way out of the deprivation trap. However, many such studies conducted after the publications of SCR and subsequent plan of action laid out find that such hopes of addressal of historical disadvantages stands substantially belied even after 7 years of the implementation of the recommendations of SCR. There are some other recent documents, especially the Social Development Report (2012) highlighting the misplaced focus of minority oriented programs and siphoning off schemes and funds intended for minority welfare in the country to majority population or non-Muslim minorities.

Social development has been one area in which India has been outperformed by the otherwise poorer neighbors like Nepal, Pakistan and Sri Lanka. It was understood that, among many other reasons, policy initiatives and implementations often aimed at accelerated growth did not simultaneously translate into inclusive development has also lead to huge social and economic inequality between rich and poor as well as the socially privileged and dis-privileged groups. Thus, economic growth with social inequalities experienced by countries like India calls for a serious relook at the policy framework of the past few decades. It is realized that the huge new inequalities are feeding into existing ones in a society where certain groups are already disadvantaged. The recent Human Development Report 2011, published by the Planning Commission of India highlights the fact that despite affirmative action, a high incidents of poverty persists among the Scheduled Castes (SC) and Scheduled Tribes (ST) as well as Muslims. One third of the Muslim population, the report shows, continues to live Below Poverty Line.

The History of Public Policies for the Minorities in India

The historical accounts of constitutional provisions and public policies for lower castes and religious minorities have largely addressed the questions of discrimination, deprivation and exclusion suffered by these communities. Scholars like Zoya Hasan (2009), for instance, focus on how the state proposes to deal with the problems of these groups and the repercussions of such provisions and policies in the protection and promotion of the interests of the deprived and the disadvantaged. However, she argues that the well-being of minorities has suffered more due to the lack of attention to issues of institutionalized inequality and deprivation than is commonly supposed (2009: 41). It was partially explained by the fact that public policies for these two groups fall into two distinct types as empowerment was the focal point for the lower castes whereas for the minorities protection of their religious identities formed the core of policies. Against the background of partition and Hindu Muslim violence surrounding it, the policies towards minorities consisted of measures aimed at recognition and protection of religious identity.

A closer analysis of the policy initiatives towards the protection of minority rights in India clearly reveals that there was a tendency to over-emphasize identity which resulted in a situation where the inequalities and deprivation were not adequately recognized and hence not frontally addressed. In other words, the readiness and political will to enhance the social welfare and rights of the un-privileged sections that marked the policies towards the lower castes was seriously missing in the case of Muslims in India. Probably, as many scholars have suspected, this clear reluctance to be similarly proactive with regard to minorities, despite mounting evidence of their deprivation and disadvantages, could reveal the early seeds of development deficits and exclusions among Muslims in the country.

This differential treatment of disadvantaged castes and minorities has had an overwhelming influence of public policies and outcomes for these groups. For a long time the state avoided the subject of development of minorities and these was one factor responsible for keeping them backward. There was very little serious public or policy debates with regard to minority development, no agreed thinking over precisely what constituted the interests of minorities and the policies needed to alleviate their problems. In these circumstances it is hardly surprising that the actual status of minorities did not figure in the formulation of public policies until the submission of the Sachar Committee Report in 2006.

Social policies in India are conventionally based on the simultaneous recognition by the constitution of cultural rights of faith-communities and the development rights of the structurally and historically deprived groups *within every* community of faith. In this recognition lies the secular foundation of our social policies. Political commentators like D.L. Sheth (2010) observe that issues like providing Schedule Caste status to ex-untouchable groups of minority religious communities ought to have been addressed and resolved in the existing framework of secular social policies. In effect, a new discourse was initiated which sought to shift the focus of social policies *from backwardness to communality of groups*, wherein religious minorities are treated as totalities in politics and as undifferentiated units of development discourse and policies. This shift has long-term negative implications for the secularization process.

Sachar Committee Report and Policy Recommendations

As one of the most comprehensive and meticulously crafted document on socio-economic conditions of Muslims in India, Sachar Committee Report exposes many myths surrounded by the development profile of minorities in India. The crux of the report lies in community's position in major socio-economic indicators of development as, sometimes, even worse than the country's acknowledged historically most disadvantaged communities, the Schedule Castes and Scheduled Tribes. The report argues that the current development profile of the community was not an evidence of favoured treatment, but a testimony of cumulative and comprehensive official discrimination and neglect.

Serious concerns over the question of identity, security and equity of the community raised by SCR also signaled the importance of addressing these interconnected priorities of development and claimed that the extent to which these issues are addressed would determine the development deficits of majority of Muslim people. The report also argued against piecemeal approaches and emphasized that policy framework to deal with the problems of the Muslims should also recognize matters like mainstreaming and inclusiveness of the community, enhancement of diversity in residential work and educational spaces, measures to enhance equity in order to reduce the sense of discrimination that the community perceives etc. (Basant and Shariff 2010: 15).

The Sachar Committee Report (2006) finds that despite being more urbanized than other socio-religious communities, Muslims in India have fallen behind on all education parameters since independence. The community suffers from low literacy rate, higher percentage of school drop outs and lower average years of school attendance. The report attributes, among many other causalities, under-investment in government schools, discrimination and lack of encouragement among local dominant groups as the root cause of these disadvantages in the educational sector. The representation of the community members in higher education, which serves as the catalyst for socio-economic mobility, has been abysmally low and has even been lower than the former untouchable communities in the country.

While winding up discussion on the varied forms of deprivation among Indian Muslims the Report makes some observations of which a few are cited below

- Notwithstanding the degree of development varies in different states it was observed that the community exhibits deprivation in almost all aspect of development. By and large, Muslims rank somewhat above SCs/STs but below Hindu-OBCs, Other Minorities and Hindu-General (mostly upper castes) in almost all indicators considered. Among the states that have large Muslim populations, the situation is particularly grave in the states of West Bengal, Bihar, UP and Assam.

- In addition to development deficit, the perception among Muslims that they are discriminated against and excluded is widespread. Effective policies to deal with relative deprivation of Muslims in the country should sharply focus in inclusive development and 'mainstreaming' of the community while respecting diversity.

Policies for Social Inclusion: The Highlights of Ranghanath Misra Committee Report (2007)

A year later the pronouncement of Sachar Committee Report which demonstrated the multiple dimensions of marginality and exclusion among India's largest religious minority, i.e. the Muslims, the Government of India resolved to constitute a national commission with five members in the committee, popularly known as Ranganath Misra Committee (2007) to be entrusted with the following terms of references:

1. To suggest criteria for identifying the socially and economically backward sections in the religious and linguistic minorities in the country.
2. To recommend measures for the welfare of the above-mentioned sections including reservation in education and government employment.
3. To suggest the necessary constitutional, legal and administrative modalities for the implementation of its recommendations.

In order to understand the lifestyle of minorities in India, the committee has looked into the diverse socio-economic profiles of these communities including demography, rural-urban distribution, sex composition, literacy and educational status, marital status and livelihood pattern. Similarly, to probe into the magnitude of the quality of life the following indicators were used:

1. pattern of landholding
2. source of income
3. health status

While Sachar Committee Report had exclusively focused on socio-economic and educational status of Muslims in the country and the three inter-related problems that they have been experiencing, namely the issues related identity, security and equity, the Ranganath Misra Committee Report lays emphasize on the linguistic and religious minorities in the country and also suggesting some of the practical measures and recommendations for the welfare of these communities including reservation. The committee also acknowledges the present constitutional and legal obstacles for the implementation of specific reservation for the minorities and suggest some of the administrative modalities to tackle these issues

While elucidating the recommendations and modalities for the implementation of welfare and development measures for the religious and linguistic minorities in India, the Ranganatha Mishra Committee has observed the following:

a) The criteria for identifying the socially and economically backward classes should be uniform based on social, educational and economic indices equally applicable to all. In fact those educationally and economically backward are, by and large, also socially backward. (144)
b) The committee suggests that there should be single list of socially and economically backward including religious and linguistic minorities based on common criteria. The committee strongly felt that education is crucial for the development and enhancement of social and economic status, thus equal and quality education should be extended to all. The committee particularly notes the educational status of vast majority of Muslims in the country is far below many other religious communities like Sikhs, Christians and Jains. (145)
c) The Ranghanatha Mishra Committee report notes that work participation is an important sign and criterion for identifying the economic status of households and communities.
d) With regard to reservation the commission was of the view that ideally the criteria for reservation should be socio-economic backwardness and not religion or caste. Further it is said that the Article 16(4) should be the basis for providing reservation benefits to minority groups who are socially and economically backward.

Community's Perspective on Remedies

In the wake of Sachar Committee recommendations scholars like Rakesh Basant and Abusaleh Sheriff (2010) have looked into the diverse and multiple views on the remedies for problems faced by Muslims. They observe that while a significant proportion of people were in favour of reservation in education and employment, there was no unanimity on this as remedy. While some argued for the reservation for all Muslims, others wanted it only for Dalit Muslims. Still others preferred an adequate inclusion of Muslims in the OBC category and a few argued in favour of economic criteria-based reservation. Finally there were also some who felt that no reservation is required if equal access and non-discrimination can be ensured.

Similarly, there were differences in views on the need for community specific programs to alleviate their conditions. While some were in favour of such programs, others argued for better implementation of existing programs for the poor. The need to encourage community-based initiatives, however, was felt widely. More the need to enhance political participation by removing anomalies for stressed. It was in response to community's perspective on the remedial measures to reverse developmental deficits that mainstreaming of inclusiveness of the community as well as the enhancement of diversity in residential, work and educational spaces were seriously felt in the community. It was in this backdrop the proposal for setting up Equal Opportunity Commission (EOC) and developing a diversity index was accentuated in the Sachar Committee Report.

Taking Stock of Development Deficits: The post-Sachar Report

Conscious of the ground reality of neglect, penury and historical disadvantages that Indian Muslims have been suffering from, the UPA government took a number of steps and established new institutions and policies to address the concerns of minorities. These concerns included the setting up of the Ministry of minority affairs, National Commission for linguistic and religious minorities and National Commission for minority Educational Institutions. The Prime minister's new 15 point programme for the welfare of minorities was intended to focus action sharply on issues linked with social, economic and education uplift of minorities and provide for earmarking of outlays in certain schemes in order to monitor the progress. The flagship program of Ministry of Minority affairs in the 11th Plan, i.e. the Multi-Sectoral Development Programme (MSDP) was intended to focus on development deficits in 90 Muslim concentrated districts of the country.

- The scale of government interventions is too small to account for the large numbers who live with these deprivations.
- The implementation of the program is limited, because it does not

sufficiently identify and address the actual obstacles which bar the educational and economic attainments of Muslim people, and their fair access to public services.

- The institutional structures designed to implement these initiatives—right from the Union ministry to implementing officials at different levels—require further conviction, clout and clear mandate to directly battle the socio-economic structural discrimination and denial encountered by the community.

The relative malfunction and breakdown of the plan of action can be partially attributed to the failure of institutional machinery created by the government to deliver those modest initiatives. For instance, Harsh Mander's report observes that "In districts, the officials who were assigned to execute these programs were de-motivated, untrained and often carried mainstream prejudices against Muslim people. They are accused to preparing plans without ever consulting the intended recipients: Muslim youth, women and impoverished workers.

The efficacy of positive discrimination such as reservations for reducing social economic marginalization of disadvantaged sections is said to have its negative and positive consequences. Some scholars feel that such policies are more likely to be successful if the beneficiary community is fairly homogenous and its members have been and continue to be subject to mistreatment and stigmatization by other communities (Basant and Sharrif 2010). It was in this perspective that heterogeneity within different Socio-religious communities was used against policies of reservation and only financial support was granted. However Sonalde Desai and Veena Kulkarni (in Basant and Sharrif 2010) observe that secular growth in education (through policies directed at the whole population) devoid of positive discrimination has not been beneficial. In other words, the role of secular changes in the educational outcome of Muslims visa-vis the positive discrimination has made widening the gap between Muslims and other socio-religious communities.

Similarly, the recent Social Development Report (SDR) about the conditions of minorities in the post-Sachar scenario reveals that the benefits intended for minorities were being cornered by either the majority population or non-Muslim minorities. Among the major reasons for the failure to fulfill the promises laid down in the Sachar Committee Report, the misplaced focus of minority oriented programs, lack of funds and fear of 'minority appeasement' were highlighted by the SDR (2012). The report also criticizes the integrity and competence of the Ministry of Minority Affairs as it was yet to find its place independent of its parental ministry, i.e Ministry of Justice and Empowerment.

Evaluating the progress in the implementation of policies after Sachar Report, Javed Alam Khan and Pooja Parvati (In Hasan and Hasan 2012) observes in their work on 'Government's commitment towards development of Muslims' that even after six years of supposed policy initiatives in this direction, there remain gaps in policy provisions and concomitant budgets, utilization of funds and fine-tuning the design of government programs specific to the development of minorities. Their focused study in Uttar Pradesh and Haryana states of North India reveal that despite targeted schemes the Muslims have been disadvantaged due to the mismatch between priorities and action as well as the diversion of funds for non-Muslim population. These scholars also lament on the negligible budgets and the weak participation in Planning and implementation for some of the most vulnerable Muslim population India. The survey conducted by the authors in four gram panchayats of Barabanki district of Uttar Pradesh clear demonstrates that lack of awareness among Muslims on any policy initiatives exclusively for Muslims including the much hyped Multi-Sectoral Development Program (MSDP). The survey also finds some of the development deficits like low levels of girls' education, inadequate health facilities, lack of access to credit to landless weavers coupled with official apathy and discrimination towards minority policies as some of the fundamental reasons for the failure of policy implementations in the district (See Khan and Parvati 2012: 259).

For Zoya Hasan and Mushirul Hasan (2012) Muslims lag further behind in the field of education, work participation, income betterment and ownership of productive aspects, which, in turn, have aggravated the deprivation of Muslims like their SC & ST counterparts. Hasan and Hasan (2012) show that inadequate planning, continuous discrimination and diversion of funds meant for Muslim welfare to non-Muslims and non-minorities have affected the efficacy of development programs targeting minorities. Similarly, the scholars also express their apprehension about the efficacy of MSDP in alleviating the socio-economic deprivation of Muslims as there has been a mismatch between identified development deficits and the interventions followed. District as the basic unit of intervention has also been criticized for its relative neglect of specific Muslim areas where development initiatives were necessary and instead focusing on elsewhere in the district where Muslims are not present in substantial numbers (Hasan and Hasan 2012: 245).

Conclusion

Scholastic documents on the conceptual review as well as the social reality of minorities in India, as attempted in this paper, invariably suggest that Muslims are the most vulnerable minorities in the country and the reality of exclusion and discrimination has become difficult to deny. Many recent development literature including the Social Development Report (2012) highlights the fact that educational and Health services have become the conspicuous sites of discrimination and deprivation, wherein beyond discriminatory practices of market forces, formal and informal structures perpetuate exclusion.

In contrast to a strong cross party consensus for the uplift of historically disadvantaged caste groups, the basic problem for minorities is the lack of consensus on policies. The political valour and vision that informed the appointment of the committee was not matched by that required to build an appropriate and adequate response to the multiple development deficits suffered by majority of Muslim people in India. It is in this context that proposal for promoting empowerment and ending exclusion will hold the keys to affirmative action program. Similarly, greater representation of minorities in decision making institutions would be necessary to make sure that their voice and interest are articulated and heard in the public domain. In this direction the need to enhance diversity in different spaces has been largely considered as a valid ground through which the participation and performance of different socio-religious communities and intra-community axioms like gender, class and caste can be ensured. Scholars and policy analysts have generally understated many dimensions of the recommendations including the proposal to move away from reservation-based prescriptions and the urgency to think more in terms of innovative policies even in the areas of affirmative action.

Endnote & References

Alam, Javeed 2008. 'The Contemporary Muslim Situation in India: A Long-term view' *Economic and Political Weekly*. Vol. 43, No.2, pp 45-53.

Basant, Rakesh and Abusaleh Sharifff 2010. *Handbook of Muslims in India: Empirical and Policy Perspectives*, New Delhi: Oxford University Press.

Galanter, Mark 1984. *Competing Equalities: Law and Backward Classes in India* New Delhi: Oxford University Press.

Government of India 2006. *Prime Minister's High Level Committee Report* (Sachar Committee Report), New Delhi : November.

Government of India *Report of the National Commission for Religious and Linguistic Minorities* (Ranghanatha Misra Committee Report), New Delhi, May 2007.

Government of India. 2011. *India Human Development Report 2011: Towards Social Inclusion.* New Delhi: Planning Commission.

Hasan, Zoya & Mushirul Hasan (eds.) 2012. 'Social Development Report 2012: Minorities at the Margins' *Council for Social Development* New Delhi: Oxford University Press.

Hasan, Zoya 2009. *Politics of Inclusion: Castes, Minorities and Affirmative Action* New Delhi: Oxford University Press.

Kabeer, Naila 2008. *Social Exclusion: Concepts, Findings and Implications for the MDGs* Institute of Development Studies, University of Sussex, Brighton.

Kohli, Atul (ed.) 2001. *The Success of India's Democracy,* Cambridge: Cambridge University Press.

Mander, Harsh 2011. *'Promises to Keep': Investigating Government's response to Sachar Committee recommendations'* New Delhi, Centre for Equity Studies.

Sen, Amartya 2004. *Social Exclusion: Concept, Application and Scrutiny,* New Delhi, Critical Quest.

Sheth, D.L. 2010.' Minority politics: the shifting terms of policy discourse' *Seminar.* 602 October.

14

The Oncoming Challenges of Public-Private Partnership into Rural Drinking Water Supply: A Case Study of District Sehore, Madhya Pradesh

Manzoor Ali

Following the 'Libertarian' philosophy which advocates for 'free market economy' without any regulation from State, the Indian government in 1990 decided to change the policy from 'Import Substitution Industrialization' (ISI) to open market. The decision was a 'minority' decision. Rob Jenkins argued that "India's shift to a market-oriented development strategy during the 1990s was made possible by the political skill of elites operating within established, yet flexible, state and non-state institutions. This often showcased the less democratic elements of the liberal parliamentary tradition—what has been called 'reform by stealth'. Underhanded tactics, aided by propitious international circumstances during most of the 1990s, may well have sufficed to promote the initial stages of India's process of marketisation..." (Rob Jenkins, 2002), Atul Kohli concurred with the above proposition and noted that "When the policy shift was announced, the main forces supporting such a shift included the narrow political leadership, the technocratic policy elite, a segment of Indian capital, and external actors, expressing their preferences mainly in the form of policy conditionalities set by the International Monetary Fund (IMF)" (Kohli Atul, 2006).

Almost all the sectors have been opened up for private players even sector like defence[1], railways, education, mining are not remained untouched. Initially, community and political opposition to such an action have deterred the government. Government has had to back off and make the private sector wait longer. On the other hand, international experience of complete privatization caused International Finance to shift their strategy. Actually, in privatization, Private capital has to invest a lot of money and to get it back companies increase the tariff which have been resisted by the people. Hence, companies have to leave the place without recovering their actual expenditure. The loss of money caused them to bring host government as guarantor for any such loss in various form called as exit policy. Hence, privatisation was begun to be seen as 'dirty' action/policy. World Bank document (2003a) too recognized this. Hall, Lobina and Motte (2005) captured the World Bank (WB) sentiments as "it was 'responding to country demand by offering a broad menu of options for public and private sector infrastructure provision'. In every instance, campaigns were taking place against policies which were advocated by the government of the day, sometimes with the support of traditional leftist parties, and invariably—in developing countries—with the support of development banks. In many countries, the policies were reversed or significantly delayed" (Hall, Lobina & Motte, 2005). The Country Assistance Strategy (CAS) 2009-12 observes, "A World Bank Independent Tribunal took place in September 2007, with the motto 'World Bank out of India', showing the strong feelings against the WB". The reasons for such strong criticisms and feelings, the Bank report notes, are, "coming out of the structural adjustment experience and the [Bank's] view of privatization as a panacea for all public sector ills" (Dwevidi, 2010). These criticisms did not lead to an end to the agenda of privatization but now continued under the aegis of Public-Private Partnership (PPP).

Memon and Butler (2004) considered PPP as a form of privatization. The poor performance of the State agency in delivery of services and lack of funds to further invest in creating infrastructure and its Operation and Maintenance (O&M) have been the catalytic rationale behind the introduction of PPP across the globe. The potential benefits expected from PPP, as assessed by the government are—cost effectiveness, higher productivity, accelerated delivery, clear customer focus, enhanced social services and recovery of user charges. However, the critics of PPP argued that "it is policies that enrich the few at the expense of the majority and for which no democratic mandate can be secured" (Datta Amrita, 2009).

PPP in India

PPP sub-group report on social sector (2004) argued that "PPP, moreover, has had its origin in the general distrust of bureaucracy and the oppressiveness of State. Involvement of community, family neighborhoods and voluntary organization under PPP is observed to have led to empowerment of citizens" (Report of the PPP Sub-Group, 2004).[2] However, this is completely erroneous and the nomenclature of the contract is misleading. In PPP, there is no scope for citizens to participate. It is purely a contract between government and private entity about the respective roles in funding, accountability, risk-sharing etc. So, it should be called as 'Government-Private Partnership'.

Indian government took clue from International Finance Institution and hinted for PPP based investments. With the onset of economic reforms, the government was planning to introduce private entities in many sectors. Eighth Five Year Plan (1992-97) document argued that "if private initiative comes forward to participate in creating such infrastructure like power plants, roads, bridges, medium and minor irrigation projects, social housing, industrial estates, on reasonable terms and with full protection of people's interests, such initiative must be positively encouraged" (Eight FYP, 1992). Ninth Plan period onwards, government advocated for private investment as it ensures the growth rate which ultimately benefits the social sector as well. This has been re-emphasized in Twelfth Five year Plan as well.

- Robust GDP is pre-requisite for economic and social progress of '*aamadmi*' and private investment is the key for ensuring that robustness.
- This private investment aims to achieve 'Developing Capabilities'—Human, Infrastructure and Institutional.
- Hence, 12th FYP envisaged the further opening of social/critical sector for private investment in form of PPP.

Today, India is the largest market for Private Participation in Infrastructure (PPI) in the developing world. In the South Asian region, it has attracted 98 per cent of regional investment. According to the database of PPP cell, a total of 758 PPP projects worth Rs. 383, 332 crore are either operational or in completion stage. Karnataka is leading with as many as 104 PPP projects followed by Andhra Pradesh (96); Madhya Pradesh (86); Maharashtra (78), Gujarat (63) and Rajasthan (59). By the end, 12th FYP is expecting Rs. 5631692 crore worth of investment in infrastructure sector. Table 1 shows the total number of PPP projects across India along with its value.

Table 1: Sector-wise Contract Award Method

Sector	*Total No. of Projects*	*Total No. of Projects based on Contract Award Method*				
		Domestic Competitive Bidding	*International Competitive Bidding*	*Negotiated MoU*	*Unsolicited*	*Value of Contracts (Rs. Crore)*
Airport	5		18,808.0			19,111.0
Education	17	620.3	25.0			1,849.7
Energy	56	10,205.0	555.0	16,014.6		67,244.6
Health care	8	275.0	217.0	16,014.6		1,833.0
Ports	61	7,536.8	26,569.4	36,249.0	4,150.0	81,038.2
Railways	4	696.6		873.0		1,569.6
Roads	405	71,489.5	76,340.7	1,259.2		176,724.9
Tourism	50	2,254.1	1,127.3			4,486.1
Urban Development	152	8,239.7	11,359.1	275.0	119.0	29,475.0
Total	**758**	**101,316.9**	**135,001.6**	**54,670.8**	**4,269.0**	**383,332.1**

Source: Ministry of Finance.

There are different models of PPP such BOO, BOT, BROT, BBO etc. BOO is Built-Own-Operates which is complete privatization. The contractor constructs and operates a facility without transferring ownership to the public sector. Legal title to the facility remains in the private sector, and there is no obligation for the public sector to purchase the facility or take title. BOT is Built-Operate-Transfer. The private partner builds a facility to the specifications agreed to by the public agency, operates the facility for a specified time period under a contract or franchise agreement with the agency, and then transfers the facility to the agency at the end of the specified period of time. In India, most of the infrastructure projects such as roads, ports and airports, are based on BOT. BBO stand for Buy-Built-Operate. A BBO is a form of asset sale that includes a rehabilitation or expansion of an existing facility. The government sells the asset to the private sector entity, which then makes the improvements necessary to operate the facility in a profitable manner. Modified Design-Build (Turnkey) Contracts is traditional Design-Build (DB) contract, private contractor is engaged for a fixed-fee payment on completion. The primary benefits of DB contracts include time and cost savings, efficient risk-sharing and improved quality. The government may collaborate with the private developer/service provider in any one of the following ways:

- *As a funding agency:* providing grant/capital/asset support to the private sector engaged in provision of public service, on a contractual/non-contractual basis.

- *As a buyer:* buying services on a long term basis.
- *As a coordinator:* specifying various sectors/forums in which participation by the private sector would be welcome.

PPP in Drinking Water Sector

Since the beginning of economic reform, the thrust has been on laying the foundation for a better environment for private sector in water supply. Collection of water tariff and O&M cost from both rural and urban areas was the basic requirement. The Dublin Conference (1992) set the tone to treat water as economic goods rather than public property. Hence, the conference encouraged privatization of water sector in developing countries. It declared that water has an economic value and must be treated as an economic good. It also stated that access to water and sanitation are fundamental human rights. This was the triumph of market environmentalism. Karen Bakker (2007) explains it as "Proponents of market environmentalism in the water sector argue that water is an increasingly scarce resource, which must be priced at full economic and environmental cost if it is to be allocated to its highest-value uses, and managed profitably by private companies whose accountability to customers and shareholders is more direct and effective than attenuated political accountability exercised by citizens via political representatives." (Bakker, 2007)

Market environmentalism effected India's policy on water supply. Eighth Five Year Plan mentioned that "wherever, house-service connections are given, it is suggested that appropriate water-tariff is levied and realized whereby operation and maintenance becomes self-sustaining to the extent possible. Private Sector efforts for construction and maintenance of drinking water projects should be encouraged and mobilised to the maximum extent feasible" (Eighth FYP, 1992)[3]. However, this Plan period did not seen much private investment as the chance of recovery of investment was less. Nevertheless, Ninth FYP repeats the policy to augment the private investment. It noted that "Private sector efforts in construction and maintenance of rural water supply and environmental sanitation should be encouraged and mobilised to the maximum extent".

According to the Government of India, PPP in water sector has been introduced in three phases. In mid-1990s—when several international projects were taken up, but they failed; around 2000—the pace of PPP in water and sanitation subsided and lastly, post 2005—where there are some early successes. These PPP projects in the three phases mainly fall under four segments of the water value chain namely: a) Bulk Water Generation, b) Treatment (Desalination, Waste water), c) Distribution of Water, and d) Network Rehabilitation. The much talked about PPP program was Swajaldhara where it was envisaged that ninety per cent of the cost would be borne by the government and remaining ten per cent by community. Also, it notes that O&M should be handed over to private companies which would be paid by consumers through a user charge. A study (Sampat, 2007) showed that the policy for water and sanitation at the international level shaped our domestic policy Swajaldhara replaced supply driven approach by a demand driven one. The demand has to come from village committee, after villagers have reached a consensus to share the capital cost initially and O&M cost later. Swajaldhara enforced village committee with lots of responsibility. But control of Village Committee by the elite may affect the accessibility of water to the poor and marginalized section which was substantiated by the field work in Rajasthan.

But, the disappointing result of PPP in water sector did not deter the government to further this agenda. In fact, government declared that PPP is nothing close to privatization. "Under PPP, water is not privatized, but the service (or supply) is put in private hands"[4]. 12th FYP put water in economic service category. National Water Policy (2012) calls for privatization of water service to recover the O&M cost. The draft policy calls for the abolition of all forms of water subsidies to the agricultural and domestic sectors, but says "subsidies and incentives" should be provided to private industry for recycling and reusing treated effluents. After meeting the livelihood necessities, water should be treated as economic goods. Progressive tariff charge should be used. Until Swajaldhara, PPP has been introduced mainly in the urban sector hoping that collecting user fee would be easier and large. A total of 390 projects worth Rs. 45,955.55 crore have been sanctioned for Water and Sanitation under Jawaharlal Nehru National Urban Renewal Mission (JNNURM) as shown in table 2.

Previous experience of introducing PPP in water supply in urban sector has shown that it is not as efficient as had been promised and also lacking in ability to mend the social gaps. Hubli-Dharwad project funded partially by World Bank promised to supply 24/7 water supply. But, continuous water supply depends on other factors such as adequate and reliable source of water supply. Such a system also requires high degree of leakage control and continuous maintenance of pressure, which in turn, calls for large investments

Table 2: Sector-wise release of funds under Sub-Mission for Urban Infrastructure and Governance

(Rupees in lakh)

Sr. No.	Sector	No. of Projects Sanctioned	Cost of projects sanctioned	ACA Committed	ACA released
1.	Drainage/Storm Water Drainage	73	8,40,007.38	3,46,165.08	2,24,855.35
2.	Water Supply	157	20,48,589.03	10,08,819.48	6,68,880.71
3.	Sewerage	112	14,98,002.28	7,14,210.87	4,12,594.95
4.	Solid Waste Management	44	1,97,286.44	1,02,262.42	62,172.37
5.	PreservationofWater Bodies	4	11,670.54	6,861.20	3,912.42
	Total	**390**	**4,595,555.67**	**2178319.05**	**1372415.8**

Source: jnnurm.nic.in

and good O&M. It has higher cost-implication. Once, 24/7 water supply costs higher, it has a negative impact on social equity as in the case of Hubli-Dharwad. Hubli, in a declared slum that is part of the demonstration zone, slum-dwellers claimed that 70/450 households had not been given 24/7 (as of July 10, 2007) because they had failed to regularize their connections. Also, public stand-posts were removed from the area. The removal of public stand-posts was part of the implementation of the 24/7 water supply project in the city. Hence, D. Raghunandan claimed that 24/7 water supply is a myth. He further add that, "If water is actually supplied 24/7 to some pilot areas, the truth is that it can only be done by taking away water from some other area" (Raghunandan, 2012)). In the case of Greater Bangalore Water and Sanitation Project (GBWASP), which was meant to connect people living on the outskirts of Bangalore to piped water and sanitation, brought Beneficiary Capital Contributions (BCC). More than 35% of the project's total capital expenditure (which is Rs 447 crore) is being sourced from future customers through upfront payments. Even the payment did not ensure timely water supply by GBWASP. Kejriwal & Bhaduri (2005) exposed the problem of Delhi Jal Board collaboration with World Bank for water supply. Delhi government was to recover three-fold expenditure on the project through user charges. Due to public opposition, the project was shelved only to return half a decade later. Madhya Pradesh also tried privatization of water through the loan granted by World Bank and Asian Development Bank (ADB) under two projects Madhya Pradesh Urban Water Supply and Environment Improvement Project (MPUWSEIP) and Madhya Pradesh Water Sector Restructuring Project (MPWSRP). The project causes disconnection on non-payment, removal of public standposts, increase in water tariffs and privatization of irrigation schemes.

PPP in Rural Water

In the rural area, before Swajaldhara, following the World Bank and GoI review, GoI had introduced the Sector Reform Pilot Projects (SRPP) in April 1999 with the implicit strategy of these reforms premised on the understanding that "people will be willing to maintain and operate water supply schemes only if they *owned* the assets; had been involved in the projects *throughout* from choosing structures to installations and repairs; *know* that the government will *not* maintain the asset; had *sufficient* funds for maintenance and had to pay for operation and maintenance of the system. These sector reforms were to be implemented on a pilot scale in selected villages in 67 districts in 26 States in the country, which probably represents the world's largest government supported yet demand-based rural drinking water programme. The Water and Sanitation Programme—South Asia (WSP-SA) and UNICEF had provided institutional support to the RGNDWM for the Sector Reform Pilot Projects" (Sampat, 200). Later on, all the reform initiated under Sector Reform was placed under Swajaldhara. Case study of Swajaldhara in 18 districts of Rajasthan showed that introducing capital cost sharing and O&M cost hampered the prospects of poor to access the water. "...in Khadbamniya in Rajsamand district people who could not afford to come up with the Rs. 1,000 initial contribution could not avail of the water supply. Similarly in Rajpura in Rajsamand, despite a strong sense of community ownership, the people who could not afford to pay this sum as initial cost could not access water from the new scheme, as was seen in many households in Chhatarpura too" (Sampat, 2000).

Isabelle Fauconnier (1999) defines equity in the context of privatization of water and sanitation as—access to water, capacity to pay for it & access to planning and decision making in the services. In case of urban water supply we have seen that privatization or PPP has hampered the chances of poor. Similar criteria of capital cost sharing and O&M cost would hamper the rural poor access to water. In India, where 77 per cent of its population lives on Rs. 20 per day, 11th FYP recognized that rural community *is not averse to paying charges* for a reliable supply (11th Five Year Plan). It also suggested that community should bear O&M cost. 12th FYP concurs with the proposal of O&M. In rural areas the Village Water and Sanitation Committee (VWSC) has role to collect user fee from the beneficiaries. Further, government wants to devolve functions (NRDWP, 2010)[5] given below to VWSC.

a) transfer of responsibility *for infrastructure creation* of hand pumps to Panchayati Raj Institutions (PRIs)

b) transfer of responsibility for *infrastructure creation of Single Village Piped Water Schemes* to PRIs
c) transfer of *responsibility for O&M of Hand Pumps* to PRIs
d) transfer of *responsibility for O&M of Single Village Piped Water Supply Schemes* to PRIs.
e) *Proportion of hand pumps whose O&M* has been transferred to PRIs
f) Proportion of Single Village Piped Water Schemes whose O&M has been transferred to PRIs
g) The VWSCs should be Standing/Sub-Committees of GPs
h) Proportion of Drinking Water sources for which water quality testing done during the previous years as per the IMIS

This paper examines the ground reality of access to water by Scheduled Castes (SCs) and Scheduled Tribes (STs) in two gram panchayats of two blocks of Sehore district, Madhya Pradesh and oncoming challenge of user charge. The district has been chief minister's area as Mr. Shivraj Singh Chauhan are presents Budhani tehsil of Sehore district. This is the reason why author selected the district to examine the implementation of rural water programme. Gram panchayat Rala and Dondi belongs to Nasrullahganj and Sehore blocks. Author has used Focused Group Discussion (FGD) and interviews with relevant government officials and Panchayat's representative to extract the relevant information. However, as women respondents were less in numbers there has been gender imbalance in the information.[6] This could be a weakness of this paper.

Status of Water in Sehore District

The study district is located 32 kilometers from the State Capital, Bhopal and stands on the foothills of the Vindhyachal Range in the middle of Malwa region. Administratively, the district is constituted of eight revenue Tehsils and five Blocks having 499 Panchayats, 1008 revenue villages and 1270 habitations. Sehore has the population size of 1.3 million which is 1.8% of the Madhya Pradesh demography as per latest Census 2011, a growth of 21.51% over 2001 figures. The density of population in the district in 2011 is 199 people per sq. km. than 164 people per sq. km in 2001. Out of the total Sehore population for 2011 census, 18.95 percent live in urban regions and 81.05% of the population lives in rural areas. Nearly 80% of the population of the district lives below poverty line. The district has 22% Scheduled Caste concentrated habitations (279) and 16% Scheduled Tribes

Table 3: Drinking Water Scenario in Sehore District of Madhya Pradesh

S.No.	*Blocks*	*Panchayats*	*Villages*	*Habitations*	*Number of SC Concentrated Habitation*	*Number of ST Concentrated Habitation*	*Fully Covered Drinking Water Habitation Scenario*	*Not Covered/ Partially Covered Drinking Water Habitation Scenario*	*Slipped Back Drinking Water Habitation Scenario*
1	Ashta	135	275	354	156	12	267	87	1
2	Budni	63	137	141	5	38	101	38	3
3	Ichhawar	70	141	184	32	66	155	27	12
4	Nasrullaganj	87	165	195	7	79	119	34	18
5	Sehore	144	290	396	79	12	239	155	18
	Total	499	1008	1270	279	207	881	341	52

Source: Habitation level data provided in http://indiawater.gov.in/imisreports/nrdwpmain.aspx

concentrated habitations (207). Average literacy rate of Sehore in 2011 is 71.11% compared to corresponding figure of 63.07% in 2001.

Access to water resources is highly dependent on the ground water. For irrigation, industry and for drinking water, ground water is considered as main source irrespective of the fact that the district has a few non-perennial rivers like Narmada, Chambal Rivers. About 62% of irrigation in the district is from ground water, though the level of irrigation in the district is very low, only 27.5% of total geographical area is being irrigated. The total number of dug wells and tube wells in the district during 2005-06 were 33048 and 14698 respectively.

On the drinking water front, Sehore city and outskirt areas have entire supply from ground water. There has been a steady rise in ground water development in the district. The stage of ground water development in the district during 2004 was 62%, which has increased considerably from 1997 estimates. However, the stage of ground water development has reached to 81% in Sehore and Astha block of district. The Net annual ground water available in the Sehore District is 752.55 MCM and draft from all uses is 469.80 MCM, Net ground water available for future use is 274.18 MCM. The Public Health Engineering Department (PHED) in Sehore district claims that drinking water services covers 90% of its population. The traditional patterns of drinking water through handpumps model captures 81% of the total population followed by Piped Water Supply 14% and Open Well 2.86%. The coverage is uniform across various segments of society including SC, ST, Other Backward Classes (OBCs) and General category of population. However, the field experience shows completely different picture altogether.

Case Study: Rala is a gram panchayat. It has five villages i.e. Rala, Sarvarganj, Chitikheda, Pardi, Okwalia. Within Rala there are one SC and one ST habitation (*tolas*). The gram panchayat has ST women Smt. Chintabai as *sarpanch* and Manohar Patel, a backward caste, as *up-sarpanch*. Devolution of power, financial and decision making was the aim of 73rd and 74th Amendment Act which envisages PRI as a tool for inclusive development. The Act has also reserved seats for SC/ST and women.[7] But, in this case study ST woman *sarpanch* told the author that she is just a rubber stamp. She has never been consulted for any decision taken by other members. Empowerment is a distant dream for these sections. The Banerjee and Duflo (2011) argument that women leaders almost always make a difference could not be verified in this case. This village has population of approx. 4000. Out of total 2175 have voting right. It is a fully covered village with Piped Water Supply (PWS) and Handpump (HP) water supply, claimed by government.

Tolas	*No. of HP*
Rala	6
Sarwarganj	1
Chitikheda	3
Pardi	1
Okwalia	4
Dalit habitation	0
ST habitation	0
Total	15

But, the fact is that the SC/ST habitations neither have HP nor have PWS. Women have to carry water for cooking and other purpose from road side HP which is 0.5 km from their habitation. Inclusive approach of National Rural Drinking Water Programme (NRDWP) is compromised in this sample study. PRI members argued that due to lack of road, bore vehicle was unable to enter the SC/ST habitation. So, they have provided HP near their locality.

Box 1: Recurring Monthly/Annual Cost for Piped Water in a Village

1 Pump Operator salary	4000/4500 p.m.
Electric Bill	1000 p.m.
O&M	500
Total	5500-6000 p.m.
Annual Cost	66000-72000

Source: Interview with PRI officials of Rala GP, Nasrullahganj, Sehore

When enquiring about Piped Water Supply, the PRI members argued that due to lack of water pressure, PWS does not reach the habitation. What are the Tribal Sub-Plan (TSP) and Scheduled Caste Sub-Plan (SCSP) outlays allocated for?[8] In any case, the villagers pay Rs. 100 p/m as user charges to meet the recurring cost and once SC and ST habitation get covered by PWS they have to pay user fees. In case of non-payment they are liable for disconnection.

Box 2: Initial amount to start-up Piped Water Supply

3 per cent (1 per cent for SCs/STs villages) capital cost sharing by the community is refundable. The total money is 'Fixed Deposit' in State account. 1/5th of amount along with incurred interest shall be given back to GPs in a span time of 5 years. Our Sample district Sehore have village like Dondi which is ready to deposit 3 per cent of their contribution. In Gram Sabha meeting villagers have given their consent for contribution. 5 GPs of Raisen district have already deposited contribution.

Source: Interview with PHED official, Bhopal.

A vital point one can derive from this story is that SCs and STs are facing discrimination while accessing water in the sample area. Secondly, they have to share capital cost, pay for the user charges and O&M once they start availing piped water supply. Now, if we consider the financial situation of SCs/STs in Madhya Pradesh it is really bad with 43 per cent and 59 per cent poverty level respectively[9]. When asked that it would not be possible for common people (read SCs/STs) to contribute for O&M and capital cost as well, officials remarked that "when they can have mobile phone why can't they pay these cost". In fact, they believe that poor people have developed taste for freebee and do not care what they get. "It will discipline them", said an official. Liberal interpretation of Article 21, Right to Life, of the Constitution by Supreme Court brings Safe and clean drinking water under its purview. It is the rights of an individual. Hence, State cannot charge its citizens while performing its Constitution bound duty.

Another gram panchayat Dodi has total 1469 population. Population is divided into two *tolas* (habitation) i.e. Ratikheda and Dodi. This village has two dalit wards but no ST population. The village has 10 landless family and 25-30 families are beneficiary of land reform and holder of patta. It has 18 HP but only 8 are operational. Author was told that in summer only 2 HP would remain functional. Depleting ground water is major problem of this village. All the 18 HP procure by PHED is not capable of pulling out water as it is INDIA II mark HP which cannot pull water below 150 feet. Water level has gone down even below 300 feet making all HP fall under slippage category.[10] This poses great difficulties for the villagers. To ward off the water scarcity, during fieldwork author got to know, villagers agreed to give user charges. Secretary of the Dodi gram panchayat told that as villagers are ready to pay administration is planning to have household PWS. But, they add a caveat that PWS, initially, will be extended to those who are able to pay and the user fee depends on the number of household connection. But, this puts dalits community at the receiving end. As the economically weaker group they have to depend on ground water sources which remain dry most of the year. Women folks and younger male family members have to move far to fetch water. Dalit community lack both logistics and social capital to negotiate with water deficit. They cannot go to anybody house and take water. They have to depend on the benevolence of the other community for the help. Here, water deficit is reinforcing the caste hierarchy and subverting the democratization process at the grass root.

Conclusion

It is crystal clear that as privatization was not the panacea for all the problems so is the PPP. "It is also observed that PPPs lead to inequalities in society by increasing the salaries and perks for PPP consultants, officials and lawyers of the private companies. This often translates into decreasing salaries and benefits to public sector employees, sometimes even leading to retrenchment of lower grade public sector employees, who are then again hired by private corporations at lower salaries without benefits. With the inclusion and insistence on payment of high user charges for the services delivered, PPPs also lead to reduced access to services for the poor and the marginalised sections of the society." (Dwivedi 2010) In general, government has to face number of challenges if PPP introduced in the sector of rural drinking water. These are as follow:

- It is going to increase out-of-pocket expenditure.
- It is not a foolproof to deal with social equity issues.
- PPP is nothing but a form of privatization. Private entity experiencing loss of revenue in BOO (Built, Own, Operate i.e. complete privatization) model of PPP changed their strategy to pursue a BOT (Built, Operate, Transfer) model in which risk is actually shared by government whereas private entity makes money through tariff charges which keeps increasing by the operational in-charge.
- Experiences of PPP around the world deflate the argument of increase of efficiency in service delivery.
- To attract the private investment government has to give a wide range of concession, which would be costlier for government.
- Private investment will not be held accountable in PPP mode.

- Jobs created under PPP would be of contractual in nature. No labour rights protection.
- To efficiently manage the existing institution/s may cause retrenchment of workers.

PPPs do not address the availability, quantity and quality issues with water supply for all the people of the project areas. There is increasing evidence to show that PPPs seem to be a manifestation of a perverse form of privatization where "all the risks are borne by the government, while the companies do not invest a penny" (Bhaduri and Kejriwal 2005). (Author is grateful to the SAMARTHAN's (Bhopal) staffs for their help in conducting fieldwork in two gram panchayats in Sehore District)

Endnotes & References

1. Ministry of Commerce and Industry pitched for raising the limit of FDI in the defence sector to at least 49 per cent. Currently, FDI up to 26 per cent is allowed in the defence sector and the department of Industrial policy and promotion's (DIPP) proposal to raise it to 74 per cent.
2. Report of the PPP Sub-Group on Social Sector, GoI, Planning Commission, New Delhi, 2004.
3. Eighth FYP (1992), Chapter: Housing, Water Supply and Sanitation, Planning Commission, Vol. 2, GoI, 1992.
4. Position Paper, The Water and Sanitation Sector in India, Department of Economic Affairs, GoI, 2009.
5. National Rural Drinking Water Programme, Guideline, Ministry of Drinking Water and Sanitation, 2010
6. How much information women have is another question author thought off as women least participate or allow to participate in panchayat's meetings. Most decision about the water such as place of hand pumps, community toilets, water security plan, etc. were taken by the male members of the village's committee.
7. Aiyar Mani Shankar led Expert Committee on "Leveraging Panchayat Raj Institutions for effective delivery of public goods and services" argued to freeze the rotation of reserved seats to two or three terms to incentivise good work and facilitate capacity building of panchayat leadership.
8. The Government of India initiated the concept of Tribal Sub-Plan (TSP) in Fifth Five Year Plan period and the Special Component Plan (SCP), now called Scheduled Caste Sub-plan (SCSP) in Sixth Five Year Plan. SCSP and TSP are seen as a critical initiative in closing the development gap between the Scheduled Castes/Scheduled Tribes when compared to others. This umbrella strategy purports to direct Plan resources across Central Ministries in GOI and Departments in the States, at least in proportion to the SC/ST population at the national level (16.2% and 8.8% respectively) and similarly at the State level, to accelerate the pace of development of SCs/STs so that the gaps in their development when compared to others is bridged at the earliest. SCSP/TSP is therefore a key instrument for fulfilling the objectives of inclusive growth in India. Source: National Advisory Council

9. Madhya Pradesh Rajya Ajeevika Forum, Annual Action Plan, 2012-13.
10. With the involvement of SAMARTHAN in this village villagers are able to formulate their demand for PWS. PHE responded their demand positively and PWS is under way.

References

11th Five Year Plan (2012): Planning Commission, Government of India.

12th Five Year Plan (2012): Planning Commission, Government of India.

8th Five Year Plan (1992): Planning Commission, Government of India.

Bakker, Karen (2007): "The 'Commons' versus the 'Commodity': Alter-Globalisation, Anti-Privatisation and the Human Right to Water in the Global South", *Antipode*, 39/3: 430-455.

Bhaduri, Amit and A. Kejriwal (2005): "Urban Water Supply—Reforming the Reformers", *Economic and Political Weekly*, XL/53: 5543-5545.

Cullet, Philippe (2011): "Realization of the Fundamental Right to Water in Rural Areas: Implications of the Evolving Policy Framework for Drinking Water", *Economic and Political Weekly*, xlvi/12: 56-62.

Datta, Amrita (2009): "Public-Private Partnerships in India: A case for Reform?", *Economic and Political Weekly*, xliv/33: 73-78.

Dwivedi, Gaurav (2010): Public-Private Partnership in Water Sector—Partnerships or Privatisation? (Madhya Pradesh:ManthanAdhyan Kendra).

Government of India (2004): Report of the PPP Sub-Group on Social Sector (New Delhi: GoI).

Hall, David, E. Lobia and R.de la Motte (2005: "Public Resistance to Privatisation of Water and Energy", *Development in Practice*, 15/3-4: 286-301.

Kohli, Atul (2006): "Politics of Economic Growth in India: 1980-2006", *Economic and Political Weekly*, 1251-1259.

Memon, F.A. and Butler D. (2003): "Role of Privatisation in Water Sector", International Journal on Water Policy and Practice: Water Perspectives, 1/1: 28-36.

Raghunandan D. (2012), Newsclick, August 27, 2012

Report of the PPP Sub-Group on Social Sector, GoI, Planning Commission, New Delhi, 2004.

Rob Jenkins (2002), The Ideologically Embedded Market: Political Legitimation and Economic Reform in India, Unpublished work, 2002.

Sampat, Preeti (2007): "Swajaldhara or 'pay'-jal-dhara: Right to Drinking Water in Rajasthan", *Economic and Political Weekly*, 42/52:102-110.

15

Globalization and its Effect on Local Self-Government: The Ideological Value of Democratic Decentralization in Question

Sibtosh Bandyopadhyay

Globalization means integrating the economy of a country with the world economy. Globalization has no specific meaning in academic world. Academically speaking, globalization provides a related process of development through which the world is turning into one big capitalist market. Democracy, development and interdependence are the three basic principle of globalization Anthony Giddens (2002) defines the concept of Globalization as, "growing interdependence between different people, religion and countries in the world as a social and economic relationship come to stretch world wide".

On the other hand, democratic decentralization does not mean absence of state power or non-functioning of state apertures. Instead, a continuous flow of administration or a political process where state itself-transfers its power and authority to the grassroots level institutions. It is needless to mentions that the transferring process enriched the rearrangement the state power. Professor Pronab Bardhan define decentralization as, "is a rage in today's world...include lose of legitimacy of the cultural state and a corresponding belief that decentralization (as against the predatory state) can bring a range of benefits directly to their local people" (Bardhan, 2000). The idea of globalization and its effect on democracy is not a new discourse in modern political science, but what is new is the constant weakness of democratic institutions particularly in third world countries. In our country, the role of panchayat or municipality as self-governing organizations are somewhat distinct in this accepts. In one side, these political institutions have confirmed people's interference in the decision making process at grass-root level and on the other hand, as an auxiliary agency, state is gradually salutation by existing political system. Therefore, prior prevention is taken for anticipated conflict between constant demand of peoples participations and limited scope of representation in the decision making process at grass-root level. The role of the state is just like a 'referee' of a football match, but never the participant. The state will provide financial security and act as an advisor for planning strategy. The grass-root level democratic institutions turned towards more pro-people to make the strategy meaningful. The researcher has tried to access the problem and prospect of democratic decentralization process under the banner of globalization. The study further seeks to examine the political attitude of people towards local self-governing institution and their representatives. These attitudes have been examined in terms of confidence or trust of voters on their elected candidates.

Globalization and its Effect on Local Democracy

Seeds of globalization process were shown in the first decade of the 19th Century. First long wave of democratization, movement also started in that time (1828-1926) which was led by the western colonial power. Capitalism, westernization and imperialism this entire phenomenon reached its apex point in the 19th Century. 'Globalization-1' had been started in that time. This globalization is popularly known to us 'Victorian Globalization'. Huntington wrote in his famous work, 'Third Wave' (1991), that a movement of democratization process had been started in Europe on and from 1928 and it spared all over the world. Nevertheless, a reverse wave of democratization movement had also started in that time; its epic center was Europe and extends all over the globe.

There was a huge impact of 'Victorian Globalization' in our country. A new gesticulate of western civilization did emerge; on the other hand, people's agitation or demonstrations against colonial power started particularly in metropolitan areas and an english littered young cohort primarily involved in it. To safeguard their imperial interest, colonial administrators realized the necessity of formation of urban local government in India. In the early stage of the 19th Century, some municipal local self-government had been gradually emerged, i.e., Madras (1688); Bombay (1762); Calcutta (1762). This first wave of democracy and Globalization-1 was subject to criticism by some scholars. They were agreeing that the dynamics of the 'Victorian Globalization' leads to imperialism and this form of globalization provokes international war. So, the First World War was the product of 'Victorian Globalization'. The scholars are identified two types of political movement under the epoch of 'Globalization-1'

First Wave of Globalization (1828-1926)

'Victorian Globalization'—Democracy—Expansion of Local self-Government

(First Reverse Wave of Globalization (1922-1945)

Imperialism——Fascism——First World War

Globalization in the 21st Century and its Effect on Democratization Process

Modern globalization (II) is a phenomenon of the 21st Century which has a historical legacy of the past. It has been finally formulated by the 'third wave of democratic movement' since 1974 after the student movement in China and Southern Europe. But it never assured the global progress of democratization movement.

Second and Longest Wave of Globalization (1974 onwards)

'Modern Globalization'—Liberalization, Privatization and growth of Multi National Corporation—Neo-Imperialism—Cultural Fundamentalism

Looking over last two decades of world politics one can say that globalization, privatization and liberalization are now a global phenomenon. Authoritarian regime is gradually collapsed, protest movement against neo-colonialism shows a tremendous apathy among the common people's of third world countries. The whole scenario creates a paradigmatic change in the cultural level of human civilization. To convey the whole endeavor Francis Fukuyoma (1989) said "...what we are witnessing is not just the end of the cold war, or the passing of particular period of postwar history, ...the end point of mankind's ideological evolution and (the) universalization of western democracy as the final form of human government....The state that emerges at the end of history is liberal in so far as it recognizes and protects through a system of law man's universal right to freedom and democratic in so far as it exists only with the consent of the government". This argument creates a new platform of controversy. Anthony Giddens reacted and said, "...it seems very doubtful that history has come to stop in the sense that we have exhausted all alternatives open to us. Who can say what new form of economic, political or cultural order may emerge in the future? Just as the thinkers of medieval times had no inkling of the industrial society that was to emerge with the decline of feudalism, so we can not at the moment anticipate how the world will change over the coming century".

Globalization and the Crisis of Representation

There is a theoretical dilemma in between parallel existence of globalization and popular participation of people's in these democratic institutions. The term 'grass-root democracy' generally used in this context. In the third world countries, constant demand of participation or involvement in the decisions makings process sometimes create irrational pressure, which might sprout of dictatorial political system. In the west, Indo-American society has sorted out this problem by in habiting representative democratic culture. In our country, the absence of democratic culture or slow rate of its flow prevents the democratic culture of local self-government. The unending problem of representation in the third world are correlated with others problems like food, shelter, over populations, illiteracy, unemployment, lack of capital and technology. Thus, it is utterly impossible task of solutions separately for a single problem. Therefore, as a crisis savior state is again invited (rolling back the state) by the civil society. However, this character of the state is somewhat distinct than the 'Twentieth Century State'. State is appeared as an aid-proving agency to the civil society.

Globalization and democracy are not a homogeneous phenomenon or a process. Globalization does not ensure global progress of democratic movement. Critics have been asserted that ongoing process of globalization definitely threatens the micro level democratic institutions. There is a widespread view that globalization introduced a new form of beliefs and ideas in civil society. These processes tend to develop its own ideology which rationalizes the culture of 'fundamentalism'. Modern globalization generates fundamentalism in two major areas of democracy. First, in civil society more specifically in third world countries sponsored fundamentalism this means traditional assertiveness of a community to maintain its identity in a global plural society. On the other hand, globalization generated fundamentalism in economic site of modern representative democracy. Jorge Sores has rightly observed the fundamentalist approach of globalization and he has defined the total process in terms of 'market fundamentalism'. George Sores has argued that market fundamentalism plays a crucial role in the global capitalist system. It provides the ideology that not only motivates many of the most successful participants but also drives policy'. (Sores 1998:126-128)

However the basic ethos of globalization is '**structural adjustment**' which never entertain the social welfare activities of a democratic government. Therefore, the popular slogan of a representative government (education, health and clothes for all) has now become a joke. Most democratically elected governments in the third world countries have lost their credibility. In our study, we face many peoples that they are in doubt about the state capacity of taken decision regarding the question of protection of individual rights. Even they are hesitant about the democratic culture of modern representative governments. Therefore, the challenge of promoting minimum standard of livelihood of people and the slogan of democratic decentralization is unquestionably linked to the challenge of upholding democratic values. This is actually a global crisis of representation. To highlight the cases and issues of decline of democratic culture in South America, Scott Main Waring argues that a crisis of democratic representation refers to one end of this continuum...where patterns of representation are unstable and citizens believed that they were not well represented. Such a crisis can be gauged by both attitudinal and behavioral indicators. The attitudinal indicators involve citizen perception: large numbers of citizen are dissatisfied with the way in which they are represented, or they do not feel represented at all. The behavioral indicators are actins by citizens rejecting existing mechanism of democratic representation—for example, withdrawing from electoral participation, voting for new parties.

Political unrest, civil war, communal riots, strikes etc. are the common tendency of third world political system because of the adverse effect of globalization. To assess the reason, we may point out that the courses modernization and liberalization enhance the desire of political participation among people. The necessity of political institution arises to act as a mediator for people's ongoing demand of political involvement. But the improper ratio of number and quality of political organization might collapse the stability of political system. For that reason people's representatives are now facing a tremendous problem, which is popularly known as 'crisis of identity'. In civil society, people's representatives are become failed to maintain there credibility. There are some pre elections declarations of a political party i.e., equal distribution of wealth, as well as to provide a minimum standard of living condition of people, up-gradation of social and political life etc., however, what is actually happening in the name of democratic declaration is perhaps depressing. A newly elected government may not be capable to uphold their promises or declarations. This is not for the failure of democratic culture of a political system but for the culture of globalization. Most of the democratically elected local governments are not in position to provide money to the social welfare fund.

A Study Report

In post-independence period, as an organ of urban local self-government Municipality or Municipal Corporation may be regarded as a great leap forward towards the process of democratic decentralization. The involvement of people in urban administration and attainment of self-reliance were the two basic objectives of the post Indian political system. Two aspects may be identified in this endeavor; today a major segment of Indian population lives in urban area. In colonial period, a privileged group had been emerged in urban society. They were very much influenced by the western education and culture of democratic values. They were well equipped in English language and primarily occupied a prestigious post in colonial administration. There was a huge disparity of culture and in education between the city dwelling native administrators with the common people antedate independence. Colonial administrator used them for their own interest.

On the other hand, people's agitation or demonstrations against colonial power started particularly in metropolitan areas and an English littered young cohort primarily involved in it. To safeguard their imperial interest, colonial administrators realized the necessity of formation of urban local government in India. In the early stage of Nineteenth Century, some municipal local self-government had been gradually emerged, i.e., Madras (1688); Bombay (1762); Calcutta (1762).[1] The idea of urban local self-government in modern India is undeniable a colonial legacy.

Secondly, the modern cities are not a homogeneous community. In a village, peoples related with each other as a member of civil society. However, the interaction between the erudite sections of civil society with the dysfunctional segments is a common phenomenon of modern urban life. They carry on to be the reason of social tension. Hence, the solution of these problems some major steps have been taken. These were the purpose of bringing together into a single administrative unit to solve the urban problems.

In post-1978 period, two major objectives of Left Front seemed to dominate. They were: (a) democratic decentralization at grass-root level, (b) reformation of existing political power structure and eradication of poverty. Municipality or Municipal Corporation also gets a prior importance as an agent of urban local self-government. The implementation party based municipal election at a regular interval open the new frontiers and channels of responsibility that requires more involvement of people in urban local self-government in terms of policymaking.

This is a case study of some municipalities in Hooghly district. In Municipal administration the researcher meets 38 members to focus on their regular attendance in the meeting of ward committee. As per available data, it is found that the percentage of ward Committee meeting and People's participation in it, is not satisfactory. Total 5 councilors out of 38 respondents stated that they are regularly participated in ward Committee meeting of their concerned ward. Field survey among members in several municipalities in Hooghly District revealed that nine of them consider that there is no significance of the routine wise ward committee meeting and their participation in it. Four members are remained silent. The mission and vision of ward committee meeting is not a-political. Therefore, 5th councilors regarded that the meeting of ward committee is held on regular basis and they are habituated to participate in it. However, only one of them placed the previous proceedings of ward committee meeting. Eleven councilors said that no meeting of the ward committee has taken place at all for many years. Most of the councilors were very much confused or remained silent about the function of ward committee.

From the ample interview among the citizens in several municipal areas, it has been found that 17% citizens do not have any idea about local self-government. It is interesting that a majority portions of people (72%) are just have heard the term 'democratic decentralization', but they unaware of even some of the simple function about the ward committee. 33% citizens are familiar with the term 'local self-government' and 'democratic decentralization', but they never take participate in meeting. Nominal percentages (0.6%) of citizens are aware about the significance of 'democratic decentralization'.

Preservations of democracy at grass root level and people's participation in decision making process it is the prime concern of municipal administration. However, in reality, the democratic structure of urban administration is gradually declined and condensed to a legal-political institution. There is no urgency of control over urban administration. However, what is actually happening in urban West Bengal in last two decades is just opposite. Because of that, people lose charm on elected representatives and activity of urban governance. Even the elected candidates are neither enthusiastic nor active. The survey report shows that only 61% candidates are eager to contest in future election. A majority of members 37% (out of the seventy-five) thinks that they can serve people better even without contesting the municipal election. A half portion of representatives (48%) believes that municipal administration is hampering the faith on democracy at the grassroots level. A puzzling factor in this classification is that the 54% member thinks for an alternative arrangement of representative democracy at the grass root level in the place of municipal governance. 12% municipal representatives are extremely worried about their election ticket for the next term, because undoubted obedience to the party is the only assurance for that, which is also a tough task. Only 8% elected member believes that urban governance is following the right path in favour of democratic decentralization.

This depression was not only a common phenomenon among the elected member of municipality but also widespread among ordinary people. Field survey among citizen in several municipalities and a municipal corporation in Hooghly district revealed that 42% common people (out of a total 40) consider that there is no significance of the routine wise municipal election and their participation in it. 68% of the respondent thinks that the promises of the party and the political leaders in pre-election period have no connection with their post election activity. An overwhelming majority of the citizen (72%) is very much disgusted about the role of the party and political leaders in relation with urban governance and they are not even interested to participate in any kind of activities in municipal administration.

Conclusion

It may be concluded from the above discussion that democracy creates some possibilities. The practical application of these possibilities is solely dependent on the political realization of representatives. In another way, it is not easy to harvest the fruit of democracy just announcing the ideology of democracy. However, the difference between the actual implementation of policies and the announced objective is quite damaging for the entire system. Anyway, it is a genuine problem for a state or a political party. This crisis or challenge is now a universal phenomenon. People's indifference towards representative institutions is not only a common to India alone; it is also noticed in western countries to some extent. Two reasons can be identified for this crisis or self-contradiction. 1. Modern representative democracy is a combination of liberal democratic system and capitalist mode of production. Thus, representative democracy failed to overcome the hurdles of capitalism and liberalism even in after 200 years. 2. Irrespective of free competitive market economy, the system confines democracy in a limited periphery. The increased number of political participations has become a susceptible crisis for representative system.

It is difficult to overcome the above-mentioned problems even under the regime of other political parties. The co-existence of opulence in the vast periphery of poverty stricken urban area has an enormous impact, which is reflected in the ever-increasing public demand and government's tremendous effort to have control over the situation. Still, the international academic world acknowledged the development of municipal system in West Bengal for last three decades. Nevertheless, development alone cannot pump the respiration to democracy. It is observed that People's dependence on the representatives and accountability of an elected representative has played a crucial role in involving the people in political system. Mainly, that is the drawback of every political system. In West Bengal, this is the major drawbacks of representative democracy. If we look at the political scenario across district, we find that lack of trust in municipal governance, inaccuracy of political elite and isolation of the representatives from the masses is a common phenomenon. On the other hand, lack of confidence of the elected representative has almost reached at apex point.

The survey report makes it clear that, 47% councilors have no idea about participatory planning, 23% members are familiar with the word 'participatory planning' or the concept of 'democratic decentralization'. The findings lead to conclusion that only 10% members are having a specific concept of 'participatory planning' or the process of 'democratic decentralization'. Thus, democratic institutions at the grassroots level should be free from political control and interference. Moreover, the responsibility of representatives should have original creativity apart from their political obligation. But what is actually happening in urban West Bengal in last three decades? That is the major departure from the Eight Planning Commission's suggestion. In addition, due to that, the urban West Bengal is turned to an open arena for political fight.

In this respect renowned economist, Amarto Sen and Jean Dreze emphasized on the 'culture or practice of democratic institutions'. Both the scholars used the term '**practice of democracy**'. It is never enough to form the democratic organizations, but the proper maintenance and use of those organizations are vital. In the first place, we are more or less in advanced position, but on the other, we have long way to go. Urban governance system failed to balance the both. The success of democracy through local self-government in West Bengal is solely dependent on the equilibrium of these two aspects.

Endnotes & References

A considerable part of municipal government in pre-independence period is discussed in the research work of several scholars. See, for example, Bandyopadhyay, Madhusudan. Evolution of Municipal Governance in Historical perspective, (in Bengali) (Calcutta: Indian Book Distributing Co, 1991, pp.13-15); Masani, R.P. Evolution of Local Self-government in Bombay (Humphre: Milford; OUP, 1929).

Amarta Sen. Identity and Violence: The Illusion of Destiny (London: Alen Lane), 2005.

Friedman, Thomas, The World is Flat: A Brief History of The Globalized World in the 21st century (London: Allen Lane, 2005).

Giddens, A: Sociology (2002) Blackwell, New Delhi, p. 690.

Habermaass, J., Legitimation Crisis (1976) Boston 1975 origi. German 1973).

Habermaass, J., The Post National Constellation, Policy Press, 2001, p. 107.

Hungtington, S.P., Third Wave, 1991, pp. 16-17.

Kinnvall, C. Globalization and religious nationalism: The Search for Ontological Security (London: Routledge, London, 2008)

Kishore Mahabubani : Can Asian Think (Singapore Times Books International) 1998.

Main Waring Scott, The Crisis of Representation in the Andes, Journal of Democracy, Vol :17, No. 3, July 2006, p.23.

Roland Pennock, Democratic Political Theory, Princeton University Press, 1979, pp. 309-11.

Samir Amin, Obsolescent Capitalism: Contemporary Capitalism and Global Disorder (London: Zed Books Limited), 2004.

Several scholars administration in post independence period, see for details Maheswari, S. State Government In India, (New Delhi: Macmillan, 2000), pp.132, 366-367; Bhattacharya, Harihar. Making Local Democracy Work In India, (New Delhi: Vedam, 2002), p.167; Roy, Uttam K. Ganguly, Madhubanti. 'Integration of Top down & Bottom up approach in Urban and Regional Planning: West Bengal Experience of Draft Development Plans (DDP) and beyond'; (Goa : National Town & Country Planners Congress, 2009), pp. 1-8 and also see, http/www Wbma.gov.in, (Department of Municipal Affairs, Government of West Bengal have been analyzed the design of municipal Administration.

Soros. G., The Crisis of Global Capitalism, "New York', Perseus Book Group pp. 126-128

Tulchin S. Joseph, Democratic Governance, Lynee Rienner Pub, pp. 43-66.

Willam K Tabb, The Amoral Elephant, "New York' 2002, p. 69.

16

Issue of Land and Forest in NREGA & FRA: Study of Sonebhadra District of U.P.

Vinay Kumar Tiwari

Land and Forest has been an important source of sustenance and livelihood for millions of people across the world. Forest provides all the basic needs such as food, fuel, wood, fodder, medicine and timber etc. At the same time forest related activities are major source of income as the forest produces and products are sold in both rural and urban markets to meet the consumers need. More ever gathering of forest produces and trading these forest produces provides an important sources of livelihood income to many people. Land is the important issue during the colonial and anti colonial period of the movement. During the colonial period agricultural was stagnation, as the Zamidars were interested only in rack renting of the peasantry. They were unconcerned about investments and the colonial states also was not favourably disposed towards agricultural development as Zamidari system on which they relied, was itself the greatest drag on agriculture. In the post-independent period Zamidari system was abolished but was not accompanied by any redistribution of land although its distribution was highly skewed. The present paper highlight the relationship of land and forest livelihood and a question of implementation of Government sponsored right based development programme like MNREGA and Forest right act through case study in Ghorawal block, Sonebhadra district of U.P. The Sonebhadra District is the largest district of Uttar Pradesh, lies in the south-eastern corner of the states, with 6788 square Kilometers area 3,782.86 sq km covered by forest. The local people call the district as the energy capital of India because of the vast natural and mineral resources the area possesses. Sonebhadra shares borders with Bihar state to the north-east, Jharkhand state to the east, Chhattisgarh state to the south and Madhya Pradesh state to the west and Mirzapur and Chandoli district of Uttar Pradesh state. The district headquarter is located in the town of Robertsgang. It has hilly terrains with dense forest cover. The Gond, Kharwar, Pannika, Bhuiyan, Baiga, and Chero are the major tribes who altogether constitute around 70 percent of total population of the district.

Forest is the very basis of our survival and have been identified as a necessary resource which plays a significant role both in social and economic development of a community and can improve the quality of life in general (Bajwa, 1987:210). It contributes to all aspect of life, providing food, fodder, fuel, medicine, building materials for all sorts of household incomes as well as providing a variety of culture and symbolic functions for many communities. This is significant for indigenous people, tribal's and communities living in and near the forest, as the forest produces like timber and non timber forest produces are an indispensable part of their livelihood strategy.

According to World Bank (2002) more than 1.6 billion people depends to verify degrees on forests for their livelihood. Out of this, 60 million people are almost wholly dependent on forests and 350 million people live within or adjacent to dense forests for substance and income. In developing countries, about 1.2 billion people rely on agro forestry farming to sustain agricultural productivity to generate income. Worldwide, forest industries provide employment to 60 million people and 1 billion people depend on pharmaceuticals' derived from forest plants for their medicinal needs (Kikhi and Kikhi, 2011:4). In India alone it is estimated that over 50 million people are dependent on NTFPs for their subsistence and case income.

For the tribal in India, forest has always been an important resource and has immense direct and indirect value. Building material, fuel, food supplement material for craft medicine are all acquired from the forest and it also provides as animal insects plants, vegetable, fruits, flowers seeds tubers mushroom, honey as dietary supplement. Such forest products are used for home consumption and also sold in local market to supplement the livelihood income. During the colonial period agricultural was stagnation, as the Zamidars were interested only in rack renting of the peasantry. They were unconcerned about investments and the colonial states also was not favourably disposed towards agricultural development as Zamidari system on which they relied, was itself the greatest drag on agriculture. In the post independent period Zamidari system was abolished but was not accompanied by any redistribution of land although its distribution was highly skewed. But the fact that the vast majority of peasants were granted proprietary rights was itself a great land marks. Thus the emerging rural scenario is characterised by sharp cleavage between two opposing classes. On the one hand there is a class of big land owner who control a large part of the land and other resources and who have gained all round through state policies. They are acquiring surpluses which are not being used in raising the productive base of the rural economy. On the other, there is a vast class of agricultural labourers, marginal and small farmers who find that work on land is not sufficient to provide them subsistence but in the absence of non form employment they stick to it howsoever unremunerative it may be.

The U.P. Tenancy Act 1939 put an end to arbitrary ejectment but the Act suffered from certain loopholes. Taking advantage of these loopholes the landlords continued to get a larger number of ten ants evicted every years. Land revenue had always been a big burden for small peasants throughout the colonial period and even in early years of independence. It was only when agriculture prices began to rise in the late fifties and after the advent of new agriculture technology a decade's latter, that the burden was lessened. The utter ruin of peasantry under the British rule brought it in the vortex of the national movement for independence and it was this basic factor which transformed it into a power full mass movement for independence. The peasantry was mobilised on the slogan of "land to the tiller" and abolition of Zamidary system. Consequentially after the independence on the recommendations of Zamidary abolition Committee, U.P. Zamidary Abolition and Land Reform Act, 1950, was passed in January 1951, but the Zamidars challenged the Act in the High Court and Supreme Court, the Act could be enforced only after July 1952. This gave the Zamidars ample time and opportunity to evict tenants and to corner the Gram Samaj land.

Land Distribution for Kol Tribal's

The Kols are a tribal group who inhabit large tracts of land in central India, comprising Madhya Pradesh (MP) and the adjoining areas of southern Uttar Pradesh (UP), i.e., the districts of Allahabad, Chitrakoot (which formed part of Banda district until 1997), Varanasi, Mirzapur and Sonebhadra. They are a proud people with a long, though unrecorded, history of living in harmony and communion with nature and the environment. They trace their lineage to the legendary Shabari of the Ramayana, who has been revered by generations of Hindus for her extreme devotion to Lord Rama during his exile. She is best remembered for having fed him berries after first tasting them to make sure they were sweet. Interestingly, while the Kols are included in the list of Scheduled Tribes (STs) in MP, they have not been accorded the same status in UP where they are classified as Scheduled Castes (SCs). They have been demanding ST status in Uttar Pradesh as well, but without much success.

During the last century, the Kols have been treated very harshly by the dominant sections of the region, especially in the southern districts of UP. They suffer high levels of exploitation, immiserisation and marginalisation at the hands of the feudal landed landlords, who combine economic exploitation with social discrimination. Needless to say, these feudal landlords belong to the upper Brahmin and Thakur castes; they find it easy to victimise and exploit the Kols by disposing the tribal's of their lands. They do this mainly through subterfuge and in collusion with the local administration, whose members belong to the same social, economic and caste groups as themselves; and when that fails, they use brute force. Because the concept of private ownership and legal title is alien to tribal society, the Kols have been unable to establish legal ownership to the land that they have cultivated for generations. In the face of relentless exploitation by the feudal interests, the Kols have had only two options or survival strategies available to them—retreating into the forest to eke out a living through their intimate knowledge of the forests and their wealth, or becoming bonded labourers in the service of the very same feudal landowners who exploit them.

The first of the two options is becoming increasingly unavailable to them due to the extension of state control over forests and the recent tendency to close forest areas for any kind of human activity in the name of environmental protection—a process began in the middle of the nineteenth century, when the colonial government extended its control to cover forests as well. As the post-colonial government through it forest department expanded its control to cover more and more forest areas, it tended to look upon the forest dwellers, in this case the Kols, with increasing suspicion and sought to evict them, declaring them to be encroachers and squatters. Today, forest officials consider the Kols to be the main destroyers of the forests as they are engaged in cutting fuel-wood and selling it in nearby urban centres. They forget that for generations these people have not only lived in harmony with the forests, but have also been responsible for their preservation. If today they are forced to carry headlands of fuel-wood for sale in urban areas, it is only because of the compulsions of sheer survival.

In the post-independence era, the Kols have been displaced from the forests due to two main reasons: (a) the construction of major projects like dams and hydro-electric and large thermal power stations in areas inhabited by them, such as Sonebhadra district, and (b) the establishment of sanctuaries and wildlife parks in forest areas, such as the Ranipur Wildlife Sanctuary that was created in 1978 and extended over 23,000 hectares of forest land. They have thus become victims of the forces of modernisation, development and progress, and more recently, of programmes for environmental preservation and conservation that, ironically, seek to improve the lives of ordinary people like them.

Rantola Incident

A case of murder has been lodged against 15 policemen, including four sub-inspectors in connection with a fake encounter here two year ago, which had resulted in the killing of two persons, lodged the case against the policemen. These include Jai Nath Mishra, Kamlesh Pratap Singh, Rajesh Kumar Singh, Rameshwar Ram—all sub-inspectors—Rakesh Singh, Kesh Bihari Rai, Shahjahan Khan, Ashok Kumar, Pramod Kumar Yadav, Dinesh, Satish Kumar, Chandrika Yadav, Rana Pratap Singh, Shiv Shankar Singh and Ravindra Nath Maurya, all constables. Before two years ago in an encounter in the Rantola area of the Sonebhadra district, the cops had gunned down two youths—Prabhat Srivastava and Rama Shankar Sahu—and later identified them as criminals. The cops, concerned, however, did not hand over the two bodies to the relatives of the deceased and instead cremated the corpses. Later, the relatives of both Srivastava, a student of Allahabad University and Sahu, a native of Garhwa in neighbouring Jharkhand, charged the police with murdering two innocent youths and later labelling them as criminals. Compelled by the protests on the issue by the voluntary organisations, the then district magistrate of Sonebhadra had ordered a magisterial probe into the entire episode. In the probe then ADM Ramkrishna had on the basis of available facts the 15 cops guilty for murdering the two innocent youths and recommended necessary action against the errant police personnel.

CASE STUDY 1

Shayama Charan Kol age group 35 years male who is resident of Pade village, Ghorawal block district Sonebhadra. His early life was very good after some times the village situation was changed. The entire village community suffering from the exploitation of zamidar socially, physically and mentally. To outcome of these problem he want to change the situation that's why he join the CPI-ML Party a political organisation working for tribal, dalit right. This organisation is based on an ideology Marx. To protect his village from the problems of exploitation by the zamidar he turn himself as a Naxal and wants to kill the zamidar. He served as village communist leader of CPI-ML. Organisation and actively participated in to the various issue of movement like issue of employment and involve protest movement successfully. But after two years he shifted into Jan Sangarsh Morcha (JSM) another organisation working for the welfare of tribal rights and actively participated in to the local movement on the issue implementation of MGNREGA, Kol reservation, and F.R.A. The basic factor is that the member of CPI-ML organisation was corrupt. They involve in their family member and spend night stay in their home with his wife and sexually exploit. To outcome of these problem he shifted into JSM and served as a village kol leader and actively participated in dharana pradersan and other organisational activity.

Right Based Approach to Development

Right, human right and right based are relatively recent additional term to the development lexicon (Tomasevski, 1993; Sano, 2000). While the human right based approach to development (H.R.B.A.) was generally neglected until the end of 1909s, in the past decades it has received an astonishing amount of attention, particularly UN agencies, international civil society organisation and donor agencies. The H.R.B.A. is an important tool not only for poverty reduction but also in efforts to combat poverty since it entails a comprehensive re-definition of the aims and approach to creates claims and not charity and hence the approach off development differs consequently and the whole process of thinking and of defining the nature of problem changes as well (Uvin, 2004, p 129).

According to Kofi Annan, 2006 emphasized that "basic human right—the right to a decent standard of living, to food and essential healthcare, to opportunities for education or decent work or to freedom from discrimination are precisely what the world poorest need most. Yet by virtue of their enfeebled status they are the one of the ones least able to achieve or defined such universal rights.

Rights Based Policies In India

India has made impressive step in pursuit of a right based development agenda and in term of the justifiability of economic, social, and cultural, rights including right to food (FIAN: 2007). Freedom from hunger or access to adequate food and nutrition is generally perceived as a Constitutional right in India.

The State has also introduced a number of Acts to change the term of its engagement with citizen through a new trajectory of governance in the context of livelihood (MNREGA), human development (right to education), governance (right to information), political space for women (50% reservation for women in P.R.I.), and control over natural resources 9 forest right for tribal communities). Moreover, a major efforts is currently on to provide a legislated right to food (ICPR, 2011).

Work and Social Security

Its aim to achieve full and productive employment and decent work for all,including women and young people. The millennium declaration also speaks of a commitment to take measure to ensure respect for and protection of the human right work and their families. In 2005, Parliament passed the National Rural Employment Guarantee Act, which is the central Government response to the constitutionally manifested right to work and a means to promote livelihood security in India rural area.

Indeginious People and Minorities Right

In 2006, the S.T. and other traditional forest Dwellers Act was passed which recognised and vests the forest right and occupation in the forest land in the forest dwelling S.T. and traditional forest dwellers who have been residing in such forest for generation but whose right could not be recorded. The major right that are granted under the Act inter alia are, the right to cultivate forest land to the extent under occupation, the right to own, collect, use and dispose of minor forest produce, rights inside forests which are traditional and customary e.g. grazing etc. This Act is to address the problem of tribal community which are dependent on forest and to undo the historical justice done to them by depriving them of their rights.

Issue of Implementation

The implementation of policies is primarily the responsibility of executive arm of the state. Opportunity must be created to enable the poor to exercise their right to participate in the implementation stage as well. The state should take up the responsibility such as obligation to respect, the obligation to protect and the obligation to fulfil an also state is primarily responsibility for realizing the human right of the people living within its jurisdiction. Other state and non state actor are also obliged to contribute to, or at the very least not to violate, human rights (Gaiha, 2003). Such opportunities are likely to arise in community level activity, which in turn are more likely to flourish within an institutional framework of representative of local Government. Decentralization of Government and a deepening of democracy are therefore essential components of the human rights approach to poverty reduction.

The life in present time is full of struggle in the affected villages. People deal a life of crisis in economy and village get deprived from a list of civil amenities. People of these villages grow mostly arhar, maize, paddy, wheat and occasionally vegetables on their small land holdings and depend on collection of Mahua, Tendu Patta, honey and dry twig, which offer them a supplementary income. Some people are doing work as a daily wage labourer.

Protest Movement for Implementation of NREGA and FRA

Ever since the announcement of the implementation of the NREGA and FRA. Jan Sansrsh Morcha (JSM) and CPI (ML) have launched a vigorous campaign aimed at monitoring every stage of the NREGA and agitating for its complete implementation they are doing protest in front of block office, tehshil and district level.

By the end of March, huge ads appeared in local papers advertising the provisions of the NREGA, and District Administrations issued Press statements about the number of job cards issued—but none of this is visible on the ground. Two months after the NREGA was declared to be in force, the bulk of people are yet to get job cards. The Administration's answer is that job cards have already been issued and complaints are being looked into. The standard excuse is that those who do not do manual labour are being denied job cards!

The JSM held dharnas and demonstrations at Ghorawal block office District Sonebhadra and demanding the 100 days job security under MNERGA Act. In Ghorawal block about 500 people of different village participated in dharana predershan under the guidance of Jan Sangarsh morcha with the slogan "job card nahi to block nahi" and demanding 100 days job security under MGNREGA Act.

Case Study: 2 About the Implementation Mahatma Gandhi NREGA Work

Most of the government schemes are not available in the villages because of corruption in the system I found massive corruption and serious irregularities in the implementation of the NREGA in the poor Kol and Baiga tribal.

Pade is an extremely backward and poor village of Ghorawal block of Sonebhadra district, in this village has 1000 households belongs to kol. The NREGS has miserably failed to provide wage employment in this village. I found massive corruption and serious irregularities in the implementation of the NREGS in this poor village.

Pyarelal (380), Subedar (400) and Damaru (318) are very poor dalits of Chheetarapur but have not received even a single day of NREGS work in last 4 years. Ramdin (27) and Asharam (13) are very poor labourers but have got no NREGS work in last 4 years. Moreover, the job card of Aasharam has fake job entry for 21 days. Ashok Kumar (48) and Mahendra Kumar (37) have never ever got any NREGS employment. Phulchand (40) too has got no NREGS work in last 4 years but his job card has fake job entry for 47 days.

Vardia is an extremely deprived village of Shivdwara Gram Panchayat of Ghorawal block of Sonebhadra district. Most of these Kol households are living in acute hunger and semi-starvation condition. Most of their children are suffering from acute malnutrition and severe under nutrition. The youth of this villager exploited by the fake cases of forest department and police case in Naxal movement operation.

Baba Kol (160) is a very poor dalit of Lohandi village of Ghorawal block but he did not get even a single day of NREGS employment in last 4 years. However, her job card has fake job entry for 99 days. In other words, though this poor dalit did not get even a single rupee of benefit from the NREGS since its launch, corrupt executing officials were able to pocket about Rs 8000/ of NREGS fund through fake job entries on the job card of this deprived dalit.

Tribals Air Grievances, Demand F.R.A. Implementation

Over 1000 tribal's who belongs to Kol and Baiga community and members of Jan Sangash Morcha (JSM) and forest workers from Ghorawal block district Sonebhadra converged at the tehshil office Ghorawal to protection they are being denied their rights and subjected to atrocities by the government machinery. They openly aired their grievances in a public hearing organised by the Jan Sangarsh Morcha an organisation working for the right of tribal people and demanded implementation of the Forest Rights Act (FRA), 2006, in letter and spirit. As the jury constituting prominent lawyers, retired judges and civil society representatives heard, forest dwellers stood up one by one to place their grievances.

Jokhan Kol (80) a resident of Varidia village of Ghorawal block Sonebhadra district, who lost his voice after allegedly being tortured by forest personnel in 2007 after they set afire crops and houses of the villagers, Sant Lal Baiga a resident of Shivdwara (Bagan basti) village Gohorawal block from Sonbhadra narrated how he has been slapped with several criminal cases and harassed for asserting the rights of forest workers

A resident of Magardahtola and Bhaisiya villages, Sonbhadra, complained about being displaced from their land. Shayama charan kol a member of Jan Sansarsh Morcha and a forest rights activist, said Kol tribal's in Sonebhadra district have not got the status of scheduled tribe so far, hence they are not eligible for land under FRA.

Roma, another forest rights activist, said according to FRA all tribals should get individual and community rights on the forest land. Also, she said, forest workers living for past 15 years in the forests are covered by FRA. The state government has made its intentions clear to implement FRA and withdraw cases against tribals and forest workers but officials at the district level are creating obstacles in execution of orders.

Conclusion

Land is the important issue during the colonial and anti colonial period of the movement. During the colonial period agricultural was stagnation, as the Zamidars were interested only in rack renting of the peasantry. They were unconcerned about investments and the colonial states also was not favourably disposed towards agricultural development as Zamidari system on which they relied, was itself the greatest drag on agriculture. In the post independent period Zamidari system was abolished but was not accompanied by any redistribution of land although its distribution was highly skewed. But the fact that the vast majority of peasants were granted proprietary rights was itself a great land marks. Thus the emerging rural scenario is characterised by sharp cleavage between two opposing classes. On the one hand there is a class of big land owner who control a large part of the land and other resources and who have gain during the period around and directly following

Independence in 1947, the internal situation in the party was chaotic. The party shifted rapidly between left-wing and right-wing positions. In several areas the party led armed struggles against a series of local monarchs that were reluctant to give up their power all round through state policies

The life in present time is full of struggle in the affected villages. People deal a life of crisis in economy and re village get deprived from a list of civil amenities. The right based approach like MGNREGA and FRA offers the potential to empower people to actively demand their rights. Constructing extremes poverty as a denial of human right, highlight the severity of such a condition to all members of society and appeal to people sense of justice in pursuing them to accept societal obligation to eliminate it. Using the right in development requires attention to both side of the equation from claim for right by citizen to the obligation and duties off the state to uphold those rights. However the implementation is very challenging and needs adequate time and resources.

Endnotes & References

Bajwa, G.S. (1987). "Environmental Management: problems and Prospects", in R.K. Sapru (ed.) Environmental Management in India, Volume ii, New Delhi: Ashish Publishing House, pp. 205-217.

Development Challenges in Extremist Affected Areas (2008). " Report Of An Expert Group to Planning Commission". New Delhi: Government of India (2011).

Food First Information and Action Network (FIAN). 2007. Right to food report India, http://fia.org

Gaiha, Raghav (2003), "Does the right to food Matter." *Economic and political Weekly*, Vol. 38 Pp 4269-4276.

Kumar, Anand (2004), "Political sociology of poverty in India: Between politics of poverty and poverty of politics". New Delhi : CRPC—IIPA Working paper 3.

Kikhi, Chozule and Kikhi, Kedilezo (2011), "The role of women in natural resources management, Kohima: Department of Planning and Coordination.

R.V. (1989), Tribal, Dalit and Government Lands, *Economic and Political Weekly*, 24 (24), 2355-2358.

Rupavath, R. (2009). Tribal Land Alienation and Political Movement: Socio-Economic Patterns from South India. Cambridge Scholars Publishing.

Shankar, Kripa (1990), "Land transfer :A case study". Gyan Publishing house New Delhi.

Sano, Hansa-Otto (2000), " Develolpment and human rights : the necessary, but partial integration of human rights and development," *Human Rights Quarterly*, 22(3), 734-52.

Tomasevski, Katariana (1993), "Development Aidand Human Rights Revisited, New York, NY: Pinter.

Uvin, Peter (2004), "Human rights and development, Bloomfield, C.T. Kumarian Press.

____ (2007), "From the right to development to the right based approach: how human right entered development," *Development in Practices*, 17(45) pp. 597-606.

PART IV

GENDER AND POLICY INTERVENTION

17

Gender Equality and Women Empowerment in India: With Special Reference to Millennium Development Goal

Sumit Saurabh Srivastava

The paper focuses on the Millennium Development Goal 3 (MDG 3) which aims at promoting gender equality and empowering women. The paper attempts its achievements and pitfalls in the context of India. The introductory part elaborates on the concept of women empowerment in existing literature. Later on the paper builds upon the outlining the Target of MDG 3 and its indicators to monitor the progress of achieving the same. The paper posits the performance of India along with these indicators and presents its situational analysis. Simultaneously the paper also elaborates upon the impending challenges and obstacles in the process of achieving the broader goal of gender equality and empowering women. The paper concludes by arguing that although many significant steps have been taken by the Indian State to promote gender equity which have manifested in concrete positive outcomes yet there is much to be done.

The social identity of gender is a marker which deeply affects the capability of any individual. As has been widely quoted and understood that gender is the social construct of sex which is biological in nature. Every society has its norms and values related to behaviour, activities and attributes which are assigned to men and women known as gender roles. These gender roles became the marker on the basis of which individual is included and/or excluded from the assets and resources of the society. Since time immoral, women have been historically excluded from the mainstream of the social and public sphere. Their exclusion has been even 'formalized' and 'sanctioned' by the respective society's traditions and customs. As argued, "...although the specific nature and degree of these differing norms vary across societies and across time, at the beginning of the twenty-first century they still typically favor men and boys, giving them more access than women and girls to the capabilities, resources, and opportunities that are important for the enjoyment of social, economic, and political power and well-being."[1] India is not an exception to this case. The traditions, norms and values of Indian society are more inclined towards patriarchy. At the very basic level, it denotes a system of social functioning where the male always has the control and authority over the female. This can be seen in the patrilocal and patrilineal aspects of the Indian society.

It was on 6-8 September 2009, the United Nations in its 55th session, the 189 nations adopted the resolution leading to United Nations Millennium Declaration. These Millennium Development Goals are related to tackle and effectively solve the issues of poverty, hunger, disease, illiteracy, environmental degradation, and discrimination against women. To successfully monitor in order to achieve them, all the MDGs have specific targets and indicators.[2] The Declaration later on transformed into the Millennium Development Goals (MDGs): Eight Goals for 2015.[3] Millennium Development Goal (MDG) 3 (Three) "Promote Gender Equality and Empower Women" focuses on the issue of gender equality and women empowerment. It realises that without giving proper attention to such issue, the other goals may not be achieved to their optimum. The MDG Target 3.A aims to "Eliminate gender disparity in primary and secondary education, preferably by 2005, and in all levels of education no later than 2015." Following are the key indicators to monitor the progress of MDG Target 3.A:

3.1 Ratios of girls to boys in primary, secondary and tertiary education

3.2 Share of women in wage employment in the non-agricultural sector

3.3 Proportion of seats held by women in national parliament

In the High-level Plenary Meeting of the General Assembly on the Millennium Development Goals at its sixty-fifth session during 20-22 September 2010 the UN General Assembly once again committed itself for achieving the goals. In the *Outcome Document* it argues that "We are committed to making every effort to achieve the Millennium Development Goals by 2015, including through actions, policies and strategies defined in the present outcome document in support of developing countries, in particular those countries that are lagging most behind and those Goals that are most off track, thus improving the lives of the poorest people."[4] Regarding MDG 3: Promote gender equality and empower women, it committed itself to "Empowering women, in particular women living in poverty, through, inter alia, social and economic policies that guarantee them full and equal access to all levels of quality education and training and vocational training, including technical, managerial and entrepreneurial training, and to affordable and adequate public and social services."

Understanding Gender Equality and Women Empowerment

Before dwelling upon the performance of India vis-a-vis the above-mentioned indicators, it is pertinent at this place to conceptualise empowerment in general and women empowerment in particular. It is necessary so as to understand the location of gender equality and women empowerment as outlined in the MDG 3. The notion as well as the process of empowerment is based on the power and powerlessness. The gender inequality results from the sense of unequal power which both men and women tend to enjoy in any given social setup. In this way, as the power structure is more inclined towards the men, the women are rendered powerless in the varying degree. This sense of powerlessness then gradually manifolds in furthering the exploitative system of patriarchy thus leaving the women in the background or so to say in the private sphere only. The public sphere i.e. the site of social interaction thus becomes exclusionary to the women. In affects their personality as well as life chances in a very negative way and manner. In a sense, she becomes disempowered in multiple ways.

Empowerment on the other hand is "giving power to a certain unprivileged section of society" in this case the women (Mohanty, 1995: 1434). For Beteille, "The idea of empowerment may be invoked in virtually any context: in speaking about human rights, about basic needs, about economic security, about capacity building, about skill formation or about the conditions of a dignified social existence" (1999: 590). In a more abstract and recent conception, empowerment can be also located in capability approach i.e. "what is each person able to do and to be?" (Nussbaum, 2011: 18). For Kabeer (1999: 435-464), the notion of empowerment is intrinsically related to the conditions of disempowerment. Empowerment entails a process of change. This process of change necessarily requires availability of choices. The process of making choice is related to the availability of choices. The ability of choosing the alternatives depends on three factors i.e. resources (pre-conditions), agency (process) and achievements (outcomes). Resources are not necessarily material in nature but they may include social resources also in terms social capital. Agency is the self assertion of the individual i.e. the realisation on the part of the individual that he/she is capable of performing the task which earlier he/she was unable to do. Both these two variables then lead to the outcomes of the action which speaks of both agency and autonomy of the women in various spheres of her life (Mishra and Tripathi, 2011: 58-65). Additively there has to be a sense of 'participation' within the notion of empowerment (Narayanan, 2003: 2484-2486).

The process of empowerment is closely linked to the notion of power. It is the process of achieving power and gradually consolidating within him/herself. It is multi-dimensional in nature as it includes the social, political, economic and psychological aspects of the individual's personality. It can very well reflect on one's control over the material resources and a sense of assertion at the level of ideas. Similarly, it has been argued that empowerment process should be broken down into four levels of power i.e. power over, power to, power to and power within[5]. Thus, "to be empowered women must not only have equal capabilities (such as education and health) and equal access to resources and opportunities (such as land and employment), but they must also have the agency to use those rights, capabilities, resources, and opportunities to make strategic choices and decisions (such as is provided through leadership opportunities and participation in political institutions)."[6]

The notion of women empowerment has also been crystalised at the global/international levels. According to United Nations Population Information Network (POPIN), Women's empowerment has five components: women's sense of self-worth; their right to have and to determine choices; their right to have access to opportunities and resources; their right to have the power to control their own lives, both within and outside the home; and their ability to influence the direction of social change to create a more just social and economic order, nationally and internationally.[7] United Nations International Conference on Population and Development (Cairo Conference, 1994) also focused on the issue of women empowerment. It effectively blended this principle to the urgent action required in the context of population growth. It argued for promoting cooperation and equality among men and women, involving women in the decision-making process at all stages and providing equal access to education for women as well as for men. Subsequently, the Beijing Conference (1995) dedicated itself to "enhancing further the advancement and empowerment of women all over the world, and agree that this requires urgent action in the spirit of determination, hope, cooperation and solidarity, now and to carry us forward into the next century."[8] United Nations Development Programme developed the Gender Empowerment Measure (GEM) estimated in Human Development Report 1995 which seeks to measure relative female representation in economic and political power. It considers gender gaps in political representation, in professional and management positions in the economy, as well as gender gaps in incomes.[9]

Back at India, gender equality and women empowerment have been mediated through the constitution of India. Some of the constitutional provisions for gender equality and women empowerment are Article 14, Article 15(1), Article 15(3), Article 16, Article 39(a), Article 39(d), Article 42 and Article 51 (A)(e) among others. Although there are various ministries and departments working for the empowerment and advancement of women, in a significant way, National Commission for Women was set up as statutory body in January 1992. Additively, the idea of women empowerment was also operationalised in the second National Family Health Survey (NFHS-2) of India conducted in 1998-99.[10] It was in the year 2001 that the Government of India formulated the National Policy for the Empowerment of Women with a focus on "to bring about the advancement, development and empowerment of women."[11]

Similarly, *Report of the Working Group on Empowerment of Women for the XI Plan* by Ministry of Women and Child Development, Government of India highlights that "The extent of empowerment of women in the national hierarchy is determined largely by the three factors—her economic, social and political identity and their weightage.... Therefore for holistic empowerment of the woman to happen—social, economic and political aspects impacting a woman's life must converge effectively."[12] Thus, we can see that there are enough mechanisms in place to ensure the unbridled process of women empowerment in India. However, as it has been argued many times that formulation of any policy or programme is another thing and its successful implementation at the ground level is another thing; it will be worth to analyse how these measures are performing at the ground level. The foregoing paragraphs look at the empirical evidence on the indicators of women empowerment and gender equality at the national level.

India vis-à-vis MDG 3

The present section focuses on the performance of India in achieving the MDG 3 i.e. promoting gender equality and empowering women. Although the rest of the MDGs do have a strong gender component attached to them, however the paper has restricted itself only to the MDG 3.A which is to eliminate gender disparity in primary and secondary education, preferably by 2005, and in all levels of education no later than 2015. The indicators to monitor the progress of the above Goal include:

3.1 Ratios of girls to boys in primary, secondary and tertiary education

3.2 Share of women in wage employment in the non-agricultural sector

3.3 Proportion of seats held by women in national parliament

The Government of India released the first *Millennium Development Goals—India Country Report* for the year 2005 on 13th February 2006. The Report highlighted some of the major initiatives and policies formulated and being implemented for achieving MDGs. These included Mahatma Gandhi National Rural Employment Guarantee Act, *Sarva Siksha Abhiyan*, Total Literacy Campaign of the National Literacy Mission, 73rd and 74th constitutional amendments providing reservation for women among others.[13] The paper in following paragraphs will reflect upon the achievements and challenges in respective indicators.

3.1 Ratios of girls to boys in primary, secondary and tertiary education

According to the Census 2011, the female literacy increased by 11.79 percent points from 53.67 in 2001 to 65.46 percent in 2011. The 86th Constitutional Amendment Act, 2002 has made elementary education a Fundamental Right for children in the age group of 6-14 years by providing that "*the State shall provide free and compulsory education to all children of the age of six to fourteen years in such manner as the State may, by law, determine*". Article 21-A of the Constitution of India and its consequent legislation, the Right of Children to Free and Compulsory Education (RTE) Act, 2009 became operative in the country on 1st April 2010. Coming to the status of girl education in India, ratio of girls to boys in primary and secondary education can be defined as the percentage of girls to boys enrolled at primary and secondary levels in public and private schools. Various schemes and programmes with specific objectives to improve upon girls' education have been implemented with varying success ratio. An important step in this regard is *Mahila Samakhya* (MS) initiated in 1989. Currently, the programme is being implemented in 121 districts

(563 blocks) of Ten States viz. Andhra Pradesh, Assam, Bihar, Chhattisgarh, Jharkhand, Karnataka, Kerala, Gujarat, Uttar Pradesh and Uttarakhand.

The Mid-Day Meal Scheme as the largest school feeding programme in the world covers nearly 10.44 crore children in 12.12 lakh elementary schools across the country. One of its offshoots is to address the low enrolment rate of the girls in schools. In order to focus on the educationally backward blocks in the country regarding girl's education, National Programme for Education of Girls at Elementary Level (NPEGEL) and the Kasturba Gandhi Balika Vidayalya (KGBV) Scheme are functioning. The latter aims "to ensure access and quality education to the girls of disadvantaged groups of society."[14] As of now till 2012-13, 3609 KGBVs have been sanctioned in the country. 366519 girls are enrolled in these KGBVs.[15] Table 1 brings out the salient features of overall girls education in India. It is important to note here that the educational need and aspiration of girl child is more than often muted by the prevailing traditional and patriarchal practice of 'son preference'. The girl is often at the receiving end as her engagement with school negatively impacts her time and energy available for household chores and caring of the younger (older) siblings. At the same time, parents of the girl are of the strong opinion that there has to have a helping hand for the women of the household. At the same time there is lack of infrastructure more in the rural areas thereby compounding the safety and security concerns regarding the girl child.[16]

Table 1: Girls Education at Glance, 2010-11

Enrolment, Gross Enrolment Ratio (GER) and Gender Parity Index (GPI)		*All Categories*			*SC*		*ST*	
		Total (Boys+Girls)	*Girls*	*% of Girls*	*Girls*	*% of Girls*	*Girls*	*% of Girls*
Enrolment {in lakhs}	School Education	2485.68	1169.91	47.07	221.41	18.93	111.97	4.50
	Open School Education	4.76	1.51	31.70	0.15	10.57	0.16	11.12
	Total (School Education)	2490.44	1171.42	47.04	221.56	18.91	112.13	9.57
	Higher Education	266.51	111.30	41.76				
Gross Enrolment Ratio (GER)	Class (I-V)	116.0	116.7		132.7		136.7	
	Class (VI-VIII)	85.5	83.1		90.6		87.0	
	Class (IX-X)	65.0	60.8		67.5		49.1	
	Class (XI-XII)	39.3	36.1		36.1		24.8	
	Higher Education	18.8	16.5					
Gender Parity Index (GPI)	Class (I-V)		1.01		1.01		1.00	
	Class (VI-VIII)		0.95		0.97		0.96	
	Class (IX-X)		0.88		0.91		0.86	
	Class (XI-XII)		0.86		0.90		0.76	
	Higher Education		0.79					

Source: Statistics of School Education 2010-11/{National Institute of Open School (NIOS)}All India survey on Higher Education 2010-11 (Provisional).

Source: *Annual Report 2012-2013*. Department of School Education and Literacy, Department of Higher Education, Ministry of Human Resource Development, Government of India, p. 182.

The National Programme for Education of Girls at Elementary Level (NPEGEL) was launched in July 2005 and is an important component of *Sarva Siksha Abhiyan*. The programme provides for development of a "model school" in every cluster with more intense community mobilization and supervision of girls enrolment in schools. As per *Report to the People on Education 2011-12*, "Up to June 2012 under NPEGEL around 41,779 Model cluster schools have been developed in 3,353 blocks of 42 districts covering about 41.2 million girls through different strategies. Around 2065 ECCE centres are operational to relieve girls from sibling care and facilitate in attending the school" (p. 28). In this regard it is pertinent to note that as per the *Millennium Development Goals: India Country Report 2014*, "the ratio of Female literacy rate to Male literacy rate for 15-24 years increased from 0.67 in 1991 to 0.80 in 2001 and stood at 0.88 in 2007-08" (p. 50). Regarding the higher education scenario in India, one can see the constant increase in both the percentage of girl's enrolment as well as the number of girls' colleges as reflected in Table 2.

Table 2: Girls in Higher Education

Year	*Girl Students enrolment*	*% of Girls in total Students enrolment*	*No. of Girls colleges*
2006-07	4820216	40.6	2208
2007-08	5167192	40.6	2360
2008-09	5649102	41.4	2565
2009-10	6080373	41.6	3612
2010-11	7048688	41.5	3982

Source: Compiled from *Annual Report 2012-13*. Department of School Education and Literacy, Department of Higher Education, Ministry of Human Resource Development, Government of India.

3.2 Share of women in wage employment in the non-agricultural sector

Economic empowerment is an integral part of the overall development of women. It is through her regular employment that she has a sense of 'ownership' and most importantly she is comparatively independent from her male relatives in terms of expenditure and economic liabilities. According to the *Statistical Profile on Women Labour, 2009-11* by Labour Bureau, Ministry of Labour and Employment, Govt. of India, as per Census 2001, female workers constituted 25.63 per cent of the total working population. At All-India level the percentage share of females as workers in the household industry and other workers stood at 6.46 and 21.75 respectively. In 2001 female work participation rate stands at 25.63 percent whereas for rural areas it is 30.79

and for urban areas it is 11.88. As far as average daily employment of women in factories is concerned, the percentage share of women to total employment stood at 8.41 in 2008 as compared to 10.6 in 1961. The Report also points out that the percentage of women to total membership in Trade Unions (Worker's and Employer's) varied from 7.1 in the year 1981 to 30.9 during the year 2006 whereas for the year 2008 it was 22.5. Table 3 presents the trend of overall employment in organized sectors (both public and private) by sex. The low presence of women in labour force can be explained by the fact that " ... increasing burden of household work prevents women from being in the labour force for a continued period through the year" (Rustagi, 2009: 164).

Table 3: Employment in Organised Sectors—Public and Private
(Lakh persons as on 31st March)

Year	*1995*	*2000*	*2003*	*2004*	*2005*	*2006*	*2007*	*2008*	*2009*	*2010*	*2011*
Public Sector											
Male	168.66	164.57	156.75	153.07	150.86	151.85	149.84	146.34	147.04	146.66	143.77
Female	26.00	28.57	29.05	28.90	29.21	30.03	30.18	30.4	30.91	31.96	31.71
Total	194.66	193.14	185.80	181.97	180.07	181.88	180.02	176.74	177.95	178.62	175.48
Private Sector											
Male	64.31	65.80	63.57	62.02	63.57	66.87	69.80	74.03	78.88	81.83	86.69
Female	16.28	20.66	20.64	20.44	20.95	21.18	22.94	24.72	24.98	26.63	27.83
Total	80.59	86.46	84.21	82.46	84.52	88.05	92.74	98.75	103.77	108.46	114.52
Both Public and Private Sector											
Male	232.97	230.37	220.32	215.09	214.42	218.72	219.64	220.37	225.92	228.49	230.45
Female	42.28	49.23	49.68	49.34	50.16	51.21	53.12	55.12	55.80	58.59	59.54
Total	**275.25**	**279.60**	**270.00**	**264.43**	**264.58**	**269.93**	**272.76**	**275.49**	**281.72**	**287.08**	**289.99**

Source: *Economic Survey 2012-13*. Statistical Appendix. Ministry of Finance, Government of India, pp. A-56.

As per the *Millennium Development Goals: India Country Report 2014*, "In 2011-12, the 68th round NSS results had estimated the percentage share of females in wage employment in the non-agricultural sector as 19.3% with the share in rural and urban areas as 19.9% and 18.7% respectively. It is projected that at this rate of progress, the share of women in wage employment can at best reach a level of about 22.28% by 2015" (pp. 07). However a major area of concern is the wage discrimination/difference between that of male and female workers. Khanna (2012) has pointed out such difference while working on National Sample Survey (NSS) Employment-Unemployment Schedule (EUS) for the year 2009-10. Table 4 reflects upon wage discrimination based on gender.

Table 4: Shares (Distribution) and Average Daily Wages, by Gender, 2009-10

Dependent Variables	*Share (%)*			*Avg. Daily wages (Rs.)*			*Average gender wage differential (%)*
	Men	*Women*	*Pooled*	*Men*	*Women*	*Pooled*	
Sector: Rural/Urban							
Rural	34.8	36.2	35	251	162.78	234.99	54.19
Urban	65.2	63.8	65	364.49	315.74	356.09	15.44
Sector: Public/Private							
Private	68.14	60	66.72	248.61	196.84	240.49	26.3
Public	31.86	40	33.28	508.21	373.61	480.02	36.03

Source: Khanna, Shantanu. 2012. *Gender wage discrimination in India: Glass ceiling or sticky floor?* Working Paper No. 214. Centre for Development Economics, Department of Economics, Delhi School of Economics, Delhi. p. 34.

3.3 Proportion of Seats held by Women in National Parliament

Third indicator to monitor the progress of the process of achieving gender equality and women empowerment is proportion of seats held by women in national parliament. The emphasis on women's political participation is all the more important for three reasons as "First, equality of opportunity in politics is a human right. Second, equality of political participation is important to ensure that women's interests are fairly represented in decision-making. Third, evidence suggests that women's participation in political decision-making bodies improves the quality of governance."[17] The *National Perspective Plan for Women* (1988) strongly recommended a 30 per cent reservation in the local government. Table 5 and Table 6 present the scenario of women political representation at the national level.

Both Tables 5 and 6 reflect a very dismissal picture of women's political representation. At the outset it can be argued that women in general have not imbibed political culture and thus they do not participate in the political processes. However, a deep reading into the scenario of politics reveals some facts which are heavily against the women in politics. Kishwar (1999: 142-147) has outlined various such factors as "...women are severely handicapped in politics because they cannot cultivate close association with men without jeopardizing their position in the family..... The breakdown of institutional politics in favour of gangster politics.... lack of literacy among women...' among others. On the other hand there has been a sustained and vibrant struggle within the women's movements in India to increase the political representation of women. The struggle has centred around the Women's Reservation Bill.

Table 5: Share of Women in Lok Sabha

General Election	*Year*	*Total No. of seats*	*No. of Women Member*	*% to the Total*
11	1996	543	40	7.36
12	1998	543	44	8.07
13	1999	543	49	9.02
14	2004	543	51	9.5
15	2009	543	59	10.1
16	2014	543	62	11.41

Source: Reservation Of Seats For Women In Legislative Bodies: Perspectives
Online Available: http://rajyasabha.nic.in/rsnew/publication_electronic/reserv_women_pers2008.pdf

Table 6: Women Members of Rajya Sabha: Number and Percentage

Year	*Number*	*Percentage*
2000	22	9.01
2002	25	10.20
2004	28	11.43
2006	25	10.41
2008	23	9.50
2011	25	10
As on June 2014	29	12.28

Source: Reservation of Seats for Women In Legislative Bodies: Perspectives
Online Available: http://rajyasabha.nic.in/rsnew/publication_electronic/reserv_women_pers2008.pdf

The 81st Constitutional Amendment Bill, popularly known as the Women's Reservation Bill (hereafter WRB), was introduced in the Parliament on 12th September 1996 aiming to achieve 1/3 reservation in the total number of seats in House of the People in a State or Union Territory.[18] The bill seeks to reserve for women 181 of the 543 seats in the Lok Sabha and 1,370 out of a total of 4,109 seats in the 28 State Assemblies. However due to stiff opposition from all the political parties, it was referred back to the Law Ministry in November 1996 for further modifications. Even after a provision under Article 331 for the nomination of a woman of the Anglo-Indian Community, it was not passed due 'lack of political will on the part of the government' (Rajalakshmi, 2003). Those who argued in favour of WRB focused on feminization of Parliament and those opposing it pointed out the preferential treatment factor and issue of 'elite' women hijacking the whole cause. The 84th Amendment Bill was introduced in July 1998. However due to caste based protests from political parties like *Rashtriya Janata Dal* (RJD) and *Samajwadi Party* (SP), the Bill was not even introduced (Menon, 2000: WS-37: 3837).

The WRB was again introduced for the fourth time in May 2003. With the General elections in 2004 around, both the BJP-led National Democratic Alliance and Congress-led United Progressive Alliance campaigned that if elected, the respective party would seek to pass WRB. Congress Party returned to power as part of the United Progressive Alliance in 2004 and subsequently issued Common Minimum Programme (CMP) including one-third reservation for women in state assemblies and the national parliament. It was after a long sustained vibrant struggle for the WRB that it was passed by Rajya Sabha on 8th March 2010. The viability and subsequent appraisal of this step needs more time than at disposal.[19] Due to various hurdles to WRB, under the broad rubric of civil and political rights, various alternatives were proposed to WRB (Omvedt, 2005: 4746-4752). Pointing out to the limitations of WRB in its current context one of the alternatives argued that "the role of independents in our elections at national and state levels is both marginal and declining" and "the success rate of women in elections is consistently and significantly higher than that of men". Thus, the way out is "to make it mandatory for every recognised political party to nominate women candidates in one third of the constituencies" (Narayan et al. 2000).[20]

Conclusion

The paper looked into the issue of gender equality and women empowerment as enshrined in Millennium Development Goals (MDGs) in the backdrop of achievements and challenges in Indian scenario. It can be concluded that in terms of ratios of girls to boys in primary, secondary and tertiary education, there is a significant level of positive change towards enrolment of girl students. As per the *Millennium Development Goals: India Country Report 2014*, "In primary education, the Gender Parity Index (GPI of GER) has gone up from 0.76 in 1990-91 to 1.01 in 2010-11 showing 33% increase, in secondary education the increase is from 0.60 in 1990-91 to 0.88 in 2010-11 thereby showing 47% increase, and in higher education, it is increased from 0.54 in 1990-91 to 0.86 in 2010-11 registering an increase of 59%" (p. 06). However the gender gap is explained by NFHS III 2005 06 "The main reasons of females never attending school are 'expensive cost of education', 'not interested in studies', 'education is not considered necessary' and 'required for household work'."[21]

Regarding the issue of share of women in wage employment in the non-agricultural sector, it is little apprehensive as there is lot to be done. The wage difference between male and female worker is still visible in most parts of India. One needs more initiatives on the part of State in minimising this. Also the issue of issuing land rights to women needs consistent advocacy and support from the government. At the same time the political agency of women has to be effectively translated into women's representation at the national level politics. The latter as is bridled with challenges as the contemporary political scenario marred with corruption, violence and muscle power is not inducive to women in particular. However, the performance of India vis-a-vis various indicators of MDG 3 is certainly can be seen as a harbinger of satisfaction and sense of achievement and commitment towards future goals.

Endnotes & References

1. UN Millennium Project 2005. *Taking Action: Achieving Gender Equality and Empowering Women.* Task Force on Education and Gender Equality.
2. *The United Nations Millennium Declaration* [Online] http://www.un.org/millennium/declaration/ares552e.pdf
3. *The Millennium Development Goals: Eight Goals for 2015* [Online] http://www.undp.org/content/undp/en/home/mdgoverview.html
4. *Resolution adopted by the General Assembly.* Online Available at: http://www.un.org/en/mdg/summit2010/pdf/outcome_documentN1051260.pdf
5. *The Women Empowerment Approach: A Methodological Guide.* Commission on Women and Development. Bruxelles. 2007.
6. UN Millennium Project 2005. *Taking Action: Achieving Gender Equality and Empowering Women.* Task Force on Education and Gender Equality. p. 33.
7. *Guidelines on Women's Empowerment.* United Nations Population Information Network (POPIN). Online Available at: http://www.un.org/popin/unfpa/taskforce/guide/iatfwemp.gdl.html
8. *Fourth World Conference on Women: Beijing Declaration.* Online Available at: http://www.un.org/womenwatch/daw/beijing/platform/declar.htm
9. For an alternative to GEM for developing countries see Mehta, Asha Kapur. 1996. "Recasting indices for developing countries: A Gender Empowerment Measure", *Economic and Political Weekly,* October 26, pp. WS80-WS86.
10. For details see Kisahor, Sunita and Kamla Gupta. 2004. "Women's empowerment in India and its States", *Economic and Political Weekly,* February 14, pp. 694-712.
11. National Policy for the Empowerment of Women (2001), Ref.: http://wcd.nic.in/empwomen.htm
12. Report of the Working Group on Empowerment of Women for the XI Plan by Ministry of Women and Child Development, Government of India. http://wcd.nic.in/
13. For details see *Millennium Development Goals: India Country Report.* 2005. Central Statistical Organization, New Delhi, Government of India. [Online] Available at: http://www.unicef.org/india/ssd04_2005_final.pdf

14. Guidelines For Implementation of Kasturba Gandhi Balika Vidyalaya (KGBV), http://www.education.nic.in/kgbv_guidelines.asp
15. Highlighting the importance of KGBVs, Kumar and Gupta (2008) have stated that "it is indeed a timely effort to address the accumulated problems arising out of systemic anomalies and cultural barriers impeding girls' development." For details see Kumar, Krishna and Latika Gupta. 2008. "What is missing in girls' empowerment?", *Economic and Political Weekly*, June 28, pp. 19-24.
16. In the similar context, Nuna (2009: 47) has stated that "Parents find it very hard to support girls' education at any level if education facilities are not available within a village boundary. The problem gets compounded with the lack of physical infrastructure in schools and continuous shortages of women teachers in rural areas." Nuna, Anita. 2009. "Bridging the gender gaps: An analysis of the educational situation with special emphasis on Higher, Technical and Professional Education", in Bhaswati Das and Vimal Khawas (eds.) *Gender issues in development: Concerns for the 21st century*. Jaipur: Rawat Publications. Pp. 20-58.
17. UN Millennium Project 2005. *Taking Action: Achieving Gender Equality and Empowering Women*. Task Force on Education and Gender Equality. Pp.: 104-105.
18. The Constitution of India (Eighty-Fourth Amendment) Bill 1998: Be it enacted by Parliament in the Forty-Ninth Year of the Republic of India...The following article shall be inserted, namely 330A (1) Seats shall be reserved for women in the House of the people... (3) As nearly as may be, one-third (including the number of seats reserved for women belonging to the Scheduled Castes and the Scheduled Tribes) of the total number of seats to be filled by direct election to the House of the People in a State or Union Territory shall be reserved for women and such seats may be allotted by rotation to deterrent constituencies in that State or Union territory.
19. A plethora of work has emerged in this context of WRB. See Menon, Nivedita. 2004. *Recovering Subversion: Feminist Politics Beyond the Law*. Permanent Black, Chicago. Basu, A. 2010. 'Gender and Politics', in Niraja Gopal Jayal and Pratap Bhanu Mehta (eds), *The Oxford Companion to Politics in India*, Oxford University Press, New Delhi, pp. 168-180. John, Mary E. 2000. 'Alternate Modernities? Reservations and Women's Movement in 20th Century India', *Economic and Political Weekly*, October 21—November 3, vol. 35, no. 43/44, pp. 3822-3829.
20. Forum for Democratic Reforms (a loose alliance formed by *Lok Satta*, *Lokayan*, CSDS and *Manushi*). Also see Narayan, Jay Prakash. *Women's Reservation Bill: A Remedy Worse Than the Disease*. *Lok Satta*. Online available: http://www.loksatta.org/remedy.pdf
21. *Women and Men in India 2011*. 13th Issue. Central Statistics Office, Ministry of Statistics and Programme Implementation, Government of India, Sardar Patel Bhavan, Sansad Marg, New Delhi, pp. xxiii.

References

Beteille, Andre. 1999. "Empowerment", *Economic and Political Weekly*, March 6-16, pp. 589-597.

Government of India. 2013. *Millennium Development Goals: India Country Report 2014*. Social Statistics Division, Ministry of Statistics and Programme Implementation, New Delhi.

Government of India. 2012. *Statistical Profile on Women Labour 2009-2011*. Labour Bureau, Ministry of Labour and Employment, Chandigarh/Shimla.

Government of India. 2013. *Report to the People on education 2011-2012*. Ministry of Human Resource Development. New Delhi.

Kabeer, Naila. 1999. Resources, Agency, Achievements: Reflections on the Measurement of Women's Empowerment. *Development and Change*. 30: 435-464.

Kishwar, Madhu. 1999. *Off the beaten track: Rethinking gender justice for Indian women*. New Delhi: Oxford University Press, pp. 135-152.

Menon, N. 2000. "Elusive 'Women': Feminism and Women's Reservation Bill", *Economic and Political Weekly*, October 28. XXXV (43-44): WS-35-44.

Mishra, Nripendra Kishore and Tulika Tripathi. 2011. "Conceptualising, women's agency, autonomy and empowerment", *Economic and Political Weekly*, March 12, Vol. XLVI, No. 11, pp. 58-65.

Mohanty, Manoranjan. 1995. "On the concept of 'empowerment'", *Economic and Political Weekly*, June 17, 1434-1436.

Narayan, Jay Prakash, Madhu Kishwar et al. 2000. "Enhancing Women's Representation in the Legislatures: An Alternative to the Government Bill for Women's Reservation." *Manushi*. No. 116, January-February.

Narayanan, Pradeep. 2011. "Empowerment through participation: How effective is this approach?" *Economic and Political Weekly*, June 21, 2484-2486.

Nussbaum, Martha C. 2011. *Creating Capabilities: The Human Development Approach*. Ranikhet: Permanent Black.

Omvedt, Gail. 2005. 'Women in Governance in South Asia', *Economic and Political Weekly*, October 29—November 4, vol. 40, no. 44/45, pp. 4746-4752.

Rajalakshmi, T.K. 2003. "A failure of will." *Frontline*, 20(11), May 24 to June 06. Web Address: http://www.hinduonnet.com/fline/fl2011/stories/20030606003003600.htm

Rustagi, Preet. 2009. "Women's work and Indian labour market" in Bhaswati Das and Vimal Khawas (eds.) *Gender issues in development: Concerns for the 21st century*. Jaipur: Rawat Publications, pp. 143-169.

18

Social Movements and the Gender Component

Sumita Parmar

Contemporary times are marked by the emergence of what are being labelled the New Social Movements or NSMs. This umbrella tern covers movements that are fuelled by diverse people united by their commitment to a specific cause or issue. The issues themselves are wide ranging both in their focus as well as the people who are involved with them. Social movements are not new phenomena and have existed since long. What is new however, is the very broad range of issues that have generated interest and motivated people of varying hues to come under one banner to work/agitate for a particular cause. Although earlier movements were primarily either political or concerned with economic issues, such as the demands for voting rights or better wages, contemporary times have seen these movements expanded in their orbit of action and going beyond the political or the economic to encompass a wide range of socio-cultural issues ranging from questions of conservation and the environment to human rights and issues of violence. Thus a specific issue becomes the thread that binds the participants who might have little in common otherwise and who are likely to go their own ways once the concerned issue is resolved or the particular purpose for which they have gathered has been achieved.

Movements comprised solely of women first became visible in the nineteenth century in the west when educated women united over issues of double standards practised by men vis-a-vis marriage and sexualities. Ironically, more than one and a half centuries later, the double standard, both in marriage as well as sexual practices, although reduced, still persists. However, the nature of the movements themselves has undergone many changes. Given the pervasiveness of the secondary position of women in almost all societies, irrespective of what laws and constitutions promise, women's movements strive for equity and justice across the globe. They seek redressal and solutions to a whole spectrum of problems. As the International Encyclopedia of Marriage states:

> Women's movements are among the most global of modern social movements. From nineteenth-century Canadian women's suffrage campaigns to recent direct actions for sustainable development in India, wherever women's movements have been established, national organizations and local grassroots groups have worked together for the interests of women and girls. Varied, even conflicting, understandings of women's interests arise from differences in gender, race, class, cultural, religion, and sexuality, as well as from global divisions of wealth and power. Nevertheless, the pervasiveness of oppression against women has led to the establishment of international women's movements with common agendas, connected to struggles for autonomy, democracy, and secure livelihoods around the world. (Women's Movements 2014)

The proliferation of these movements has given rise to the birth of theories about them that inform and help us in comprehending them. They do this by contextualizing them and putting them into larger frameworks thus bringing about perspective. These theories analyse available empirical evidence combined with the dynamics created by the intersections of the varying stakeholders who constitute the movements and attempt to generate a nuanced understanding. The fluidity of their nature makes their study both challenging and important. There are no clear demarcations or definitions and what lends cohesion and coherence is the specific space that a large group of like-minded persons through their joint interest in a particular issue create.

A study of these movements indicates that they are generally characterized by a gendered component and women form a core constituency as participants. The reason is not far to seek. Women are inherently involved in the issues that touch their daily lives, and have a direct impact on its quality and tone. Therefore, women frequently play a significant role in them, sometimes in positions of leadership and at others as affected parties and. In fact, history is witness to the fact that women have played significant roles in different social movements in different parts of the world and their contributions have changed the political, social and cultural landscapes. These contributions, hitherto unrecognised, have been empirically established in recent times thanks to the work of feminist sociologists. In fact the work of feminist social movement scholars is central to the new theories of the New Social Movements.

History also bears testimony to the fact that in spite of their involvement in social movement's women are frequently side lined and not given decision making and leadership positions when the aims have been achieved. Thus social movement's analyses indicate that the politics of social movements have often resulted in women becoming marginalized in the very movement in which they played crucial roles and participated as equals alongside men. The case of the Civil Rights movement of the 1960s in America is a good example when women were relegated to secretarial positions and sidelined after the movements had achieved some measure of success. Earlier, in the case of the fight against slavery in the 1840s women formed a substantial and important part of the anti-slavery movement. However, they were not welcomed as equals or co-protesters by the men. For instance, the women delegates to the World Anti Slavery Convention in London in July 1840 were sidelined and confined to silent attendance only! The following extract taken from a letter written by Lucretia Mott to her friend Maria Weston Chapman describes the meeting and the marginalized status of the women participants. The feelings of the writer are representative of the general reactions of the women:

> ... the name "The Worlds Convention" was merely a "poetical license"—(alias—a rhetorical flourish—)—and that the 'Com.' [Committee] in their wisdom had seen meet to ordain and enact, that women should not compose part of their august body. That they further 'as wise men should, had a resolution prepared for this said 'Conference' as one of its first measures, 'That all the arrangements of said committee be sanctioned and approved by the Conference. Of course we would not "thrust ourselves forward" into such a meeting, but having come so far to see what could be done for the Slave, and being [thus?] prevented doing anything ourselves, we were willing to be mere lookers on and listeners from without, as, by so doing we should be the means of many more women having an invitation to sit as spectators—which we found was accounted a very high privilege, in this land—by their women, who had hitherto, most submissively gone forth into all the streets, lanes, high-ways and bye paths to get Signers to petitions, and had been lauded—long and loud, for this drudgery, but who had not been permitted,—even to sit with their brethren, nor indeed

> much by themselves in public meetings—having transacted their business, as we were informed, by Committees....(Lucretia Mott, 1840)

The above described experience finds resonance in the experiences of women the world over. India has been and is home to an astonishing range of social movements, some of the more prominent ones having been initiated and sustained by women. The issues that concern women cut across the urban/ rural divide as do they the caste and class divide. Violence, limited opportunities, constraining patriarchal norms impact on the lives of women from different sections in different ways, but they touch all women. In the words of Raka Roy:

> The women's Movement of the seventies and early twenties received considerable attention for its campaign against dowry and for tougher rape legislation. While these campaigns were carried out in the name of all women, particular attention was nevertheless paid to the needs of poor women. (Roy Raka and Katzetstien, 2005)

Two outstanding movements of our times that bear testimony to the resolve and determination of women and that were initiated by women are the Chipko movement of Uttarkhand (then Uttar Pradesh) known globally as a nonviolent way of protesting and the anti-attack movement of Andhra Pradesh. Both these movements were spontaneous in their initiations and were sustained in the first case by rural and in the second by poor, illiterate women. The Chipko Movement (the word *Chipko* translates into "sticking" in Hindi—as in clinging to or sticking to something) which started in 1974 Uttarakhand can be called a pioneering movement since it addressed the issue of environmental protection at a time when the Government was relatively indifferent and unconcerned about the matter and public awareness about it in India was very little. The rational of the Movement is echoed, forty years later in the words of Vandana Shiva, in 2014 who says, "a paradigm shift to earth–centred economics, politics and culture is our only chance of survival." (Shiva, Vandana, 2014)

The sequence of events pertaining to the Chipko Movement read like a fictional narrative. The felling of trees bears a direct effect on the life of rural women. Several of their activities are closely intertwined with the forests and nature. Any change in their natural habitat impacts significantly on their lifestyle. Maria Mies puts it succinctly:

> On the more earthly level, diversity and interrelationships are characteristic of all sustainable agricultural systems. Biodiversity in this context implies

> co-existence and interdependence of trees, crops and livestock, which maintains cycles of fertility through biomass flows. Women's work and knowledge is concentrated in these invisible "spaces between'. (Mies and Shiva, 2010)

But in the village of Reni and in the surrounding areas, large scale cutting down of forests had been going on with subsequent deforestation. The men and women of the village realized that continued deforestations would severely damage the environment and therefore they decided to protest and try and stop any further cutting of trees in the area. But the nexus of the government agencies and contractors was a powerful one and no heed was paid to the protesters. The contractors were given the authority to go ahead and cut the trees. Unknown to the villagers a date was set and on the fixed day the contractors arrived with their labourers to begin the work. As they were approaching the site, they were seen by a girl of the village who raced ahead and informed the villagers of the impending doom. As luck would have it, the men of the village had all gone out for work and there were only women present in the village at that time. Undaunted, the women, led by a woman called Gaura Devi, went to the site and tried to reason with the contractors. As was expected, the contractors turned abusive and refused to pay any heed to them. The situation was tense and called for drastic action. This was provided when the women decided to cling to the trees, hugging them and telling the labourers that they would first have to cut them and only then could they harm their beloved trees. The contractors, along with the officials accompanying them, did not know what to do and how to handle this unprecedented situation. They had to give in before the resolve and the anger of the women and return with their mission unaccomplished. The rest of what happened after this novel way of protest is history. That action of the women of the village grew into the Chipko movement which snowballed into a mass movement resulting in the protection of the forest giving rise to similar movements in the rest of the country. What makes this a unique case is that women were proactive and successful in achieving their purpose. As it became a popular movement, the people felt confident enough to take on the powerful lobbies that were interested in the cutting of the trees. The sense of empowerment combined with determination and commitment ensured their success. The CM became an inspiration to many others and motivated people to resist or fight or draw attention to issues that they felt were being either neglected or simply wrongly managed by the Government or vested interests under the tacit protection of the government.

The anti-arrack Movement originated in a small village called Dubagunta in Nellore District of Andhra Pradesh which is plagued by the problem of alcoholism. The sale of distilled liquor in the rural areas of the state disrupted the life of the women and children impacting negatively on them. The men would work hard but end up spending their hard earned money on liquor, beating up their wives, getting into debt and becoming ensnared by the money lenders. The women of the districts were at their wits end and did not know how to address this problem and salvage their lives from complete ruin. The story of the anti arrack movement reads no less like a fictional narrative than the chipko movement of the North. Apparently, the government with collaboration with some NGOs had been running an adult literacy programme under the National Literacy Mission for the people of the area. The programme was being carried out with imagination and some out of the box thinking. Literacy was being taught through stories and one of the stories that were used was about the problem of a woman whose husband was an alcoholic. Life had become unbearable for the woman, and although she had tried hard she had been unable to solve with the problem. Finally, in desperation, the woman committed suicide. It was a story that the women attending the class could identify with. As they heard the sad story, slowly the women of Dubagunta who had come for their literacy class began to relate their own stories and the kind of problems they also faced. They saw that arrack consumption was a common problem and wondered whether they could address it in a united manner.

They decided that if the supply of arrack could be stopped, then their men would no longer be able to buy the liquor and consequently their problems would be solved. They marched together to the arrack shop and forced it to close down. The news of the forced closing down of the liquor shop by the united pressure of the women spread like wildfire throughout the district and soon other villages saw similar scenes. The women organized themselves becoming empowered in the process and took on the fight with the contractors and the government. They asked why, when there were no educational or medical facilities provided by the government, should there be so many shops selling liquor and that too with the cooperation of the Government. This battle crossed caste and class lines and was in that sense unique.

Both these two movements so different in their aims were similar in the spontaneity of their beginnings and are evidence of the fact that women could bring about fundamental changes through proper organizing and leadership.

It is noteworthy to observe that there is a symbiotic relationship between social movements and women's groups—whether they are Self Help Groups or community level social work groups. Particularly in times of disaster, these types of groups play a proactive role in the organizing and provision of care and support to affected persons and after the crisis is over, the women from these groups develop the confidence to take part in and play important roles in larger social movements. Conversely, those women who are involved in social movements, again through the development of self-esteem and confidence will play positive roles in times of crisis.

Slightly different in its genesis, but nevertheless an equally pioneering effort was made by Ela Bhatt in Gujarat. Bhatt led the women of varying trades working in the informal sector in a movement to unite and form a trade union in 1972 calling it SEWA (The self-Employed Women's Association) in Ahmedabad. SEWA became a women's movement which not only catered to the problems that small scale women entrepreneurs faced, but protected the women by giving them proper guidance in their economic affairs and by opening a bank for them. This was the first bank to be opened for poor women in India. It also supported them in facing and resolving everyday problems like harassment by the contractors, troubles at home, and exploitative interactions with the police etc. SEWA is now firmly established and internationally recognized. In January 2001 when Gujarat was hit by a severe earthquake and there was large scale destruction of property and loss of life, SEWA did stellar work involving women to build homes and shelters in order to reclaim their lives (Desai, 2007).

In more recent times disturbing trends vis-a-vis women entering the public space, the articulation of women's voices and the highlighting women's issues have become evident. There is an effort to push for and impose religious and caste identities on women by reactionary forces and vested interests. Fortunately, this is being countered at two levels—the micro and the macro. At the micro levels, grassroots organizations concentrating on sustainable development in the remote and rural areas dilutes the impact of the unprogressive forces. On the other hand, at the macro level, globalization and the growth of international trade and commerce make it possible to organize across boundaries. Growing awareness among people and the desire to live qualitatively and not simply materially better lives, has become an important factor in the dynamics of the contemporary social movements.

Endnotes & References

"Women's Movements." International Encyclopedia of Marriage and Family. 2003. Retrieved July 02, 2014 from Encyclopedia.com: http://www.encyclopedia.com/doc/1G2-3406900450.html

Desai Madhavi (2007), *Gender and the built environment in India*, New Delhi : Zubaan, p.188

Lucretia Mott (1840) to Maria Weston Chapman, 29 July 1840, Boston Public Library. "Women's Movements." International Encyclopedia of Marriage and Family. 2003. *Encyclopedia.com.* (July 2, 2014). http://www.encyclopedia.com/doc/1G2-3406900450.html

Mies Maria and Shiva Vandana (2010),, *Ecofeminism*, Jaipur : Rawat Publications, p.171

Roy Raka and Katzetstien Mary Fainsod (2005), eds. *Social Movements in India, Poverty,* Power *and Politics,* Oxford : Rowman and Littlefield Publishers, Inc., p. 18.

Shiva, Vandana (2014), *Making Peace with the Earth*, New Delhi : Women Unllimited, p. 7.

Women's Movements (2014), International Encyclopedia of Marriage and Family. 2003. *Encyclopedia.com.* 2 Jul. 2014, http://www.encyclopedia.com

19

Disability and Mainstreaming Gender: It's Linkage with Inclusive Development

Sudhir Singh

Disability is part and parcel of every society. Its roots could be traced back to evolution of human race. Since the inception of the human race there has been a gap of resources between rich and the poor. At the out set of 21st century it has been further aggravated with the free flow of the tenets of globalization. But these prevailing imbalances into their resources could not only reflect with the status of the people with disability but it has doubly making an impact on the community. Disability is a point of discrimination in all societies either it is developed or developing countries. It is particularly a matter of social stigma which prevails since centuries. In developing countries too they are confronting with gamut of discrimination embedded with social stigmas. According to International Groups of Disabled Rights "In our view, it is society which disables....Disability is something imposed on top of our impairments, by the way we are unnecessarily isolated and excluded from full participation in society. Disabled people are therefore an oppressed group in society" (UPIAS/Disability Alliance, 1976).

In developing countries the situation of common development has remained pathetic due to variety if reasons. Majority of developing countries have emerged independent after the Second World War. Many among them have adopted democracy as the way of governance. Democracy insists on the common development with special component of the development to the marginalized. In a broader term it is called inclusive growth. Simply it means to bring all segments of the society together into the developmental process. By all cannons of social justice, the disability includes as one of the worst group within marginalized groups. The component of human rights has emerged as one of the most publicized agenda of the international system with the end of the cold war. It has further expanded in post 9/11 international scenario. Human rights and democracy however are dependent on each other. In other words human rights could not be realized in the absence of democratic framework. Because with the component of social and economic rights the beauty of democracy is to provide civil and political rights to the people on the basis of equality. But even in democracies, which are morally compelled to implement the egalitarian agenda of human rights, it is observed that it has kept mum on the compliance of these cardinal principles of democracy. Today right from the Egypt to Libya, the wave of democratization is extremely intense. But the United States which consider itself as one of the important harbinger of the global democracy regime could not pursued this agenda into its vessel clients State like Saudi Arabia due to maximize its vested agenda. India is considered as one of the largest democracies of the world but in the case of Burma it has not been able to promote democratic values despite severe torture to democratic activists by military junta it is engaging the Junta to maximize its national interest to contain the influence of its arch rival China there. But despite these isolated infringements these countries have expressed its desire to support democratic values across the globe. Post cold war and post 9/11 international system has further aggravated this wave of democratization and human rights. Disability is one of the most vital human concern and 1993 Vienna Convention of international human rights have first time adopted disability as one of the most crucial component and more than 150 countries of the contemporary world are signatories of this declaration. Again under the aegis of the U.N. majority of world governments have signed the declarations which ensure the compliance of all rights to disables in 2007. Globally it has been established as one of the most deprived sector of the humanity therefore beside many international laws, many municipal laws have also been enacted for the promotion and protection of the rights of the disable community.

Disable people as part of the society deserves equal rights like able people. They are not asking for any charity but just asking for rights to realize their eternal urge of equality which has remained as one of the most important cardinal principle of democracy rights from the French Revolution of 1789.

The United States has been calming since a long time that it is the sole harbinger of the international regime of human rights. But even with the end of cold war, when communism has been evaporated from the universe, the United States despite their rhetoric of human rights have extended all round support to many authoritarian regimes for the sake of their national interests. Despite these prevailing realities, it is a fact that with the process of globalization human rights have become one of the most important components of international system. Even authoritarian regimes have become compelled to pay lip services to the cause.

For democracy as I have stated earlier it is the life blood to provide all kinds of amenities to the common people with exclusive stress on destitute. Kautilaya, the great Indian Philosopher has insisted in his famous book *Arthsastra* that a king must nurture their subject as a new born baby is being nurtured by their parents. One could trace the origins of democracy and human rights from his writing. He was the prime minister of the greatest Indian empire called Mauryan Empire. We are aware about the fact that monarchy was not accountable for the people because merely it was of the opinion that it derives its legitimacy from the almighty god therefore it is only accountable for the god. In democracy, people are the custodian therefore the elected rulers must be accountable for the people and people are most benefited element by all theoretical frameworks. But in reality prevalence of chronic poverty across the globe particularly in less developed and developing countries exclusively in those countries which have adopted democracy as a mode of governance is a blatant denial of the fundamental rights of the common people. In many developing countries it is matter of governance but in majority of them lack of resources and rampant corruption is denying the basic tenets of democracy to the common people.

It almost fits into the Indian context. India is a developing country and in 2011 World Bank had announced that within next two years, India will be surpassing China is GDP growth. (*Times of India*, 2011) Despite being a newly emerged country, India has done tremendous progress in all round development. Today after seven decades of our independence, one of the biggest concerns remains and that is inclusion of the marginalized into the mainstreaming process of development. It is one of the most crucial factors, which sustains a kind of unrest in our society. Poverty is a great denial of democracy and human rights. It is true that since last few decades we have been able to upgrade the life standard of 300 million people. But according to the Planning Commission still around 35 per cent people lives below the poverty line. According to the 2011 census, India has 121 crore population and still existing gender gap vindicates the point that gender has been discriminated despite growing literacy and prosperity. Currently 12th Five Year Plan (2012-2017) is in operation. According to the Approach Paper of the 11th Plan "The 11th plan provides an opportunity to restructure policies to achieve a new vision of growth that would be much more broad based and inclusive, bringing about a faster reduction in poverty and helping bridge the divides that are currently the focus of so much attention. The first steps in this direction were initiated in the middle of the Tenth Plan based on the National Common Minimum Programme adopted by the government. These steps must be further strengthened and consolidated into a strategy for the 11th plan." (11th Five Year Plan, 2006) The Approach Paper of the 11th Plan stressed on gender development. According to the paper" "The gender divide is another dimension of the problem which needs urgent attention. Gender bias is deeply ingrained in our society and is reflected in indicators like sex ratios, literacy levels of boys and girls, Maternal Mortality Rates [MMR], etc. however, even these data do not fully reflect the discrimination against women. The 11th Plan strategy for gender balancing must take care of the special needs of women such as clean cooking fuels, care for pregnant and nursing women etc. Gender balancing would require appropriate provisions in government policies/ schemes across Ministries/ Departments and sectors." (11th Five Year Plan, 2006)

We are aware about the census data 2011. It reveals that gender ratio is decreasing despite positive indications from other realm of human development. If the status of common women has not been improved then what kind of hope we could foresee for the women with disabilities. They are forced to face barrage of hostilities despite that the fact that India is growing as an economic power at the global stage. Poverty is rampant and empirical experience reveals that poverty hamper's the aspiration of the people with disability in general and women with disability in particular.

Nobel Laureate Prof. Amartya Sen has advanced international thinking about global poverty as a human rights issue. Sen's work in ethics and economics has emerged as a key influence on international decades about global poverty and human rights, and has depended and expanded theoretical thinking about this issue in important and innovative ways. Global poverty has moved rapidly up to the international human rights agenda in recent years. Virtually all governments have recognized the protection and promotion of human rights aimed at survival and development of the human person;

including the human rights to life, the human rights to a standard of living adequate for health and well being and the human right to education-as ethical, legal, political and economic imperatives for the 21st century. Global poverty causes these internationally recognized human rights to be violated and denied and has been described by Mary Robinson, the former United Nations high commissioner for Human Rights, as the worst human rights problem the world faces today. (Robinson, Mary, 2004) There are inherent relationship between disability and poverty. Disable community requires better medical attention and poverty prevents them to avail this urgent need. It is resulted into the variety of hazards for the people of disabilities. Disability is one of the most important components within marginalized groups. According to the international agencies, the number of disable people in India is 8-10 per cent but government of India insists that they are less than 3 per cent only. Here lies the seed of discrimination against PWD. Disable people constitute sizable portion of our population but due to governmental apathy and societal negligence their welfare schemes are inadequate, which kept them excluded despite all round claim of the government about their development.

India could not be strong without accommodating disable population into the mainstreaming process of development. Disable community remains one of the most discriminated in Indian context because of the double discrimination. India is a country where still even at the out set of the 21st century societal support or opposition matter's for the formation and implementation of any legislation for any nature. Disable community particularly confronting with the societal stigma. Because society still plays extremely important role in our system therefore disable people's all round development has been jeopardized.

Noted disable rights activist, Anita Ghai has cited one worst experience of a disable person and according to her "Destiny, fate, god, past sins ... Call it whatever you will ... it is not justified ...it would have been better if I had been allowed one day instead of dying everyday". (Ghai Anita, 2001)

Activist and scholars have acknowledged the expanding of borders of feminist research to include women with class, ethnic, national and other diversities. The widening sphere means that awareness about women problems in many sectors including the home, the workplace and other domains are slowly and steadily unveiled before us. In spite of the increasing range of issues that are being recognized as important, we note that a space for disabled women has yet to be found in serious feminist research. We discovered that as social group disabled women have hardly found a place in any existing theory. This reduced us to conclude that we need a space demarcated for women with disabilities in present day researches.

John Rawals is well known for his theory of justice and still considered as the one of the most authoritative theorist on justice. But Rawal's ignored gender in his theory of justice. For a feminist critic of Rawal's theory of justice, S.M. Okin has argued that under the Rawlinson paradigm, injustice against women within the house hold is invisible. Justice if not viewed within the family can only result in strengthening patriarchal norms. (Okin, 1989) We noted that the specificity of disabled women status has been linked to the general group of disable, thus meeting the legitimacy of their claims to the experiences of different disabilities, for instance, those with hearing problems have commonality of issue, which are not gendered. We realized that within this setting, the placing of women within the general understanding of disability sector, whether visual, locomotors or any other is fragmented, as far as they were seen with gendered lenses. The disability alone categorization was therefore insufficient to understand their problems. This is proved by the fact that disabled women are nearly invisible element, not only in the general disability movement but more so in the women, s movement. Through our experiences of working with the disability sector, we have realized that women within the disability movement, at least in the initial phase, are included because it is politically correct to include women then for any other reason.

While as women they face similar problem, as disabled women they experience problems different from the non-disabled. Therefore, their problems need to be addressed by both the feminist and disability movement. Despite this, we noticed that within the women movement at large they remained rightly invisible. In the context of women with disabilities, the contemporary debate therefore attempts to provide a comparative, relational based conception of feminism, which has been excluded from the general majority of a global feminist literature and movement. We believe these women are overlooked, this regarded and neglected as a group within majoritarian feminists strategies.

In 1995, Parliament has passed an act called People With Disability Act (PWD Act, 1995) for the all round protection and promotion of disable community rights. According to this Act, 3 per cent reservation has to be provided to disable community in all government employment. Today after 19 years of the compliance of the Act, it has not been implemented in its true proportion in any department either with the central or state governments. So is the state of many other developmental welfare schemes targeted for the betterment of the disabled people.

Disable people are marginalized but women within disability are worse. Women are doubly discriminated one as a disabled and another as a women. The state of overall women in our country is pathetic and women with disability are subjected to variety of societal and governmental apathy's. There are several other domains of women where neglect has been perpetuated by all corners against them both by the society as well as by the state. But the status of women with disabilities is extremely pathetic and need urgent attention by all concerned. At all India level, the states of women with disabilities are not at par with able women. It is also pertinent to mention here that without bringing women with disabilities into the mainstreaming process of development, we could not ensure the real concept of sustainable development. With this angle of development there is an urgent need to look into women with disabilities with separate identity within disability. Inclusion of this component is required to accommodate not into the planning process but in its implementation too. For this purpose a broad based awareness is badly required. Given the enormity of this issue this paper will try to cover the status of disable women in India.

Disability is a feminist issue, but is largely ignored in citizenship debates. A process of exclusion diminishes the well-being of both those affected and those, who consciously or unconsciously, participate in such a process. Women with disabilities/disabled women, largely inhabiting these margins, may experience the illusion of inclusion. The public imagination conceives of most people with disabilities, especially women, as passive citizens. They represent a source of increasing demand for services in an environment of ever-diminishing state and public finances. Dominant ideologies within the disability arena are changing from welfare to rights, yet people with disabilities still do not appear as active members of the community. Forced to claim 'special rights', their status as citizens with existing rights (albeit unacknowledged/inaccessible) is negated. Their rights however have emerged as an important concern for the state as well as the civil-society. But in a country like India, it is extremely turbulent their genuine citizenry rights. First it will be established than one could process their exclusive rights. Although they have emerged a critical arena of international human rights regime but it has not been translated into action despite many legislation and civil-society efforts. One could not separate the status of women with disability with the status of common women into the Indian society.

People who experience disability find themselves propelled from the 'normal' range of taken-for-granted 'rights', into the realm of passivity and lack of agency. Downward social mobility and social status often converge with acquired disability status. (Jenkins, 1991) Since Athenian times, men with disabilities, along with women, slaves and so on, have been excluded by law from citizenship status, physically prevented from taking any active role in democratic societies or indirectly constrained by discriminatory and oppressive institutions and ideologies. At one extreme they have been viewed as sub-human—'freaks'—and, like some indigenous peoples, the objects of extermination policies, justified through 'scientific' discourses. Recently a more benevolent and enlightened approach has seen the construction of people with disabilities as fully human and 'capable' of some assimilation into mainstream society. Efforts have been made in India both by the state and the civil-society to mainstreaming gender disability into the developmental as well into the planning process. But fact of the matter is that disability as a component has yet to include into the mainstreaming process despite gamut of assurances. First it needs to be incorporated than the women with disability will be better justified.

Now the question arises that how we will be bringing women with disabilities into the mainstreaming process. There may be variety of measures for the achievement of this goal but the most practical is there empowerment. The researches in this arena carried out by many agencies have insisted that majority of disable people are able to work without any aid and appliances. If we will provide them employment than they will not only able to earn their bread and expanses for medical requirements but could promote the overall movement of disability too. This aspect is extremely important for the women with disabilities because they are doubly discriminated into the society first as the women and secondly as a disable. Their employment will put self confidence within their personality and they will act with better confidence to cope all challenges in their life. There are multiple perspectives on empowerment and the particular meanings given to the construct, according to persons, settings, goals, and other variables. Research on empowerment has largely focused on groups that are typically considered disadvantaged, disempowered or ostensibly powerless (Thompson & Spacapan, 1991) Luke, Rappaport, and Seidman (Luke, Rappaport & Seidman, 2002) suggested that empowerment is more than a mere process, solution, or exemplar as is, for instance, prevention. Instead, they posit that empowerment is the process to which the primary energies of psychologists, counselors, social workers, and others should be directed and through which most of the goals for social and individual change will be most appropriately accomplished. Zimmerman and Warschausky, in their rehabilitation research, asserted further that a focus on individual or person-centered notions of empowerment precludes us from seeing the implications for community or social change. Empowerment, they argue, should not be treated simply as some personality variable that would neglect the construct's social relationship. For instance, among service providers to mentally disabled clients, empowerment has become a program principle (Cohen, 1989) that underlies group self-help designs, mechanisms and consequences. Nobel Laureate, Amartya Sen has also argued that incorporation of gender into the mainstreaming of development is the key to the success of the initiative of human development for any society. The government of India has already started the process but it has yet to take off properly and component of disability is absent from this debate. It is vindicated only with one fact that government of India counts disable community as merely 2.3% of total population despite the fact that UN agencies are often mentioning that it is not less than 10%. Here lies the crux of the problem because when government will not accept their real number it means that the planning process will allocate resources in a different manner. Needless to say that it has marred the prospects of the actual empowerment of the disable community, which remains as a severe issue of concern for our desire goal of sustainable development. When in totality disable community has not been given its due share than asking for separate arrangements for the women with disabilities seems to a castle's in the air.

However given the actual situation at the grass root level in India, we have to formulate our strategies to cope with the situation under which women with disability get benefited. First of all poverty is important in the context. Planning Commission has accepted that around 35% people are below poverty line and numbers of welfare measures have been carried out to bring them from this deprived situation. But here again governmental apathy remains mater for grave concern for all concerned. For an example, the government has given exclusive attention for the plight of the SC/ST community through a number of corrective measures. But at the same time, it has not been much concerned for the same level of efforts for the welfare of disable community. One could trace this imbalance within the governmental policies regarding resources allocation for the welfare of the disable community. The fact is the government data, itself insisted that there is strong link between disability and social marginalization. The NSSO data 1991 suggests that 40% of the disable poor belong to the SC/ST community. Thus, if empowerment schemes of the SC/ST do not have a disability component, a large section of the community will be deliberately doomed to marginalization.

In Indian context, where poverty is rampant and traverse all artificial barriers, better employment opportunities could improve their situation in a massive manner. For that in 1995 People With Disability Act had been enacted by the parliament, which provide 3% reservation to the people with disabilities in all governmental services. But the majority of people with disabilities particularly women with disabilities didn't have adequate educational as well technological qualification therefore they are not eligible for these positions. Majority of women with disabilities are from unorganized sector and particularly from the enormously vast rural sector. The work activity status of disabled persons depicts that about 46% of disabled populations both in rural and urban areas were without work. Only 1.8 and 7.3% disable persons in rural and urban areas respectively were regular employees in 2002. Even the nature was only in low profile jobs with bare minimum income. Provide employment opportunities for disable persons is the top priority to make them self-reliant, unfortunately, very few employment opportunities are provided to the disable persons due to social, cultural and work potential bias against them. It is more suited for the denial of job opportunities for the women with disabilities. The National Centre for Promotion of Employment for Disabled Persons [NCPEDP] in collaboration with the National Association for Blind, Delhi, conducted a survey for disabled persons since the enactment of PWD Act, 1995. (NCPEDP Study) the survey was conducted in 119 NGO's. major findings of the surveys are as follows

- Only 12.89% disabled people were among the professional staff members of these organizations. Disabled women again formed a dismal 4.47% of the group. The administrative structure of the respondent organizations seems to be dominated by non disabled males.
- About 50% of the disabled people placed by the respondent organization in the last two years were self-employed. Only 1/4 of the beneficiaries were disable women.
- According to the data, about 90% of the people were earning less than 2,000 per month. In fact, 47.50% of them earn below Rs. 1,000 per month.
- Though 1,628 private sector companies were approached in the last

two years for placement by the respondent organization, only 1,557 disabled people found jobs in this sector. While 804 public sector companies were approached, only 220 disabled people get jobs in this sector for the last two years.

- Only 33.61% of the respondents organizations register their beneficiaries with employment exchanges. Only 212 disabled people were placed through this channel out of the total job placement of 4,812 disabled persons.
- While 5,618 disabled people received vocational training in the last one year, only 4,812 people were placed in the last two years.
- Only a handful of organizations provide training in industry related skills to disabled people. Majority of the NGO's provide training in skills like art and crafts, making stationery item's etc, which limit their options to self-employment.

Concluding Remarks

India is sustaining a high pace of growth since last many years despite odd global scenario. In the contemporary world, beside China there is hardly any country which could equate Indian pace of all round development. But the fact remains that women remains at the receiving end by any parameter of human development index than man and even 2011 census data proves this argument. Women need to be included into the mainstreaming process of development than only the real concept of sustainable development could be achieved. As far as women with disabilities is concerned there problem is twin first as a women and second as a disable. For the proper mitigation of the challenges we need to develop the capacity level of the women with disabilities. As NSSO data reveals they are able to work and we know that they need better medicinal as well as societal care for the betterment of their life therefore we need to ensure their economic empowerment. Merely governmental sector is unable to provide this opportunity to one of the most hapless segment of our society. It needs all concerned efforts and we must do this. Private sector will be a great help. We need to harness the concept of corporate social responsibility because due to the growing clout of the process of globalization, market forces are strengthening and they need to allocate adequate resources for this unfortunate section of our society. Only all concerned sincere efforts could ensure all round well being of the women with disabilities. Being a democratic society we need to implement all legislation for the promotion and protection of the cause. Since we believe in the concept of welfare state therefore it is the duty of the society to provide basic societal support to women with disability. Our traditional values propelled us to extend all possible support to women but women with disabilities need more support from the society than the government because government neither could nor be successful till we will be not providing positive support to women with disabilities.

At the outset of the 21st century it is an open secret that women with disabilities in particular live not at par with common citizens of our country. They are asking for parity not for charity and we need to realize this fact in a candid manner. The new Modi government has adopted a model of Kautilaya's notion of the state that it must take care of each of its citizen as new born baby is being taken by their parents. It is an era of participatory democracy therefore it is the moral duty of the rulers to ensure that each need must get their due. The 2014 mandate is unique and one of the propelling factors of this mandate is an urge of good governance. One must hope that this government will to abide by its pledge. Civil society role however will remain crucial. Societal awareness could be pivotal for the compliance of this egalitarian goal. Consciousness is increasing in this field but more need to done to provide tenets of human rights to women with disabilities.

Endnotes & References

Cohen, M.B. (1989), Social work practice with homeless mentally ill people: *engaging the client. Soc.* Work, 34(6), 505–509

Ghai, Anita (2001), *Disability and Life Course; Global Perspectives* (eds) Marginalization and Disability, Experiences from the Third World; Mark Priestley, Cambridge University Press, Cambridge, 2001.

Jenkins, R. (1991), 'Disability and social stratification', British Journal of Sociology, Vol. 42, No. 4: 557-80.

Luke, D.A., Rappaport, J. & Seidman, E. (2002), *Setting Phenotypes in a Mutual Help Organization: Expanding Behavior Setting Theory*, pp. 217–238 (2002).

Okin, S.M. (1989), *Justice, Gender and the Family*, New York, Basic Books.

Robinson, Mary (2004), *Health, Human Rights and Development*, OECD Forum. Available at http: //www.oecd.org/dataoecd/7/27/31787614.pdf.

Role of NGO's Vis-a-Vis the Employment Scenario in India with reference to people with Disabilities, NCPEDP and The National Association for the Blind, Delhi Research Study.

Thompson, S.C., Spacapan, S. (1991), *Perceptions of control in vulnerable populations*. J. Soc. Iss. 47(4), 1–21

Times of India (2011), New Delhi, January 2011.

Towards Faster and More Inclusive Growth; An Approach to the 11th Five Year Plan, *Planning Commission,* Government of India, New Delhi, 2006, p. 1.

UPIAS/Disability Alliance (1976), *Fundamental Principles of Disability,* UPIAS, Disability Alianc, London.

20

Gendering Public Policy in India: A Review

Koushiki Dasgupta

The problems of locating women in public policies are connected with three general concerns. The first question is related with the construction of an exclusive category of 'women'. Since women are a heterogeneous category including different castes, class, religions and cultures, it is difficult to make women a singular category of enquiry. Patriarchal oppression or socio economic discriminations against women may have been taken as components of unity but it is not enough to describe women as a category in the public policy making projects. Secondly, women productivity or her involvement as a worker in both formal and informal sector has no yet been acknowledged properly and her contributions in the public and private work spaces are undercounted or underestimated. Therefore, the policy makers are sometimes caught into the quandaries of vague information that their knowledge on women looks too much flawed to make any decision. The third question arises out of the figuration of women identity within a framework of ambivalence. She has been looked at wearing a double mask—one identifying her to the national community and the other to the particular culture she belonged to.

The nationalist construction of women as a cultural embalm of the nation too often create conflict between women's right as equal citizens and a community's cultural practices. This conflict is better grounded on gender discriminatory practices and it equally influence the nuances of public policy making in India. In 1937, a National Planning Committee was constituted with the task of reporting on different areas of national life and drawing an outline for Indian's planned development after independence. The Sub Committee on Women's Role in Planed Economy was to deal with women's life considering "her social economic and legal status, her right to hold property, carry on anti trade, profession or occupation and remove all obstacles or handicaps in the way of realizing and equal status and opportunity for women..." (Chaudhuri, 996). The report titled 'Women's Role in Planned Economy' was divided into three parts. The first one discussed on the individual status of women on the areas of 'civic rights', 'economic rights', 'property rights' and 'education'. The second section dealt with 'marriage and its problems', and 'family life', the third section dealt with numerous issues like caste, widows, remarriage of widows, unmarried mothers, abortion etc. The subcommittee demanded equal voting rights for women Right to work, right to employment, right to equal access to public services, equal wage for equal work, equal right to health, leisure, property rights, recreation and others were some of the rights demanded by the subcommittee. In the report trade unionism amongst all categories of women was encouraged and it was accepted as principle of equality between man and women (NPC Series, 1947). The report of the committee felt that the works of a housewife, 'which at present receives no recognition either from the State or society, should be recognized as having an economic value and that work in the home should not be considered in any way inferior to the other type of work done outside the home (NPC Series, 1947). Interestingly this subcommittee grounded most of its claims on the basis of the 'special contribution of women made to the nation' and as the 'guardians and trustees' of the future generations. Here lies the ambivalence of policy making that the articulation of equal citizenship or the articulation of property rights and economic freedom was correlated with the responsibility of creating a cultural 'environment in the home' so that the children or the 'future generations' could have the proper education. Thus women were entrusted with the task of ensuring the nation's cultural future and her role as a mother was emphasized. The report stated, "we do not wish to turn women into a cheap imitation of man or to render her useless for the great task of motherhood and nation building (Chaudhuri, 996). The planning committee proposals did not recommend any structural changes to the condition of women and soon in 1934 the All India Women's Conference asked for the removal of legal inequalities between man and women (AIWC Annual Report, 1934). But the male reformers did not share the same ideas with the AIWC except a few Congress leaders. While Women's Conference talked about uniform laws for all women regardless of community (AIWC

Annual Report, 1935), a section of the leaders were afraid of a probable disruption in Hindu social system, the others were not even bothered for the legal reforms because they felt that the Hindu women were not suited for public life and they were happy with their family life.

It was expected that after independence women would be understood differently in the development paradigm. Surprisingly in an era of planning she was not even represented properly, however, the Indian state had always planned up its policies on women. Starting from family planning to maternal mortality, the state time to time made numerous declarations on girls' literacy, women education, and women employment. Apart from general policy making the state took interest on the improvement of widows, tribals, working women, minority women and others. Inspite of its efforts, the state somehow lacked the ability to take practical actions on these areas. Many of its policies are never translated into a reality and remained at a level of commitment only. The National Institute of Public Finance and Policy had shown that the amount of expenditure fixed for the women is not enough compared with the actual number of beneficiaries. Side by side there is some vague areas in policy making process that what categories or scheme would be taken for a gender differentiated impact.. A good policy making process is one that is committed to producing high quality decision with a high degree of legitimacy, power and accuracy (Moore, 1998). It also requires a close involvement of the persons who have to implement the policy on ground. Since independence various commissions and tasks forces in India looked at the condition of women and made recommendations for the betterment of their statutes in the society in terms of economic independence, education, health opportunities etc. But it was seen that the benefits of policy making were not reaching all women, particularly those that were poor. The government of India is willing to make policies in favor of women empowerment but lack of knowledge on the root causes of social inequalities or a kind of apathy towards wide scale structural social change is making all the efforts more or less halfhearted (Datta, 2002). One of the main problems of policy making in Indian is extreme fragmentation and lack of coordination between the government departments. Sometimes they fail to formulate one common agenda aligning to all the sectors of a particular department. Other than this inadequate time spent on policy implementation, inadequate professionalism on the part of the policy makers and advisors create unwanted difficulties in the execution of a policy. However, the most serious problem on the part of the government is that the state often takes an indifferent or lethargic stand in dealing with the structural problems built into the Indian social system. For example, several schemes were undertaken in the past for the betterment of the distressed widow women without going into the root causes of distress (Mari, 1999). It is noticed that in gender reinforcing schemes, the traditional roles of women are highlighted in most of the cases. In order to ensure women's economic independence, jobs were created only for home based works. In the Community Development Programme, introduced after independence in 1952, better home making skills were taught with a belief that they would become better housewives. From the Second to the fifth Five Year Plans welfare remained as the primary issue instead of empowerment. For the first time in the Sixth Five Year Plan, a chapter was included on Women and Development. On the shift from women as targets of welfare policies to groups of development, the government concluded that, "This shift represents reassertion of the principle of women's equality of rights—to participate effectively in the process of development, ensuring thereby movement in the direction of the constitutional goals. (Ministry of Social Welfare, 1985)

Question emerged that how far these community development measures are helpful in eliminating poverty. Poverty in developing countries is deeply embedded in the socioeconomic structure based on unequal distribution of wealth and resources. For example the policies of forming self help groups may be cited. It was expected that the micro credit programmes would generate income among women and women themselves would be benefitted from the higher status achieved as a result of being able to provide additional income. This concept of cooperativization is from the Gandhian philosophy and it is now widely applied in rural women's development schemes. Group formation and micro finance networking is a common feature of rural women development schemes in most of the poor societies of India, Bangladesh or Africa but the over emphasis on a poverty often fails to recognize different constraints on poor rural women and can not necessarily guarantee an overall empowerment of their lives, mostly due to the fact that 'neither their views nor the interests of grass roots women have been taken into consideration at the time of policy formulation (Rajagopal & Mathur). Two major Self Help Group networks in India have access to institutional credit. The National Agricultural Bank for Rural Credit and the *Swarnajayanti Gram Swaeozgar Yojana*. But in most of the cases it is seen that the women are targets of action and their voices are rarely heard. In the self help schemes, the self has been problamatised with the bureaucrat's own image rather than the women for whom the schemes wee made. The act of government officials directing what kind of activities the women should involve in, indicate the reflection of the same power structure prevalent in rural societies. These schemes do not leave women into an autonomous space of action and more or less ignored individual agency as a factor in determining women efforts. Women remaining in bellow poverty lines often fail to connect with the women *panchayet* members due to castiest, political or class differences and fail to get the necessary information. In addition to this, women face gender specific difficulties both at the home and at the outer world. The male members of her family especially her husband controls her life in a patriarchal social structure and she often fail to repay the credit taken out of a micro finance scheme due to domestic disturbances. However, no generalization is required in terms of the issues related to women in self help group's rather individual experiences and situational compulsions must be accounted for a better understanding of the existing problems in a particular socio cultural context (Koczberski, 1998).[12] If the self help group services aim to build up entrepreneurial potentials among rural women, then individual initiatives must be acknowledged instead of group assistance in particular cases. In different situations women were refused for lone on an individual basis and such a system spoiled the individual capacity building initiatives at an early stage. The state must motivate the individual woman but it is not done usually in case of rural women. Women lack the skills and motivations for nontraditional economic activities. If they get the required support and assistance from the state and from the community, women leaders may come out as an inspiration for many others. Definitely the idea of a group generates community bonding in a society but it must be remembered that, 'Men and women look for groups to which they can belong, certainly forever, in a world in which all else is moving and shifting, in which nothing else is certain. (Hobsbawn, 1996)

If one looks at the development projects where women were included on gender specific terms, it will be evident that here women have been identified as vulnerable groups and the projects are simply characterized as welfare projects. The projects interested in generating women's income, tried to make it through the schemes in conformity with the traditional roles of women. However, some policy proposals asked for the solution to equality into widening access to factors like technology and education. The welfare oriented approach of 1950s has been changed to production oriented approach in 1970s and towards empowerment in early nineties. It has been stated that women had to be brought into the development process through access to employment and to move women into national economics. In case of the tribal and lower caste women, these strategies are too much difficult to accommodate. Though there is a substantial presence of tribal women in the Indian work force, women do not have direct rights over disposal of the produce. Dependence on natural resources, environmental degradation, industrialization and other factors contribute equally for the decline of tribal economy in general. The government of India initiated several policies and programmes for the upliftment of the tribals, but tribal development policies in India failed to recognize the gender connotations. The tribal women are not separately addressed into the planning proposals (Bhandari & Channa, 1996). They are included into the broader tribal development programmes. Other than poverty eradication programmes and maternal benefits to rural women the state hardly realize the needs of the rural women including the tribal women. In the development literature women are seen as 'objects' not as 'agents', however, any development activity should start with the involvement of the target population (Sen, 1990). But in state planned development programmes the cultural and historical context of tribal marginalization hardly get any attention, many studies tend to ignore the diversities among tribals with reference to their access to state generated resources. As a result of misconceived development policies, tribals have faced increasing alienation due to agricultural experiments, technology transfer and large scale deforestation. The tribals are getting deprived of their traditional resources due to the entry of several multinationals into the tribal areas—rich in mineral and other natural resources. The external forces are as powerful as to make the tribal women seeking alternative ways of livelihood outside the region leading to migration. A good number of studies are available on the condition of tribal women, however, their participation in the decision making process has not yet been ensured. This issue is actually related with the broader issue of women participation in politics. In case of seat reservation policy for women (Lok sabha Debates, 1996), some counterproductive elements like proxy representatives, separation of male representatives from women development programmes and other factors are affecting the overall process. Inspite of numerous obstacles to women's political effectiveness, there is evidence that women leaders in local bodies do manage to articulate their perspectives in matters like land rights to women, water supply issues, roads, fuel, health, education and others.

One of the most important forms of gender inequality across the world is that the policies and programmes are not cleanly motivated for promoting women's control over their income and resources. Indian government passed laws ensuring women's right to land or property but her rights are yet to be practiced and her control over the capital is yet to be established. Unless women are bought into recourse generating process, she can't enjoy income security at the highest level. However, her participation into the socio-economic process cannot be done unless gender violence is tackled with strong hands. Violence against women reduces quality of life, reduce her mobility and participation into the social process. It is noticed that domestic violence can push households into economic crisis in a manner the state can face loss due to the absence of women form paid work and a gross decline in her productivity after an incident of violence. On the other violence in public may give rise to conservative forces which can put a check on women's public appearances and participation (Kelkar, 2005). These factors are the stumbling blocks before making women 'agents' of the development process. Providing space to women in the planning process is not enough since 'the agenda of globalization promotes democracy for those who can participate in the bargaining process (Monhanty, 1995)·

In 1975, also the International Womens Year, the government appointed Status of Women Committee issued a report on women in independent India. The report declared that even though there were more educated women than the past, women were not adequately represented in the economic sector and public life. The state policies are not reaching the dalit, adivasi women at a local level the state is depending more on the women groups, NGOs and on individual initiatives to reach to these marginalized women. In order to end gender violence the state must do something more that policy making. In states like Punjab there are 875 girls to 100 boys and overall there are 927 girls to 1000 boys in India *(New York Times,* 2001). Indian governments has already passed legislation banning sex selective abortion or pre natal sex determination, but the government seems more or less ignorant or helpless in introducing structural changes to the society. Enactment of laws, introducing the power of rights and finding ways to move women out of what they looked like disadvantaged, seemed descent for several years, but it is not enough. State generated policies and programs may open some channels of self exploration, it would not lead women to a position of writing her destiny beyond the socio cultural nuances of a patriarchal structure. Terms like 'integration', 'gender mainstreaming', 'welfare' or even the so called 'empowerment' are falling short of expectations. Gendering public policy needs the women speak for themselves in all issues of the society and it would be possible only when there is a cultural change, a perception that women are not objects of control but an equal partner of the development process.

Endnotes & References

AIWC Annual Report (1934), In the areas of marriage, guardianship of children and inheritance, the AIWC proposed its demands, Ninth Session, Karachi, pp. 17-31, 70-71.

AIWC Annual Report (1935), Tenth Session.

Bhandari, J.S. and Channa S.M. (1996), *Tribes and the Government Politics*, New Delhi.

Chaudhuri Maitrayee (1996), 'Citizens, workers and the emblems of culture: An analysis of the first plan document on women' in Patricia Oberoi, (ed), *Social Reform, Sexuality and the State,* New delhi, pp. 211-35.

Datta Rekha (2002) in R Datta and J Kornberg (eds), *Women in Developing Courtiers: Assessing Strategies of Empowerment,* Boulder Co, p. 80.

Hobsbawn, E. (1996), 'The Cult of Identity Politics', in *New Left Review*, 217, p. 40.

Kelkar Govind (2005), 'Development Effectiveness through gender Mainstreaming: Gender Equality and Poverty Reduction in South Asia' in *Economic and Political Weekly,* 40:44, 4690-4700

Koczberski, G. (1998), 'Women in Development : A Critical Analysis' in *Third World Quarterly,* 19 (3), p. 403.

Lok Sabha Debates (1996); Women's Reservation Bill was tabled in the Lok Sabha on 12th September, 1996. This bill was introduced on behalf of the United Front government led by Shri H.D. Devegowda as part of an assurance given in the common Minimum Programmed of the United Front. See Lok sabha Debates, 2nd Session, 11th Series, Vol.5, Nos 28-30, 11-13 September, 1996, pp. 513-514.

Mari Bhat, P.N. (1999), 'Widowhood and Modernity in India' in Martha Chen (eds), *Widows in India,* New Delhi.

Ministry of Social Welfare, Government of India (1985), *Women in India*, Country Paper, New Delhi.

Monhanty Monoranjan (1995), 'On the Concept of Empowerment', *in Economic and Political Weekly*, 17 June, pp. 1434.

Moore, Mark H. (1998), *Creating Public Value-Strategic Management in Government,* Cambridge.

National Planning Committee Series (1947); *Women's Role in a Panned Economy*, pp. 215-216.

New York Times (2001), Week in Review, May 6, p. 4.

Rajagopal S. and Mathur, K., 'Women's Empowerment Through State Benevolence' in *Economic and Political Weekly*, 35(33), p. 2910.

Sen Amartya (1990), 'Gender and Comparative Conflicts' in Tinker Irene (ed) *Persistent Inequalities, Women and World Development*, New York, p. 149.

21

A Socio-Historical Underpinning of Public Policy for Social Justice and Women Empowerment

Vijaylaxmi Saxena

Development in the modern context connotes that all the advances in science, technology, democracy, values and societal organization fuse into the mega humanitarian project of producing a far better world. In its stronger sense, development means using the productive resources of society to improve the quality of life of the peripheral people. In the true sense development means improving the conditions of life. Majority of developing countries thus provide a great deal of emphasis on creating and strengthening infrastructure facilities and reflecting development as higher expectations of the material welfare. These expectations are generally crystallized at the level of planners and policy makers and it is the experience of many that such expectations do not find affirmation through the responses of the people on whom such a benefit is meant to be bestowed. The proponents of alternative development feel that the chasm between the perceptions of the people at large seems to be widening. It is seen that in the dominant development paradigm economic development is considered to be synonymous with large projects and thus excluding the 'marginalized' communities. Seeing development in terms of the substantive freedoms of people has far-reaching implications for our understanding of the processes of development and also for the ways and means of promoting it. On the evaluative side, this involves the need to assess the requirements of development in terms of removing the unfreedom from which the members of the society may suffer. The process of development, in this view, is not essentially different from the history of overcoming these unfreedoms. While this history is not by any means unrelated to the process of economic growth and accumulation of physical and human capital, its reach and coverage go much beyond these variables. In focusing on freedom versus evaluative development, it is not being suggested that there is some unique and precise "criterion" of development in terms of which the different development experiences can always be compared and ranked. Given the heterogeneity of distinct components of freedom as well as the need to take note of different persons' versus diverse freedoms, there will often be arguments that go in contrary directions. The motivation underlying the approach of "development as freedom" is not so much to order all states—or all alternative scenarios—into one "complete ordering," but to draw attention to important aspects of the process of development, each of which deserves attention. Even after such attention is paid, there will no doubt remain differences in possible overall rankings, but their presence is not embarrassing to the purpose at hand (Sen; 1999).

According to UNDP report—Human development is about more than income. It is about widening people's choice to lead lives they value. This means expanding the capabilities of people to live long, healthy and creative lives, to acquire knowledge, to have access to the resources needed for a decent standard of living, and to enjoy dignity, self-respect, and the respect of others. Policies in support of human development goals try to create an environment in which these capabilities can be enhanced. (UNDP 2003: 1).

The traditional disabilities due to caste and gender were social and not just economic. Deep-rooted ideas of purity and pollution governed the social standings of different castes and sexes; men and women were deemed to be of unequal moral worth as were the different 'varnas': and the social hierarchy was underpinned by a legal order in which privileges and disabilities were carefully modulated according to caste and gender. The law has now changed; social attitudes have also changed though to a much smaller extent. Despite the changes, women and persons of inferior caste continue to suffer from many disadvantages (Beteille, 1999). As an agenda towards development, there is a talk about the empowerment of the poor, of backward communities, of women and of variously disadvantaged sections of society. Empowerment is seen by many politicians, policy makers, social activists and a growing section of the intelligentsia generally as the only effective answer to oppression, exploitation, injustice and the other anomalies with which our society is beset. The focus on empowerment has given a new emphasis to the building of economic and social capabilities among individuals, classes and communities. As one would expect, interventions of various kinds are being considered and recommended. Capacity building through craft training, especially for women, whether for full-time or part time employment, is seen in a similar light in the idea of empowerment is ascertain theory of social change, in particular of change from a hierarchical to an egalitarian type of society, or in a slightly different language, from an aristocratic to a democratic type of it (Beteille, 1988). The issues of empowerment is about social transformation; it is about radical social transformation; and it is about the people—ordinary, common people, rather than politicians, experts and other socially or culturally advantaged persons. Above all, it is about power, although the concept of power contained in it is generally left unspecified. Empowerment is both a means to an end and an end in itself. The term adapts itself differently situations, and its signification is both variable and fluid. (Beteille, 1999).

A significant path in the direction of empowerment has been through the expansion of citizenship. One possibility may be the benefits to be gained from a comprehensive system of quotas; it cannot be argued that such a system will have no social costs whatsoever. The Constituent Assembly in fact took an ambivalent attitude towards numerical quotas, admitting the need for them, but only in very special cases and for a limited period of time. After all, it had adopted strong provisions for equal opportunities for all, and creating additional provisions for special opportunities for some was bound to put strains on the former. Ambedkar himself, while advocating special provisions for the specially disadvantaged, had argued that those provisions should not be made so extensive as to eat up the general provision of equality of opportunity for all.

It was hoped at the time of independence that the special provisions would not be needed for very long and that they would gradually be pared down as the country advanced economically and politically. What has happened is the opposite. There has been some economic and political advance no doubt; but the pressure for more comprehensive quotas in the interest of equality and social justice has grown relentlessly. An initial move in the 1950s to have quotas in employment for the OBC in addition to those for the SCs and STs was aborted; but what was aborted in the 50s came to be adopted in the 90s. The committee on the status of women had in the 70s recommended against the adoption of quotas for women in parliament and in the state assemblies and which recently has been accepted in principle after a lot of hue and cry.

Situating Dr. Ambedkar and his philosophical contribution on the representation of underprivileged vis-à-vis the State, we find that he has left its imprint on the social matrix of the country after independence, and shaped the political and civic contours of India today. It may not be erroneous to presume that it would have been a different India without him and, in all probability, a much more inequitable and unjust one. He attempted to forge India's moral and social foundations anew and strove for a political order of constitutional democracy that is sensitive to disadvantage, inherited from the past or engendered by prevailing social relations. His vision on the critical role of the state and his strategy towards developmental and ameliorative, and consequently an interventionist approach, as against the Gandhians and the Liberals, is pragmatically significant. To him, the state was invested with a pivotal role in the economy. But, whenever such a pivotal role for the state is alluded to, it is based on the premise of a regime of rights that suggested the reasons and limits of intervention. Ambedkar was deeply suspicious of embedded identities asserting themselves in the name of ethnic, linguistic and cultural claims, relating such assertions to the problem of majorities and minorities. When identity assertion tool place, he felt, the minorities are likely to be the victims. He qualified majoritarianism, with strong grids of the rule of law, special privileges to minorities, and the existence of a civil society which could nurture democracy as a civic virtue. His opinion that policies and institutions deeply affect the question of representation found expression in his suggestion before the Simon Commission, that if adult franchise was introduced he would favour a joint electorate with reservation for Depressed Classes and if limited franchise was continued he would demand a separate electorate. He thought that governance must reflect sociological reality as closely as possible lest those wielding power to their advantage suppress the excluded groups (Rodrigues: 2002).

Ambedkar said, there are diverse types of disadvantages that men and women suffer and a common yardstick cannot be applied for their amelioration. It is not enough that equal resources and opportunities are assigned to people, for if people suffer from disadvantages such resources and opportunities may not beget equal results in spite of the best efforts of social agents. Therefore, the disadvantaged need to be extended certain preferences that result in giving a fair opportunity to them. He envisaged such support at various levels from collective decision-making to placement in jobs and services. Eventually he thought that such considerations need to become civic virtues rather than the authoritative dispensations of the state.

Ambedkar's View on Social Justice and Empowerment of Women

Locating Ambedkar's vision of social justice one finds that he pleaded for 'just society' and 'casteless society' having the element of liberty, equality and fraternity. His attitude towards justice was humanistic as well as nationalistic. The basic premise of social justice thus remains to be the emancipation of the underprivileged, exploited and oppressed section of the society and a guarantee for their freedom and mobility. He emphasized that the freedom of mind is the real freedom and a proof of one's existence.

One centrally pervading theme of the writings of Dr. B.R. Ambedkar was the attainment of 'social justice' and the establishment of a 'Just society'. He not only provided a ruthless criticism of the existing social order but also came up with an alternative vision and alternative model of social order based on justice, liberty, equality, fraternity and annihilation of caste. Ambedkar was convinced that for ensuring social justice, it was essential to demolish chaurnavarna system (See Ambedkar, 1987).

Various interventions by Ambedkar during 1919-54 capture his understanding about the problem of deprived castes. He reiterated his position that the problems of untouchables are rooted in the historical denial of basic human rights. So the remedies against discrimination were placed with the framework of citizenship rights. He addressed the problems of 'structural inequalities' and suggested following policies for social inclusion and justice:

1. Claim for equal rights: Ambedkar demanded political representation, however, he started with a claim for equal rights to the untouchables that he called 'citizenship rights'.
2. Measures for equal opportunity and participation.
3. Policies for empowerment to compensate for historical inclusion and denial of equal rights like to resources, education and employment (See Ambedkar, 1987; 1989; 1992).

To understand philosophical and liberating ideas of Dr. Ambedkar towards building an inclusive society—a society that overrides man-made differences and ensures inclusion in the restricted areas enshrining equality of opportunity as well as opportunity among the members of the society—which is essential for healthy nation and democratic principles. According to Ambedkar, democracy is not merely a form of Government. It is primarily a mode of associated living, of conjoint communicated experience. It is essentially an attitude of respect and reverence towards our fellow men."

After 1990s, Indian state adopted neo-liberal economic policies. This discourse process may be prerequisite to bridge socio-economic equality for healthy socialist democracy. In such a situation idea and view of Dr. B.R. Ambedkar acquires prominence and provides viable alternative to problem of Indian social fabric, especially on and about operational mechanism of caste system and its possible elimination. It may not be inappropriate to state that Dr. Ambedkar is the first thinker who systematically advocates for inclusive society based upon principles of secular and democratic values.

Post-colonial India witnesses several changes with regard to marginalized section in general and Daltis in particular. Indian constitution provides certain provision to safeguard interest of Scheduled Caste, Scheduled Tribe and Minority and accordingly initiate the process to evolve an inclusive Indian society. This however is not an easy process and comes as a bolt from blue. Jotibarao Phule, Narayan Guru and E.V. Periyar Ramaswami conscious effort and persistent fight help motivated intellectuals from the marginalized communities in colonial India. In fact Dr. Ambedkar's vision and mission for emancipation of Dalits who constitutes majority of Indian population is a unique effort. Dr. Ambedkar's fight was not concession of a few Dalits, rather a conscious effort to build an inclusive Indian society by analyzing vis-à-vis understanding socio-economic inequality and their possible remedy (Omvedt; 2001).

The discourse of inclusive Indian society is part of the large mission propounded and practiced by Dr. Ambedkar in his effort to build Indian society as values of equality and social justice. Probably Dr. Ambedkar is the first person who seriously thought about social equality and inclusive Indian society as an essential feature for emergence of healthy nation-state and democracy. Further Dr. Ambedkar lifelong battle has given a systematic direction to multiple strategies for development of downtrodden and marginalized mass in general and Dalits in particular as a means to achieve inclusive society. The strategy of inclusive development suggested by Dr. Ambedkar encompasses constitutional safeguard, legislative measure, public policy measure, spiritual aspect and tireless battle for social justice and oppression. This movement has a significant bearing on our present day society and polity. This movement has called for a reinterpretation of values of humanism, democracy, equality and liberty in Indian context.

Ambedkar's effort towards upliftment of women can be gauged through the famous statement by him as "I measure the progress of a community by the degree of progress which women have achieved". His basic idea towards subordinate group was—"Learn to live in this world with self-respect. You should always cherish some ambition of doing something in this world. But remember that the age of selflessness has ended. A new epoch is set in. All things are now possible because of your being able to participate in the politics and legislature of your country".

Dr. Ambedkar the revolutionary of 20th century has played a vital role in securing the basic human rights for the women in general and Mulnivasi women in particular. Dr. Ambedkar continued the pioneering work of Mahatma Jyotiba Phule and his wife. Right from the beginning of his struggle for the eradication of caste prejudices, he started involving women in the struggle. He realized that the real progress of the mulnivasi could not be achieved without liberating the women themselves. He started motivating the women. His first demand of adult franchise, which was met in the early 20s after resistance from the brahmins, gave voting rights to untouchables as well as to women. That was the beginning of an era of liberation for women. (Omvedt, 2011)

Dr. Ambedkar then brought women, the mulnivasi women in particular into the struggle. In December 1927 during the Mahad Tank struggle, on the first day (of the second leg) when the procession was taken out, women marched in the procession along with men. Second day, Dr. Ambedkar exclusively addressed women. He told them to participate in the struggle against the tyranny of caste system. He emphasized to them that men alone cannot fight this menace. The main theme of his speech was "Importance of participation of women in the struggle of depressed." He also wanted to prepare the women for a cultural change. He told them to change their style of dressing, to do away with unwanted ornaments, which they used to wear all the time and told them to send their girls to school, keep cleanliness etc.

The 1930s saw the organization of independent meetings and conferences by dalit women in the Ambedkarite movement. This was an obvious consequence of Ambedkar's practice of organizing a women's conference along with every general meeting and Sabha that he called. In these 'parishads' of the 1930s, dalit women delegates passed resolutions against child marriage, enforced widowhood and dowry; critiquing these practices as brahmanical. Women's participation in the Mahad Satyagraha, their support to the Independent Labour Party and the Schedule Caste Federation have been well documented [Moon and Pawar 1989: Amiihihi Itihaas Ghadtawila: Anibedakari Chalvalitil Streevancha Sahabhag, Stree, Mumbai]. Women in large numbers supported Dharmantaar as a need for a religion that would recognize their equal status. Women's participation in the Ambedkarite movement must be read in the context of the fact that in Ambedkar's theory of caste there is also a theory of the origins of sub-ordination of women and that he saw the two issues as intrinsically linked.

He argues that "the absence of intermarriage or endogamy is the one characteristic that can be called the essence of castes" (Ambedkar 1992). Thus it is the superimposition of endogamy on exogamy and the means used for the same that hold the key to the understanding of the caste system. Ambedkar then draws up a detailed analysis of how numerical equality between the marriageable units of the two sexes within the group is maintained. Thus he argues that practices of sati, enforced widowhood and child marriage come to be prescribed by brahmanism in order to regulate and control any transgression of boundaries, i.e., to say he underlines the fact that the caste system can be maintained only through the controls on women's sexuality and in this sense women are the gateways to the caste system [Ambedkar 1992:90]. In his speech at the gathering of women at the Mahad satyagraha, he draws linkages between caste exploitation and women's sub-ordination by underlining this; calls upon women to contest the claims of upper caste women's progeny to purity and the damnation of that of the lower caste to impurity.

Dr. Ambedkar was an ardent supporter of family planning. He emphasized the need of family planning way back in 1938. At that time nobody even dreamt of it. He even criticized his own parents in public speeches because he himself was the 14th child in the family. This showed his concern for the well being of the women. Dr. Ambedkar had also been encouraging women to organize themselves. One such historic women's conference was held on 20 July 1942 at Nagpur. Some 25,000 mulnivasi women participated in the conference. Dr. Babasaheb Ambedkar was highly impressed by the large gathering. In his speech he told the women to be progressive and told them to abolish traditionalism, ritualism and customary habits, which were detrimental to their progress. He also advised them not to indulge in early marriages, not to infuse inferiority complex among the children.

Through the constitution of India, as the chairman of the constitution drafting committee, Dr. Ambedkar was instrumental in granting equal status to all the citizens irrespective of sex, religion etc. Dr. B.R. Ambedkar has tried to slow down the barriers in the way of advancement of women in India. He laid down the foundation of concrete and sincere efforts by codifying the common Civil Code for the Hindus. To him, the prevailing two schools of Hindu Law viz. 'Mitakshara' and 'Dayabhag', created and sustained inequality.

One can realize that he saw the Hindu Code Bill as a basis for the reform of Hindu society. Although he certainly did not believe that this reform could be carried out through legislative fiat alone, he sought to lay down some minimum principles within the legislative framework of personal laws. For this purpose he made a study of the Mitakshara and Dayabliaga systems of Hindu laws governing marriage, divorce and inheritance, as well as looking at the practices of smaller communities within the Hindu fold. He considered that the most progressive principles in the existing Hindu codes should be incorporated into the 'modern' Hindu Code Bill. Ambedkar insisted on enshrining in the Hindu Code Bill some basic tenets on which there should be no compromise: the right to divorce for the woman, the out-lawing of polygamy for those married under Hindu law, and the granting of some unconditional rights of inheritance for widows and daughters were among these.

He also insisted on the recognition of inter-caste marriages as valid under Hindu law. Although a Special Marriage Act which contains such rights and freedoms for those wishing to enter into a civil marriage contract was already in existence before 1947, only a small minority of persons actually opted for this. Ambedkar's concern was that these minimum tenets be put into the Code for Hindu personal laws so that women entailing into marriage based on religious practice should have the benefit of these rights. The record of the debates on the Hindu Code Bill in the Lok Sabha between 1947 when the motion was tabled, and the time of Ambedkar's resignation as law minister, shows the violence of the opposition of orthodox forces to these proposals. It is interesting to note that these forces articulated their reactionary positions on the question of caste as well as gender: it was of course said that giving the woman the right to divorce would destroy the traditional family etc.

This bill was so dear to Dr. Ambedkar that he resigned from the government in protest against the dropping of the bill. After his resignation, the bill was passed in bits and pieces. The property rights section was immediately passed. This itself was a landmark in empowering women and the entire credit for this goes to Dr. Ambedkar. The other sections of the Hindu Code Bill were passed in the form of following acts: Hindu Marriage Act 1955; Hindu Succession Act 1956; Hindu Minority and Guardianship Act 1956; Adoption and Maintenance Act 1956.

What is important is that behind Ambedkar's efforts to put the bill through parliament is his vision that women are central to the fight against the caste system. That the subjugation of women is central to the functioning of the caste system and that woman is in his words, the gateway to the caste system. Thus the brahminical forces that uphold caste must take control of these gateways in order to perpetuate the system of caste hierarchy and caste oppression. The need to enact a juridical code that provides for emancipation of women in the areas of marriage, divorce and inheritance is essential because side by side with a Constitution giving political and economic rights to citizens,

In recent past, a lot hue and cry is being made over 'Women's Reservation Bill' by the different sections of the Indian society, different political or apolitical organizations but nobody seems to be honest in its perspectives. However, 33% reservation to women in Parliament and state legislative bodies speaks about the Ambedkar's vision of political empowerment.

Public Policy for Women Empowerment and Development—Global Context

Gender inequality is rooted in social stratification based on the roles and responsibilities assigned to men and women and the differential valuation of these roles. Thus women's position and degree of empowerment is determined by the ways that gender identities, gender roles and gender relations are conceived at the family, household, community and societal levels. The differential valuation of the tasks performed by men and women remains the root cause of attitudes that result in differential investment in men and women with regard to such development forces as secular education, skill formation, and income generating activities. The crux of the problem in gender relations lies in the fact that gender roles, rights and obligations are not just different but they are highly unequal. In almost every sphere of human functioning in India, the roles defined for women are subordinated to those defined for males, the rights for women are fewer or less emancipating than those of men, and women's obligations are more limiting than those of men, resulting in gender disparity at every level, cutting across all types of class and caste powerlessness.

One can infer from Giddens's (1984) structuration theory to help conceptualize gender as a structure that creates stratification, with an emphasis on the recursive relationship between structure and individuals. Like Giddens, we embrace the transformative power of human action. Social structures not only act on people; people act on social structures. Indeed, social structures are created not by mysterious forces, but by human action.

It is true that the nation's identify does lay in the culture and more specifically in its womanhood, the Indian male supremacists have, very smugly, denigrated 'female exclusiveness'. Thus, most of the Indian women have been suffering from the lack of self and space, disempowerment, disprivilege, disadvantage, sexist discrimination, gender inequity, invisibility, asymmetries, marginalization, devalorizaiton and reification.

Consequently various women empowerment specific policies and plans have been executed. Naturally therefore the Eighth Five-Year Plan (1992-1997) marks a definite shift from 'development' to 'empowerment' of women. Special Marriage Act, 1954; Hindu Marriage Act, 1955; Hindu Succession Act, 1956; Hindu Minority & Guardianship Act, 1956; Hindu Adoption and Maintenance Act, 1956; Immortal Traffic Prevention Act, 1956; Dowry Prohibition Act, 1961 & 1984; Maternity Benefit Act, 1961; Medical Termination of Pregnancy Act, 1971 ; Child Marriage Restraint (Amendment) Act, 1978; Family Court Act, 1984; Indecent Representation of Women (Prohibition) Act, 1986; Commission of Sati (Prevention) Act, 1987; The National Plan of Action for Women, 1976; National Perspective Plan for Women, 1988; Shramashakti, 1988; National Commission for Women, 1990; Support to Training and Employment Programme for Women, 1987; Rashtriya Mahila Kosh; Mahila Samridhi Yojana; Indira Awaas Yojana; Jawahar Rozgar Yojana; Streeshakti Mission; DWCRA; TRYSEM; National Rural Health Mission; National Rural Employment Guarantee-Scheme; the 73rd and 74th Constitutional Amendment Acts of 1993 and the support services launched and effectualized by the Govt, of India bear ample testimony to desire and preparedness of the State of India to facilitate empowerment of women in India for the ultimate efflorescence of the Indian HR. With reference to the thrust laid on empowerment of women by the state of India, the concept of empowerment is anatomized with a view to facilitating a holistic study of women empowerment, per se, in India.

Action for gender equality does largely depend on empowerment of women, that is "equitable access to resources, power, and decision-making". Women empowerment requires a realignment of power, decision making at the household, institutional and all levels of society. Participatory in nature, empowerment is a dynamic process aiming at transfer of power to women, dispriveleged and disadvantaged variously in any androcentric political construct. "The empowerment of women concerns women gaining control and power over their own lives. It involves awareness raising, building self-confidence, expansion of choices, increased access to and control over resource."

No doubt, women's position and degree of empowerment is defined by gender and gender relations in society. Gender represents not just the biological sex of an individual, but also the different roles, rights, and obligations that are attached by society to individuals born with male or female sex characteristics. Within the feminist framework, positive peace is defined as the absence of indirect or structural violence within various domains of society, economic structures, environment, political and democratic processes. Negative peace is the absence of personal, physical and direct violence, which includes unorganised, direct violence like child, spouse or partner abuse, rape and so on (Mazaruna & McKay, 1999). Contemporarily, there is a strong need to advocate for women to be part of the peace-building process. Women, by virtue of their sex, being creators of life (mothers) and nurturers of life and with regards to many cultural norms, are deemed more caring, peaceful and non-violent. As mothers, wives and primary socialisers, they play an important role in shaping society and protecting their families.

In 1990, the National Commission for Women was established to safeguard the rights and legal entitlements of women. One of the main objectives of India's Ninth Five Year Plan was to provide employment opportunities for women. Only one fourth of the country's women (25.6%) were involved in officially recognized economic activities. Among these working women, only 35.7% were literate. The majority of working women lived in rural areas (87.3%) and were involved in cultivation and agriculture activities (71.8%) (Government of India, 2001b).

The enactment of the 73rd Amendment of the Constitution in 1993 has reserved 33% of the seats in local governments such as, Panchayats and Municipalities for women so as to encourage their participation in societal decision-making. Since 1994, the Micro Credit Scheme (MCS) has also been in operation in India. During 1998-1999 more than 100,000 poor individuals, mainly women, benefited from MCS assistance through 32 Micro Finance Institutions or NGOS. The national infant mortality rate (IMR) is declining gradually, but the female IMR is always higher than the male IMR. Recent government figures show the IMR for males to be 57 while it is 64 for females (SRS, 2005). The sharp decline in the sex-ratio of the population between 0 and 6 years of age in the 1990s (945 in 1991 to 927 females per 1000 males in 2001) has drawn the attention of the public and policy makers.

On higher education and Indian women, Chanana (2011) rightly suggests—like women elsewhere, Indian women are heterogeneous and the societal system of stratification is reflected in differential access to women from different socio-economic groups but the gender gap affects all of them.

Gender is one of them. Therefore, looking at educational policy and whether it promotes gender equality in higher education will tell a lot about the equality commitments of the system towards women. Further, women still do not enjoy parity with men in *participation and outcomes* although *access* has improved. On the whole, their entry into higher education is not unproblematic. Therefore, higher education as an instrument to achieve high status as well as equality is an appropriate site to examine attempts to promote gender equality in society.

'Empowerment of Women' has indeed become a widely popular, and so far, unquestioningly accepted, concept among the Third World feminists, including the Indian ones, and has, as often happens, to take the wind out of the sails of the momentum of the ideology and practice of social movements to render them rudderless, been promptly co-opted by the Indian establishment. So, we have calls for, and attempts at, the 'empowerment of women'—Political, social, economic, cultural, and what have you-by the Indian Women's Movement, a movement to look for which at the moment has become like looking for a needle in a haystack of the goings-on of a multitude of disparate, autonomous, scattered groups without sufficiently coordinated voices or uniform practices congregating and becoming proactive only occasionally on certain specific issues.

Empowerment is a meaning-loaded word and concept, like all words and concepts. Words are symbols that we use to name a thing which may be an object, an occurrence, a situation or a process and concepts are descriptions of an existent idea or general notion. To devise words and concepts is an exceptionally human capability. Paulo Freire (1972) calls this the 'naming of the world.' He writes that human existence cannot be silent, nor can it be nourished by false words, but only true words, with which men transform the world.

The concept of 'empowerment of women' implies a mediating of the relationship between the two genders by power and thus has inbuilt within it latent conflict, one up-manship, hierarchisation and a constant glancing behind one's shoulder to make sure that the other sex is not trying to out-power or over-power one. This state of affairs, it is certain will definitely not lead to a cessation of sexual struggle for power and sexual politics but escalate it adding to its surreptitiousness, mistrust, a working against each other.

For many development organizations, power is defined as 'power over', meaning that, in the case of GAD, women will gain power at the expense of men. This view suggests that women 'should be empowered to participate within the economic and political structures of society—occupying positions of power in terms of political and economic decision-making' (Rowlands; 1997). This reformist approach accepts current social structures rather than seeking transformation. Like earlier Women in Development (WID) approaches, this accepts the way in which decisions are made and the processes through which resources are allocated, but considers that women should be given positions in the hierarchy of power to ensure equality.

Others look at 'power to', which has empowerment as the ability to act in particular ways. What is important about this approach is that it does not produce a zero-sum game where women's advantage is men's disadvantage, but that the increased empowerment of women will improve the community as a whole. Increased ability to act, whether in matters to do with market production or house hold reproduction, will have a positive effect on all members of the group.

There is a need for addressing the women towards democratization through following measures:

- The necessity to protect girls and women against violence, especially gender based violence;
- The need to protect women against further violence and injuries by engendering de-mining and small arms programs;
- The need to better address the specific situation of former girls and women combatants;
- The need to actively support women's inclusion and leadership in politics;
- The need to prevent the perpetuation of gender injustice;
- The prevention of women and girls's re-victimization;
- The need to address women and girls' specific needs in economic reintegration programs;
- The mainstreaming of women needs into macro and microeconomic programs.

The empowerment process is difficult to measure quantitatively. Various authors have used education, work participation, and exposure to mass media, the means or sources by which women are expected to develop decision-making authority, greater freedom of movement, autonomy, and attitudinal changes in favour of gender equality, as indicators to measure empowerment.

Education is an essential foundation for all social, economic and cultural development (Sen, 1994).

In brief one can highlight the various dimensions of empowerment as follows:

- **Psychological**—Self-image and identity; Creating space; Acquiring knowledge
- **Cultural**—Redefining gender rules and norms; Recreating practices
- **Social**—Leadership in community action; Action for rights; Social inclusion; Literacy
- **Economic**—Attaining income security; Ownership of productive assets; Entrepreneurial skills
- **Organizational**—Collective identity; Establishing representative organization; Organizational leadership
- **Political**—Participation in local institutions; Negotiating political power; Accessing political power

Microfinance and Women

Microfinance for women has been a popular poverty-alleviation strategy among development agencies since the mid-1980s. It has also been considered an effective vehicle for women's empowerment. Support consists most typically of the provision of small loans, either to individuals or groups.

The rationale for providing women with loans has been that:

- Women are disproportionately represented among the poorest in society and need more help than men in securing sustainable livelihoods.
- Women are discriminated against in the formal labour market and so are usually obliged to seek an income on the margins of the economy, in the informal sector.
- Women-headed households are on the increase as a result of economic recession, changing labour needs, increasing urbanization, and the break-up of extended family structures. In some male-headed households, women are now the main source of income.
- Women-headed households are usually more vulnerable in times of crisis, as they have fewer resources to draw upon.
- Studies show that repayment rates on loans and contributions to family well-being are often higher among women than among men (Mayoux 1999).

In recent years, doubts about the efficacy of microfinance as a vehicle for women's empowerment have arisen (Mayoux 1999; Kabeer 1998) in large part as a result of growing criticism that faith placed in microfinance as a poverty-alleviation strategy has been grossly exaggerated (Hulme and Moseley 1996). With regard to women, Linda Mayoux provides a strong critique of the naive belief that microfinance by itself creates a 'virtuous spiral' of economic, social, and political empowerment, without it being considered necessary to develop explicit strategies to address other dimensions of poverty or gender subordination. She considers as highly simplistic the view that mere participation in such a scheme is sufficient for women's empowerment. Indeed, a number of studies in Bangladesh show that while for some women it may be empowering, for many others it is marginal both in economic and socio-political terms (Kabeer 1998; Goetz and Sen Gupta 1996). In some cases, it increases domestic violence.

Transnationalism, Dalit Women and Mobilization

Dalit solidarity organizations have now begun lobbying foreign private corporations and development agencies operating in South Asia regarding affirmative action (DSN UK, 2005a, 2005/06; IDSN, 2005, 2006). The final evidence that the international 'alternative' movements are determined to keep the *dalit* issue firmly on the international public agenda, came with the award of the 2006 Alternative Nobel Prize to Ruth Manorama, an activist for the rights of *dalit* women, and for *dalit* rights in general. *Dalit* issues are now a staple of the agendas of the international alternative movements.

In a recent work, Manisha Desai emphasized that "transnational feminist practices have become the dominant modality of feminist movements across the world, since the Fourth Women's World Conference in Beijing." Transnationalism Desai defined as "both organizing across national borders as well as framing local, national, regional, and global activism in 'transnational discourses'." (2005:319) No doubt, transnational activism and the appropriation of a discourse of human rights has played a significant role in shaping the activism and the organizational formation of the Dalit (formerly untouchables) Women's movement.

Thus, Beijing served as an important venue for the Dalit Women's Movement. It was the first time they were able to express themselves directly on an international stage. Yet, this was not the last time they were to be present at UN forums. In fact, for Dalit women, as well for the Dalit and Women's movements in general, the UN has offered spaces for affiliated nongovernmental organizations (NGOs) and a host of transnational advocacy networks active in the area of human rights.

The virtual invisibility of Dalit women led Vimal Thorat to assert in 2001 that "both the Dalit movement and women's movement have consciously ignored the Dalit women's issue." Thorat noted that despite two generations of articulate committed Dalit professional women these "articulate women are not invited by Dalit forums, especially the political parties. Why?" Thorat's ire was directed not only at the Dalit movement but at the Indian women's movement. Stated Thorat, "this betrayal of Dalit women's issues is matched by the utter disregard and tokenism with which Dalit women's issues are taken up by the women's movement." Despite this invisibility Thorat did acknowledge that "nevertheless, the Dalit's women's articulations are growing." (Thorat 2001) Cited in particular was the formation of the National Federation of Dalit Women (NFWD) in Delhi in August 1995 in the lead up to the Beijing Conference in September of that same year.

Thus, apart from the UN, another key site for transnational feminist activism since the Beijing Conference of 1995 has been the World Social Forum (WSF) (Desai 2005, p 325). The Dalit Network Netherlands (DNN), in collaboration with the NCDHR, the NFDW, the All India Dalit Women's Rights Forum, the Feminist Dalit Organization, Nepal, and the IDSN, organized a conference on human rights and dignity of Dalit women in The Hague, November 20-25, 2006.

Another phase is "internationalizing Dalit rights." For this phase, NCDHR states that it has made "major strides in giving visibility to the plight of the Dalit community." These strides have been made through NCDHR's participation in all World Social Forums (WSF), the World Conference Against Racism (WCAR, the 40-day Dalit Swadhikar Rally throughout India, "The Situation of the Dalits in India" at the European Parliament in Brussels in 2006, and the first International Conference on the Human Rights of Dalit Women at The Hague in 2006, the recognition of the problems of Dalit Human Rights by the United Nations in August of 2001, recognition by the European Union in May of 2007, and lastly, recognition by the United States Congress in July of 2007. NCDHR also won the RAFTO award in 2007 for its work at progressing human rights. The NCDHR website does not make declarative statements about the final accomplishment of this phase as yet.

AIDMAM is the All India Dalit Mahila Adhikar Manch, a forum for Dalit women to work towards altering the double-burden of Dalit females-being Dalits and women. It seeks to challenge the structures that enable discrimination, whether patriarchal, caste or class based, or economic. The DAAA is the Dalit Arthik Adhikar Manch, a branch of the NCDHR that focuses on changing the economic and educational practices in India which leave Dalits behind while other castes move forward. The NFDRLM consists of the National Federation of Dalit Land Rights Movements. This organization focuses on Dalit access to land and an agricultural livelihood. Lastly, the NDMJ is the National Dalit Movement for Justice, a broader movement within the NCDHR. It mostly consists of Dalit survivors of violence or discrimination as well as sympathizers and seeks to enforce justice. It does so by attempting to, "establish [Dalits] as equal citizens in the society under Dalit leadership within our rising consciousness...to promote and protect Civil Political Rights of Dalits for ensuring... fair justice"

One thus finds that the exclusive nature of many national projects may, in turn, shape those very people who are excluded into an alternative inclusive community-one which then contests its own exclusion from the nation. One possible alternative inclusive community is beyond the local or national level, but rather may be found at the global level of transnational social movement networks. These networks act as sites of global inclusivity, gathering people from around the world who share grievances.

Conclusion

In conclusion, let us inspire by Ambedkar's words for overcoming exploitation were: "You must abolish your slavery yourselves. Do not depend for its abolition upon god or a superman. Remember that it is not enough that a people are numerically in the majority. They must be always watchful, strong and self-respecting to attain and maintain success. After independence, one observes that women's position in Indian society is highly gender stratified. The low status of women in India has been a matter of concern for many years, and the Indian government has implemented various policies and programs to improve their situations. The Indian Constitution (1950) has stressed gender equality in all spheres of life. Since 1950 (Article 45) the Government of India has taken various efforts to provide free and compulsory education for all children between the ages of 6-14 years. Even as the literacy rate in India has increased, the gender gap remains very significant, with a literacy rate of 75.8% for men in contrast to a female literacy rate of 54.2% (Government of India, 2001a). Yet, many girls face barriers in accessing education, including poverty, negative attitudes towards educating a daughter, social norms, fear of threats to chastity, and fear of violence.

'Empowerment of Women' has indeed become a widely popular, and so far, unquestioningly accepted, concept among the Third World feminists, including the Indian ones, and has, as often happens, to take the wind out of the sails of the momentum of the ideology and practice of social movements to render them rudderless, been promptly co-opted by the Indian establishment. So, we have calls for, and attempts at, the 'empowerment of women'—Political, social, economic, cultural, and what have you—by the Indian Women's Movement, a movement to look for which at the moment has become like looking for a needle in a haystack of the goings-on of a multitude of disparate, autonomous, scattered groups without sufficiently coordinated voices or uniform practices congregating and becoming proactive only occasionally on certain specific issues. In recent years, doubts about the efficacy of microfinance as a vehicle for women's empowerment have arisen. Further, one possible alternative inclusive community is beyond the local or national level, but rather may be found at the global level of transnational social movement networks. These networks act as sites of global inclusivity, gathering people from around the world who share grievances.

Endnotes & References

Ambedkar, B.R. (1987). Dr. Babasaheb Ambedkar's writings and speeches (BAWS), Vol. 3, Bombay: Government of Maharashtra Publication.

Ambedkar, B.R. (1989). Dr. Babasaheb Ambedkar's writings and speeches (BAWS), Vol. 4, Bombay: Government of Maharashtra Publication.

Ambedkar, B.R. (1992). Ambedkar and Social justice, New Delhi: Ministry of information and broadcasting, Publication division.

Ambedkar, B.R. (1982-90): Castes in India, Speeches and Writings of Dr Bahasaheb Ambedkar, Vol I, Bombay: Government of Maharashtra.

Beteille, A (1983): The Idea of Natural Inequality and Other Essays. Oxford University Press, Delhi.

Beteille, A (1999): 'Empowerment', Economic and Political Weekly, Vol. 34, No. 10/11 (Mar. 6-19, 1999), pp. 589-597

Chanana, Karuna (2011). 'Policy Discourse and Exclusion-Inclusion of Women in Higher Education in India', *Social Change* 2011 41: 535

Desai, Manisha. (1999). Transnationalism: the face of feminist politics post-Beijing, *International Social Science Journal.* 57:2, pp. 319-330.

Freire, Paulo (1972) The Pedagogy of the Oppressed, Harmondsworth: Penguin

Government of India (GOI), 2001a: Census of India, 2001: Population totals.

Goetz, A. M. and R. Sen Gupta (1996) 'Who takes the credit? Gender, power and control over loan use in rural credit programmes in Bangladesh', *World Development* 24(1):45-63.

International Dalit Solidarity Network. 2003. "Statutes of the International Dalit Solidarity Network." Adopted September 16, 2003. http://www.idsn.org/statutes.html (Accessed 18 May, 2005).

Hulme, D. and P. Moseley (eds.) (1996) Finance against Poverty, London: Routledge

Kabeer, N. (1998) 'Money Can't Buy Me Love'? Re-evaluating Gender, Credit and Empowerment in Rural Bangladesh', *IDS Discussion Paper* No. 363, Brighton: IDS

Kymlicka, Will (1989). *Liberalism, Community, and Culture*, Oxford: Oxford University Press

National Alliance of Women (NAWO) (2007) "Final Strategy Paper to take forward the Implementation of the CEDAW Concluding Comments." http://www.unifem.org.in/Strategy%20paperON%20CEDAW%20-%20UNIFEM.pdf (accessed 3December, 2011).

National Federation of Dalit Women (2002) "How Dalit Women's Lives Mirror Descent Based Discrimination." http://www.dalits.org/CERDStatementRuth.htm, (accessed 24 October, 2011).

National Federation of Dalit Women (2001) "NGO Declaration on Gender and Racism." In: Anupama Rao (ed.), *Gender and Caste*, London: Zed Books Ltd., pp. 363-367.

Mayoux, L. (1999). 'Questioning virtuous spirals: microfinance and women's empowerment in Africa', *Journal of International Development*, November-December: 957-984

Misra, Jugal Kishore. 2006. "Empowerment of Women in India," The Indian Journal of Political Science, Vol. 67, No. 4 (Oct.-Dec., 2006), pp. 867-878P

Omvedt, Gail. (2011). Understanding Caste—From Buddha to Ambedkar and beyond, New Delhi: Orient BlackSwan.

Rodrigues, Valerian (ed.) (2002) *The Essential Writings of B.R. Ambedkar*, New Delhi: Oxford University Press.

Sen, Amartya, (1999). *Development as a Freedom*, New Delhi: Oxford University Press.

See http://www.ambedkar.org

United Nations, 1995b: Fourth world Conference on Women, Platform for action, women and poverty, Beijing, China, September 1995

United Nations Document. (1996). CERD/C/304/Add.13 http://www.unhchr.ch/tbs/doc.nsf/0/30d3c5041b55e561c12563e000500d33?Opendocument (accessed 20 April, 2010).

22

Impact of Central Sponsored Schemes on Women Empowerment with Special Reference to Health and Education

Renu Srivastava

Society is made by men and women but after the construction of any civilized society we see the difference between these two pillars of society. There is much evidence of extensive gender based inequality even in the elementary matters of health care and nutrition in many regions across the world (Singh, 2010). We live in democratic scenario so the women rights is not only a legal right but it is also a human right and Women empowerment becomes a most important contemporary issue in India as well as world. Women empowerment is the outcome of the concept of liberty or freedom and justice.

The term of empowerment has different meanings in different socio-cultural and political context, and does not translate easily into all languages. It is a multi dimensional approach. Empowerment is the expansion of assets and capability of poor people to participate in, negotiate with, influence, control, and hold accountable institutions that affects their lives (Narayn, 2005:14). The Oxford English dictionary defines the verb empower as "to enable." In contrast to the earlier definition of empowerment as delegation (of authority and resource sharing), enabling implies motivating through enhancing personal efficacy. In the management literature on power and empowerment, often both meanings are fused together, and their relationships to each other are not clear. For instance, Whetten and Cameron (1984) alluded to power as both gaining control over limited resources and as a sign of personal efficacy. Likewise, Neilsen (1986) considered empowerment both as giving subordinates resources and as increasing their sense of self-worth. However, Burke (1986) recognized the distinctiveness of the two meanings, but like most management researchers preferred to use empowerment in the sense of delegation rather than in the sense of enabling (Kanungo 1988).

Objective

This paper trying to focusing some objective related to central sponsored schemes and its impact on women empowerment, which are as follows:

1. To study the central sponsored schemes related to women's health and education.
2. To examine the impact of these schemes on women empowerment.

Methodology

The present study is based on theoretical in nature. The analysis is base on secondary data. The secondary data has been collected from various government reports, books, articles and various reputed journals. The secondary source of information has been taken from internet, books and various reputed journal like Economic political weekly.

Development Approach of Women Empowerment

In Indian context we can see gender equality in our preamble, fundamental rights and as well as in our directive principles. Constitution gives positive discrimination right to the state for gender equality. After the implementation of our constitution government had adopted welfare approach to make any schemes for women and after that in next phase government had adopted equality and health promotion based approach. After 80th century finally government adopted skill development and empowerment based approach for women's development. Simultaneously in international world united nation organization had been make a framework on women empowerment by organizing four conferences at Mexico, Denmark, Nairobi and Beijing. At the 1995 Fourth World Conference in Beijing, women's empowerment was introduced to an expanded audience of state actors and governments. The signatories of the conference pledged to advance women's empowerment world wide. Arnoff (2011) quoted Batliwala (2007) and describe the Beijing conference vision of women's empowerment stressed three main fundamentals:

- It was a socio political process;
- Power was the critical to empowerment; and
- The process promoted shifts in political, social, and economic power between and across individuals and groups.

This international environment affected the Indian approach about women empowerment. The decades of the 1980s and the 1990s have been characterized by a variety of pressures on the government of India and state governments, especially from international bodies and from groups within for affirmative action in favor of women as well as incorporating gender issues in policy planning. One of the primary objectives of the Ninth Five-Year Plan (1997-2002) is to create an enabling environment where women can freely exercise their rights both within and outside home as equal partners along with men. The Ninth plan document further states that this will be realized through early finalization and adoption of the 'National Policy for Empowerment of Women' (Rajgopal & Mathur 2000).

In eleventh five year plan empowerment of women's approach adopted by government. The Government has been implementing various schemes for the socio-economic advancement and development of women in the country. This study describes the health and education related schemes for women. Health and Education is the key factor for effective and inclusive empowerment and it is as a mean to promote development in social and economic condition therefore the government has been implementing various schemes related to women. The lack of education means the lack of self-reliance, self-confidence for which women are not able to come out of their problems. So educating a woman means educating a family.

Central Sponsored Schemes Related to Women's Education

Mahila Samakhya (MS)

Mahila Samakhya has started in 1989 and Education for Women's Equality—is the Government of India's (GOI) main programme targeted at tackling gender inequality. It promotes gender equality and women's empowerment by supporting women to organize into collectives, called Mahila Sanghas. These help women to resist violence; to gain better access to education and health services; to open up economic options such as microfinance; and to enhance women's role in local government. MS is run by the Ministry of Human Resource Development (MHRD) and education is usually at the core of activities. The Sanghas campaign for and support girls' participation in formal schooling, build and manage centers for non-formal education for girls, often with boarding facilities, and organize women's literacy and numeracy programmes. The purpose of the current phase of MS is to consolidate and double the size of the programme and to promote gender equality and women's empowerment in a total of 167 Districts across 11 Indian states.

The objectives of the MS programme are as follows:

1. Expansion of the programme to form an additional 21,000 Sanghas in 420 additional EBBs;
2. Raised confidence and capacity of one million Sangha and federation women members with increased engagement of other women community members;
3. Mahila Sang has playing an active role in monitoring village level educational, health, rural employment and other relevant activities;
4. Greater participation of women and girls in formal and non-formal education;
5. Women empowered to improve the quality of life of themselves and their families.

MS is a national programme funded through national resources with additional external funding by the United Kingdom's Department for International Development. During the 11th Plan period, the coverage of MS is expected to almost double nationally to cover 21,000 additional sanghas in 420 additional EBBs–(Educationally Backward Blocks). Education is a major component of MS and it is seen as integral for women's empowerment. Various interventions provide for education inputs, these vary inform across states but are common in their philosophy of women's empowerment with education. Broadly defined, it ensures that women are better aware of the rights and entitlements and are able to acquire the needed information from various programmes and schemes SSA, NPEGEL (National Programme for Education of Girls at Elementary Level), KGBV, NRHM, and MNREGA. Various trainings have been held for sangha women on issues of legal literacy, health and HIV AIIDS, accessing banking/institutional facilities, skill building (masonry, maintenance of tube wells, stoves etc), development of entrepreneurial skill. This has also led to better practices (nutrition, health, hygiene) at household and (dealing with discrimination issues) at the village level.[1]

The achievements of the Mahila Samakhya programme can be well positioned in terms of the qualitative indicators of empowerment of women suggested at the Beijing conference in 1995. As prioritized by the Conference the programme can demonstrate increase in self-esteem individuals and confidence of collectives in the form of Sanghas and federations, increase in articulation of knowledge, health, nutrition, reproductive rights, law and literacy among poor rural women. Programme strategies and interventions have retained their focus on enabling this process. The sustained struggle of the Sanghas against violence and discrimination against women is showing some results in terms of reported decrease in violence against women (VAW) in most areas. The change of attitude of society in the project villages is now reflected in more enrolment of girls, opening of dialogues on practices like witch hunting, addressing issues of trafficking and engaging with boys and men in the community and homes, homes through forums/manches, engagement with PRIs and others.[2]

Srava Siksha Abhiyan (SSA)

Education is the base of society. It gives a vision to understand any thing so education is important for us. Sarva Shiksha Abhiyan (SSA) forms the cornerstone of government interventions in basic education for all children. SSA, launched in November 2000 as an umbrella programme, was to support and build on primary and elementary education projects. The programme aims to ensure five years of primary education for all children in the age group of 6-14 years by 2007 and eight years of schooling by 2010 (Kainth 2006).

The objectives of SSA:

1. All children in school, Education Guarantee Centre, Alternate School, 'Back-to School' camp by 2003; extended to 2005.
2. Bridge all gender and social category gaps at primary stage by 2007 and at elementary education level by 2010.
3. Universal retention by 2010.
4. Focus on elementary education of satisfactory quality with emphasis on education for life.

In the initial years of the scheme beginning 2001 till 2003-2004, the programme was under-resourced. In 2004-05, a cess of 2% on all Union taxes and duties were levied to earmark funds for the programme (GIO 2010).

Table 1: Girls Enrolment between 2003 and 2007

States /UT	*Girls Enrolment (2003)*	*Girls Enrolment (2007)*
Andhra Pradesh	47.07	45.35
Assam	47.84	49.76
Bihar	44.77	45.79
Chandigarh	44.97	44.69
Haryana	47.29	49.08
Himachal Pradesh	48.02	45.65
Madhya Pradesh	48.34	46.51
Rajasthan	40.06	44.31
Tamil Nadu	47.8	47.12
Uttar Pradesh	45.77	48.23
West Bengal	49.5	50.10
All States/UT	46.4	47.10

Source: Planning commission of India 2010.

The above table shows that the girls enrolment between 2003 and 2007. Here we can see that girl's enrolment has increasing from 2003 to 2007. This shows the positive impact of Sarva Shiksha Abhiyan (SSA). In Uttar Pradesh the girls enrolment is higher than other state.

Kasturba Gandhi Balika Vidyalaya (KGBV)

Kasturba Gandhi Balika Vidyalaya is a residential school which cover shared to reach girls especially the deprived ones belonging predominantly to the SC, ST, OBC community and minority groups. This is an intervention for girls residing in small and scattered habitations far off from the nearest school.

Objectives of KGBV

The main objectives of the Kasturba Gandhi Balika Vidyalaya scheme are:

- Facilitate retention of girls
- Ensure greater participation of girls in education
- Develop and promote facilities to provide access to girls belonging to disadvantaged groups like SC and ST
- Improve quality of education
- Stress upon the relevance and quality of girls' education for their empowerment.

There are presently 6000 blocks in the country and about 2,500 KGBVs have been opened blocks. This means an addition of 3,500 KGBVs are needed in covering the remaining. The Kasturba Gandhi Balika Vidyalaya scheme launched in 2004 is designed to encourage greater participation of girls in education at upper primary level. Under the Scheme 1180 residential schools at upper primary level have been sanctioned for girls belonging predominantly to SC/ST/OBC and Minority communities in educationally backward blocks with higher gender gaps and low female literacy. A minimum of three-fourth of the seats are reserved providing uniforms for the girls from marginalized or minority communities and the remaining are for girls from families below the poverty line (NCERT, 2008).

Health Related Schemes

Indira Gandhi Matritva Sahyog Yojana (IGMSY)

The Indira Gandhi Matritva Sahyog Yojana (IGMSY) is a flagship program of the government of India introduced in 2010 under the Ministry of Women and Child Development. It is a conditional cash transfer scheme that targets pregnant and lactating women 19 years of age and older who have had two children. Its goal is to partly compensate them for wage-loss during childbirth and childcare and to provide conditions for safe delivery and good nutrition and feeding practices. The scheme was implemented on pilot basis in 53 selected districts. The beneficiaries in 2011-12 were: 3.05 lakhs; and during 2012-13, 3.76 lakhs. All pregnant women of 19 years of age and above are eligible for the benefits, except those who receive paid maternity leave. The cash transfers under the Scheme are subject to the following conditions:

- The first transfer (at the end of second birth/pregnancy trimester) of Rs. 1,500 requires the mother to:
  - o Register pregnancy at the Anganwadi centre (AWC) within four months of conception
  - o Attend at least one prenatal care session and taking IFA tablets and TT (tetanus injection), and
  - o Attend at least one counseling session at the AWC or healthcare centre.
- The second transfer (three months after delivery) of Rs. 1,500 requires the mother to:
  - o Register the birth
  - o Immunize the child for OPV and BCG at birth, at six weeks and at 10 weeks
  - o Attend at least two growth monitoring sessions within three months of delivery

- The third transfer (six months after delivery) of Rs. 1,000 requires the mother to:
  - o Exclusively breastfeed for six months and introduce complementary feeding as certified by the mother,
  - o Immunize the child for OPV and DPT
  - o Attend at least two counseling sessions on growth monitoring and infant and child nutrition and feeding between the third and sixth months after delivery[3]

National Rural Health Mission (NHRM)

The Goal of the Mission is to improve the availability of and access to quality health care by people, especially for those residing in rural areas, the poor, women and children. The National Rural Health Mission (2005-12) seeks to provide effective healthcare to rural population throughout the country with special focus on 18 states, which have weak public health indicators and/or weak infrastructure. These 18 States are Arunachal Pradesh, Assam, Bihar, Chhattisgarh, Himachal Pradesh, Jharkhand, Jammu & Kashmir, Manipur, Mizoram, Meghalaya, Madhya Pradesh, Nagaland, Orissa, Rajasthan, Sikkim, Tripura, Uttaranchal and Uttar Pradesh.

GOALS

- Reduction in Infant Mortality Rate (IMR) and Maternal Mortality Ratio (MMR)
- Universal access to public health services such as Women's health, child health, water, sanitation & hygiene, immunization, and Nutrition.
- Prevention and control of communicable and non-communicable diseases, including locally endemic diseases
- Access to integrated comprehensive primary healthcare
- Population stabilization, gender and demographic balance.
- Revitalize local health traditions and mainstream AYUSH
- Promotion of healthy life styles

Outcomes

- Infant Mortality Rate reduced to 30/1000 live births
- Maternal Mortality Ratio reduced to 100/100,000
- Total Fertility Rate reduced to 2.1

- Engaging 250,000 female Accredited Social Health Activists (ASHAs) in 10 States
- Health Day at Anganwadi level on a fixed day/month for provision of immunization, ante/post natal checkups and services related to mother and child healthcare, including nutrition. Improved facilities for institutional delivery through provision of referral, transport, escort and improved hospital care subsidized under the Janani Suraksha Yojana (JSY) for the Below Poverty Line families[4]

Accredited Social Health Activist (ASHA)

The objective of the Indian Government's National Rural Health Mission (NRHM) is to strengthen the healthcare delivery system with a focus on the needs of the poor and vulnerable sections among the rural population. One of the main tenets of the mission is to identify one ASHA (Accredited Social Health Activist) per 1000 population in the rural areas with the purpose of supporting the community to access public health services. She is expected to create awareness on health and its determinants, mobilize the community towards local health planning, and increase utilization of the existing health services. The ASHAs play a critical and effective role in bridging the gap between NRHM and the communities therefore it's important to keep the ASHA motivated to perform her duties efficiently and address issues related to provision of quality services (Bajpai, & Dholakia 2011). The average age of ASHA workers is 30 years, with majority 71 (53.8%) of them in the age group of 26 to 30 years.129 (97.7%) of them are married and 115 (87.1%) were Hindu by religion.80 (60.6%) of ASHA had formal education till 8TH standard as recommended in NRHM (Shashank, J.K., Angadi, M.M., Masali K.A., Wajantri P., Bhat, S. & Jose A.P., 2013). The ASHA programme is the most visible face of the NRHM, and is likely the world's largest community health volunteer programme, with approximately one ASHA for every 1000 population in rural India. There are presently a total of 849331 ASHAs selected across the country, of which 492784 ASHAs are in the high focus states, 53619 in the NE sates, 298286 in the Non High focus states and 4642 in the Union Territories. The proposed total is 8,80,739, of which 93.73% have been selected overall with over 97% of selections completed for the high focus states. Although it was only intended to cover high focus states and tribal areas in the non high focus states, in 2008 the remaining states opted for the programme. About 74% of women with a child up to 6 months and about 71% of women with a child under two who had an episode of illness in the past month, reported receiving services from ASHA indicates that nearly 30% of the population is still not reached. ASHAs were very active and effective in promoting institutional delivery and immunization (GOI 2011).

Conclusion

Women empowerment is the multi dimensional process. Education and health is the key factor of this process. The above study shows that central sponsored schemes have improve the health and education status of women in all states. The maternal mortality rate (MMR) has reduced because of health facilities. These schemes are generating employment among women's. May be ground realities differ from the government data but present time most people are aware from the importance of health and education. This is the positive impact of these schemes. Change is the continuous process and every change takes place in our mind.

Endnotes & References

1. http://mhrd.gov.in/sites/upload_files/mhrd/files/AideMemoireJRM08.pdf
2. http://mhrd.gov.in/sites/upload_files/mhrd/files/AideMemo_MSJRM2013_Formated.pdf
3. http://en.wikipedia.org/wiki/The_Indira_Gandhi_Matritva_Sahyog_Yojana_%28IGMSY
4. http://www.nird.org.in/brgf/doc/Rural%20HealthMission_Document.pdf

References

Arnoff, Elly (2011), "A Literature Review on the Conceptualization of Women's Empowerment," paper presented at University of North Carolina, Available at https://cdr.lib.unc.edu/indexablecontent?id=uuid:aaa16cd4-e931-4ad6-9c83-0532040e53ec&ds=DATA_FILE Access on dated 06 November, 2013.

Bajpai, N., & Dholakia R.H. (2011), "Improving the Performance of Accredited Social Health Activists in India" Working Paper Series, South Asia, Columbia University.

Batliwala, S. (2007), Taking the Power out of Empowerment: An experiential account", *Development in Practice*, Vol. 17, Nos. 4-5, pp. 557-565.

Conger, J.A., & Kanungo, R.N. (1988), "The Empowerment Process: Integrating Theory and Practice," *Academy of Management Review*, Vol. 13, No. 03: 471-482.

GOI (2010), "Evaluation Report on Sarva Shiksha Abhiyan Programme" Planning Commission, New Delhi.

GOI (2011), "Report of the Working Group on National Rural Health Mission (NRHM) for the Twelfth Five Year Plan (2012-2017)" Planning Commission, New Delhi

Kainth, G.S. (2006), "A Mission Approach to Sarva Shiksha Abhiyan," *Economic Political Weekly*, July 29.

Narayan, Deepa (eds.), (2005), "Empowerment and Poverty Reproduction: A Sourcebook", Rawat Publications, Jaipur.

NCERT (2008), "National Consultation on Kasturba Gandhi Balika Vidyalaya" August 11-12, New Delhi.

Rajagopal, S. & Mathur, K. (2000), "Women's Empowerment Through State Benevolence", *Economic Political Weekly*, Vol. 35, No. 33:2908-2910.

Shashank, J.K., Angadi, M.M., Masali K.A., Wajantri P., Bhat, S. & Jose A.P. (2013), A study to evaluate working profile of Accredited Social Health Activist (ASHA) and to assess their knowledge about infant health care," *IJCRR*, Vol. 5, No. 12, pp. 97-103.

Singh, Abha (2010), "Towards Women's Empowerment" Singh, S.K. (eds), Women's Empowerment in India: Philosophical Perspectives, Originals, Delhi.

Index

Accredited Social Health Activist (ASHA), 316
Adoption and Maintenance Act 1956, 296
Advocacy Groups, 11
Aggressive Promotion Strategies at Subnational Level, 81
Agni II, 145
Agni Intermediate Range Ballistic Missile, 144
Agriculture, 159
Aharari, Ehsan, 113
Air Com. Jasjit Singh, 129, 144-45
All India Dalit Mahila Adhikar Manch (AIDMAM), 304
Ambedkar, Dr. B.R., 291-95
Annan, Kofi, 237
anti-arrack Movement, 265
Armed Forces Special Powers Act (AFSPA), 187
Asian Development Bank (ADB), 212

Balachandran, G., 143
Ban Ki-moon, 49
Banerjee, Dipankar, 141
Bangladesh, 86
Bardhan, Prof. Pronab, 222
BCIM, 85-86
Beneficiary Capital Contributions (BCC), 212
Bhambari, 88
Bidwai, 120
BIMST-EC, 86
Block Development Council, 190
Border Haats, 87
Border States, 85
Built, Operate, Transfer (BOT), 220
Built, Own, Operate (BOO), 209, 219
Bulk Water Generation, 211
Buzan, Barry, 111

Cabinet Committee on Security (CCS), 151
CAG, 28
CCI, 28
Census 2011, 250
Centre for Women's Development Studies (CWDS), 12
Chandrasekhar, 175
China, 50, 116
China-Pakistan-United States Triangle, 113
Chipko Movement, 263-64
City Twinning, 84
Civil Society Organizations, 11
Classical realism, 110
Cold War, 107, 109, 111-12, 114-15, 124-25, 131, 138, 142, 224, 269
Command-and-Control Structure, 150
Comprehensive Test Ban Treaty (CTBT), 108, 122, 130, 134, 147
Conference on Disarmament (CD), 148
Contemporary Reforms, 29
Credible Minimum Deterrence, 139
Cultural, 103
    Empowerment, 302

Dalit Network Netherlands (DNN), 304
Dalit solidarity organizations, 303
Davis, Zachary S., 111
Dayabhag, 295
Dayabliaga, 296
De-bureaucratization, 29
Demick, 52
Democracy, Practice, 230

Democratic Decentralization, 228
Development of Information Technology, 21
Development Program Landings (DPL), 161
Disability, 268, 272, 274
Distribution of Water, 211
District Planning and Development Board, 190
Draft Nuclear Doctrine (DND), 152
DRDO, 134
Dreze, Jean, 230
Drugs, 48

Economic Empowerment, 302
Economic, 103
Educationally Backward Blocks (EBBs), 311
Employment-Unemployment Schedule (EUS), 253
Empowerment, 247, 300, 308
Environment, 44
EU's climate-energy package, 45

Family Planning Grants Commission, 174
Family Planning, 176-77
Farzmand A., 22
Federalism, 77-78
First Wave of Globalization, 224
Fissile Material Cutoff Treaty (FMCT), 130, 148
FMCR, 134
Foreign Trade Offices, 83
Forest, 233
Forest Rights Act (FRA), 241
Fourth World Conference, 309
FRA, 239
Frankel, Benjamin, 111
Freire, Paulo, 300

Gandhi, Mrs. Indira, 128
Gender Empowerment Measure (GEM), 249
Gender Equality, 247
Gender Inequality, 297
Ghose, Arudhati, 120
Giddens, Anthony, 222
Girls in Higher Education, 252
Global Expansion Impact, 42
Global Nuclear Disarmament, 150
Globalization, 8, 18, 21, 24, 42, 43, 79, 222
  and its Effect on Democratization Process, 224
  and its Effect on Local Democracy, 223
  and Crisis of Representation, 225
  Dimensions, 3
  Impact of, 38
Globalization-1, 223
Greater Bangalore Water and Sanitation Project (GBWASP), 212
Growing Subnational Paradiplomacy, 80

Halqa majlis, 193
Halqa Panchayat, 190
Handpump Water Supply, 217
Hasan, Mushirul, 203
Hasan, Zoya, 196, 203
Health Care services, 162
Hindu Marriage Act 1955, 296
Hindu Minority and Guardianship Act 1956, 296
Hindu Succession Act 1956, 296
HIV/AIDS (GIPA), 47
HIV/AIDS (PLWHA), 46-47
HIV/AIDS Issue, 46
Hubli-Dharwad project, 211

IBRD, 158, 160
IDA, 160
IMF, 24
Indeginious People, 238
India
  Country Strategy, 158
  Family Planning Programme, 172
  Trade Promotion Organisation (ITPO), 81
India's HIV/AIDS Control Programme, 158
India's New Economic Policy (NEP), 78
India-China War, 114
Indira Gandhi Matritva Sahyog Yojana (IGMSY), 314
Infant Mortality Rate (IMR), 300, 315
International Bank for Reconstruction and Development (IBRD), 157
International Centre for the Settlement of Investment Disputes (ICSID), 157
International Conference on Population and Development (ICPD), 46
International Finance Corporation (IFC), 157
International Labour Organization (ILO), 48
International Womens Year, 286
Internationalizing Dalit Rights, 304
IRDA, 28
Isabelle Fauconnier, 213

J&K
  Decentralization, 187
  Existing Three Tier Model, 190
  Panchayati Raj Act 1989, 189
  Poor-Governance in, 185-86
  Probable Constraints in Empowering PRI, 191
  Trajectory of Public Policy on Participatory Democracy, 188
  Village Panchayat Act, 1935, 188
  Village Panchayat Act, 1958, 189
Jan Sangarsh Morcha (JSM), 237, 239
Jervis, Robert, 112
Jones, Charles, 111

Kapur, Ashok, 121
Karen Bakker, 210
Karve, Dr. R.D., 172
Kashmir Valley, 186
Kasturba Gandhi Balika Vidayalya (KGBV), 251, 311, 313
Kaul, H.N., 172
Khrushchev, 138
Kol Tribal's, Land Distribution, 234

Lasswell, Horold, 41
Little, Richard, 111
Local self-government, 228

Madhya Pradesh Urban Water Supply and Environment Improvement Project (MPUWSEIP), 212
Madhya Pradesh Water Sector Restructuring Project (MPWSRP), 212
Mahila Samakhya (MS), 250, 310
Marquand, David, 39
Maternal Mortality Ratio (MMR), 271, 315
Mazdoor Kisan Shakti Sangathan (MKSS), 14
Media, 80
Mehta, M.C., 13
Micro Credit Scheme (MCS), 300
Microfinance and Women, 302
Mies, Maria, 263
Military, 103
Millennium Development Goal 3 (MDG 3), 245, 247, 250, 257
Millennium Development Goals (MDGs), 246, 256
Minimal Nuclear Deterrence, 136
Minimum Credible Deterrence, Credibility, 138
Ministry of Human Resource Development (MHRD), 311
Minorities Right, 238
Mishra, Brajesh, 134, 136
Missile Technology Control Regime (MTCR), 134, 149
Missiles for Deterrence, 144
Mitakshara, 295, 296
MNREGA, 232, 238-39, 311
Modern Globalization, 224-25
Modified Design-Build, 209
Mohan, C. Raja, 125, 129
Mukerjee, R.K., 170
Multilateral Investment Guarantee Agency (MIGA), 157
Multi-Sectoral Development Programme (MSDP), 201
Myanmar, 86
Myrdal, G., 169

Nair, V.K., 140
National Centre for Promotion of Employment for Disabled Persons (NCPEDP), 277
National Commission for Women, 12, 299
National Family Health Survey (NFHS-2), 249
National Federation of Dalit Women (NFWD), 304
National Perspective Plan for Women, 254
National Planning Committee, 280
National Policy for Empowerment of Women, 310
National Programme for Education of Girls at Elementary Level (NPEGEL), 251-52, 311
National Rural Drinking Water Programme (NRDWP), 217
National Rural Health Mission (NHRM), 315
National Sample Survey (NSS), 253
National Security Advisory Board (NSAB), 136, 153
National Tribal Policy, 167
NATO, 142
NCDHR, 304-5
Nehru, Jawaharlal, 117
Network Rehabilitation, 211
New Social Movements or NSMs, 260
NGOs, 12
No-First-Use, 130, 142
Non-Proliferation Efforts, 117

NRHM, 311, 316
Nuclear Command Authority (NCA), 151
Nuclear Proliferation Treaty (NPT), 118, 149
Nuclear Suppliers Group (NSG), 149

ONGC Tripura Power Company (OTPC), 86
Organizational Empowerment, 302

Panchayat Adalat, 190
Panchayati Raj Institutions (PRIs), 213
Peaceful Nuclear Explosion, 128
People With Disability Act (PWD Act, 1995), 273, 277
Piped Water Supply (PWS), 217
Planning Commission of India, 178
Pokhran II, 131, 133-34, 152-53
    Debate, 152
    Indian Official Pronouncement, 136
    Strategic Factors, 112-13
Police Agenda, Global Context, 44
Policies for Social Inclusion, 199
Policy Advice Market, 9
Policy Analysis, Technocratic View, 6
Policy Making, Supreme Court, 12
Policy
    Changing Discourse, 9
    Process of Negotiation, 7
Political, 103
    Empowerment, 297, 302-3
Pollution, 44
Population Explosion, 45
Population Information Network (POPIN), 248
Population Policy, 169, 170, 172-75
post-Cold War, 34, 110, 112, 116, 269
Post-Independence Reorganization of States, 60
post-Pokhran II, 129, 150, 152
    Nuclear Strategy, 135-48
Poverty, 45
pre-Independence Internal Boundaries, 57
Private Participation in Infrastructure (PPI), 208
Privatization, 52
Psychological Empowerment, 302
Public Health Engineering Department (PHED), 216
Public Policies, History, 196
Public Policy
    Making, 98
    and Corporations, 100
    Early Debates on, 37
    Globalisation, 38
        State, 22-23
    its Origin, 35
    New Global Era, 27
    Realistic Alternative: Decentralized, 102
Public-Private Partnership (PPP), 207-8
    Drinking Water Sector, 210
    Rural Water, 213

Ranghanath Misra Committee Report, 199
Ranipur Wildlife Sanctuary, 236
Rantola Incident, 236
Rashtriya Swayamsevak Sangh (RSS), 147
Rawals, John, 273
Reagan, Ronald, 18
Regionalisation, 79
    Parties, 80
Regulatory Reform, Changes, 99
Rejecting Nuclear Ambiguity, 130
Resettlement Plan, 164
Right Based Approach to Development, 237
Rights Based Policies, 238
Robinson, Mary, 272
Roman Catholic Church, 176
Roy, Raka, 263

Sabharwal, 48
Sachar Committee Report, 198, 201
Sagan, Scott, 124
Sarva Siksha Abhiyan, 252
Scheduled Castes (SCs), 196, 214, 235
Scheduled Tribes (STs), 196, 214, 235
Second World War, 268
Sector Reform Pilot Projects (SRPP), 213
Self Help Groups, 266
Self-Employed Women's Association (SEWA), 266
Sen, Amarto, 230
Sen, Prof. Amartya, 271
Sheth, D.L., 197
Singh, Jaswant, 132, 135, 148
Single Line Administration, 189
Sino-Pakistani connection, 116
Sister Town, 84
Social Development Report (SDR), 202, 204
Social Empowerment, 302
Social, 103
Social Policies, 197
Solarz, Stephen, 132

Special Economic Zone (SEZ), 82
Srava Siksha Abhiyan (SSA), 311-12
Sridharan, Kripa, 129
State Paradiplomacy, Prospects, 84
State, Contemporary Debate, 24
State's Paradiplomacy, Pitfalls of, 88
States Activism, Foreign Economic Policy, 77
States Reorganization Commission (SRC) Report, 62
States, Use of International Forum, 83
States' Paradiplomacy, New Trend, 87
Stigler, Joseph, 25
Strategic Forces Command (SFC), 151
Strobe Talbott, 135, 148
Structural adjustment, 226
Subrahmanyam, K., 140, 146
Supreme Court, 28
Swarnajayanti Gram Swaeozgar Yojana, 283

Terrorism, 48
Thatcher, Margaret, 18
The Naya Kashmir, 188
Third Wave, 223
Tightening Export Controls, 149
Tourism, 85
Trade and Industry, 50
TRAI, 28
Treatment (Desalination, Waste water), 211
Tribal Development Efforts, 166
Tribal Development, 164
Tribal Peoples' Development Plan, 164
Tribal sub-Plan (TSP), 166

U.P. Tenancy Act 1939, 234
UN Office on Drugs and Crime (UNODC), 48
UN Volunteer (UNVs), 47
UNDP, 46, 47, 289
UNESCO Population Commission Report, 170
United States (US), 35-36, 117
UNO, 169

Vajpayee, Atal Behari, 122, 130, 132, 136, 139, 145, 148, 150
Victorian Globalization, 223
Village Water and Sanitation Committee (VWSC), 213
Violence Against Women (VAW), 286, 312

Waltz, Kenneth, 110
Waring, Scott Main, 226
Wattal, P.K., 175
WHO's AIDS programme, 47
Wilson, Charles, 101
Women Empowerment, 247, 249, 300, 306
Women in Development (WID), 301
Women's Reservation Bill, 255
Work and Social Security, 238
World Bank, 24, 45, 157-59, 160, 162, 163, 164, 207, 233, 270
World Bank's Country Strategy, 158
World Commission on Environment and Development (WCED), 44
World Conference Against Racism (WCAR), 304
World Social Forum (WSF), 304
WRB, 256
WTO, 4, 24, 81